ECONOMIC
DEVELOPMENT
Challenge and Promise

ECONOMIC
DEVELOPMENT

Challenge and Promise

Edited by

STEPHEN SPIEGELGLAS

Associate Professor of Economics and Statistics
The Drexel Institute of Technology

CHARLES J. WELSH

Associate Professor of Economics
The Drexel Institute of Technology

PRENTICE-HALL, INC., *Englewood Cliffs, New Jersey*

©1970
By PRENTICE-HALL, INC.
Englewood Cliffs, N.J.

13–223354–1
Library of Congress Catalog Number: 70–78491

current printing (last number)
10 9 8 7 6 5 4 3 2 1

Prentice-Hall International, Inc., London
Prentice-Hall of Australia, Pty. Ltd., Sydney
Prentice-Hall of Canada, Ltd., Toronto
Prentice-Hall of India Private Ltd., New Delhi
Prentice-Hall of Japan, Inc., Tokyo

Printed in the United States of America

PREFACE

The years since World War II will undoubtedly be recorded in history as a period in which world attention began to be focused on the underdeveloped countries. A universal concern to alleviate their plight became evident. This concern is seen in aid programs of many industrial countries and in the work of the United Nations and its specialized agencies. It is also seen in the attention given to the problem of underdevelopment by universities, to the extent that both undergraduate and graduate courses in economics of development are today firmly entrenched in curricula of institutions of higher learning almost everywhere.

Concurrently, economists (as well as other scientists) have been devoting a great deal of time to this issue. Their research has led to a veritable flood of published material, both theoretical and practical in nature, that has greatly contributed to the understanding of the development process. New theories were designed and, in light of the immediate response that they have elicited, few remain either unchallenged or unaltered. At the same time, many studies on various developing countries and their development experience have led to a greater appreciation of the practical problems and have modified the views of economists concerning the type of strategy best suited for economic development. One can cite, for instance, a decreased emphasis in recent years on the role of capital resources and an increased emphasis on human resources development. One can also cite the recent critical appraisal of import-substituting industrialization and the strong stress on the need to develop exportable manufactured goods by the developing countries.

Along with all textbooks on economic development, this book of readings reflects the more recent exchange of ideas and shifts of emphasis. Of course, full coverage of topics is impossible. Given that a book of readings is compiled essentially to provide supplementary material, the adoption of a suitable sequence of topics became a major consideration. Even a cursory examination of textbooks on economic development will reveal, however, that there is not such a thing as "a sequence." By necessity, our order of topics is a compromise; therefore, a matrix is provided on pages x and xi that shows how each selection fits into the scheme and sequence of the seven widely used textbooks. Other main considerations have been the necessity to include a sufficiently wide coverage of topics and a desire to produce a book of readings designed both for economics majors and those not majoring in economics.

After a huge quantity of published material, foreign as well as domestic, was examined, thirty-three readings were selected. Each represents either an outstanding contribution, an issue of controversial significance, or a clear synthesis of ideas expressed in various scientific journals and books. We are, of course, well aware that in spite of our goal to compile a book of readings within the confines of an objective framework, our own preferences and predilections are undoubtedly showing.

We wish to acknowledge our thanks to the authors, journals, and publishers for their permission to reproduce the selections appearing in this book of readings. We are very grateful to Dean James M. Parrish for his encouragement in our undertaking.

STEPHEN SPIEGELGLAS
CHARLES J. WELSH

CONTENTS

vii

	Alpert	Enke	Hagen	Higgins	Kindleberger	Krause	Morris
1. Bauer	1	2	1 6	1	20	1 3	1
2. Lewis	2	1 28	2 7	17	1 2	2 5	1 15
3. Johnson	1 2	16	17	18	11 Appendix / 11	10 12	13 15
4. Watson and Dirlam	4	16	17	17 18	3 5	12	14
5. Cairncross	4	9 15	8 13	6 18		12	9 14
6. Tripathy	4	6 15	17	18	5	12	14
7. Bos	4	15	17	18	5	12	14
8. Qayum	4	9	17	16 18	3 Appendix / 3	12	2 14
9. Myint	11	4	7 20	8 9 16	3	3 4	2
10. Bhatt	11	16 17	7	15	11 12	7 10	2 15
11. Harbison	6	19 22	9	19	6	5	5 6
12. Waines	6	21	9	19	6 Appendix	5 5	5
13. Rosenberg	9 10	11	6 10	12 23	2 5	3 4	8 9
14. Millikan and Blackmer	6	28	2	12	2 10	3	3
15. Coale	5	2 18 20	12	1 2	15	4	5
16. Eckaus	11	5	8	10 18	8	8	8
17. Shearer	5 11	6 18	14 18	10 18	8 14	8	8 15
18. Johnston and Mellor	11	7 8	3 5	14	4 12	6 10	4

The matrix above keys the thirty-three readings in this book to related chapters in the following seven widely used textbooks:

Reading	Alpert	Enke	Hagen	Higgins	Kindelberger	Krause	Morris
19. Long	7	8, 28	3	20	12	6	4
20. Krebs	11	7, 25	4, 5	14, 21	12	7, 8, 9	7
21. Hirschman	4, 12	7	5, 7, 19	21	12	4, 7	7, 12
22. Ellis	9	12	15	22	13	13	9
23. Hicks	9	14	13	23	13	13	12
24. Kaldor	9	12, 13	15	24, 25	13	13	9, 12
25. Cairncross	12	23, 24	19	13	16	8	11
26. Keesing	12	25	19	13	16	6, 8	11
27. Vartikar	12	28	19	26	16	6, 8	11
28. Marshall	12	24, 25	19	13	16	11, 14	11
29. Meade	13	25	19	13, 26	16, 18	6	11
30. Johnson	13	26	19	13	18, 19	19	11
31. Singer	16	27	16	28	17, 19	15, 21	10
32. Carlin	16	27	16	28	17, 19	15, 21	10
33. Little and Clifford	15	27	16	28	14, 18	21	8, 10

Alpert, Paul. *Economic Development: Objectives and Methods.* New York: The Free Press, 1963.
Enke, Stephen. *Economics for Development.* Englewood Cliffs, N.J.: Prentice-Hall, Inc., 1963.
Hagen, Everett Einar. *The Economics of Development.* Homewood, Ill., Richard D. Irwin, Inc., 1968.
Higgins, Benjamin Howard. *Economic Development: Principles, Problems, and Policies.* Rev. ed. New York: W.W. Norton & Company, Inc., 1968.
Kindelberger, Charles Poor. *Economic Development.* 2nd ed. New York: McGraw-Hill Book Company, 1965.
Krause, Walter. *Economic Development; the Underdeveloped World and the American Interest.* San Francisco: Wadsworth Publishing Company, 1961.
Morris, Bruce Robert. *Economic Growth and Development.* In cooperation with C. Wendell King. New York: Pitman Publishing Corporation, 1967.

ECONOMIC
DEVELOPMENT
Challenge and Promise

PART 1

INTRODUCTION

Nowadays the inhabitants of the underdeveloped countries no longer accept chronic poverty and low levels of living as inevitable, and they demand that their economic conditions be altered and their lot improved. This "revolution in expectations"—a strong desire for and insistence upon a better future—raises, however, fundamental issues of development economics and at the same time introduces social and political problems that no government can ignore. Viewed in all its implications, economic development of underdeveloped countries must therefore be classified among the most crucial problems of this day and age, and inasmuch as two-thirds of the world's population is involved, it must be clearly recognized as a matter of universal concern and an issue of utmost significance for the future of mankind.

In view of the urgency of economic development dictated by political undercurrents, it is well to recall that a description of living conditions prevailing in a great majority of these countries, even not so long ago, portrayed such a distressing picture as to evoke great concern about the foreseeable prospects for improvement. As generally described, many underdeveloped countries lacked even rudimentary prerequisites for development and were faced with insurmountable obstacles, generally identified in terms of specific vicious circles.

After a decade or so of pronounced improvement in many countries, some economists began to question, however, the earlier pessimistic views, and their writings suggest that the previous stress on obstacles to economic development might have been greatly overdone.

An expression of such optimism can be found in Selection 1, in
which BAUER attempts to disprove the validity of the vicious circle
of poverty thesis. The author rejects indentification of the underdeveloped world in terms of stagnation and retrogression and
argues, with considerable supporting evidence, against the pessimistic assertion that the differences in rates of growth and levels
of income between the rich and poor countries must be permanent.

Any optimistic statement concerning prospects of developing
countries tends to contain an implicit assumption that economic
development is desirable. Not only is the process of economic development expected to lead to significant material betterment, but it is also
expected to contribute greatly to the improvement of human life
through better health and education, increased leisure, and the like.
The industrial countries, with their higher levels of technology and
standards of living, are considered examples to be emulated. This,
at least, is the position taken by leading groups and intellectuals in
developing countries. Unfortunately, no exhaustive sampling studies
of public opinion in these countries are available that would reveal
how deeply this thinking permeates all strata of population. History
teaches that there are no benefits from development without costs and
that material progress often results in loss of individuality, greater
unhappiness, and increased social tension. Thus, it is debatable whether
the average man really considers economic development an unqualified
blessing and whether higher rates of growth and higher levels of
living, in fact, compensate most people in developing countries for the
loss of their cherished values. In the transitional period, they most
likely do not. Almost never do people willingly abandon traditional
ways of thinking and of doing things (a different assumption would be
contrary to known facts about human behavior). However, one might
conjecture that in the longer run the positive factors will predominate.

These and similar considerations are the subject of Selection 2.
In it LEWIS emphasizes the ambivalent nature of the attitude of
most people toward economic development and exhaustively discusses
reasons for its attraction and dislike. The author finds that many
objections to economic development are actually more apparent
than real. He points out that acceleration of the process of change
necessarily involves hardships and underscores that a society must
be prepared to incur substantial costs if it ever expects to enjoy the
benefits accruing from development.

The willingness of the people in developing countries to make
sacrifices is a necessary, even if insufficient, precondition for economic
development. It goes without saying that the process of economic
development is extremely complex and is affected by many factors.
In view of great differences that exist among these countries, innumerable combinations of goals, strategies, and approaches are certainly

possible, and each combination requires a multitude of decisions on various aspects of development.

It is not surprising that governments are the chief decision-making agents in development. They often assume that role through dire necessity. Not only is there a great shortage of entrepreneurs, but the private sector is generally too weak to break through vicious circles. In addition, there is quite often a mistrust of the market forces and a conviction that economic development must be planned and cannot be left to the guidance of an unplanned system. Unfortunately, the capability of governments is also limited, mainly because the unavailability of trained personnel precludes the simultaneous performance of a number of important tasks. Thus, it should be apparent that only a few governments in underdeveloped countries can simultaneously perform the tasks of coordinating and organizing economic activity on the one hand and of originating innovative activity on the other. As is well known, the latter task is best left in the hands of private entrepreneurs. It would appear, therefore, that the public and private sectors are complementary and that there is a role to be played by both sectors, the former providing the physical infrastructure, the over-all guidance as well as a favorable climate for economic development, and the latter providing the necessary innovative activity.

A careful analysis of this entire issue is provided in Selection 3, in which JOHNSON appraises the relative merits and demerits of centralized and decentralized planning. The author finds that each alternative has its own appeal, the former in terms of greater social justice and the latter in terms of greater efficiency. He then proceeds to scrutinize the specific objections voiced against assigning a major role in development to the market forces and concludes that developing countries could gain a great deal if the public and private sectors would jointly spearhead the process of economic development.

Selection **1**

Is There a Vicious
Circle of Poverty?

P. T. BAUER

From: "The Vicious Circle of Poverty," Weltwirtschaftliches Archiv,
Vol. 95, No. 1 (1965), pp. 4–18. Reprinted by permission of Weltwirtschaftliches Archiv.

I

1. I intend to discuss the validity of the widely held notion that the underdeveloped (or poor) countries[1] are caught in a vicious circle of poverty and stagnation,
or, as it has been put rather pithily by the late Professor Nurkse, that a country is
poor because it is poor. The great upsurge of interest in the last twenty years or
so in the economics of poor countries and of their development has so far not
yielded many illuminating generalisations. The thesis usually known as the vicious
circle of poverty is perhaps the principal generalisation of this literature. It is not
quite so dominant now as it was a few years ago. But it is still prominent in the
academic, official, and popular literature in this general area. It also serves as
background or as basis for important policy proposals and measures, notably
for the suggestion that appreciable economic progress in poor countries requires
drastic sacrifices at home, supplemented by large-scale aid from abroad.

2. The thesis states that poverty itself sets up well-nigh unsurmountable obstacles
to its own conquest. It is presented in several distinct and different variants, which,
however, are not exclusive but cumulative. The most frequent is that the low
level of income renders saving impossible, thus preventing the capital accumulation
necessary for an increase in income. Others include the suggestion that the narrow
markets of poor countries obstruct the emergence and extension of the specialisation necessary for higher incomes; that demand is too small to permit profitable
and productive investment; that government revenues are insufficient for the
establishment of effective public services; that malnutrition and poor health keep

---

[1] In accordance with current practice I use this term to include most of Asia, Africa, and
Latin America. As should be clear and will be noted in the text, the distinction between developed
and underdeveloped countries is imprecise, arbitrary, and impermanent.

productivity low, which prevents a rise in income; and there are others as well. International private investment cannot alleviate the situation, since one aspect of the vicious circle is a lack of profitable private investment opportunities.

3. I quote at some length from influential sources to show the importance of the thesis in the literature, to illustrate the reasoning behind it, and to forestall criticism that I am quoting out of context.

4. One is from a study submitted to a United States Senate Committee by the Center for International Studies of the Massachusetts Institute of Technology, a well-known and very influential organisation in this field. ". . . the general scarcity relative to population of nearly all resources creates a self-perpetuating vicious circle of poverty. Additional capital is necessary to increase output, but poverty itself makes it impossible to carry out the required saving and investment by a voluntary reduction in consumption."[2]

5. Another formulation which has often been quoted is by the late Professor Nurkse, whose book *Problems of Capital Formation in Underdeveloped Countries* is one of the best known and influential writings in this field. He writes under the heading "The Vicious Circle of Poverty"[3]:

> *In discussions of the problem of economic development, a phrase that crops up frequently is"the vicious circle of poverty". . . .*
>
> *A situation of this sort [a vicious circle of poverty], relating to a country as a whole, can be summed up in the trite proposition:"a country is poor because it is poor."*
>
> *Perhaps the most important circular relationships of this kind are those that afflict the accumulation of capital in economically backward countries. The supply of capital is governed by the ability and willingness to save; the demand for capital is governed by the incentives to invest. A circular relationship exists on both sides of the problem of capital formation in the poverty-ridden areas of the world.*
>
> *On the supply side, there is the small capacity to save, resulting from the low level of real income. The low real income is a reflection of low productivity, which in its turn is due largely to the lack of capital. The lack of capital is a result of the small capacity to save, and so the circle is complete.*
>
> *On the demand side, the inducement to invest may be low because of the small buying power of the people, which is due to their small real income, which again is due to low productivity. The low level of productivity, however, is a result of the small amount of capital used in production, which in its turn may be caused at least partly by the small inducement to invest.*
>
> *The low level of real income, reflecting low productivity, is a point that is common to both circles.*

6. Such quotations could be multiplied easily from the writings of well-known authors such as Professor Gunnar Myrdal, Dr. H. W. Singer, and many others.

---

[2] *Study Submitted by the Center for International Studies of the Massachusetts Institute of Technology to the Senate Committee Investigating the Operation of Foreign Aid* (Washington, D.C., 1957), p. 37.

[3] Ragnar Nurkse, *Problems of Capital Formation in Underdeveloped Countries* (Oxford: Blackwell, 1953), pp. 4sq.

7. It will be readily realized that this thesis can be expressed in the form of a model, that is an analytical device setting out the essential variables in the explanation of particular phenomena. The model of the vicious circle of poverty and underdevelopment is a particular model designed to explain the continuation through time of a zero or negligible rate of economic growth. The essential variables and relationships in most growth models are these: the growth of income is a function of the rate of capital accumulation, that is, of investment; investment depends on saving; and saving is a function of income. Hence the growth of income depends on the growth of capital and the growth of capital depends on the growth of income. Thus the model behind the thesis of the vicious circle of poverty pivots on the suggestion that the low level of income itself prevents the capital formation required to raise income.

8. This thesis is demonstrably and indeed obviously invalid. If it were valid, innumerable individuals, groups, and communities could not have risen from great poverty to riches as they have done throughout the world in both rich and poor countries. This in itself should be sufficient to disprove the thesis as a general proposition. The thesis is refuted also by the very existence of developed countries all of which started poor, with low incomes per head and low levels of accumulated capital, i.e., with the economic features which define underdeveloped countries today. Yet they have advanced, usually without appreciable outside capital and invariably without external grants. This would have been impossible on the arguments of the vicious circle of poverty and stagnation. As the world is a closed system and clearly began in a state of underdevelopment, the thesis is indeed inconsistent with the phenomenon of development.

9. It is also refuted by the rapid economic advance of many underdeveloped countries in recent decades, which for obvious reasons is particularly relevant in this context. I shall give some instances of this progress in broader terms and others in more detailed and specific terms.

II

10. According to the statistics of the Economic Commission for Latin America over the period 1935 through 1953, the gross national product in Latin American countries increased at an annual rate of 4.2 per cent, and output per head by 2 per cent.[4] Over the period 1945 through 1955 the rate of growth was even faster, as total output increased by about 4.9 per cent annually and output per head by 2.4 per cent, an appreciably higher rate than in the United States.[5] Latin America is largely pervaded by the money economy so that statistics of the gross national product are somewhat more meaningful than for most underdeveloped countries.

---

[4] United Nations, Department of Economic and Social Affairs, *Analyses and Projections of Economic Development*, I: *An Introduction to the Technique of Programming*, a study prepared by the Economic Commission for Latin America, United Nations Publication, Sales No.: 1955. II.G.2 (New York, 1955), p. 10.

[5] *Idem*, *Economic Survey of Latin America*, 1955, Incl. an *Essay on Government Income and Expenditure*, 1947–1954, prepared by the Secretariat of the Economic Commission for Latin America, United Nations Publication, Sales No.: 1956. II.G.1 (New York, 1956), p. 3.

11. South East Asia, and in particular Malaya, and West Africa are other under-developed regions where there has been rapid and readily demonstrable progress since the latter part of the nineteenth century. In these areas there are no series of national income figures going back before the Second World War and the present figures are somewhat hazardous. The national income of Malaya (gross domestic product per head per year) was about £100 in 1961,[6] the latest year for which official figures are available, and in Ghana it was about £75 in 1962, again the latest available figure. These are low figures by Western standards[7] but they never-theless reflect substantial advance since the beginning of the century, when these were essentially subsistence economies.

Regardless of the availability or limitations of national income statistics, there is no lack of information on the rapid progress of these economies in these years. The rubber industry of South East Asia began only around 1900. In 1963 it pro-duced about 2 million tons of rubber annually (in spite of the disorganisation in Indonesia, the country with the largest area under rubber), worth about £400 million. More than two-thirds of the output is on Asian-owned properties. In 1900 total domestic exports from Malaya were worth about £8 million annually; in 1963 they were about £300 million.[8] In 1900 there were no exports of plantation rubber from Malaya; in 1963 they exceeded 800,000 tons, rather more than half from Asian-owned properties. There has also been a very rapid increase in the entrepot trade of the country, which reflects largely the spread of the exchange economy in Southeast Asia. Thus while total Malayan (including Singapore) exports and imports together (including re-imports) in 1900 were around £50 million, in 1963 they were about £1,000 million.

12. In West Africa the progress of Ghana (the Gold Coast until 1957) and Nigeria since the end of the nineteenth century has been striking, rapid, and well docu-mented. There is ample evidence of this progress from sporadic national income figures and, more relevant and revealing, from statistics of population growth, foreign trade, government revenues, literacy, health, infant mortality, and so on. The rapid progress of Ghana is reflected in statistics which are somewhat more reliable and meaningful than elsewhere in Africa or Asia. As already noted, by the early 1960's the national income per head was about £75; in real terms it had dou-bled since 1910 and quadrupled since 1890. The total population approximately quadrupled between 1890 and 1960 from about 1.6 million to about 6.5 million.

13. Statistics of foreign trade are of particular interest for West Africa because well over 99½ per cent of the population is African: all agricultural exports (the bulk of all exports) are produced by them and practically all imports are destined for

---

6 The statistics of national income per head in this paragraph are calculated from the figures of the gross domestic product presented in the United Nations' *Year Book of National Accounts Statistics, 1963* (New York, 1964), pp. 85 and 107; and from the population figures in the United Nations' *Monthly Bulletin of Statistics*, Vol. XVIII (Dec. 1964), pp. 2sq.

7 It should be noted, however, that the conventional statistics much exaggerate the income differences between the developed and underdeveloped countries. This is discussed in Section V below.

8 The external trade of Malaya and Singapore in 1963 is derived from data in the official *Monthly Statistical Bulletin of the States of Malaya*, Kuala Lumpur (Oct. 1964), pp. 89 sqq., and from the Singapore *Monthly Digest of Statistics*, Vol. III (Oct. 1964), p. 43.

their use. To take Ghana-Gold Coast first. In 1890 there were no exports (or production) of cocoa; by the mid-1930's these were about 300,000 tons annually, and by the early 1960's they were over 400,000 tons, all from farms established, owned, and operated by Africans; there are no foreign-owned cocoa farms. In 1890 combined imports and exports were less than £1 million annually; by the 1930's both imports and exports were in tens of millions; since the mid 1950's imports and exports have each been around £100 million annually. Over this period there was a spectacular increase in imports of both consumer and capital goods. In 1890 there were no imports, or negligible imports, of flour, sugar, cement, petroleum products, or iron and steel. In recent decades most of these have been on a massive scale.[9] In the early 1890's there were about 3,000 children at school; by the mid-1950's there were over half a million. In the 1890's there were neither railways nor roads, but only a few jungle paths, and transport of goods was entirely by human porterage and by canoe. By the 1930's there was a substantial railway mileage and a good road system; by then journeys by road required fewer hours than they had required days in 1890.

14. Substantially the same applies to Nigeria. Around 1900 exports and imports were each around £2 million annually; by the 1930's they were in tens of millions and since the mid-1950's they have been around £150–200 million annually. Here again practically all exports are produced by Africans and practically all imports are destined for their use. In 1900 there were no exports (or production) of cocoa from Nigeria and exports of oil palm products were one-tenth of their present volume. And here again there has been a phenomenal increase in imports of mass consumer goods and capital goods over this period; in recent years there has also been a substantial increase in the local production of commodities previously imported.

15. The economic development of West Africa is only the most striking instance of a more general experience in Africa since the end of the nineteenth century. There has been substantial material advance in many parts of the continent, those parts with which the developed world has established contact. And the advance has taken place from extremely backward and indeed savage conditions. By Western standards, sub-Saharan Africa was materially almost unimaginably backward in the third quarter of the nineteenth century. For instance, there were no schools and no man-made communications in the interior (with the irrelevant exception of a few primitive paths chiefly cut by slave-traders or raiders). Apart from slave-trading and raiding there was then very little contact between the different parts of the interior of Africa because of the absence of communication facilities which have since been developed in many parts of the continent.

16. Statistical information of the kind just presented can be multiplied easily. But by itself it cannot convey the profound and pervasive changes which have taken place in many parts of the underdeveloped world in recent decades and which have changed the conditions of existence. In many areas this progress has meant the suppression of slavery and tribal warfare and the disappearance of famine

---

[9] In recent years local production of some commodities (for instance, cigarettes) has replaced imports; this does not affect the argument of the text.

and of the worst epidemic and endemic diseases. It has meant the development of communications, the replacement of local self-sufficiency by the possibilities of exchange, and the emergence and growth of cities. For instance, Malaya, which in the 1890's was a sparsely populated country of Malay hamlets and fishing villages, has been completely transformed by the rise of the rubber industry and has developed into a country with populous cities, thriving commerce, and an excellent system of roads. In West Africa slave raiding and slavery were still widespread at the end of the nineteenth century; in 1900 the towns of Northern Nigeria, which are now centres of the groundnut trade, were important slave markets.

17. One further specific example: Hong Kong was an empty, barren rock in the first half of the nineteenth century. By the end of the century it was a port and a minor entrepot centre. In recent years it has become a major manufacturing centre, exporting manufactures on a massive scale. Throughout the Western world severe barriers have come to be erected against imports from Hong Kong to protect the domestic industries of the United States, Great Britain, Germany, and France from the unsubsidised competition of the industries of Hong Kong, an underdeveloped country, 8,000 or more miles away. This rapid progress has occurred in spite of the presence in Hong Kong of three features often said to reinforce the vicious circle of poverty, namely, lack of natural resources, extremely severe population pressure, and a very restricted domestic market.

18. The level of income in underdeveloped countries is by definition low, but this is compatible with advance, indeed even rapid advance, if that advance has begun only comparatively recently, and has started from a very low level. This is the position in many underdeveloped countries.

The thesis of the vicious circle of poverty postulates either that low average levels entail zero rates of change, which is readily refuted by observation; or, alternatively, the thesis identifies a low level with a zero rate of change, which is a simple error in logic. It is remarkable that such a crude notion should have been so widely accepted.[10]

III

19. I now turn to two points which may be of some interest of their own and are also designed to forestall possible objections.

20. First, the foregoing discussion is not intended to suggest that there has been material progress throughout the underdeveloped world. There are substantial groups and large areas in the underdeveloped world which have progressed little in recent times. They include the aborigines in many parts of the world, the desert peoples of the Sahara and elsewhere, and the tribal populations of Central and

---

[10] It seems particularly paradoxical that the notion should have been espoused most widely and uncritically in countries with a Protestant culture, that is, a culture which values self-achievement and is genuinely opposed to a philosophy of charity in the form of giving something for nothing. On the other hand, a Protestant culture seems more conducive to a guilt feeling and this has played a part in the arguments in favour of foreign aid, and among these arguments the vicious circle of poverty has been prominent.

East Africa. And over large areas of South and East Asia (including large parts of rural India, Pakistan, and China), progress has been comparatively slow, and much of it has been absorbed in the form of increased populations. These are areas largely of subsistence agriculture. There is nothing abnormal or unexpected even in extreme material poverty in these circumstances. In particular, it has nothing to do with a generally operative vicious circle of poverty. There is no general rule or prescriptive right ensuring that all countries or regions should reach the same level of economic attainment or the same rate of progress at any given time or over any given period. Economic progress and achievement depend very largely on human qualities and attitudes; on social and political institutions, which derive from these; on historical experience; and also on natural resources and on various other factors. There is nothing surprising, abnormal, or reprehensible in differences in economic attainment.

21. Second, recognition of the material progress in so many parts of the underdeveloped world is not a plea for laissez-faire or for any other policy. The advance has often created formidable problems calling for government action. The progress which has occurred has often been rapid and generally also uneven, both in the sense that it has affected certain areas and sectors earlier and more pervasively than others and also in that its impact has been much greater on some activities, attitudes, and institutions than on others. This latter aspect in particular has often set up considerable strains. The resulting problems are often acute but they are totally different from those of stagnation. Problems of changes in land tenure arrangements and in property rights and inheritance, personal and social problems arising from detribalization and from the transformation of a subsistence into a money economy, and problems of congestion and delay in ports and on the railroads are pressing issues in a number of underdeveloped countries, which would not arise in a stagnant economy caught in a vicious circle of poverty. Indeed, the insistence on the vicious circle of poverty has served to obscure these other problems and to divert attention and energy from attempts to deal with them.

IV

22. The standard current ideology or orthodoxy of underdeveloped countries, of which the thesis of the vicious circle is an integral and indeed principal part, refers to the underdeveloped world almost wholly in terms of stagnation, starvation, retrogression, and so forth. However, there also exists a substantial and authoritative body of writings, chiefly by anthropologists, historians, administrators, and even some economists, which discusses the rapid changes in these countries since the end of the nineteenth century and the problems associated with them. This literature discusses prominently the difficulties of adapting institutions and attitudes to fast-changing conditions: the transition from communal to individual tenure of land, the results of detribalization and disintegration of communal life and values, and the difficulties of rapid urbanization, and other related problems. Here are a few examples.

23. The following is a typical passage from the writings of Mary Kingsley,

scholar, traveller, and humanitarian of the turn of the century, who wrote on the impact of the culture of nineteenth-century Europe on the African whose outlook was that of much earlier cultures[11]: "If you will try Science [i.e., anthropology], all the evils of the clash between the two culture periods could be avoided, and you could assist these West Africans in their thirteenth-century state to rise into their nineteenth-century state without their having the hard fight for it that you yourself had."

24. In 1926, well before African development became a major international issue, Dr. A. McPhee published a book with the revealing title *The Economic Revolution in British West Africa*.[12] The following passages epitomize his conclusions[13]: "In fact, the process since the 'Nineties of last century has been the superimposition of the twentieth century after Christ on the twentieth century before Christ, and a large part of the problem of native policy is concerned with the clash of such widely different cultures and with the protection of the natives during the difficulties of transition. . . . The transition has been from the growth of subsistence crops and the collection of sylvan produce to the cultivation of exchange crops, with the necessary implication of a transition from a 'Natural' economy to a 'Monetary' economy, and the innumerable important reactions from the latter phase."

25. Much the same conclusions were reached by Sir Keith Hancock, judicious and critical historian of African development. This is what he says[14]: "In some periods of European history—in our own day, for example, or in the day of the first steam-engines and power mills—the European world has seemed to be transformed; Europe nevertheless has remained the same world, spinning very much faster. But in Africa change means more than acceleration. Europe's commerce and its money-measurements really have brought the African into a new world. . . . He retains something of his old social and religious and mental life and habit—these things are very slow in dying—but they are distinct from his new economic life and habit."

26. The problems of policy were particularly baffling in the context of land tenure (though by no means confined to it), notably whether individual rights in the cultivation and ownership of land should be permitted to replace communal or tribal tenure wholly or in part, again a problem which would not arise in a static or stagnant society. According to Professor S. Herbert Frankel, well-intentioned but mistaken decisions in this field, taken before the First World War, have had far-reaching consequences in East and South Africa, retarding the more secure advances of the Africans in East Africa and leading South African policy into its present impasse. He writes in a recently published and closely argued paper[15]:

---

[11] Mary H. Kingsley, *West African Studies* (London, 1901), pp. 326sq. Quoted in: W. K. Hancock, *Survey of British Commonwealth Affairs*, Vol. II: *Problems of Economic Policy 1918–1939*, P. 2 (London, New York, and Toronto, 1942), p. 333.

[12] Allan McPhee, *The Economic Revolution in British West Africa*, Studies in Economics and Political Science, No. 89 in the Series of Monographs by Writers Connected with the London School of Economics and Political Science (London, 1926).

[13] *Ibid.*, p. 8sq. The author points out that similar changes were occurring in East Africa and quotes an interesting government report to support this.

[14] Hancock, *op. cit.*, Vol. II, P. 2, p. 283.

[15] S. Herbert Frankel, *The Tyranny of Economic Paternalism in Africa, A Study of Frontier Mentality 1860–1960*, suppl. to *Optima* (Johannesburg, Dec. 1960), p. 7.

"Looking back from the vantage point of our own times, it is clear that the root cause of the economic backwardness of various African territories as well as of the Native areas in the Union lies in the failure to modify customary control of land occupation and tenure, which has prevented the emergence of land use and ownership compatible with modern forms of commercialized production in a money economy. The failure to make of the land a viable economic factor of production has condemned the peoples on it to eke out a precarious subsistence. . . . As long as communal systems of land tenure and the ban on Native purchase of land in European areas continued, those able and willing to embark upon new methods of production were unable to obtain land holdings of suitable size, adequately protected against tribal rights and authority, and ensuring to the owner the undisturbed fruits of his labour for himself and his heirs. The enterprising, the unemployed, or the redundant were, therefore, condemned to wander to the towns or to other European areas to sell their labour."

27. Nor is this literature confined to Africa. The problems and strains of rapid advance are a major theme of J. S. Furnivall's *Colonial Policy and Practice*, which deals extensively with the experience of Burma[16]: "The dissolution of the political structure is only the first stage in social dissolution, and it is completed by the second, or economic, stage, breaking up the village into individuals. In this process two factors are operative: economic forces are released; and the checks controlling their action are relaxed. . . . In such circumstances there remains no embodiment of social will or representative of public welfare to control the economic forces which the impact of the West releases."

28. These writers were not simple sentimentalists deploring the passing of the good old days; they noted the very rapid changes and the problems created by them.

V

29. The discussion of the preceding sections bears on the suggestion that the international inequality of income is constantly and necessarily widening because the underdeveloped world is caught in a vicious circle of poverty while the developed countries are progressing steadily and often rapidly. And this ever-widening inequality is said to be both morally reprehensible and politically explosive. If the thesis of the vicious circle were valid, the conclusion would be simple, irresistible, and meaningful. But once it is recognised that the thesis is invalid, no such simple conclusion is possible.

30. The following considerations are among those germane to this issue. Whether the international inequality of income between developed and underdeveloped countries is widening or not depends among other factors on where the line between them is drawn, which is arbitrary. For instance, a number of countries which used to be classified as underdeveloped are no longer so regarded; familiar examples include Japan and Hong Kong. This is, of course, quite apart from the

---

[16] J. S. Furnivall, *Colonial Policy and Practice, A Comparative Study of Burma and Netherlands India* (New York, 1956), pp. 297sq.

fact that all developed countries began as underdeveloped. Again, for a large part of the underdeveloped world there were until recently no statistics whatever of national income or production, and the present statistics are often of very limited meaning.

In particular, these statistics often greatly exaggerate differences in incomes and standards of living between developed and underdeveloped (rich and poor) countries. This arises chiefly because the rates of exchange normally used in comparing national outputs greatly understate the domestic purchasing power of the currencies of the underdeveloped countries (relatively to those in developed countries), because they are based on the purchasing power of money over internationally traded goods, in which the comparative advantage of developed countries is much greater than over nontraded goods and especially services. Moreover, many of the goods and services conventionally included in the national income are more properly regarded as cost, rather than as output or income, and these are relatively much more important in developed than in underdeveloped countries. Further, intra family services are usually excluded from national income estimates. In underdeveloped countries the concept of the family is much wider than in developed countries, and a much larger preparation of economic activity takes place within the family so that this omitted category is much more important in the underdeveloped than in developed countries. Yet again, a large part of subsistence output and of services connected with subsistence or near-subsistence production are either wholly ignored or undervalued, and these are much more important in underdeveloped than in developed countries. And there are also other reasons for the relative underestimate of income in poor countries. These considerations obviously bear on comparisons both of income levels and of rates of progress.[17]

31. The profound changes in the conditions of life which have occurred in many parts of the underdeveloped world over the last century also much affect the meaningfulness of discussions whether the differences in real income per head between rich and poor countries have widened or narrowed over this period. Indeed it is doubtful whether the concept of income conventionally measured is helpful in indicating or expressing such profound changes.

32. The inadequacy of national income estimates for comparative purposes is reinforced by the great increase in population which has occurred throughout the underdeveloped world over the last fifty to eighty years, over which period the population of most of these countries has increased by a factor of between 2 and 5. This has come about largely as a result of suppression or reduction of famine,

[17] The relative underestimate in the conventional statistics of incomes and living standards in underdeveloped countries has been known for some time. An up-to-date and systematic discussion, both of the extent of exaggeration in the conventional comparisons and of the reasons for it, are to be found in an article by Dan Usher, "The Transport Bias in Comparisons of National Income", *Economica*, N.S., Vol. XXX (London, 1963), pp. 140sqq. He writes (p. 140): "For example, the conventional comparison shows that the *per capita* national income of the United Kingdom is about fourteen times that of Thailand. Recomputations made by the author to allow for various biases in the comparison suggest that the effective ratio of living standards is about three to one. Even if the recomputed ratio is doubled, the change in order of magnitude is large enough to affect our way of thinking about the underdeveloped countries."

disease, infant mortality, slave raiding, and tribal warfare. As a result, very large numbers of people have survived who otherwise would not be there, which obviously bears on the relevance and meaningfulness of discussions on differences in average or median incomes between developed and underdeveloped countries.

33. Economic progress is usually measured by the growth of real income per head. This procedure implies various judgments which are generally covert and unrecognised. The increase in population in underdeveloped countries has been brought about by the fall in the death rate (especially, but not only, among children) and this implies a longer expectation of life. The position of those who have failed to die has certainly improved, as has the situation of those whose children continue to live. Thus there is here an obvious and real psychic income. Its reality is clear from people's readiness to pay for the satisfaction of the postponement of death. Thus the usual way of drawing conclusions from income per head obscures important conceptual problems of the defined and measured income. It also implies a judgment that a high birth rate is a sign of an inability rather than of an unwillingness to control birth.

34. Over considerable periods in recent times, notably since 1930, the rates of population growth in many underdeveloped countries have been higher than in most developed countries. A differential rate of population increase in rich and poor countries brings about a change in relative numbers; as a result, the mean incomes could fall for the whole world, or for the underdeveloped world, even if incomes have everywhere increased. Indeed, the difference between the median incomes in rich and poor countries could widen even if incomes in the latter rise faster than in the former, if the difference in the rates of population growth is greater than that in the rise in incomes. These are, or should be, familiar statistical results of a change in the relative importance of component elements of an aggregate.[18]

35. Of course, even if international inequality in some specified sense or other were widening for such reasons as, for instance, the relatively greater ability of the populations of the developed countries to take advantage of technical progress or other differences in economic qualities and attitudes, this would not mean that the higher incomes have been extracted from the underdeveloped countries or otherwise secured at their expense, as is commonly suggested in contemporary discussion. The higher incomes and living standards in developed countries have been created there and not extracted from the rest of the world. In the material

---

[18] The discussion in the text bears on some quite specific ideas in the most influential current literature on underdeveloped countries. For instance, Professor Gunnar Myrdal writes: "As Mr. H. W. Singer has rightly pointed out, world real income per capita, and with it the standard of living of the *average* human being, is probably lower now than twenty-five years ago, and perhaps lower than in 1900, because the nations that have rapidly raised their economic standards have been a shrinking proportion of the total world population." Gunnar Myrdal, *An International Economy, Problems and Prospects* (New York, 1956), p. 2 (my italics). The relevant passage in Mr. Singer's article quoted verbatim in: *ibid.*, p. 341, reads: "If we define the 'average' world income as that of the median world citizen, the spectacular improvement which has occurred at one extreme and which has fascinated economists and other observers becomes irrelevant." Apart from the absence or the severe limitations of statistics of income, these passages rest on a misleading and unwarranted use of the concept of average.

sense at any rate, contact[19] with the developed world has benefited the poorer countries. Throughout the underdeveloped world the most advanced and rapidly advancing areas are those with which the developed countries have established contact. Conversely, the poorest and most backward are those with least contact with the developed world.

VI

36. In recent years a variant of the general thesis of the vicious circle of poverty has gained considerable influence. This is the suggestion that the presence of the developed countries sets up an international demonstration effect which serves to obstruct further any capital formation in underdeveloped countries which might otherwise take place. This is regarded as a further obstacle to capital formation and to economic development, in effect substituting another vicious circle of poverty and underdevelopment should the first vicious circle be broken through in some way or other. This has first been advanced by Professor Nurkse, who argued that contact with advanced economies is damaging to underdeveloped countries by raising the propensity to consume, thus discouraging saving and preventing investment. To quote[20]: "Knowledge of or contact with new consumption patterns opens one's eyes to previously unrecognized possibilities. . . . In the poorer countries such goods are often imported goods, not produced at home; but that is not the only trouble. The basic trouble is that the presence or the mere knowledge of new goods and new methods of consumption tends to raise the general propensity to consume. . . . The vicious circle that keeps down the domestic supply of capital in low-income areas is bad enough by itself. My point is that it tends to be made even worse by the stresses that arise from relative as distinct from absolute poverty."

37. In fact, however, the effects of contact with more advanced countries are usually very different from those assumed by the international demonstration effect. It almost invariably accelerates economic growth in less developed countries by encouraging production for the market, by suggesting new wants, new crops, and improved methods generally. This indeed is a commonplace of economic history. And at present throughout the underdeveloped world the more advanced sectors and areas are those which are in contact with the more developed countries.

38. The usual formulation of the international demonstration effect omits to note that the new types of consumer goods can be bought only if incomes are first earned to purchase them. Indeed, until quite recently the absence of new wants and the inelasticity of consumption and of standards of living were regarded as major obstacles to economic development; and the role of new categories of consumer goods, often termed incentive or inducement goods, was emphasized as an instrument of economic progress. The demonstration effect resulting from contact with more developed economies usually induces a higher economic

---

[19] The reference here, as elsewhere in this paper, is of course to peaceful contact, not to military conquest.

[20] Nurkse, *op. cit.*, pp. 61sq., *70*.

performance, more effort, more productive work, more enterprise, and often also additional and more productive saving and investment, especially direct investment in agriculture for production for the market. This influence is reinforced because the contact usually not only suggests new wants but also acquaints the population with new crops and methods of production, the adoption of which makes possible the satisfaction of the new wants. Moreover, by generating cash incomes this process also promotes investment in other parts of the economy; public investment made possible by increased revenues is only one obvious example.[21]

The usual exposition of the international demonstration effect seems to assume that the exchange economy has already permeated the entire economy, or at any rate that the supply of effort to the exchange sector and its rate of expansion are not affected by the attractiveness of the rewards obtainable in that sector. These assumptions are inapplicable to most underdeveloped countries.

----

[21] However, in the public sector of underdeveloped countries an adverse administration effect does indeed often operate. Governments, politicians, and public servants in underdeveloped countries seem to be very susceptible to it in adopting or seeking to adopt technical, educational, and social standards which are inappropriate and wasteful. The governments and public servants in these countries are being pressed to rival the standards of developed countries. Readiness to yield to these pressures may be a condition of political survival, and in yielding to these pressures the politicians and the administrators do not spend their own resources. But this is very different from the international administration effect suggested by Professor Nurkse and by those who follow him. And on balance the net effect of the international contacts has obviously promoted material progress in the underdeveloped countries, as is clear from the fact that throughout the underdeveloped world the most advanced sectors and areas are those with which the developed countries have established contact.

Selection **2**

Is Economic Development Desirable?

W. ARTHUR LEWIS

From: The Theory of Economic Growth (*Homewood, Ill.: Richard D. Irwin, Inc., 1955*), pp. 420–435. *Reprinted by permission of Richard D. Irwin, Inc.*

Like everything else, economic growth has its costs. If economic growth could be achieved without any disadvantages, everybody would be wholly in its favour. But since growth has real disadvantages, people differ in their attitude to growth according to the different assessment which they give to its advantages and disadvantages. They may dislike the kind of society which is associated with economic growth, preferring the attitudes and institutions which prevail in stable societies. Or, even if they are reconciled to the institutions of growing societies, they may dislike the transitional processes in the course of which stable societies are converted into growing societies; they may therefore conclude either that the benefits of growth are not worth the cost of the disturbance it involves, or also that growth should be introduced slowly, so that the society may have as long as possible to adjust itself to the changes which economic growth requires. We shall begin with the advantages of growth, and then consider the costs of growth in terms of the attitudes it requires and in terms of the disturbances involved in the process of transition.

THE BENEFITS OF ECONOMIC GROWTH

The advantage of economic growth is not that wealth increases happiness, but that it increases the range of human choice. It is very hard to correlate wealth and happiness. Happiness results from the way one looks at life, taking it as it comes, dwelling on the pleasant rather than the unpleasant, and living without fear of what the future may bring. Wealth would increase happiness if it increased resources more than it increased wants, but it does not necessarily do this, and there is no evidence that the rich are happier than the poor, or that individuals grow happier as their incomes increase. Wealth decreases happiness if in the acquisition of wealth one ceases to take life as it comes and worries more about resources and the future. There is, indeed, some evidence that this is the case; insofar as

17

economic growth results from alertness in seeking out and seizing economic opportunities, it is only to be expected that it should be associated with less happiness than we find in societies where people are not so concerned with growth. There is evidence of much greater mental disturbance in the United States of America than there is in other countries, and, even when allowance is made for differences in statistical reporting, it is at least plausible that the higher suicide rate is causally connected with the drive for greater success in an already rich community. We certainly cannot say that an increase in wealth makes people happier. We cannot say, either, that an increase in wealth makes people less happy, and even if we could say this, it would not be a decisive argument against economic growth, since happiness is not the only good thing in life. We do not know what the purpose of life is, but if it were happiness, then evolution could just as well have stopped a long time ago, since there is no reason to believe that men are happier than pigs, or than fishes. What distinguishes men from pigs is that men have greater control over their environment—not that they are more happy. And on this test, economic growth is greatly to be desired.

The case for economic growth is that it gives man greater control over his environment and thereby increases his freedom.

We can see this first in man's relations with nature. At primitive levels, man has to struggle for subsistence. With great drudgery he succeeds in wresting from the soil barely enough to keep himself alive. Every year he passes through a starvation period for several months, because the year's crop barely lasts until the next harvest. Regularly he is visited by famine, plague, or pestilence. Half his children die before reaching the age of ten, and at forty his wife is wrinkled and old. Economic growth enables him to escape from this servitude. Improved techniques yield more abundant and more varied food for less labour. Famine is banished, the infant mortality rate falls from 300 to 30 per thousand; the death rate from 40 to 10 per thousand. Cholera, smallpox, malaria, hookworm, yellow fever, plague, leprosy, and tuberculosis disappear altogether. Thus life itself is freed from some of nature's menaces. Not everybody considers this a gain. If you think that it is better to die than to live, and best not to be born, you are not impressed by the fact that economic growth permits a reduction of death rates. But most of us are still primitive enough to take it as axiomatic that life is better than death.

Economic growth also gives us freedom to choose greater leisure. In the primitive state we have to work extremely hard merely to keep alive. With economic growth we can choose to have more leisure or more goods, and we do indeed choose to have more of both. The opposite impression is created if a comparison is made between impoverished agricultural countries and rich industrial countries, since in the former labour is idle through much of the year, when the weather is unfavourable to agriculture, whereas in the latter men work regularly throughout the year; but this is a false comparison. If we compare not industry with agriculture, but the industrial sector in rich, with the industrial sector in poor countries, and similarly the agricultural sector in both countries, we shall find almost invariably shorter hours of work in each sector, as income grows; and also less drudgery, with increased use of mechanical power.

Also, it is economic growth which permits us to have more services, as well as more goods or leisure. In the poorest communities 60 or 70 per cent of the people are needed in agriculture to procure food, whereas in the richest countries 12 to 15 per cent suffice to give a standard of nutrition twice as good. The richer countries can therefore spare more people for other activities—to be doctors, nurses, and dentists; to be teachers; to be actors and entertainers; to be artists or musicians. Many of the "higher" activities which philosophers value— art, music, the study of philosophy itself—are in a sense a luxury which society can afford to develop only as economic growth permits it to spare increasing numbers from the basic task of growing food. It is true that only a relatively small surplus is needed to support the arts and that some of the highest artistic achievements date back to societies where the masses of the people were very poor. The raising of living standards over the past century has widened the opportunity to appreciate and practise the arts, without necessarily affecting the quality or quantity of the best art one way or the other. However, leaving aside the highest art, there has without doubt been an enormous increase in popular leisure and the popular opportunities for enjoying what were previously the luxuries open to very few. Relatively far more people hear the work of the best composers today than heard the work of Mozart or of Bach in their own times, or saw the work of Rembrandt or of El Greco.

Women benefit from these changes even more than men. In most underdeveloped countries woman is a drudge, doing in the household tasks which in more advanced societies are done by mechanical power—grinding grain for hours, walking miles to fetch pails of water, and so on. Economic growth transfers these and many other tasks—spinning and weaving, teaching children, minding the sick —to external establishments, where they are done with greater specialization and greater capital, and with all the advantages of large-scale production. In the process woman gains freedom from drudgery, is emancipated from the seclusion of the household, and gains at last the chance to be a full human being, exercising her mind and her talents in the same way as men. It is open to men to debate whether economic progress is good for men or not, but for women to debate the desirability of economic growth is to debate whether women should have the chance to cease to be beasts of burden and to join the human race.

Economic growth also permits mankind to indulge in the luxury of greater humanitarianism. For instance, at the lowest levels of subsistence there is little to spare for those who cannot help themselves, and the weakest must go to the wall. It is only as the surplus increases that men take increasing care of the leper, the mentally deranged, the crippled, the blind, and other victims of chance. The desire to care for the sick, the incompetent, the unlucky, the widow, and the orphan is not necessarily greater in civilized than in primitive societies, but the former have more means to spare for the purpose, and therefore do in fact display greater humanitarianism, Some people are disturbed by this; they think that it is against the eugenic interest of society to maintain persons who are not able to keep up in a competitive struggle, and they consider that the long-run effect will be to reduce biological vigour unless such persons are sterilized. But these are as yet in a minority.

Economic growth may be particularly important to societies where political aspirations are currently in excess of resources, since growth may forestall what might otherwise prove to be unbearable social tension. For example, in some countries, such as Great Britain, the working classes or their spokesmen are demanding ever larger wage-packets and ever-increasing expenditure on housing, education, health, and other amenities. If in such societies income per head is stable, the desires of one group can be met only at the expense of other groups, and this is bound to lead to civil strife. In these democratic days, most countries of the world are passing through a phase where bitter civil strife is inevitable unless there is a rapid increase in production per head, so that resources are brought nearer to aspirations. This is the aspect of economic growth which impresses itself most upon statesmen, so it is not surprising that democratic statesmen are everywhere very much convinced of the urgency of stimulating rapid economic growth. At the same time it must be admitted that economic growth does not always diminish strife. It may on the contrary have the effect of disturbing relatively stable social relationships, of stimulating envy and desire, and of precipitating class, racial, or religious conflict. This is related to the proposition that economic growth does not necessarily increase happiness. Neither does it necessarily increase political freedom. It increases the opportunity for dictators to control men's minds, through mass communication, and men's bodies, through highly organized police services. So it is not possible to argue that economic growth necessarily improves political relations.

Another aspect of the disproportion between aspirations and resources is to be seen in the political attitudes of countries of low international status. Peoples now in colonial status are anxious to become independent. Independent nations, numerous in population but poor in income, are anxious to have a higher status in the counsels of the nations. Rightly or wrongly such peoples think that if they were richer, and especially if they were rich enough to have powerful armed forces, they would count for more in international affairs, and there would be more respect for their nationals and for their way of life. There are some nationalists whose reaction to the modern world is to turn away from it and to urge their people to return to the old ways of life. But most of the nationalists who have acquired power believe that it is necessary to have rapid economic growth. Many people believe that great differences between countries in wealth or economic development provoke war and that the world would be nearer to peace if there were not wide disparities in standards of living. This is a very doubtful proposition, since societies which are undergoing rapid economic growth are often tempted to fall upon their neighbours. In any case, the causes of war are so numerous and so indirectly related to economic considerations that it hardly helps to discuss the case for economic growth in terms of possible effects on peace or war.

It is sometimes argued that any expectation that all the nations of the world can raise their standards of living continuously must be illusory, since the effect would be only to exhaust rapidly the world's accumulated stocks of minerals and of fuel. This argument rests upon two uncertain assumptions. First, it presumes that human ingenuity must in due course fail to find new substitutes for what is used up, an assumption which is rendered increasingly doubtful by what we are learning about the nature of the atom and about the transformation of one element into another. And secondly it assumes that future generations have an equal claim to the world's resources. Why should we stay poor so that the life of the human race may in some centuries to come be extended for a further century or so? Is there not as good a case for the present generations to make the best of the resources they find and to leave the distant centuries to look after themselves? Even if these questions are answered negatively, there remains the further point that it is not the poorest nations of the world who are using up the minerals and fuel rapidly, but the richest. If the argument has validity it may be taken as a counsel to Europe and to North America to stop raising their standards of living any further, but it is much less forceful as counsel to Asians and Africans, whose current draft on accumulated reserves is so small, to continue in their present poverty.

THE ACQUISITIVE SOCIETY

If the benefits listed above were available without cost, nearly everyone would favour them. Many people, however, consider that the attitudes and institutions which are necessary for economic growth are undesirable in themselves; they prefer the attitudes and institutions which belong to stable societies.

In the first place, they dislike the economizing spirit, which is one of the conditions of economic growth. If other things are equal, growth is most rapid in those societies where people give their minds to seeking out and seizing opportunities of economic gain, whether by means of increasing earnings or by means of reducing costs. And this propensity to economize, though it might equally well spring solely from a desire to reduce drudgery and increase the leisure available for enjoyment or for spiritual pursuits, seems in practice not to be well developed except when it is associated with a desire for wealth, either for its own sake or for the social prestige or the power over people which it brings. It is arguable that economy is a virtue, in the sense that there is the same sacred duty imposed upon man to abhor waste and to make the best use of his resources as there is to abhor murder and to look after the widows and orphans—in fact the parable of the talents says that this is so. Not everyone agrees that we have a sacred duty to fuss and bother about resources or about fleeting time; these would say that economy costs too much in nervous energy and human happiness and is rather a vice than a virtue. They might admit a duty to economize or work enough to reach some minimum standard of living, necessary for health and comfort (a dubious concept) but would argue that economy beyond this level is not worth the effort. Moreover, even those who accept economy to be a virtue may nevertheless deplore the fact (if it is a fact) that this virtue is found only in association with the vice (if it is a vice) of materialism. It is possible to desire that children should be taught to make the best use of the resources and opportunities available to them (the virtue of economy), and at the same time not to want more than they already have (to avoid the vice of cupidity). If this were done, and if the teaching were effective, there would still be economic growth; only, instead of its showing itself in ever-rising material standards of living, it would show itself in ever-increasing leisure at constant material standards; and if this leisure were not to result also in the ever-increasing vice of idleness (if this is a vice), children would have also to be taught to use their leisure in ways which resulted neither in idleness nor in the production of economic goods and services. We cannot, in practice, get very far by pursuing lines of enquiry which depend on assuming human nature to be other than it is. Man likes to have more wealth, likes to economize, and likes to be idle. None of these desires seems to be intrinsically either virtuous or vicious, but any one of them pursued to its extremes, in disregard of other duties, obligations, or rights, results in unbalanced personalities and also in harm to other persons. It is just as much possible for a society to be "not materialistic enough" as it is for it to be "too materialistic." Or, to put the matter the other way round, economic growth is desirable, but we can certainly have too much of it (more than is good for spiritual or social health) just as well as we may have too little of it.

Exactly the same comment can be made in relation to individualism, which is the second score on which economic growth is attacked. It seems to be the case that economic growth is more likely if individuals attend primarily to their own interests and those of their more immediate relations than if they are bound by a much wider net of social obligations. This is why economic growth is associated, both as cause and as effect, with the disappearance of extended family and joint family systems; with the erosion of social systems based on status (slavery, serfdom, caste, age, family, race) and their substitution by systems based upon contract and upon equality of opportunity; with a high level of vertical social mobility; and with the decline of tribal bonds and the reduced recognition generally of the claims of social groups. This is another problem which cannot be solved by making a virtue of one side of the argument and a vice of the other. There are some rights which all individuals ought to have and which should be protected against all social claims; and at the same time every individual belongs to a group, or whole series of groups, whose existence is necessary to his own social health, and whose continuance depends upon his recognizing the claims of the group and loyally accepting its authority. The growth of individualism in the past five hundred years has had its evil side, but it has also been a valuable and liberating influence. Economic growth cannot therefore be attacked for being associated with individualism as if the only good things in human relations were tribalism, social status, extended family relations, and political authoritarianism.

A third line of attack upon economic growth derives from its association with reliance on reason. Economic growth depends upon improving technology, and this in turn is greatest where men have a reasoning attitude both toward nature and also toward social relations. Now the reasoning mind is suspect, either because it is believed to result in religious agnosticism or in atheism, or also because it is considered incompatible with the acceptance of authority. As for religious belief, it is an open question whether decline of belief in God or gods is to be blamed for the evils of our time, or even whether the evils of our time are greater than those of previous ages in which religious belief was commoner. But, in any case, it is not true that belief in the importance of reason is inconsistent with belief in God.

The existence of God cannot be proved or disproved by rational means, so there is no reason whatsoever why the most rational of men should not also believe in the existence of God. Reason erodes not religion but authority, and it is only insofar as religion is based upon authority that the reasoning mind is hostile to religion. But in this sense the reasoning mind is just as hostile to science as it is to religion; for it is hostile to any attempt to claim that current doctrine is not open to re-examination from the roots upward or that only the initiated have the right to question its validity. Here again, however, as with materialism and with individualism, so also with reason; truth is not to be found by identifying virtue with one only of two opposites. For, just as materialism and spirituality are both desirable, so also society needs to have both reason and authority. The good life is founded in weaving a pattern of opposite principles, not in rejecting some and using only the others.

A fourth line of attack is pursued by those who do not like the growth of scale which is associated with economic growth. The economies of scale show themselves, in the first instance, in the division of labour and in the use of machinery. This is disliked by some who dislike machine-made goods and who prefer the products of the skilled handicraftsman. Economic growth destroys old handicraft skills, and though it creates even more new skills, machine skills and others (for specialization greatly increases the range of skills), there are many people who regret the passing of the old skills and the old craft products and who find no consolation either in the growth of the new skills or in the multiplication and cheapening of output which mass production makes possible. The principle of specializations is itself attacked, for specialization results in people having to do the same thing over and over again and this, whether it be turning nuts on bolts, or packing chocolates into boxes, or repeating the same university lecture, or practising musical scales, or taking out appendixes, is necessarily boring, until one gets so used to one's job that one can do it without giving the whole of one's mind to it.

The economies of scale show themselves also in the growth of the size of the administrative unit. Thus businesses, units of governments, and other organizations grow in scale. In the process, men are separated from the ownership of their tools and are proletarianized. Large-scale organization brings with it also peculiar social tensions; such organizations have to be run on hierarchical lines, which means that a few command while the majority obey, however much one may seek to democratize the process; these organizations have also to find some means of distributing work and reward which is at the same time efficient and accepted as just. We have not yet succeeded in learning how to run large-scale organizations without creating unrest, and many people therefore think that we would be better off without them.

Large-scale organizations are also disliked because of the discipline they impose; day after day men must rise at the same hour, arrive at their place of work at the same hour, do much the same things, and return home at the same time. Some think that this makes life drab and monotonous and reduces human beings to the mechanical role of cogs in some vast wheel. They would prefer that men should not be tied to the clock and should have greater freedom of choice from day to day, though it is by no means clear either that the man who works in the one-man business is less a slave of the clock, or that having regular habits is something to be deplored.

The economies of large-scale organization also result in the growth of towns, especially when this is associated with growing real income per head, which increases the demand for manufactured products and for services relatively to the demand for agricultural products. Insofar as the revolt against large towns is associated with a preference for agricultural occupations, it is really a revolt against technological progress. For it is technological progress which enables a country to produce with 15 per cent of its population enough food to feed the whole, and if we are to return to the days when 70 per cent of the people were needed upon the land, either we must abandon all that agricultural science has taught us, or else we must reduce hours of work to about ten a week. It is technological progress in agriculture which results in the growth of urban occupations, but it is the economies of large-scale organization which result in these urban occupations being concentrated in ever larger towns. That this is undesirable is by no means clear. The majority of people, when given the chance of working in the town or in the village, choose the town—this is why towns grow at the expense of villages; only a minority prefer the village to the town, and many of those who denounce the town are in fact careful to avoid living in villages. If towns are thrown up in a great hurry, without proper planning or control, they can indeed be slummy, drab, ugly, and unhealthy; but in these days there is no reason why new towns (or even old ones for that matter) should not be as beautiful, gracious, healthy, and inspiring as any village, as well as providing far wider opportunities for exercising body, mind, and soul than any village could ever hope to offer.

Finally, economic growth may be deplored in so far as it is dependent upon inequality of income. That this dependence exists cannot be denied since growth would be small or negative if differential awards were not available for hard work, for conscientious work, for skill, for responsibility, and for initiative. It is arguable in any given situation whether the existing differentials are too great or too small, in the restricted sense of being greater or less than is required to achieve the desired rate of economic growth. But it is not arguable, as the rulers of the U.S.S.R. soon discovered, that significant economic growth could be achieved even if there were no differentials at all. Now, part of the revolt against economic growth on this score is no more than an argument that in some particular place or time the differentials existing are greater than are necessary for the achieved level of growth and are due to faulty social organization. To this extent the argument simply becomes one of altering social institutions (inheritance of property, ownership of land, taxation, educational opportunities, etc.) in ways which alter the distribution of income or of property without reducing the rate of economic growth. But there are also situations where the degree of differentiation which economic growth demands is not acceptable even when it is fully admitted that smaller differentiation would reduce growth—for example, situations where foreign teachers or technicians cannot be had except at salaries which are high by local standards, or where pioneering foreign or domestic entrepreneurs are unwilling to initiate developments unless they are allowed the chance to make and keep profits at a rate far in excess of what is locally thought to be "reasonable." The economic test in such matters is that of supply and demand: "reasonable" differentials are those salaries or profits which are objectively necessary in the situation to secure the required supply of skill or initiative. But what is "reasonable" on this test may well be "unreasonable" by some other standard of merit or social justice.

Three conclusions follow from this analysis. First, some of the alleged costs of economic growth are not necessary consequences of growth at all—the ugliness of towns or the impoverishment of the working classes, for instance. Secondly, some of the alleged evils are not in fact intrinsically evil—the growth of individualism, or of reasoning, or of towns, for example. As in all human life, such things can be taken to excess, but they are not intrinsically any less desirable than their opposites. From this it follows, however, thirdly, that the rate of economic growth can be too high for the health of society. Economic growth is only one good thing among many, and we can take it to excess. Excessive growth may result in, or be the result of, excessive materialism, excessive individualism, excessive mobility of population, excessive inequality of income, or the like. Societies are not necessarily wise to choose to speed up their rate of growth above its current level; if they do, they will enjoy substantial benefits, but they may also incur substantial costs, in social or in spiritual terms, and whether the potential gains exceed the potential losses must be assessed separately in each situation as best we may. It is because economic growth has both its gains and its losses that we are all almost without exception ambivalent in our attitudes toward economic growth. We demand the abolition of poverty, illiteracy, and disease, but we cling desperately to the beliefs, habits, and social arrangements which we like, even when these are the very cause of the poverty which we deplore.

PROBLEMS OF TRANSITION

Special problems arise when it is a matter of introducing economic growth into societies which have existed for some centuries at low levels more or less of economic stagnation. For it is then necessary to transform beliefs, habits, and institutions; and though in due course when the new beliefs, habits, and institutions have been going for some time, and have become firmly rooted, a new dynamic equilibrium may be reached which is in every sense superior to the old static social equilibrium, nevertheless the transition may produce temporary but very painful situations.

One of the more obvious of these is changing peoples' habits of work. For example, suppose that copper is discovered in a very primitive country where all the people have land of their own which enables them to live to their own satisfaction, though at very low levels of health, of material standards, or of culture. These people do not want to work in copper mines, and it may be that they will not voluntarily accept employment at any wage which would make it remunerative to work the mines. On the other hand, it is also possible that if they were forced to work in the mines the wealth they could thereby produce would make it possible to give them very much higher standards of material well-being, of health, of education, and of culture. Suppose also that if initially forced they would after a while acquire such a taste for the new kind of work, such an appreciation of their high standards, and such contempt for their previous ways of life that in due course they would be glad to work in the mines after the force was removed. Is the temporary use of force justified in these circumstances? This abstract example is by no means a mere academic exercise, since it is not at all dissimilar to what has happened in some parts of Africa, where the people have been forced to work in mines or on plantations, whether by orders issued through their chiefs, or because this was the only way of earning money to pay the taxes imposed on them for this purpose, or because they were driven off their lands. What actually happened in these cases is more complicated than the facts given in our abstract example, because of the additional fact that those who exercised force in these circumstances did it primarily to enrich themselves and not because they wished to benefit the Africans. In some of these cases there is also the further fact that the Africans have not even benefited materially; on the contrary, their former villages are ruined economically, their way of life has been destroyed, while they themselves live in barracks, slums, and shanty towns in material no less than in spiritual impoverishment. We have always emphasized in this enquiry that it is possible to have economic growth, in the sense of increasing output per head, without the majority of the people being any better off, because the increased output enriches only a powerful few. Most people in the world would agree that such developments are immoral and would condemn economic policies which benefit the few at the cost of the many no matter how great the increased output that would result. This, however, is quite different from the abstract case we are examining, since it is one of the presuppositions of this case that the effect will be greatly to increase both the material and the cultural standards of the people involved, and that they themselves will in due course prefer the new way of life to the old. Faced with this example people react in different ways. Some rest their case on opposition to compulsion: however good the ultimate effects, they say, no man should be coerced for his own good or for the good of his descendants. Others rest their case on happiness; even if the people come to prefer the new way of life to the old, they say, they are not really any better off because they are not any happier; hence they have had a painful transition to no purpose, since they have gained nothing that matters—a questionable argument, as we have already seen, since it is doubtful whether happiness is an appropriate test of change. Still others react differently and would justify coercion if it greatly benefited the coerced. Thus, Negroes in the New World condemn the act of slavery which took them there, but in truth not all of them regret that their forefathers were not left in the jungle villages of West Africa. So also there will always be politicians and statesmen, while the world lasts, who will not hesitate to coerce their subjects for the ultimate good of the coerced.

The question of the limits of permissible force is currently very acute since it has been demonstrated by the U.S.S.R. that a ruthless government can raise real output very rapidly if it is willing to deal severely with those who oppose its plans. All underdeveloped countries are being invited, by communist or other propaganda, to yield up their liberties in return for a promise of rapid economic growth. The invitation is somewhat misleading. They are told that the loss of liberty would be temporary, that the "dictatorship of the proletariat"—or the caudillo, or the army leader, or whoever it may be—is only a transitional phase, to be followed by the "withering away" of the state; but we may well doubt whether liberties once surrendered are ever so easily regained. Neither does the invitation guarantee a rising standard of living; output may rise rapidly, but the dictator may decide to use it for purposes other than raising the standard of living of ordinary people. In any case, it is quite clear that it is not necessary to have a dictatorship in order to have economic growth. One or two democratic governments of underdeveloped countries—Burma, the Gold Coast—have shown that they have the will and the courage to find the resources which are necessary for growth and that this can be done within the democratic framework by leaders who enjoy widespread confidence and support. It is up to other democracies to show that they can do the same.

Another painful transition is that which has to be made in social relations. The opposition of reason to authority, the movement from status to contract, and the change from social stability to vertical social mobility all upset existing relationships, whether in the matter of class, religion, political obedience, or family ties. This is clearly enough the case if the transition comes to a head in violent revolution, but even without this the transition is painful because it frustrates existing expectations and rights in every sphere. Many people are opposed to economic growth on this account. Some take the view that the old relationships are as good as the new or even better—they dislike the new freedom of family relations, the alleged "rights" of the "common man," and the destruction of the old social harmonies. Others, who do not believe that the old relationships were particularly harmonious and who prefer the new, nevertheless question whether the difference is worth the cost. This, clearly, is an issue which can be decided only in terms of the valuation which one sets upon such matters as increased knowledge, equality of opportunity, better health standards, longer life, and the other fruits of economic growth.

Then there is the transition which has to be made in moral values. In the old society children are brought up into a code of behaviour, duties, and loyalties. The new society has a different code. Good behaviour in one society may be bad behaviour in the other. The duties and loyalties shift from one set of persons and institutions to another set—from the age group to the trade union, from the chief to an employer, or from the family to impersonal customers. In due course the new code may be established and may work as smoothly as its predecessor, but meanwhile the community may pass through a trying time, during which the old morality has been cast off before the new has taken hold. Such transitions have been particularly painful in the past because we have not understood what was taking place. The transition is made much easier if the morality of the old society and the morality of the new society are both well known, and if those who are responsible for setting or guarding the moral standards of the community (especially the priests, the teachers, and the legislators) deliberately set out to preach the new morality, right from the beginning of the change. But, in the first place, it is only recently that we have come to understand these matters and to appreciate in particular the extent to which moral codes are bound up with and appropriate to particular social and economic patterns. In the second place, those who guard the moral standards of the community usually consider it to be their duty to guard the old code; they are hostile to the change and regard the new code as immoral. And thirdly, even if they were won over to the new code, much of their authority disappears in the transitional phase, because of the growth of reliance on reason and because of the public's loss of confidence in the institutions and practices with which these guardians have hitherto been identified. Thus the new code is not introduced systematically or authoritatively. It is picked up only gradually, and in parts. New beliefs and old beliefs mix inconsistently. And there is much frustration and bewilderment when people do what they know to be the right thing to do and find themselves ridiculed, scolded, or punished for behaving in that way.

Painful transitions are inherent in the transformation of a society from one way of life to another; they cannot be altogether avoided except by avoiding change itself. This no one can do. The propensity to change is inherent in the nature of man. For man is essentially curious and therefore forever accumulates knowledge, which alters his way of life. He is also prone to dissatisfaction, wanting more than he has, or moving about, or coveting his neighbour's status or possessions. He has also a sense of adventure, which makes him take chances, and a sense of rebellion, which is a constant challenge to hierarchical relations. It is therefore a waste of time to think in terms of stopping social change and a waste of sentiment to regret that all established institutions must pass away. For social change arises just out of those parts of our nature which distinguish us from the rest of the animal kingdom.

All the same, though we cannot prevent change, we can accelerate it or retard it. We have already emphasized that the rate of change can be too high, as well as too low. In the present context our problem is not the appropriate rate of growth of output, but rather the appropriate length of the period of transition from one pattern of social attitudes and institutions to another. Here there is no easy generalization; there is as good a case for getting transitions over quickly as there is for allowing plenty of time for adjustment.

In practice, we have no opportunity to choose retardation. The leaven of economic change is already working in every society—even in Tibet—thanks to the linkage of the world which has been achieved in the past eighty years by steamships, by imperialism, by aeroplanes, by wireless, by migration, by Hollywood, and by the printed word. There have, in particular, been two developments which make it imperative not to retard but to accelerate further growth. One of these is the fact that aspirations have grown faster than production. And the other is the fact that death rates are falling faster than birth rates.

In all the underdeveloped world, aspirations now greatly exceed production, and the gap is growing. The masses of the people are beginning to believe that their poverty is unnecessary and that it could be ended by changing their allegiances. Some few believe that it could be changed by their own individual endeavour, but many more believe that the solution lies in repudiating their landlords, their employers, their priests, or their present political rulers. Some politicians also have great aspirations, whether it be to raise the material and cultural standards of their people, or also to raise the standing of their country in international affairs. Now a large gap between aspirations and production can be very dangerous, since it produces frustrations from which almost anything may emerge. Many people fear that the result will be "communism" (a word which no longer has any precise meaning). Some fear the spread of native breeds of "fascism" (a word which has to be interpreted to include the traditional warlordism of many Eastern countries, as well as the Latin American "caudillo"). Others again see a strong likelihood that power will pass to religious fanatics (to mullahs, Mahasabas, rabbis, and the like). It is not therefore surprising that the leaders of many under-developed countries give a very high priority to measures for rapidly increasing production. Whether they will have the courage, and the necessary internal and external support, to raise the necessary resources may be doubted. And it is also doubtful whether in any case aspirations will not continue to outdistance production. But those who believe that it would be wrong to speed up production because of the effects on social relations, or on moral codes, usually forget both that these are already changing rapidly and also that the results of frustrated aspirations may be even more dangerous to existing patterns than speeding up production would be.

The population dilemma is even less escapable. Underdeveloped countries untouched by external influences seem to have stable populations, with birth and death rates both very high by current standards. Once these countries are drawn into the modern world, with the consequent eradication of local famines and introduction of public health and medical care, the death rate begins to drop rapidly and may fall from forty to ten per thousand in less than two generations. It then becomes necessary to begin to increase total production by rates of one or two or three per cent per annum, to keep up with rising population. Also, unless there is plenty of land available, it also becomes necessary to take steps to reduce birth rates to the same spectacular degree as death rates. This seems, however, almost certainly to require that production should grow even faster than popula-tion, since most of the explanations of the reasons why people adopt family limita-tion ultimately turn upon rising standards of living. In such a situation we cannot really choose to retard the growth of production; on the contrary, in practically every one of the countries usually called underdeveloped the situation is that the current rate of growth of production is not adequate to permit the population problem to be tackled seriously. Again those who argue for retardation have usually overlooked what is happening to population and have forgotten that the consequences of a population explosion may be much more damaging to existing social structures and moral codes than the consequences of any likely increase in production would be.

Selection **3**

Is There a Role for Market Forces in the Development of Developing Countries?

HARRY G. JOHNSON

From: Money, Trade and Economic Growth; Survey Lectures in Economic Theory (*Cambridge, Mass.: Harvard University Press, 1962*), *pp. 151–163. Reprinted by permission of George Allen and Unwin Ltd. and Harvard University Press.*

Economic development is a field of study in which economists have only recently begun to specialize, and in which consequently there is as yet no settled body of economic doctrine. I must therefore begin with the warning that what I am about to present is not the agreed view of a representative group of economists, but rather my own opinions. Though I have drawn on the literature of development and of economic theory in forming these opinions, I cannot say that the results constitute an authoritative statement of the present position of economics.

The fundamental causes of economic growth are not a subject with which economists have dealt much in the past, and they are not a subject with which economists can claim to be qualified by training and technique to deal now. My subject is not, however, the causes of economic development, but planning and the market in economic development; this involves the theory of markets, and on that subject economists by profession have a great deal to say. Indeed, from the time of Adam Smith, the theory of markets has been the core of economics as a social science.

It is true that the full ramifications of the market as an instrument of social and economic organization were not appreciated from the start by the classical economists. The English classical economists understood the functions of commodity markets, but they did not link the theory of distribution to the pricing process. The integration of the theory of factor prices with the theory of commodity markets was left to J. B. Say, and later Walras and Marshall, to work out. But the relation between the market and economic development lay at the centre of the foundations laid by Adam Smith. Smith was concerned with economic development, and at the heart of his work was the market, determining the extent of specialization and division of labour and the limits to increasing productivity.

In recent times, there has been a retreat both in economic theory and in economic policy from the nineteenth-century ideal of the unfettered market as a principle of economic organization. But the economic pros and cons of this retreat have been fully debated, and the economist consequently has a great deal to say about the relative merits of the market as contrasted with other methods of economic organization and the circumstances appropriate to each.

The subject of planning and the market in economic development is, therefore, one which falls definitely within the field of the economist. Before I go on to discuss it, I must define more precisely what I mean by it. "Planning and the market" may be interpreted in two different ways. First, it may refer to the contrast between direction of the economy by Government and the policy of laissez-faire. This is not my subject, though in a wider philosophical and historical context it offers much to discuss. For example, though laissez-faire and direction are often regarded as opposites, if one looks to the history of economic development one finds (as Professor Easterbrook has shown[1]) that economic development is almost invariably a process in which planning and direction on the one hand and freedom of enterprise on the other play their part and are mixed. There is almost no case in which economic development has been entirely planned or entirely unplanned. The usual pattern is one of some framework of control by Government, within which the entrepreneur provides his services—a mixture of bureaucracy and enterprise, in which bureaucracy takes care of the major risks of development and enterprise faces and overcomes the minor ones. Another relevant point that Easterbrook makes is that an economy which succeeds in finding a formula for growth tends to repeat that pattern after it has become inappropriate. For example, Britain has gone on trying to work the internationally-orientated pattern of her nineteenth-century development; Russia has been very successful in developing heavy industry but has not yet solved the problem of agriculture.

The alternative interpretation takes planning, in the sense of a general direction of the economy, as an established principle, and considers the market as an alternative to other and more direct means of detailed control. Given the general framework of economic planning, there is still a choice between two alternative methods of looking after the details. One is by direct detailed planning by a central authority; the other is by leaving the working out of details as far as possible to the operation of the market. (There is a third alternative, in which the Government is itself the entrepreneur and investor, which I shall consider later.)

This alternative interpretation is the one I shall be using: I shall discuss the question of the market mechanism as against detailed planning as an instrument of economic development. I should like to make it clear from the start that I am going to make a strong case for the market, as the preferable instrument of economic development, on two main grounds. The first is that the achievement of the

---

[1] Professor Easterbrook's analysis was presented in the Marshall Lectures at Cambridge University in the spring of 1956. Unfortunately these lectures have not been published, but some of the ideas are available in W. T. Easterbrook, "Long Period Comparative Study: Some Historical Cases," *Journal of Economic History*, Vol. XVII, No. 4 (Dec. 1957), pp. 571–595.

desired results by control methods is likely to be especially difficult and inefficient in an underdeveloped economy; at this point I should like to remind you that a large part of Adam Smith's argument for laissez-faire was the inefficiency and corruption he saw in the Governments of his time. The second is that the remedies for the main fault which can be found with the use of the market mechanism, its undesirable social effects, are luxuries which underdeveloped countries cannot afford to indulge in if they are really serious about attaining a high rate of development. In particular, there is likely to be a conflict between rapid growth and an equitable distribution of income, and a poor country anxious to develop would probably be well advised not to worry too much about the distribution of income.

I am going to make a fairly strong case for the market, because the market figures relatively little in the literature of economic development, and the theoretical analysis which economics has developed in relation to markets is often overlooked or disregarded. Before getting down to business on the subject of markets, I should like to explore a little the question why, in the theory and policy of "economic development," so little scope is usually allowed to the operation of market forces. There have been, I think, three main groups of factors at work.

In the first place, there seems to be in human societies a set of social and psychological factors favouring intervention in the market. In this connection it is important to remember that the free market as commonly understood is essentially a characteristic of the nineteenth century—before then, and since, the common feature of economic organization has been intervention in the market. What are these factors? One of them, I believe, is the impatience of idealists and would-be reformers with the working of the market and their desire to take direct action to improve things, according to their criteria of improvement: this attitude reflects the intellectual arrogance typical of reformers. The attitude is reinforced by the fact that the defects of market organization seem obvious to anyone, or can be made to seem so, whereas the socio-economic functions of the market are obscure and difficult to appreciate. The discovery of these functions was indeed the great achievement of the classical economists and constitutes the only claim that economics has to the status of a science. The obscurity of the market's functions makes it easy, also, to confuse opposition to unattractive features of the free enterprise system which express themselves through the market, such as inequality of income and wealth, with opposition to the market as a mechanism of organization.

Opposition to and dislike of the market for the reasons I have just discussed is frequently allied with a positive belief in the desirability of Government intervention in the market and a faith in the disinterestedness and effectiveness of such intervention. Belief in the desirability of Government intervention in the western world is associated with the spread of socialist ideas and in its modern form can be traced back to Benthamite utilitarianism; elsewhere, it can probably be associated with the nature of the state as the dispenser of justice in primitive economies. Belief in the efficiency and disinterestedness of Governmental intervention is associated with the growth of the modern career civil service, with its standards of incorruptibility, particularly in Britain and countries influenced by the British example. (This explains why the belief is less prevalent in the United States than in other English-speaking countries.) It is, in my opinion, an important question for underdeveloped countries whether their civil services are of the calibre required to administer the kinds of social and economic programmes adopted in the advanced economies.

Opposition to the market as a means of economic organization is also inherent in the characteristics of an established and functioning civil service. One of these characteristics, a corollary of the standards of administrative efficiency and "public service," is a natural propensity to regulate. A good civil service, or a bad one, is rarely prepared to decide that non-intervention is the best policy; and to the bureaucratic mind the functioning of the price system as a regulator appears mere disorder and chaos. Another characteristic is an antipathy towards entrepreneurship; the entrepreneur is an agent of change, and as such disturbs the orderliness of the economy and makes it more difficult to regulate. This is not, of course, a universally valid generalization: civil services have, at times, played important entrepreneurial roles themselves, though usually under the pressure of political events. One special feature of the generally anti-entrepreneurial attitude of civil servants, noted by P. T. Bauer in his studies of West African trade,[2] is specially relevant to underdeveloped economies. This is the antipathy of the British-trained type of civil servant, literate and "responsible," to the semi-literate and socially unacceptable type of individual who possesses the knack of making money by trading—the small-scale entrepreneur on whose activities economic development from a low level may well depend.

These characteristics of civil services are important in considering the uses and limitations of control methods in economic development. The economist, or any other intelligent man, can easily think up ways in which market processes could be improved on by means of controls, assuming that he administers them himself and has infinite time in which to do so. But would the conclusion in favour of controls be the same if it were accepted that their administration had to be entrusted to a "responsible" civil servant of the British type, let alone a civil service with a less ingrained tradition of honesty and distinterestedness?

A third factor antithetical to the market has been the character of modern economics itself, as applied to economic planning. Modern economics has been strongly influenced by the theoretical revolutions of the 1930s, which were inimical to competition and the market. On the one hand, both the theory of monopolistic competition and the new welfare economics have been excessively concerned with criticisms of the efficiency of the market mechanism, criticisms formulated from a static viewpoint not obviously relevant to growth problems. On the other hand, the Keynesian revolution fostered aggregative thinking to the neglect of older ideas of substitutability in production and consumption (which in turn have receded into the limbo of mathematical economics); and the habit of aggregative thinking has to some extent been reinforced by the modern emphasis on statistical verification which has necessarily postulated simplicity of economic relationships.

---

[2] P. T. Bauer, *West African Trade: A Study of Competition, Oligopoly and Monopoly in a Changing Economy* (Cambridge: Cambridge University Press, 1954), especially Chaps. 11–12, pp. 145–171.

In addition to these theoretical developments, development economics has been strongly influenced by the nature of the major problems with which economics was concerned before it turned to "development," namely, mass unemployment and war finance, which inculcated the habit of thinking about economic structure as given and of applying criteria other than consumers' choice. Two features of wartime economic planning are frequently overlooked in the attempt to carry over its concepts and techniques to peacetime planning. In the first place, the battery of controls applied in wartime rested very heavily on a strong appeal to patriotism. The application of similar techniques might be possible in an under-developed country which could mobilize and concentrate all the instruments of communication and propaganda on the single aim of development, but the capacity of most countries to do this is doubtful, especially as development presents no single dramatic objective comparable to victory. Secondly, in spite of the propaganda and the patriotic appeal, wartime economic policy in most countries ran into serious difficulties with the resurgence of the market in the form of black markets of various kinds, shop shortages, incentive problems, and so on.

I have been discussing various reasons why thinking about economic development has been inimical to, or neglectful of, market considerations. I now want to recapitulate briefly the various economic functions of the market and the price system as a method of economic organization. I shall be brief, as the argument is a familiar one.

In the first place, the market rations supplies of consumer goods among consumers; this rationing is governed by the willingness of consumers to pay, and provided the distribution of income is acceptable, it is a socially efficient process. Secondly, the market directs the allocation of production between commodities, according to the criterion of maximum profit, which, on the same assumption, corresponds to social usefulness. Thirdly, the market allocates the different factors of production among their various uses, according to the criterion of maximizing their incomes. Fourthly, it governs the relative quantities of specific types of labour and capital equipment made available. Fifthly, it distributes income between the factors of production and therefore between individuals. Thus it solves all the economic problems of allocation of scarce means between alternative ends.

These are static functions; but the market also serves in various ways to provide incentives to economic growth. Thus the availability of goods through the market stimulates the consumer to seek to increase his income, and access to the market provides an opportunity for inventors of new goods and technical improvements to profit from their exploitation. Moreover, the market serves particularly to provide an incentive to the accumulation of capital of all kinds: first to the accumulation of personal capital in the form of trained skill, since such skill earns a higher reward; and second to the accumulation of material capital, since such capital earns an income.

The argument, then, is that a properly functioning market system would tend to stimulate both economic efficiency and economic growth. And it is important to note that the market does this automatically, while it requires no big administrative apparatus, no central decision-making, and very little policing other than the provision of a legal system for the enforcement of contracts.

All this sounds very impressive, but it is clearly not the whole of the story. What, then, are the objections to the market, how serious are they, and what should be done about them in the context of economic development? I shall discuss these questions in some detail. But first I shall state briefly the central theme of my discussion. It is that in many cases the objections to the market can be over-come by reforming specific markets, so as to bring them closer to the ideal type of market; and that to overcome other objections to the market may be very expensive and may not prove to be worthwhile—in other words, the defects of the market mechanism may on balance be more tolerable than they look at first sight.

Now, what are the objections to the market? They can, I think, be classified into two main types. One type of objection is that the market does not perform its functions properly. The other type of objection is that the results produced by the functioning of the market are undesirable in themselves.

I begin with the first type of objection—that the market does not perform its function properly. Here it is useful to draw a distinction between two quite different sorts of cases—those in which the market operates imperfectly and those in which a perfectly functioning market would not produce the best results.

Imperfect operation of the market in an underdeveloped country may be attributable to ignorance, in the sense of lack of familiarity with market mechanisms and of awareness of relevant information, or to the prevalence of other modes of behaviour than the rational maximization of returns from effort. In the first case, the appropriate Governmental policy would seem to me to be not to assume from the market the responsibility for allocative decisions, but to disseminate the knowledge and information required to make the market work efficiently and provide the education required to use it. The second case implies a more funda-mental obstacle, not only to the use of the market but also to economic develop-ment itself, and suggests that successful economic development requires a basic change in social psychology. To my mind, it raises a serious question of fact. Is it really true that people in underdeveloped countries are strangers to the idea of maximizing gains? The idea that they are is very common in the literature and policy making of economic development; one of its manifestations is the implicit assumption that both supplies and demands are completely price-inelastic. I am very sceptical about this, partly because of Bauer's work and partly because at least some of the actions of Governments in underdeveloped areas presuppose that even the poorest producers are susceptible to price incentives. I personally do not think one is justified in assuming as a general proposition that ignorance and illiteracy necessarily imply that men are not interested in making money. If it is true, there will be serious difficulties in the way of economic development; but again, the appropriate Governmental policy would seem to be to educate the people in the practice of rational economic behaviour.

Even if the market functions perfectly, it will not produce the best possible results by its own criteria if there is a difference between social and private benefit or cost. This type of case may be particularly relevant to economic development; it includes the case of increasing returns to scale and can be extended to include the possibility that technical progress or capital accumulation tend to proceed more rapidly in industry than in agriculture. But it raises an immediate question of fact—whether divergences between social and private benefit or cost are numerous and important or not. This is an important question, but one on which we do not know very much for certain. The theory of increasing returns is logically intriguing, but the influence of increasing returns still has to be disentangled from that of technical progress in historical growth. Again, it is a fact that few advanced countries are not industrial, but this by itself does not establish the wisdom of a policy of forced industrialization in an underdeveloped country. Aside from the question of fact, the existence of divergences between social and private returns does not necessarily indicate a need for the Government to replace the market mechanism; instead, the operation of the market can be perfected by the use of appropriate taxes and subsidies to offset any divergences between social and private returns.

I now turn to the second type of objection to the market, the point of which is not that the market does not work in the way it should, but that the results produced are undesirable in themselves. Here, I think, there are two major objections to the market. The first is that the income distribution produced by the market is unjust and socially undesirable. The distribution of income through the market depends on the wealth and talents of different individuals and on their individual skill in seeing a profitable opportunity of employing their money or labour. If they make a wise or lucky choice, they may obtain a much higher income. The objection is that this method of determining the distribution of income is not just. But if you attempt to intervene in the distribution of income, you immediately encounter the problem that such intervention interferes with the efficiency of the market system. If people are not allowed to enjoy the income they could obtain by their decisions, their decisions in turn will be affected, and the efficiency of the system will be impaired. There is, therefore, a conflict between economic efficiency and social justice. The extent and importance of this conflict is likely to vary according to the state of economic development. The more advanced a country is, the more likely are its citizens to have consciences about the distribution of income and to accept the high taxation necessary to correct it without disastrously altering their behaviour; and, on the other hand, the higher the level of income reached, the less serious will be any slowing down of the rate of growth brought about by redistribution policies. An advanced country can afford to sacrifice some growth for the sake of social justice. But the cost of greater equality may be great to any economy at a low level of economic development that wishes to grow rapidly, particularly as it is evident that historically the great bursts of economic growth have been associated with the prospect and the result of big windfall gains; it would therefore seem unwise for a country anxious to enjoy rapid growth to insist too strongly on policies aimed at ensuring economic quality and a just income distribution. I should add that the problem may not be in fact as serious as I have made it out to be, since in the course of time rapid growth tends in various ways to promote a more equal distribution of wealth.

At this point I should like to digress on a special aspect of the conflict between the market principle and considerations of social justice which appears in some underdeveloped countries: the conflict created by opposition on moral grounds to the payment and receipt of interest.[3] Now the view that interest is a bad thing is economically nonsensical (unless it is merely a terminological dispute) until the economy has reached a stage at which no more capital can usefully be employed. I am not here referring to the administrative difficulties of removing interest from the economy, but to the economic principle involved. The problem of underdeveloped countries centres around the scarcity of capital. If capital is scarce, there should be both an incentive to the accumulation of it by saving and a device for rationing supplies of it among alternative uses. These are the functions of interest. If you "abolish interest" in the sense of forcing interest to be called by some other name, as was the practice in the Middle Ages, the result will merely be inconvenience; but if you abolish interest in the economic sense, the result will be the loss of the economic services performed by interest. On the one hand, the amount of private saving will be reduced and its allocation to investment distorted by the restriction of investment to activities over which the saver has personal control. On the other hand, insofar as there is a pool of investment funds (created, say, by taxation or monetary expansion or made available by foreign aid), some method will have to be found for rationing it out among competing claims if it is to be used efficiently. This problem has in fact arisen in Russia, where the engineers and planners who assess investment projects have had to work out concepts, which amount to the rate of interest, to fill the gap created by the refusal of Marxian dogma to recognize that capital has a scarcity value and is productive.

The same sort of argument makes it seem undesirable for the Governments of underdeveloped countries to use their monetary policy to favour themselves with low rates of interest. Governments now often enjoy the privilege of paying a rate of interest of $2\frac{1}{2}$ or 3 per cent; this encourages them to think, and to plan, as if capital were easily available. There seems no reason why Governments should enjoy low rates of interest when capital is scarce; on the contrary, it promotes wasteful investment and also, for reasons explained below, tends in the long run to promote inequality of income distribution.

I have been discussing the objection to the results of the market system on the grounds that it produces an undesirable distribution of income. A second objection of the same sort is that the free market will not produce as high a rate of growth as is desirable. I think there is a strong case for this objection, because people's actions in regard to saving and investment depend very much on their guesses about the future. Now people are likely to know their own current requirements better than the Government. But the requirements of the future have to be looked at not from the individual or family point of view or that of the nation as a collection of individuals, but from the point of view of the ongoing society. The needs of society in the future, many economists agree, tend to be underprovided for by the free market.

Even if the conclusion that state action is desirable to raise the rate of growth is accepted, this conclusion nevertheless does not carry with it a number of corol-

---

[3] This digression was a response to the seminar discussions that accompanied the Pakistan Refresher Course; in the seminar it became clear that many students were bothered by the conflict between economic principles and the Muslim injunction against the taking of *riba*.

laries which are often attached to it. In particular, it does not necessarily imply that the state ought to undertake development saving and investment itself. Private enterprise may be more efficient than the Government in constructing and operating enterprises, so that the best policy may be to stimulate private enterprise by tax concessions, subsidies, and the provision of cheap credit. Similarly, it may be preferable to stimulate private saving by offering high interest rates, rather than by forcing savings into the hands of the state by taxation or inflation. One argument against a policy of low interest rates and forced saving is that it may in the long run contribute to the inequality of income distribution. The reason is that the poor or small savers are mainly confined to low-yielding fixed-interest investments, directly or indirectly in Government debt, because these are safe and easily available; whereas the larger savers can invest their money in higher-yielding stocks and shares or directly in profitable enterprises. There is, therefore, an opportunity here for Government both to stimulate saving for development and to improve the distribution of income.

There is another reason for being wary of the proposition that the state should undertake development investment itself—the danger that if the Government undertakes investment itself, especially if its adminstrators are not too clear on their objectives, the result will be the creation of vested industrial interests inimical to further development and resistant to technical change.

To summarize the foregoing argument from the point of view of development policy, it seems to me that much of development planning could usefully be devoted to the improvement and strengthening of the market system. This does not imply the acceptance of all the results of laissez-faire, especially with respect to the rate of growth; but there are reasons for thinking that too much emphasis on a fair or ethical distribution of income can be an obstacle to rapid growth.

The argument I have presented has been concerned mainly with one side of the case for the market. The other side concerns the costs and difficulties of controls, in terms of the manpower costs of the administration they require, and their effects in creating profit opportunities which bring windfall gains to some members of the community and create incentives to evasion which in turn require policing of the controls. I have touched on that side of the argument sufficiently frequently to make it unnecessary to elaborate on it further.

Instead, I shall comment briefly on international markets in relation to economic development, since so far I have been implicitly concerned with internal markets. Economic development planning inevitably has a strong autarkic bias, by reason both of its motivation and of the limitation of the scope of control to the national economy. Nevertheless, international trade can play an important part in stimulating and facilitating the development process. Access to foreign markets for exports can permit an economy with a limited domestic market to exploit economies of scale, and the potentiality of such exports can serve as a powerful attraction for foreign capital and enterprise. Similarly, the capacity to import provided by exports can give a developing economy immediate access to the products of advanced technology, without obliging it to go through the long and perhaps costly process of developing domestic production facilities. Economic nationalism and excessive fear of the risks of international trade, by fostering aversion to exploiting the advantages of the international market, can therefore retard economic development unnecessarily.

One further comment on the international aspects of the market and economic development seems to me worth making. Discussion of the international side of development has been mostly concerned with commodity trade and commercial policy. But in fact one of the most important ways in which the world market system is imperfect is with respect to the international mobility of capital and labour. The problem of international capital movements has received a fair amount of attention, labour mobility and immobility much less. Now, the process of economic development in the past, especially in the nineteenth century, was characterized by vast movements, not only of capital, but also of labour, about the world. The mass movement of labour between countries has now been more or less shut off by the growth of nationalism. I believe it is important to recognize this restriction on international competition and its implications for programmes of economic development. It means—looking at the world economy as a whole—that the solution to the problem of maximizing world output cannot be approached directly, by bringing labour, capital, technology, and natural resources together at the most efficient location; instead, the other productive factors have to be brought to the labour. To a large extent, "the economic development of underdeveloped countries" is a second-best policy,[4] in which gifts of capital and technical training by advanced to underdeveloped countries are a compensation for the unwillingness of the former to consider the alternative way of improving the labour to resources ratio, movement of the labour to the resources. The fact that development is a second-best policy in this respect may impose severe limitations on its efficiency and rapidity.

To conclude, I have been concerned with the role of the market in economic development, and I have aimed at stressing the economic functions of the market, in automatically taking decisions about various kinds of allocations of economic resources, and the place in economic development programmes of improvements in market organization and methods. I have been advocating not a policy of laissez-faire, but recognition of the market as an administrative instrument that is relatively cheap to operate and may therefore be efficient in spite of objectionable features of its operations. The general assumption on which I have been arguing is that economic development is a process of cooperation between the state and private enterprise and that the problem is to devise the best possible mixture.

---

4 See J. E. Meade, *The Theory of International Economic Policy, Volume II: Trade and Welfare* (London: Oxford University Press, 1955); and R. G. Lipsey and Kelvin Lancaster, "The General Theory of Second Best," *Review of Economic Studies*, Vol. XXIV(1), No. 63 (1956–57), pp. 11–33.

PART 2

NATURE
AND TECHNIQUES
OF PLANNING

It can unequivocally be stated that nowadays all developing countries accept economic planning as a device for achieving their development goals, in the belief that only through a systematic process can their aspirations be realized in the fastest and smoothest manner. Planning involves centralized decision-making, with governments guiding the developmental processes. Decisions on the direction that a developing country is to take on the road to economic development are undoubtedly among the most crucial ones that responsible authorities must make.

Plans differ in scope and in degree of sophistication. It goes without saying that the scope of a plan and the degree of its sophistication must be a function of a country's stage of development. It follows that in most underdeveloped countries unsophisticated, pragmatic development planning is preferable to planning that utilizes elaborate models. Plans must also be highly realistic; that is, only attainable over-all objectives must be formulated and only reasonable specific targets must be set.

Practical considerations require that plans be programmed if they are to serve as a device for coordinating national policy. This is clearly a demanding task that requires not only an ability to assess carefully priorities among investment alternatives and to choose correctly among available techniques, but in addition an ability to determine sufficiently precise time sequences and schedules. In most developing countries this task is beset by a number of rather serious difficulties. The lack of basic statistical data and dearth of organizational talent deserve special mention. Another difficulty stems from the fact that economic theory, which was essentially developed to explain conditions in advanced countries, does not provide sufficient guidelines for effective planning in developing countries.

These and other limitations, as well as issues relating to the nature of planning and the usefulness of programming techniques, are the subject matter of Selections 4 through 8.

In the first, WATSON and DIRLAM discuss problems facing planners. The authors emphasize that model-building should be a careful undertaking and that planners should set targets that are both meaningful and realistic.

CAIRNCROSS deals with the capital-output ratio, a concept that is inherent in growth models, and indicates the difficulties involved in the operational use of that concept.

TRIPATHY, in turn, evaluates a number of well-known criteria used in assigning priorities to investment projects and underscores the difficulties of relying on a single criterion in decision making.

BOS points out the particular usefulness of benefit-cost analysis in an appraisal of investment projects. Although his arguments do apply both to advanced and developing countries, he enumerates those aspects of a project appraisal that are particularly relevant to the latter.

In an attempt to improve upon aggregative models currently in use, QAYUM presents a simple long-term growth model of the Cobb-Douglas type, tailored to developing economies.

Selection **4**

Planning Problems

ANDREW WATSON and JOEL B. DIRLAM

From: "The Impact of Underdevelopment on Economic Planning," Quarterly Journal of Economics, *Vol. LXXIX, No. 2 (May 1965), pp. 167–178 and 186–192. Reprinted by permission of Harvard University Press and the authors;* © *1965 by the President and Fellows of Harvard College.*

One of the cruel ironies of economic life is that the societies that most want comprehensive economic planning are those least prepared to benefit from it. The economic planner carries with him a bag of sophisticated tricks invented (but seldom tested) in the most advanced countries of the world. He encounters in the backward society attitudes, institutions, shortages of crucial skills, and a lack of information that continually thwart him in his work. Instead of being able to use his techniques to elaborate and realize a grand design, he is time and again forced into awkward and professionally humiliating compromises. Often the most that he is able to say with any integrity is that some courses of action seem more (or less) desirable than others. But since no one dares to take the responsibility for inaction, over-all plans continue to emerge. These plans are concocted by methods which bear little scrutiny and which are, in fact, almost never discussed in the literature of economic development.[1] That they often achieve little, and are sometimes harmful, is scarcely surprising.

---

[1] The process of making plans, as distinct from the principles of planning, has not been regarded as an important area of study. In selecting materials for his encyclopaedic compendium, *Leading Issues in Development Economics* (New York: Oxford University Press, Inc., 1964), Professor Gerald Meier has scoured a large number of published and fugitive sources. Yet his section on "Development Planning in Practice" accounts for only 44 out of 567 text pages, and of these only a quotation from John P. Lewis' book on India comes close to analyzing how a plan is actually put together. The contributors to Professor E. E. Hagen's book, *Planning Economic Development* (Homewood, Ill.: Richard D. Irwin, Inc., 1963), concern themselves in part with this problem, but they lack the elbow-room for grubby but essential details. Albert Waterston's monographs for the IBRD's (International Bank for Reconstruction and Development) Economic Development Institute on Jugoslavian, Pakistani, and Moroccan planning have useful sections on the planning process, and certain other publications of the IBRD contain brief discussions of planning administration. With these exceptions, however, the shelves are bare. A publication of the Department of Economic and Social Affairs of the United Nations, *Planning for Economic Development* (New York: United Nations, 1963) is of little value. Its discusion of the formulation of plans offers only well-worn platitudes. The section on implementation is equally unhelpful.

It is our thesis that the handicaps which appear universally to afflict the planner in an underdeveloped country have been insufficiently considered in setting the goals of, and establishing the institutions for, planning. . . . It will not be possible to offer any magic formula for improvement. But if a higher quantum of realism is injected into the discussion, planners will be able to use the resources at hand to greater effect. They will also be able to set a level of expectations for planning that is more in keeping with what is possible.[2]

THE BACKGROUND TO PLANNING:
DEVELOPMENT IN THE PREPLANNING PERIOD

We shall begin by looking at the way in which important economic decisions are taken in an underdeveloped country which has not yet espoused planning. We shall then be able to see why discontent with these decisions arises, why planning is deemed necessary, and in what circumstances planning commences. The difficulties which the planner faces will then emerge more clearly.

Typically, the preplanning government has no independent budgetary agency along the lines of the U.S. Bureau of the Budget. Instead, all funds—those for development as well as those for routine activities—are allocated among competing ministries and agencies by a Ministry of Finance.[3] This Ministry may also be responsible for taxation and the raising of funds from other sources. Decisions about the use of funds intended for economic development are made on an annual basis and usually in a haphazard fashion. There is little long-range thinking and virtually no effort to coordinate one program with another.[4]

The improvised character of budgeting for economic development allows a diffusion of participation—to a degree that the uninitiated sometimes find astonishing—in decision making. In time-honored fashion, local interests muster support for local projects. Ambitious ministries and ministers elbow less aggressive competitors out of the way. Experts with foreign training and foreign consultants may ride their own hobby horses. If there is a monarch, or all-powerful prime minister or president, those who can get his ear are instrumental: these intimate advisers may be reinforced by powerful families. Some projects, for political or other reasons, may have high prestige (they may appear to help politically powerful refugees, create an image of industrialization, or cater to an important religious

---

[2] Throughout this paper generalizations will be ventured which, it is believed, apply to most, if not all, underdeveloped countries. Exceptions there must be; but the experience, independent inquiry, and research of the writers suggest that the exceptions are not of sufficient importance to invalidate their conclusions.

[3] The key role of the Ministry of Finance has persisted even into the planning period, particularly in former British colonies, which have modeled their administrations on that of the United Kingdom. See L. Walinsky, "Burma" in Hagen, *op. cit.*, pp. 42–43; and A. Waterston, *Planning in Pakistan* (Baltimore: Johns Hopkins Press, 1963), pp. 53–54.

[4] Disabilities of control by a Ministry of Finance are cogently summarized in A. Waterston, "Administrative Obstacles to Planning," *Economia Latinoamericana*, I (July 1964), 324–327. See also L. Walinsky, *Economic Development in Burma* (New York: Twentieth Century Fund, 1962), pp. 432–447.

group). Such pressures, of course, are not peculiar to underdeveloped areas. But they are stronger where governments and civil services are weak. They are at once a reason for, and an obstacle to, economic planning.

Compounding the confusion in recent years have been the ubiquitous, world-traveling salesmen of industrial engineering and construction firms. Allying themselves with power groups in the underdeveloped country, they corrupt, overtly or subtly, the government's decision-making process. Venal or deluded politicians plead their cause and often succeed in committing slender surpluses to investments of marginal or no value.

At this stage, the private sector is sometimes thought of as relatively unimportant in decision making: largely agricultural, with a slight admixture of petty trade. Yet in many underdeveloped areas there are large foreign-owned companies that can make extremely important development decisions. Even where there are no known oil fields, a large exploration program can give an appreciable impetus to the economy. A local mine denied foreign partners may be doomed to ineffectiveness. Decisions of airlines, or even hotel companies, often of strategic significance, are usually made in isolation and without full consideration either by the decision-makers or the country itself of the long-run consequences of the moves.

Finally, foreign-aid donors have their own projects and special interests. While local governments may be consulted, the ultimate decisions rest with the givers (who themselves have usually had little experience with planning). There is seldom a chance for the recipients to take the initiative, even if they have the technical capability to do so. Certain funds become available suddenly and unpredictably, as a result of the budgeting vagaries of the donors, and may have to be spent quickly. In an effort to justify appropriations, short-run payouts are often given primary emphasis, or, more objectionable still, the spectacular or superficially attractive project receives top priority. Something in concrete is likely to take precedence over something intangible, such as a farm-loan or marketing program. Projects which aim at long-term human development are found to be difficult to justify. With a rapid turnover of supervisory aid officials, responsibility is diminished, and there is a corresponding propensity to initiate ill-conceived projects that are not carried to fruition. Worthwhile schemes may wither, forgotten.

ESTABLISHING A "DEVELOPMENT BOARD": THE CENTRALIZATION OF AID NEGOTIATION

As governments become aware of the deficiencies in the use of investment capital, they attempt to correct matters by setting up an agency which is supposed to monopolize decisions concerning development projects. This body may be called a Development Board or something similar. The hope is that the Board will improve the quality of decisions which bear on economic development, partly by carrying out studies which will permit more enlightened choice and partly by constituting a countervailing center of power more able to resist the pressures to which the Ministry of Finance was subject. Though the move to set up a Development Board is generally taken by the government itself, the final impetus may come from a World Bank report or from the impatience of the donor countries with the multiplicity of officials with whom they have to deal.[5]

The Development Board may find time to promulgate a few goals that stir popular enthusiasm; in the hurly-burly of administration and negotiation, however, any semblance of organized planning toward these goals, or observing any sort of priority in project selection, disappears. The overriding aim of the Board—and of some well-meaning officials in the aid-giving organizations—is to keep the level of assistance as high as possible, regardless of the sometimes crippling contribution in personnel and funds which has to be made by the recipient. There is sporadic reliance on foreign experts and engineering firms which prepare feasibility studies for various projects, or on economists who appear at research institutes, deliver lectures, or prepare reports. These reports are used on a hit-or-miss basis by the Development Board to "make points" with the aid donors.

Though for many countries at this stage a blueprint for economic development is available in the form of a report by the World Bank, the usually reasonable and well-considered recommendations of these reports are more often than not ignored. Projects continue to be chosen in much the same way as in the preplanning stage: for personal, political, or religious reasons, with economic justification usually provided after the fact.[6] If an aid recipient feels strongly enough that it needs a steel mill or an oil refinery, it may at this stage be able to squeeze it out of reluctant donors. PL 480 funds are channeled to access highways to politically favored cities, regardless of the already excessive burden of highway maintenance; small towns and villages get little or nothing. Perhaps most important of all, the big-ticket projects continue to be favored by both donors and recipients, even if premature or for other reasons unsuitable.[7]

In such a climate, the Development Board does almost no planning even in the sense of applying a system of priorities. To some extent its impotence is intentional: those already in control have no wish to surrender power to a body which might become semi-autonomous. As a result, the Board is often completely bypassed on the important decisions, and the head of state or a minister negotiates directly

---

[5] British and French colonies drew up investment plans pursuant to the requirements of the Colonial Office and the Commissariat au Plan, respectively, during the preindependence period. Representative experiences of the organizations responsible for securing funds in this fashion are reviewed in S. Schatz, "The Influence of Planning on Development: The Nigerian Experience," *Social Research*, Vol. XXVII (Winter 1960), pp. 451–468, and A. Waterston, *Planning in Morocco, Organization and Implementation* (Washington, D.C.: Economic Development Institute, 1962). See also D. G. M. Dosser, "The Formulation of Development Plans in the British Colonies," *Economic Journal*, Vol. LXIX (June 1959), pp. 255–266. The origin and history of the Jordanian Development Board are summarized in IBRD, *The Economic Development of Jordan* (Baltimore: Johns Hopkins Press, 1957), pp. 425–429.

[6] For numerous illustrations of such projects in Burma, selected even after planning (or at least after the hiring of a consulting agency for planning), see Walinsky, *Economic Development in Burma, op. cit.* The rehabilitation of the Hedjaz Railway may also be mentioned.

[7] "Officials tended to overemphasize big projects . . . . In part this could be attributed to the preference of foreign lending and donor agencies for large projects. . . ." Waterston, *Planning in Pakistan, op. cit.*, p. 61. Egypt appears to have extracted the Aswan Dam funds from donors without any conclusive demonstration that the project's return justified the expenditure. An internal report of the IBRD was unfavorable to the project.

with aid sources. Ministries without technical assistants are impatient and skeptical of planning. Other ministries do not cooperate in their assigned responsibilities; they cannot be coerced by an institution whose governing body itself consists of ministers and whose director has a lower rank. The most competent, and perhaps the most powerful, figures in the development organization tend to be the accountants and auditors, since the primary function of the Board remains that of showing the aid donors that funds have been used more or less for the intended purpose.

The second stage of the preplanning period, then, witnesses the establishment of an organization which is conscious of the importance of development expenditures and attempts to consolidate negotiations for development projects. Although there are gestures toward longer-range coordination of development projects, there is little or no attempt to establish goals and priorities. Development still lives from hand to mouth.

PRESSURE FOR MORE PLANNING

The failure of individual project negotiation to achieve even the vaguely formulated goals for the underdeveloped country leads inevitably to mounting pressure for more and better planning. Those officials who know how the development program is arrived at are aware of the shortcomings of annual negotiation and budgeting. They press for longer-term commitments. They are eager to fit development activities, including those of both the ministries and the proliferating independent agencies, into the framework of a plan. They want to adopt targets, balance needs and resources, and appraise projects by applying rational priorities. Their dissatisfaction is legitimate, and can lead to constructive changes.

There are, however, other elements which urge more ambitious planning. The special interests that had not hesitated to claim available funds for their pet projects (e.g., hotels in the capital city, awarding of construction contracts to affiliated foreign firms) see that as long as the economy stagnates, their projects may not be profitable. They, too, become concerned about the economy's rate of growth. They are troubled by its failure to exhibit anything other than passive response to successive injections of funds. Again, those businessmen who did not pull any plums out of the pie will also usually favor growth, in the hope that future pickings will be better. Even the ruling political group is usually able to see the weaknesses of an economy which cannot move under its own steam. It, too, may anxiously be looking for a short-cut to growth (though the more farsighted of its members may also see that the social change entailed by growth will undermine its power).

There is also popular support for more ambitious planning. Not only is there a rapidly spreading belief amongst common people the world over that their material lot can, and should, be greatly improved in a short time span; there is also a growing conviction that economic planning can bring about this betterment. This faith derives partly from the unscrupulous propaganda of other underdeveloped countries reporting the "achievements" of their latest plan, which they compare with the alleged "stagnation" of unplanned economies. Here, too, the quest for social justice joins hands with a longing for rapid growth. Again, partly because of propaganda from planned economies, it is widely believed that planning will equitably redistribute income, raise consumption levels, and prevent the enrichment of a few businessmen, particularly foreign ones.[8]

Finally, the aid-givers, including the United Nations and the World Bank, have become convinced that more ambitious planning is essential. The donors have become restive. Alarmed at the results of nonplanning, they want to look forward to a period when aid will taper off. The United States, in a complete reversal of the Point Four philosophy, has shifted its support from technical assistance to planning.[9] Under the Alliance for Progress, the formulation and adoption of a comprehensive development program have been made conditions of receiving aid. The openly expressed hope is that plans will result in relieving the U.S. taxpayer of the burden of aid (though the recipient country may be given the impression that *more* funds will be available if projects are fitted into a plan).

Paradoxically, the application of pressures for planning as a means of reducing dependence upon foreign aid often occurs after the recipient's economy has been adjusted to a minimum level of assistance, and secondary industries depending on the income generated by continuing aid have become rooted. Any hope that assistance can actually be reduced in the immediate future because of planning is therefore likely to be illusory, since the planners can scarcely begin by destroying part of the economy already established.

THE PLANNER'S DILEMMA: LONG-RANGE PLANNING OR IMPLEMENTATION?

The planning organization often starts out in life a stepchild, or even a changeling, without official status. Perhaps it is an autonomous unit of the Development Board or an *ad hoc* committee reporting to the prime minister. Initially, it is badly understaffed and may have no authority. Its director may have a job with an official title that has nothing to do with planning.

These difficulties are, however, gradually overcome. Foreign advisers are imported to strengthen the staff and train the junior members.[10] An effort may be made, by bypassing civil service regulations, to secure especially competent

---

[8] Although the rate of growth of per capita income in Egypt is probably lower than that of any other Arab country, there is a widespread belief through the Arab world (outside of Egypt) that the Egyptian economy is growing rapidly, that the lot of the common Egyptian is greatly improved, and that success has been largely due to planning. The broadcasts of Radio Cairo, beamed at the whole Arab world and much of Africa south of the Sahara, have been mainly responsible for spreading this fiction. See, e.g., Jacques Baulin, *The Arab Role in Africa* (Harmondsworth, England: Penguin, 1962), pp. 46–49.

[9] For Point Four policy, see J. B. Bingham, *Shirt-Sleeve Diplomacy*, (New York: The John Day Company, Inc., 1954), Chaps. 1–2. A comprehensive critique of the current doctrine appears in A. L. Camargo, "The Alliance for Progress: Aims, Distortions, Obstacles," *Foreign Affairs*, Vol. XLII (Oct. 1963), pp. 25–37.

[10] Foreign advisers have drawn up the Nigerian, Pakistani, Iranian, Jordanian, and Burmese plans, to name only a few. With the recent emphasis on planning as a condition of aid, planners have been supplied under contract for many Latin American and Asian countries. Nominally, the planners are is some way attached to the administration of the planning country; in most cases, however, they are financed either by a foreign government or by a philanthropic foundation.

younger people. Eventually, it is recognized that the planning organization experts are probably more able, even in the operational field, than the civil servants in the ministries with which they deal.

At this point, however, the planning organization approaches an important turning point in its career. Because it works closely with the ministries in reviewing projects, urging the adoption of measures of feasibility and performance, and to some extent determining the deployment of ministry personnel, it inevitably begins to mix in the day-to-day activities of the ministries. The problem then arises of how deeply it should become involved in operations. The planning organization is faced with a choice of taking over much of the work pertaining to development previously carried out by the ministries and other agencies of the government, or restricting itself to something else—which, for lack of a better word, we shall call planning.[11]

The planning organization *may* become a state within a state, wielding power far in excess of that of the conventional ministries.[12] But when it manages to grab, or has conveyed to it, such power, it fails to perform its own functions properly. It becomes involved in operations, and its energies are consumed in carrying out the details of the development projects. The members of the planning organization become identified with and favor pet projects. Planning, in the sense of coordination and impartial evaluation of projects, or long-range thinking, is relegated to the background.

Yet the process by which planning shifts insensibly to operations is traceable to the underdevelopment that called forth planning in the first place. A wide-awake and conscientious planning group *can* avoid this slippery path by constantly exercising self-control. But it must be prepared to see that those who are in charge do not delay and repeat mistakes. It must refrain from substituting for the inferior techniques of other officials the obviously superior skills of the planning experts. In the face of continual pressure from all sides, it must put long-run benefits, in

---

[11]On the other hand, mobile planning teams will not be troubled by their day-to-day relations with other governmental branches because their tenure is only a matter of weeks or months, at most. High-powered economists prepared a development plan for one small Latin American country in six weeks and then departed for other assignments.

[12]The planning organization in Iran evidently enjoyed such power at one time, or so it was alleged when A. H. Ebtehaj, its ex-chief, was arrested. *New York Times*, Nov. 12, 1961, 40:4. Cf. the (temporary) success of the Klein-Saks mission to Chile in 1955, which did not resign itself to the somewhat frustrating task of "writing a comprehensive report," but instead "in effect usurped the role of policy maker." A. O. Hirschman, *Journeys Toward Progress* (New York: Twentieth Century Fund, 1963), p. 207. In contrast, however, is the situation described in a letter from an economist on a mission in Venezuela. "The best of the Latin American plans by general agreement is right here. But what it is, really, is a collection of all the projects that a normally active and exceptionally well-heeled government has thought up for the next four years, fitted to the indubitable proposition that 20 per cent unemployment and 3 per cent annual population increase imply about a 7 per cent GNP growth rate if improvement is desired. . . . Now 7 per cent becomes a 'target' and everything else . . . must be 'quantified in line with national targets,' never mind whether external markets, labor costs, cost-price trends or simple engineering technology would permit such an over-all rate. At the other end of the process, the operating agencies go their merry way implementing the decisions which their *jefe* has taken without regard to [the planning organization's] estimates. In short, planning is done by an agency which has no power, and power is exercised by agencies which have no plan." This same correspondent felt, however, that we had overemphasized the defects of planning administration.

the shape of development of self-reliant civil servants and ministries, ahead of shortrun gains.

Yet the ideal course is far from clear. Where planning is wholly divorced from operations, nothing tangible appears to come of attempts to plan.[13] The gap between the level of competence in the planning organization and that in the operational organizations may be such that no projects are devised that can conscientiously be included in a plan. Or, if projects and programs are submitted in reasonably useful form (as a result of assistance from foreign experts or planning officials), they are simply not carried out after incorporation in the plan.

The appropriate extent of control over operations by the planning organization cannot very well be determined on an a priori basis, and the question is seldom permanently settled. It would be tedious to recall how in one country after another the seat of power has shifted from one part of the administration to another, and how the planning organization has swung back and forth between operations and advice, reflecting political changes or the emergence of strong personalities. Almost inevitably, the planner's dilemma is resolved by a power struggle and not by the adoption of principles of good administration.[14]

CONSTRAINTS ON PLANNING

Once "planning" is initiated, regardless of its extent, the limitations on what can be achieved soon become apparent (though they are seldom openly admitted). On every side, the planner's freedom of maneuver seems to be restricted.

For one thing, the weight of history is heavy. The range of choice open to the planner is drastically reduced by hand-me-down projects which are already under way, or for which commitments have been made. The marginal benefits of continuing those projects already started may be greater than the marginal costs, even though the project would not be selected de novo and may actually distort the pattern of future development.

The legacy of institutions and personnel is perhaps even harder to reject. An investment bank may have been corruptly or sloppily administered; changing its top officials may be all that is needed to make it efficient. Yet the change may bring all its activities to a halt. When the aid-dispensing agencies have had a hand in setting up institutions associated with projects—community development organi-

---

[13]In the Philippines, a large number of plans have been prepared, but no effort was made to carry them out. See F. Golay, *The Philippines: Public Policy and National Economic Development* (Ithaca: Cornell University Press, 1961), *passim*. The Burmese experience was similar. The first Jordanian Five-Year Plan, completed in 1961, was held in abeyance and then subsequently revised in a Seven-Year Plan, which remains unpublished. The Nigerian Five-Year Plan has been similarly pigeonholed.

[14]A similar problem may be expected to arise in the matter of budgeting. Because the development budget may well represent a substantial part of the total budget, and because development expenditures may in some sense take priority over other expenditures, the role which the planning authority is to play in drawing up the national budget—or even that part of the budget allocated to what are considered development expenditures—has to be defined. Unless a satisfactory working relationship can be reached by the planning division with the budget agency (or the Ministry of Finance), the cabinet, and the individual ministries, a free-for-all may ensue.

zations, for instance—not only do the planners have to compromise with their principles to please those who pay the shot, but they will usually find, even when the form of the organization has been changed, that the same individuals reappear in strategic positions.

Once planning has begun, moreover, the problem of political interference may become more, rather than less, acute. As the planning organization gains in prestige, it can less readily insulate itself from the needs of the group in power: dissident groups are always ready to seize any stick to attack the ruling party and the planning group itself. The planners must balance short- against long-run considerations in selecting projects. In publicizing what they have done or hope to do, they cannot forget the fate of the Iraq Development Board and the mutilated body of Nuri As-Sa'id. Thus there remains the temptation to spend funds on make-work schemes or to choose spectacular projects of the capital-intensive type. If the long-run results of such opportunism are disappointing, the politicians are not much concerned with the long run. In the short run they may be dead.[15]

There is also pressure to include social gains in the plan: unemployment insurance, free medical care, better housing for the poor, higher pensions, and reduction or elimination of child labor. These "gains" usually precede the achievement of a high rate of growth. Sometimes they have been legislated into existence before the appearance of the planning organization. They can seldom be modified or curtailed.

Finally, there will be pressure to set unrealistic targets: to promise rates of growth which could never, even in the most favorable of circumstances, be achieved.[16] Of course, a case can be made for aiming high—the Russians have made much of this technique. Even if the targets cannot be reached, it is argued, people will work harder and achieve more than they would without them. The danger is that the unattainability of the targets will soon become evident and, by emphasizing the impotence of the government, lead to discouragement and dissidence. More important, perhaps, an insistence on high goals that cannot be achieved distorts the whole framework of the plan. It may lead to serious maladjustments in the rates of growth of different sectors, to excessive use of foreign exchange and eventually to exchange controls, to excess capacity in heavy industry, and to neglect of basic sectors such as agriculture for which it is more difficult to program a rapid advance.[17]

---

[15] W. B. Reddaway, who is favorably inclined toward Indian planning, points out that the First Indian Plan neglected to initiate schemes that required a long time to complete. *The Development of the Indian Economy* (Homewood, Ill.: Richard D. Irwin Inc., 1962), p. 192. Cf. the shift in Iranian planning from the large projects of the Second Plan to the small ones of the Third.

[16] The Pakistan First Five-Year Plan was a "disastrous" failure, particularly in agriculture. C. Wilcox, "Pakistan," in Hagen, *op. cit.*, pp. 64–66. The factual justification for the targets of the Second Plan was "only slightly stronger than that of the first." *Ibid.*, p. 71. The Second Indian Five-Year Plan, as is well known, ran into a foreign-exchange crisis, and growth was substantially below expectations. See the informative chart in I. M. D. Little, "A Critical Appraisal of India's Third Five-Year Plan," *Oxford Economic Papers*, Vol. XIV (Feb. 1962), p. 2.

[17] For a sober examination of the consequences of permitting industrialization to take precedence over the raising of agricultural productivity, see J. H. Power, "Industrialisation in Pakistan: A Case Study of Frustrated Take-off," *The Pakistan Development Review*, Vol. III (Summer 1963), pp. 191–207.

Tying the plan to unrealistic targets has other objectionable consequences for feasibility studies and other planning in the private sector, unless the forecasts used reject the officially announced rates of growth. Perhaps the solution to this problem is for planners, like businessmen, to keep two sets of books. . . .

•   •   •

MAJOR OBSTACLES RESULTING
FROM UNDERDEVELOPMENT

. . . In this section we shall focus attention on certain key shortages, or constraints, which tend to defeat the planner's efforts and to inhibit growth. The existence of these shortages in less developed regions has been noted by other writers, but only in passing. In most cases, they have been regarded—wrongly—as peripheral aberrations, temporary and capable of being surmounted if planners are aware of them, and if a "sense of crisis" is present. In reality, they are the essence of underdevelopment.[18]

A. Lack of Information

Under this heading may be included a multitude of evils, one or other of which will dog the planner all along the way—in preparing the plan, in implementing it, and in revising it through its lifetime. Most crucial, at the outset, will be the lack of statistics. Even the most advanced countries may lack many of the statistical series which planners require, but the shortage is much more serious in an underdeveloped nation: some countries attempt comprehensive plans without even tolerably reliable estimates of population or national income and no information on their past rates of growth. Other fundamental series, concerning cost of living, agricultural prices, indebtedness, land tenure, and so on, will almost certainly be

---

[18]See Hagen, *op. cit.*, p. 362. Hagen quite carefully pulls together what he calls the "difficulties" revealed by his case studies, but does not appear to regard them as much more than incidental obstacles, mostly capable of being overcome by good "planning organization" (principles for which he briefly lists in *ibid.*, pp. 333–335). In his view they do not seem to call for shrinking the area of the economy to be planned or lowering targets. On the contrary, he proposes that in spite of their conspicuous success in developing their economies, the Mexicans and Japanese should change over to hortatory and comprehensive development programs. *Ibid.*, p. 360. Cf. Vernon, *The Dilemma of Mexico's Development* (Cambridge, Mass.: Harvard University Press, 1963), *passim.*, where no credit is given to economic planning. Again, Walinsky, in his full-dress review of the experience of the Nathan consultants in Burma (*Economic Development in Burma, op. cit.*), quotes with approval the significant warning of the report which preceded the participation of the consultants in the planning process: "Success of the development program hinges more on this (adequate manpower) than any other single factor." Yet after hundreds of pages of confirmation of this very point, showing the impossibility of implementing a plan in the face of incompetence, dogmatism and corruption, he manages to remain optimistic about what can be done: "To a far greater extent than in the more advanced democratic societies, governments, in underdeveloped countries must take major responsibility for initiating and carrying through accelerated economic development." *Ibid.*, p. 586.

lacking.[19] On occasion, data in the possession of other agencies will not be furnished to the planners.

In searching for other kinds of information, the planner will find that library facilities are inadequate and works he wishes to consult cannot be obtained. This is one of several reasons why there is so little effective pooling of the experience of underdeveloped countries with similar problems. Even reports made by visiting experts a few years earlier may have vanished. Files and other records may have been lost. When projects get under way, the planner may be in the dark about their progress, there being no regular machinery for collecting and feeding back information.[20]

B. Lack of Suitable Projects Ready for Implementation

Perhaps a special case of the lack of information, this constraint deserves special mention on account of its importance. Because enough projects have not been prepared in sufficient detail, much of the time and the staff of the planning division will be occupied in working up more projects. Nevertheless, the plan, when it emerges, may be less specific than desired, and it may include some projects of questionable value merely because these *had* been prepared in detail.

In certain areas, the plan may have to be kept deliberately vague, since the desirable course of action will not be known until the results of a feasibility study or a resource survey are available; estimating the required investment or setting goals for output is not possible in such areas, and another element of uncertainty creeps into the whole plan. Again, if additional funds for development become available, and for budgetary reasons have to be appropriated quickly, it will sometimes be discovered that no suitable projects are ready. The funds may go begging, or will be applied to hastily conceived schemes on which they and other scarce resources are wasted.

C. Lack of Qualified Personnel

The lack of skilled human resources is generally more serious than any other resource lack, and is at the root of all the other main shortages characteristic of

---

[19] A notorious example is the Nigerian population figure. After the first "complete" census, there was no agreement on whether the population was 41.4 or 53.2 million. See W. G. Stolper, "Economic Development in Nigeria," *Journal of Economic History*, Vol. XXIII (Dec. 1963), p. 396. The Third Indian Plan was severely distorted by the planners' ignorance, until very late in the planning process, of the rapid increase in population that had taken place during the period of the Second Plan. See Lewis, *The Quiet Crisis in India* (Washington: The Brookings Institution, 1963), p. 24. The latest Turkish plan, according to one observer, is a workmanlike job, complete with intersectoral input-output tables. But it has one defect: the underlying statistics are either unreliable or absent. See J. K. Eastham, "The Turkish Development Plan: The First Five Years." *Economic Journal*, Vol. LXXIV (Mar. 1964), pp. 132–336.

[20] According to Lewis, projections of specific industry growth used in the Indian Third Five-Year Plan were not based on actual accomplishments under the Second Five-Year Plan, *ibid.*, pp. 125–126. Malenbaum states that in India material for studying outputs and operational behavior is "elusive at best." *Prospects for Indian Development* (New York: The Free Press, 1962), p. 63.

underdevelopment. To glimpse its importance, we need only imagine the effect of transferring populations from developed to underdeveloped nations.

High administrative officials attend to petty details. This practice occurs partly because of a shortage of trained and trustworthy assistants and partly because of an inability to delegate power. The consequence is a minor vicious circle: underlings are not trained to accept responsibility, and their superiors neglect the most important work.[21] The few able people at the lower levels of the civil service are often less effective than they could be, owing to incompetent superiors or colleagues, or because of unwieldy procedures (sometimes left over from colonial days).

The results are everywhere apparent. Schedules for such relatively simple tasks as committee reports cannot be followed. Projects do not produce according to plan. The potential output of a mine, for instance, cannot be realized, because the acceleration of production presents a series of interrelated problems that defy solution. (These may range from the unwarranted interference of directors in matters of office routine to the selection of new sites for exploitation.) Similarly, a potential increase in agricultural output from irrigation remains potential, because, even if the necessary construction is completed, it is a difficult and time-consuming process to work out and get accepted the most desirable livestock and cropping patterns.[22]

Large-scale projects, unless carried out by foreign personnel, can seldom be incorporated with assurance in a plan. This fact is sometimes temporarily obscured by the letting of major construction projects to foreign concerns and by the underplaying of projects which make heavy demands on local administrative talent. All too often, the really difficult, *but strategic*, programs which promise to establish bases for continuing growth—community development, the organization of agricultural cooperatives, the creation of agricultural extension and research stations in effective concert, the training of technicians and administrators, and the like—are sacrificed to projects such as highways and dams that can be built under contract with foreign firms.[23]

Attempts to move ahead intensify shortages in personnel. Agencies expand

---

[21]Cf. Olsen and Rasmussen, in Hagen, *op. cit.*, p. 237. The Burmese Economic and Social Board, whose membership included ministers concerned with economic activities, did not meet frequently, did not delegate responsibility, and was so concerned with the operating function that it could not plan development, or even review and appraise performance. A board of enquiry to improve implementation was composed of key civil servants who already had full-time jobs. Walinsky, "Burma," *op. cit.*, pp. 47–48. See other illustrations in Waterston, "Administrative Obstacles to Planning," *op. cit.*, pp. 310–312.

[22]In northeast Brazil the construction of numerous large dams over a period of years has been unattended by the development of agriculture. See the summary in Hirschman, *op. cit.*, pp. 43 and 76. In Iraq, according to one well-informed writer, the building of irrigation works became an end in itself, with little attention being paid to subsequent agricultural development. See M. Ionides, *Divide and Lose* (London: Geoffrey Bles, 1960), Chap. 15.

[23]The problem of establishing an effective community development project is perhaps typical. In most countries where the program has been attempted, it has been impossible to train a sufficient number of dedicated and capable persons, to keep them in the villages, and to overcome the hostility of the older and more specialized branches of the civil service to what is regarded as encroachment. See, e.g., H. Tinker, "The Village in the Framework of Development," in R. Brabanti and J. Spengler, *Administration and Economic Development in India* (Durham: Duke University Press, 1963), pp. 94–133.

and proliferate, there are frequent changes in jobs, and people shift so often that they fail to acquire a knowledge of their jobs. Able civil servants move up to head ministries, and with a change in the party in power move out of government, never to return (since they cannot reenter as juniors). Changes in foreign personnel, who are frequently in key positions, aggravate the problem.[24] Foreigners who first conceive the ideas for programs are seldom around when they finally take shape; and those who start projects have been posted thousands of miles away by the time they are in full-scale operation (if the project is not abandoned before this point has been reached). Since the chances are that one will not be around to be taxed with their failure, there is a temptation to plump for schemes on very short-run grounds.

The "solutions" which have been devised for overcoming shortages of personnel have not been conspicuous for their success; each tactic, if it does not fail utterly, at least has serious drawbacks. In the case of projects which require prolonged experience of local conditions, contracting projects or parts of projects to foreign firms adds greatly to the cost without ensuring that the work will be well done. When the foreigners withdraw on the expiration of their contract, the residue of local training will be minimal and, after the initial thrust by the foreigners, local follow-through may not be forthcoming. The importation of foreign experts to work alongside local personnel may overcome some of these disadvantages, but much will depend on the quality of these "experts" and the duration of their stay.[25] Those whose expertise is confined to a knowledge of how things are done in an advanced country, those who do not easily adapt themselves to the conditions of the underdeveloped country, and those who stay only a short time will contribute little. Those who stay only long enough to make recommendations, and do not remain to see to the establishment of an organization to implement these recommendations, will not have much effect, even where there existed a prior determination to carry out reform. On the other hand, if experts *are* able to get results, there are other dangers: lacking a sense of economic timing, they may try to do too much, and draw too much money and manpower into their own sphere. Other areas, perhaps even more important, but lacking an expert, may be neglected.

Nor, in our opinion, is the training of local personnel abroad (known in the

---

[24]Even staunch supporters of the U.S. foreign-aid program have been disturbed by the rapid turnover of personnel. See *Personnel Administration and Operations of Agency for International Development. Report of Senator Gale W. McGee*, Senate Doc. No. 57, 88th Congress, 2nd Session (1963), *passim*. According to Senator Hubert Humphrey, the job cannot be done with two-year personnel who leave the program six months after they have learned their job. "Two-thirds of the loan officers experienced in Latin-American affairs who were with the Development Loan Fund at the time it was absorbed into AID in November, 1961, have now left the Agency and those who left were among the ablest. . . ." *A Report on the Alliance for Progress*, 1963, Senate Doc. No. 13, 88th Congress, 1st Session (1963), p. 11.

[25]To give only one example, the French government has found that newly independent nations in what was formerly French Africa are unwilling to accept technicians who had African experience during the colonial period. It has therefore been necessary to send experts with no previous African experience, and the result, according to one writer, has been the repetition of many old mistakes. See E. Bonnefous, *Les milliards qui s'envolent* (Paris: Fayard, 1963), p. 188. See also Dudley Seers' "Why Visiting Economists Fail," *Journal of Political Economy*, Vol. LXX (Aug. 1962), pp. 325–338, which aptly pinpoints the difficulties facing foreign advisers and experts.

trade as the "Holiday on Ice") often a satisfactory solution.[26] Inevitably, a trip abroad is regarded as a prize in itself: it is a chance to leave a dirty, hot, culturally backward area for New York, London, or Paris, with the additional lure of a faintly possible permanent residency abroad. Selection is frequently made on the basis of the political connections of the candidates, not their ability. The people chosen, if competent, are desperately needed on the job. It seems unlikely that the marginal social benefit of a Ph.D. for a geologist with an M.A. who knows the local conditions exceeds the cost of waiting another two years to locate water-bearing strata for 100 villages. But U.S. AID officials do not make their selections on such bases. Very often, the training received is of little value in the context of the underdeveloped nation and may actually disorient the trainee. Or if the training has some application, it may not be used: on his return the trainee is given another job, either through bureaucratic inefficiency or jealousy.[27]

In most cases, it seems best to train on the job, with whatever local teachers can be recruited and foreigners where they are really needed. Such training can sometimes be effectively supplemented by short study trips to countries which are just one notch up the scale in development and have made conspicuous progress with the very problems with which the trainee will be dealing. Short-term, practically oriented courses in regional training centers can also yield good results, but until now this kind of training (which for many kinds of work could be organized at a fraction of the cost of scholarships to the United States) has been little used.[28]

Regardless of what "solutions" are used, however, only limited progress can be expected in overcoming this crucial shortage.[29] While a country is underdeveloped, the shortage of competent personnel will remain a persistent, hard-core problem to which all attempts to accelerate growth will be vulnerable. This obstacle will not disappear until the larger problem, of which it is a part, has been solved.

---

[26]Cf. R. Brabanti, "Reflections on Bureaucratic Reform in India," in Brabanti and Spengler, *op. cit.*, pp. 50 and 59.

[27]The writers are acquainted with an individual who was regarded as the most highly trained tannery manager in the world. He had studied for several years in the United States, Germany, France, England, and Jugoslavia, while waiting for a tannery to be approved, financed, and built. When it was finally completed and ready to go into production, he was fired by the directors in a trivial dispute. In another case the director of an agricultural research station and his chief assistant, both highly competent men with M.A.'s, were sent to the United States for a three-year Ph.D. program. The work of the station, which had previously been the only station carrying out important research, came to a standstill.

[28]A good example of a successful venture of this kind is the British Forestry Training Centre in Cyprus to which civil servants from a number of Eastern Mediterranean countries are sent for short-term courses. As the conditions in Cyprus, unlike those found in most parts of the United States, are similar to those in the trainee's homeland, the chances that the training will be transferable are greater.

[29]It cannot be overcome simply by more education *per se*. Middle Eastern countries are today afflicted by unemployment of high school and university graduates who have concentrated on arts courses.

Selection **5**

The Capital-Output Ratio

A. K. CAIRNCROSS

From: "*Reflections on the Growth of Capital and Income,*" Scottish Journal of Political Economy, *Vol. VI, No. 2 (June 1959), Section II, pp. 103–112. Reprinted by permission of the* Scottish Journal of Political Economy, *Oliver and Boyd Limited, and the author.*

I was brought up on a theory of capital which took little account, in any explicit way, of the interconnection between investment and innovation. Much of it was directed to explaining the phenomenon of interest and ran in terms of marginal efficiency of capital. The theory was not much concerned with dynamic and cumulative changes in which total output grew, and it either ignored them, in order to concentrate on the length of the period of production, or tended to generalize from the factors governing the behaviour of the individual unit, whether on the side of savings or investment, to the factors governing the aggregates in an entire economy. No consideration was given to the rebound on the demand for capital that follows any increase in income brought about by the use of more capital in a fully employed economy. It was also difficult to be sure, when a writer was discussing an increase in capital, whether he meant an increase in the rate of investment or an increase in the stock of capital.

The current tendency is to start with a macroeconomic analysis in terms of capital coefficients, concentrating on the growth of capital and output, and relegating problems of allocation and distribution to a back seat. The supply of other factors of production is largely taken for granted and assumed to accommodate itself to the growth of capital, which, explicitly or implicitly, figures as the controlling element. The idea of marginal efficiency, while not abandoned, is rarely brought into relationship with that of the capital-output ratio; and economists move rather uneasily between the two sets of concepts as the type of problem under discussion alters.

The capital-output ratio is a useful and natural concept for the purposes of national economic planning. This is particularly true where it is necessary to check the consistency of targets for the growth of national income against the additional capital likely to be available from current savings or foreign investment. But even in calculations of this kind there are important ambiguities.

First of all, there is a tendency to use the ratio as a measure of the productivity of capital, on the assumption that the whole of any increase in output can be attributed to the expansion of capacity resulting from investment. This tendency is conspicuous not only in many of the discussions about underdeveloped countries, where it may have some slight justification, but even in writings about advanced industrial countries, where the contribution of additional capital to economic growth is obviously far from 100 per cent. In some versions, a looser causal relationship between the growth of capital and of output is assumed, but capital is still treated as the bottleneck and a fixed relationship is taken to do no real violence to the facts.

The capital-output ratio, however, is merely a quotient measuring, in its incremental form, the relative rates of increase of capital and output. If it could be shown that it was fixed in respect of each constituent of total output by technical factors, this would not mean that technical factors alone governed the ratio for total output, since the constituents of output may vary in weight with changes in demand brought about by economic factors. There is, in any event, neither constancy through time in production coefficients, nor constancy at any one time between one firm and another, and the methods of production in use yield, to some extent at least, to the pressure of economic factors such as the relative cost of different productive agents.

If appeal is made to the facts, it appears to be true that for the few countries (all of them industrial) for which adequate data exist, there has been some degree of constancy over long periods in the average capital-output ratio. But this is not true of the *marginal* capital-output ratio. There are, in any event, good *a priori* reasons for expecting any change in the average ratio to be slow (since the yearly increments, both in capital and income, are normally small in relation to the pre-existing totals) and for expecting some of the more important constituents of the capital stock to bear a fairly constant relationship to total income. Fluctuations in the ratio do occur, and it is too early to form any firm conclusion as to the long-term trend and the resistance that would be offered by technical inflexibility to persistent economic forces such as a change in habits of thrift.

If one looks at the practice of countries engaged in national economic planning, there are further grounds for scepticism. In the USSR, for example, it is an article of faith that the capital-output ratio must go on rising; successive plans have provided for a higher rate of growth of producer goods than of consumer goods. On the other hand, in some of the underdeveloped countries there is a willingness to plan for a falling capital-output ratio; and in some South American countries, where plans are less fashionable, output does appear to have expanded in postwar years a good deal more rapidly than capital.

Apart from these considerations, there is no reason why constancy in the capital-output ratio should be accepted as demonstrating a causal connection in one direction rather than the other. If income is growing, it is almost inevitable that savings will grow, too; the more rapid the growth of income, the higher the proportion of income that is likely to be saved. The accumulation of capital may, in those circumstances, be little more than a symptom of development, rather than its cause. If, for example, all economic activity took the form of agriculture

and house building, and technique stood still in the building industry but progressed rapidly in agriculture, the growth of agricultural output might be accomplished with little or no additional investment of capital, while the increase in
income might give rise to a larger demand for houseroom and hence for capital.
Any constancy of the capital-output ratio in such circumstances would reflect the
income-elasticity of demand for housing, not the inflexibility of the technique of
producing food or building houses; and the growth of capital would be a function
of the growth of income, which in turn would be a function of technical progress.

A somewhat similar situation might occur if technical progress in agriculture
(e.g., the use of better seeds) put little demand on capital in that sector of the
economy but made it necessary to provide additional storage, transport, and port
facilities in order to handle the larger crops. The capital-output ratio in agriculture
itself might fall; but the fall could be largely or entirely offset by some conse-
quential change in another sector, a change that of itself would do little to promote
the growth of output, but might be indispensable in order that the economy should
enjoy the full advantage of technical change.

It might be supposed from these examples that this objection to a causal interpretation of constancy in the capital-output ratio rests on the unequal incidence
of technical change in different sectors of the economy. That there is such inequality of incidence is apparent enough; but even if it did not exist, the objection
still stands. For within each sector also, there is no necessary identity between
the areas of rapid change and the areas of heavy investment. The mainspring of
economic progress lies in innovation in the widest sense, rather than in capital
accumulation; and if innovation leaves the capital-output ratio unchanged, this
reflects a particular balance of forces between different elements of technical change
and the broader economic factors governing the growth of capital and income
and is in no sense a demonstration of the predominance of capital over the other
factors operating on productivity.

Some economists have put this proposition more strongly and argued that all
technical change must be capital-saving (in Sir Roy Harrod's sense of the term)
since, if there is no change in available resources, including capital, and the productivity of these resources increases, this must imply a fall in the capital-output
ratio. In one way this is true: technical progress will raise output without additional
saving, for example, by permitting existing instruments to be replaced by instruments of equal cost but greater productivity. But in another way, the proposition
is not true: if technical progress allows more machines to be made at the same cost,
capital increases at the same time as output and the capital-output ratio will remain constant if producer goods and consumer goods benefit equally from the
advance in techniques. There is, in fact, an ambiguity in the measurement of capital
of which too little store is taken in most discussions of capital-output ratios. If
one looks at the stock of capital as the cumulative product of past thrift, one
necessarily disregards the steady accretion that results from technical improvements
in the manufacture of capital goods—improvements that allow depreciation
funds to be used to better purpose on reinvestment than when a similar sum was
originally invested. Similarly, in any estimation of future capital requirements—in

the sense of fresh savings to expand the capital stock—some allowance ought to be made for the continuation of technical change in the producer goods sector before any calculation of incremental capital-output ratios.

This is by no means the only difficulty involved in the operational use of the concept. There are several additional circumstances which make it hazardous to interpret the results of empirical research. For example, in an underdeveloped country, land is one of the most important forms of capital just as food is one of the most important items of income; land values are unlike other property values and cannot easily be amalgamated with them if the amalgam is to have any theoretical significance. Much the same problems arise when estimates of capital have to be based on current yields rather than on cost of reproduction. Then there are the types of capital, notably consumers' durables, that may gradually replace producers' durables but are commonly excluded from estimates of the capital stock; and on the side of output and income, there are the numerous and important examples of nonmonetary transactions and self-supplied consumption that are usually omitted but may form a large proportion of total real income. Further difficulties of interpretation spring from divergent movements in the prices of capital and consumer goods: the process of economic development may bring about a change in the cost of labour relatively to the cost of capital and if there is any difference in capital intensity between the industries producing capital and consumer goods this will cause their prices to diverge and so disturb the ratio of capital to output.

Given the importance that has come to be attached to the capital-output ratio, it is remarkable how little attention has been given to the forces at work on it. In the prewar literature, much of the discussion abstracts almost entirely from the factors that seem to have been of first importance: technical change, urbanization, geographical discovery, etc. Instead, prominence was given to changes in technical coefficients in response to changes in the cost of capital—a process which now tends to be belittled. In keeping with the emphasis on obtaining the best allocation of resources, it was assumed that the supply of capital would be made to go round by a kind of price rationing which would exclude uses and methods offering an insufficient return. If capital became more abundant, this would increase the competitive advantage of more capital-intensive methods of production, more durable (but more expensive) forms of capital, and products making more lavish use of capital in their manufacture. This "deepening" of capital was assumed to be governed, with some reservations, by diminishing returns, so that the capital-output ratio, had it featured in the exposition, would have been likely to be represented as tending to increase.

One important reservation concerned the possibility of increasing returns. Most of the discussion on this subject related to manufacturing industry, a sector in which only a relatively small proportion of total capital was employed, and the discussion was directed more to issues of monopoly and competitive equilibrium than to the macro-economics of capital. Nevertheless the same line of argument was obviously as applicable to a railway network as to a steel mill, and in late Victorian times the importance of this reservation must have been apparent.

After the middle seventies, railway-building took a much reduced slice of national savings, and this relaxation of the pressure did not prevent the railways from carrying a rapidly expanding traffic.

The possibility of increasing returns rests largely, in the present context, on an expanding population and output. This expansion allows fuller use to be made of capacity created earlier and permits, therefore, of some economy in the use of capital per unit of output. An increase in population does not operate necessarily or exclusively in this direction, however, since it may put pressure on scarce resources and make it necessary to sink increasingly large amounts of capital in order to obtain given additions to the supply. The dominant effect of the increase, leaving these opposite possibilities on one side, and assuming also that employment rises at a parallel rate, is to make capital and output rise together and to preserve constancy in the ratio between the two. The more this process of capital "widening" enters, the greater the stability imparted to the capital-output ratio. If population is increasing rapidly and unemployment is not resulting, any other factor will have to have a very marked tendency to expand or contract capital requirements per unit of output if the change in the ratio is to be appreciable. In nineteenth-century Britain, the rate of growth of population was about 1 per cent per annum, while income and capital grew about twice as fast. Thus fully half of the growth in income and capital was controlled by a factor unlikely to disturb the ratio between the two.

A less obvious factor operating on the ratio is the pattern of demand. This was implicit in the classical formulation, since changes in the rate of interest could affect the demand for the more capital-intensive products such as houseroom and bring about a redistribution of demand in favour of those products. There is also an income element to be considered, since the pattern may change through time with the growth of income, its distribution, and all the dynamic elements that change spending habits for reasons unconnected with prices and incomes. The shift towards services and away from food is the most prominent example of a change in the pattern of demand that may have important effects on the demand for capital and the capital-output ratio. The emergence of synthetic materials and products is of comparable importance, but reflects a change in supply conditions at least as much as in demand and is cited below from this point of view.

Industrialization is undoubtedly one of the most important determinants of the ratio. It commonly involves the swallowing by the towns of large numbers of agricultural workers who are largely redundant to the needs of the rural areas from which they come. There are few things that make greater demands on capital than towns and the period of urbanization is inevitably one of high investment; but it is usually also a period in which income seems to grow rapidly, perhaps because of the spurious indices by which it tends to be measured, but no doubt also because of real economies of scale and concentration. Thus the effect of industrialization is to put a strain on available resources of capital, without necessarily deflecting the capital-output ratio a great deal. *A priori*, one might expect the large housing requirements of urban living to push the ratio up; but, as we have seen in Russia, and as we saw earlier in England, overcrowding and slums can provide a buffer if the shortage of capital is acute. Town-building may do no more than meet the bare requirements of industry for the housing of its workers and be carried through at far less capital cost than seems desirable to a later and richer generation.

A rather similar effect, although in the opposite direction, may be produced by the spread of literacy and education. This is generally recognized to be one of the keys to successful development and is likely, therefore, to go with a rapid growth in income. It is sometimes suggested that the outlay involved ought to be regarded as creative of personal capital and that when this adjustment is made, the capital-output ratio may show little change. It is doubtful, however, whether a large change would result even without the adjustment: for with better education there is a tendency to make use of more and better equipment, so that physical capital rises along with human, and the movement in the capital-output ratio is damped.

The influence of foreign trade and investment is also important. Many of the underdeveloped countries find that development is frequently associated, causally or otherwise, with a more than proportionate growth, especially in the early stages, in foreign trade, and that some at least of their most promising export lines call for heavy capital expenditure. This is particularly true where there are mineral ores and oil to be exploited and a need for extensive transport improvements before trade can be conducted. We know relatively little, however, about the capital-output ratio in the export sector of the economy in comparison with the ratio for the economy as a whole. All we can say is that there may be a divergence between the two and that foreign trade may cause the capital-output ratio to diverge from the capital-income ratio, measured from the side of consumption rather than production.

Foreign investment permits of a similar divergence between the requirements of capital needed to produce a given domestic output and the supply of savings generated by the corresponding income. It is curious, given the historical importance of foreign investment in relation to economic development, how rarely it features in models of economic growth. There is a good deal of evidence that capital requirements at some stage in growth are apt to outstrip domestic savings and at other stages to be outstripped by them. If there is international mobility of capital, therefore, and if different countries are at different stages in the cycle of growth, the explosive interaction of savings, income, and capital requirements that many economists put into their theoretical crucibles operates through a safety valve in the balance of payments rather than through wild fluctuations in the level of employment. The saving clause is, however, an important one: for if the major economies are all at the same stage, the safety valve cannot operate.

The importance of this factor was most evident in Britain in the years immediately before 1913 when total capital, including foreign investments, represented about six years' income, while domestic capital was only equal to between four and five years' output. Had the current savings of the country all been absorbed domestically, the incremental ratio of capital to output would have had to be very high indeed, especially as, over much of this period, the rate of growth of real income was extremely low. At the *average* rate of growth of 2 per cent per annum the incremental ratio, with savings at 15 per cent of income, would have had to be no less than 7.5; and if the diversion of savings to home investment had had the effect on income growth that one suspects, it might have had to be even higher.

The operations of government can exercise a similar influence. It is obvious that governments can make large drafts on national savings without any visible increase in output. This is so in wartime but it is true also of war preparations that lead to the creation of debt and of many objects of government borrowing even in peacetime. The effect of a long war, moreover, is likely to be to depress the capital-output ratio either through the destruction involved or through neglect of repairs and replacements. Hence an equilibrium that would seem impossible between a high rate of saving and low capital requirements may be maintained through erratic incursions by government into the capital market. Nor is there any reason why the incursions need only be erratic, since the government may systematically regulate the pressure on capital by operating directly on its own requirements, wherever these are capable of postponement, or through the budget surplus so far as this is politically acceptable.

Finally, we can hardly overlook the effects of innovation. It is hardly open to doubt that technical progress has been the most important instrument in raising the standard of living over the past two centuries, nor that, along with population growth and migration, it has dominated the course of investment in time of peace. To discuss the capital-output ratio without regard to the effects of innovation, therefore, is to rewrite Hamlet and leave out the Prince.

Nor is it possible to make the heroic simplification that its effects on the ratio are neutral. As has been argued above, the historical stability of the capital-output ratio could be due to quite adventitious circumstances, since the major uses of capital are highly concentrated and need show no necessary identity with the major areas of innovation. Moreover, even if, in the long run, innovation does prove to be neutral, there is no reason why this should imply neutrality in the short run to which most analysis of stability and fluctuations applies. The typical, and by far the most important innovation in the nineteenth century, was the steam engine and its by-product, railway transport. It took half a century at least to build the railway system in this and other countries; and if, at the end of that time, the capital-income ratio was no higher than before, this would prove nothing at all about the pressure of capital requirements in the interval. Current investment in railways in the early phase of railway building may easily have dwarfed the release of capital for the maintenance and replacement of other forms of transport, while eventually the stock of capital invested in all forms of transport might reach a total no higher in relation to the output of transport services than obtained before the railway age. It is not necessary to hold that this was in fact so; the point of importance is that an *acceleration* of technical progress, or the emergence of a major innovation in a stream of minor ones, is bound to increase capital requirements in advance of output and introduce a disturbance to the existing equilibrium between savings, income, and the rate of capital accumulation.

Whether technical progress does accelerate from time to time we cannot be certain since no one has yet succeeded in devising a measure that would assist judgment. Nor is it easy to say whether innovation does in fact exert its main pressure in the direction of greater capital intensity. Perhaps the big inventions— steam power, electricity, nuclear energy, synthetics of all kinds—do work this way, but the host of minor inventions and improvements that are less conspicuous and less talked about may well operate in the other direction.

Selection **6**

Criteria for the Selection
of Investment Projects

R. N. TRIPATHY

*From: "Criteria for the Choice of Investment Projects in Development
Planning,"* Indian Journal of Economics, *Vol. XLV, No. 176 (July 1964),
pp. 69–81. Reprinted by permission of the* Indian Journal of Economics.

The primary objective of a developing country is to secure the greatest increase
in its income from its available resources. The aggregate volume of investment
to be undertaken becomes meaningful when expressed in terms of concrete investment projects, and thus the programming aspect of investment planning is an
important problem in planned development.

In a free market economy the main problem of allocation of investible resources
into different industries "lies in evaluating the amount of scarce resources which
will actually be required by alternative types of production."[1] Thus, in this context, the micro-analytical criterion of marginal productivity, in which the productivity of the last unit of investment in each sector is considered from the point
of view of the profitability of the firm, is the primary criterion for the allocation
of resources. The optimum allocation of resources in terms of the criterion of
marginal productivity is achieved as a result of the operation of the market forces.
But the price system which makes the evaluation of scarce resources "fairly accurate
in more highly developed economies is often a rather unreliable guide to the
desirability of investment in an underdeveloped economy."[2] This is because
of the existence of structural disequilibrium in the use of factors of production with
labour commonly underemployed and capital and foreign exchange rationed.

---

[1] H.B. Chenery, "The Role of Industrialisation in Development Programmes," *American
Economic Review* (May 1955), Papers and Proceedings of the 67th Annual Meeting of the American Economic Association.

[2] *Ibid.* H. B. Chenery has expressed identical ideas at another place. He has pointed out
that "in underdeveloped areas it is generally recognised that both private value and private cost
may deviate far from social value and social cost. In such cases perfect competition cannot even
be used as a standard for many sectors of the economy; rather it is necessary to measure social
productivity and to provide for some form of government intervention to achieve more or less
efficient distribution of investment resources." "The Application of Investment Criteria," *Quarterly Journal of Economics* (Feb. 1953), p. 76.

Professor H. N. Khan[3] has suggested the criterion of social marginal productivity for the allocation of investment into the different industries of an underdeveloped country. This implies the abandonment of the microanalytical criterion of marginal productivity from the point of the individual firm in favour of the social criterion related to the national income as a whole and considered from the point of view of the productivity of the last unit of investment. From the point of view of the criterion of social marginal productivity, the policy implication is that those investment projects be selected of which the social marginal productivity is the highest.

The adoption of the criterion of social marginal productivity leads to the conclusion that the mechanism of market prices does not of itself make possible the optimum use of resources. "In a highly developed economy where the natural resources are more or less known, marginal productivity is approximately the same in all sectors and hence wages for the same levels of skill and degrees of effort are also approximately equal; in an economy of that type the social productivity of investment should approximate its productivity from the point of view of the firm. In that case price mechanism is a safe guide to investment. This does not apply to an economy in its early stages of development. There is a marked disparity in the degree of utilisation of the factors of production as between one sector and another. The mere transfer of factors or the introduction of new combinations thereof may bring about a substantial increase in social productivity. This increase need not necessarily be reflected in the profitability of the firm. Thus the rate of development may be speeded up if the inadequacies of the market as the governing mechanism of economic progress are eliminated and if investments are effected according to a co-ordinated comprehensive plan."[4]

But the application of the principle of social marginal productivity in the context of a planned allocation of resources may present a number of difficulties. Economic development is a dynamic process which involves changes in the size and quality of population, tastes, technological knowledge, and social and institutional factors; whereas the criterion of social marginal productivity assumes a static setting. In view of this, "the criterion of social marginal product must, therefore, be interpreted within the usual dynamic complex."[5] The interpretation of this criterion in a dynamic framework can be made only by imparting value judgments regarding the various social objectives, some of which may be conflicting. Another problem that may arise is whether a project should be preferred which maximises per capita income but at the same time involves a more unequal distribution of income as compared to another project. "Answers to these questions involve value judgments, and different individuals may reach various conclusions. Even if the social marginal productivity of each investment project were known, this would still not resolve the issue of whether national output or per capita

---

[3] "Investment Criteria in Development Programmes," *The Quarterly Journal of Economics* (Feb. 1951).

[4] Celso Furtado, "Capital Formation and Economic Development," *International Economic Papers*, No. 4, p. 139.

[5] G. M. Meier and R. E. Baldwin, *Economic Development* (1957), p. 344.

output should be maximised, and it would not be a sufficient guide to investment from the viewpoint of the most desirable distribution of income."[6]

The application of the criterion of social marginal productivity is also complicated by the element of time involved in investments of different kinds. The problem arises whether an investment which takes more time to mature should be discriminated against and those investments should be preferred the period of gestation of which is shorter.[7]

In the estimate of marginal social productivity, the element of time must be considered as a cost. Different projects take different time periods for construction; their periods of gestation differ and their rates of physical depreciation are also different. To determine the most productive investment projects, future yields of capital assets must be discounted to their present values and these discounted values should be compared with their present costs. Besides, investment decisions will differ according to the future shape of the income stream which is desired. An investment project aimed at maximising the rate of increase in national output in the short period may be considered the most preferable. But from the long-term point of view, this may not lead to the maximising of the rate of growth of national output, and an investment project which maximises output in the long period may be considered preferable.

The allocation of investment on the basis of the criterion of social marginal productivity requires the determination of the socially most productive investments. But a choice with regard to alternative investment projects may not be always possible. Some investments such as those in social overheads do not result in direct increase in national output, and thus, to make a choice between investments which result in a direct increase in output, and those which do not is not always easy. Besides, the concept of productivity is also a value concept, and not simply a physical one. Thus a conflict may arise between the value concept of productivity and its physical concept. In an underdeveloped country, the marginal social productivity of an investment project may be quite large, considered in terms of physical output; but from the point of view of value productivity, it may be quite low, because of the limited magnitude of the market for the product.

It is true that the financial yield on invested capital is an unreliable guide to the allocation of public sector investments, but in all cases it may not be possible for the public sector to neglect the value productivity of an investment project. This

---

[6] *Ibid.*, p. 345.

[7] As Prof. K. N. Raj has put it, "If the rate of output in the case of projects with shorter gestation period is higher, there is of course no problem, for they are then always preferable to projects with larger gestation period. But the difficulty arises because the rate of output realisable through projects with short gestation period is, in many cases, lower than in the case of those with longer gestation period. One has then to balance the advantage of a higher rate of output realisable through the latter against the disadvantage of having to forego the output which could be realised through the former, even at a lower rate, in the intervening period.

"Obviously the longer the period over which the value of the different streams of output is estimated and compared, and the smaller the discount for time in the evaluation of the output realisable later, the more preferable will projects with longer gestation period and higher rates of output tend to become." K. N. Raj, *Some Economic Aspects of the Bhakra Nangal Project* (1960), pp. 25–26.

serves to point out the practical difficulties in the way of the choice of investment projects on the basis of the criterion of social marginal productivity.

In order to apply the criterion of social marginal productivity to actual choice of investment projects, it is necessary to estimate the social marginal products of various investment projects. But there are a number of problems connected with the estimate of social marginal product of an investment project. Investment, especially in social and economic overheads, tends to increase the demand for certain factors of production and products, and this may make possible larger output from existing units of production. An investment on its completion makes possible new combinations of factors, which increase their productivity. "Thus every increase in output tends to widen the market for output in general, and opens out possibilities of increasing output still more through drawing in unutilised labour, making worthwhile further division of labour, as well as in other ways. Through both their supply and demand effects, an investment at one point can thus increase output at other points in the system and we have to take all of them into account in estimating the social product of the particular investment."[8]

Thus the structural interdependence of investments in different sectors leads to complicate the estimation of social marginal product. Investment in one sector induces investment in other sectors, and the problem arises to what extent in estimating the social product of the former the marginal output resulting from the latter should be added.

Prof. K. N. Raj has suggested a way out of this difficulty. He maintains that we should not allow ourselves "to be drawn into the question of how far the initial investment provides by itself the additional capital required for the subsequent induced investments, but to confine our attention to a specific time period and region, determined by the perspective of the whole investment programme: take into account the magnitude and the distribution of the investment which, within the assumptions of the programme, appear likely to take place; lump together the initial 'overhead' investment with the investments which could be regarded as induced by it; and relate the total of this to the total of the expected increases in output from them."[9] Prof. K. N. Raj has accepted that this is not a satisfactory solution of the problem, but at the same time he has pointed out that if "the rate and pattern of investment over the relevant period are already given, it should be possible, even if only very roughly, to assess how much of the further investments required to exploit the economies offered by an 'overhead' investment will in fact be forthcoming during the period, and how much would be the consequent increases in output."[10] But the reliability of such estimates will depend to a large extent on the instruments available to the planning authority for ensuring that the rate and pattern of the actual investments conform to its own planned design, as well as on various other factors affecting organisational efficiency.

For the estimation of the social marginal productivity of an investment project, Prof. A. E. Kahn has suggested that from the addition to output due to the invest-

---

[8]K. N. Raj, *op. cit.*, p. 31.
[9]*Ibid.*, p. 32.
[10]*Ibid.*

ment, the alternative output sacrificed as a result of drawing factors of production from other fields into this one has to be subtracted.[11]

Professor Kahn was thinking here in terms of the orthodox welfare economics. Thus the factors are valued at their social opportunity cost, *i.e.*, at what they could have produced in other fields had they not been drawn into the particular investment project. In an underdeveloped country where there is a huge unemployment of labour, the opportunity cost of labour may be taken as nil; and according to Professor Kahn's approach, labour becomes costless. Thus ignoring the factors other than labour, Kahn argued that in this case the social marginal productivity criterion becomes the same as the Polak-Buchanan rate of turnover criterion. This criterion would lead to a different result from that of the Polak-Buchanan rate of turnover criterion only when the social opportunity cost of labour is positive. Thus in an underdeveloped economy where the social opportunity cost of labour is zero, Kahn recommended the technique with the least capital coefficient, *i.e.*, with the maximum rate of turnover.

Such an interpretation of the criterion of social marginal productivity may be accepted if the objective of investment planning is to maximise output in the short period. But if the objective of investment policy in a planned economy is to maximise the rate of growth of output in future, such an interpretation may not be valid. The rate of growth of output is a function of the rate of capital accumulation; and the rate of capital accumulation is determined by the excess of production over current consumption. But it does not follow that investment which maximises the production of output in the short period will also maximise the excess of production over current consumption. The technique maximising the output in the short period will generate more employment, and, as a result, the excess of production over current consumption will be low. It means that "even if the alternative social product is nil, the cost of labour will be positive given by the increase in consumption due to extra employment. Thus the social marginal productivity is all right if we are not interested in the future at all. But if we take a long-term point of view, the criterion need no longer be valid."[12]

Walter Galenson and Harvey Leibenstein have differed with Prof. A. E. Kahn's interpretation of the criterion of social marginal productivity, and they have put forward the criterion of "marginal per capita reinvestment quotient"[13] as an alternative criterion for an economy which is interested in achieving a higher rate of capital accumulation and growth of output in future. They have pointed out that social marginal productivity may not be a universally correct criterion under all conditions if the purpose of the planners in underdeveloped countries is

---

[11]Investment Criteria in Development Programmes, *op. cit.* Another writer estimates the social marginal product as the value added in the domestic economy per unit of investment minus the total operating cost per unit of investment plus the balance of payments premium per unit of investment. H. B. Chenery, "The Application of Investment Criteria," *Quarterly Journal of Economics* (Feb. 1953), p. 83. Thus the criterion of social marginal productivity has been interpreted in different ways by different people.

[12]A. K. Sen, "Some Notes on the Choice of Capital Intensity in Development Planning," *Quarterly Journal of Economics* (Nov. 1957), pp. 563–564.

[13]"Investment Criteria, Productivity, and Economic Development," *Quarterly Journal of Economics* (Aug. 1955).

to maximise the rate of economic development. As they have put it, "suppose that for two firms, I and II, the rates of reinvestment of profits are respectively, 100 per cent and 20 per cent, while in other respects the two firms are in the same position at the time of observation. If some agency charged with the allocation of capital funds had to choose between the two firms, it would be indifferent between them on the basis of the marginal productivity criterion, since the prospective return per unit of investment would be the same. But if the rate of reinvestment is taken into account, firm I would clearly be favoured if the purpose were a more rapid rate of capital accumulation."[14]

But the Galenson-Leibenstein criterion is also not free from objections. It accepts the maximisation of the rate of growth of output in future as a result of a higher rate of capital formation as the objective of investment policy. But the present income may be regarded as more valuable by society than future income. The Galenson-Leibenstein criterion neglects this possibility. The society may prefer to have higher rate of immediate income and a lower rate of income in future. This preference for the present may not be due to irrational telescopic faculty but due to a very rational consideration that "our present income being less than our future income, the value of additional income to us is much at the present moment. This problem of time preference leads to a number of complexities which we shall encounter when we try to put forward an alternative criterion; but that a complete neglect of the problem is illegitimate seems clear."[15] But if the planners prefer the future rise in output to the present rise in income, they would adopt the criterion of reinvestment in the allocation of investment.

Thus the analysis of the criterion of the social marginal productivity leads to the conclusion that though this criterion is a better guide to the allocation of investment than the criterion provided by the market mechanism, its application in the actual implementation of investment policy in underdeveloped countries is not free from theoretical and practical difficulties. In the actual formulation and implementation of policy of allocation of investment, the planners in these countries may be predominantly influenced by political and social considerations rather than by strictly economic considerations.

THE MAXIMISATION OF THE RATE OF
TURNOVER AS AN INVESTMENT CRITERION

The maximisation of the rate of turnover or the maximisation of the ratio of output to capital has also been suggested as an investment criterion.[16] As Prof. N. S. Buchanan has put it, "If investment funds are limited, the wise policy, in the absence of special considerations, would be to undertake first those investments

---

14"Investment Criteria, Productivity, and Economic Development: Reply to Mr. Moes and Mr. Villard by Galenson and Leibenstein," *Quarterly Journal of Economics* (Aug. 1957), p. 473.

15A. K. Sen, *op. cit.*, p. 567.

16J. J. Polak, "Balance of Payments Problems of Countries Reconstructing with the Help of Foreign Loans," *Quarterly Journal of Economics* (Feb. 1943); N. S. Buchanan, *International Investment and Domestic Welfare* (1945).

having a high value of annual product relative to the investment necessary to bring them into existence."[17] In a model where the social opportunity cost of labour is nil due to the existence of unemployment, the social marginal productivity criterion coincides with the maximisation of the rate of turnover criterion.

But the actual application of the criterion of the maximisation of the ratio of output to capital is difficult because of the various conceptual and practical problems relating to the definition of the capital-output ratio. As pointed out by Harvey Leibenstein, the capital-output ratio would be a powerful tool of analysis if it could be reasonably assumed that the ratio is independent of the behaviour of the other variables in the system. The capital-output ratio will be a meaningless concept if factors completely unrelated to the increment to the stock of capital cause great variations in output.[18]

The maximisation of the rate of turnover as an investment criterion in an underdeveloped country has the danger of distorting the pattern of investment in a manner which may be incompatible with the achievement of a high rate of economic development in the long run. The investments in basic and capital goods industries, in public utilities, and in social and economic overheads have a low output-capital ratio, and as a result, such investments will not be favoured from the point of view of the maximisation of the rate of turnover criterion.

On the other hand, investments in consumption goods industries and into the agricultural sector would be favoured because of the smaller gestation period and high output-capital ratio.[19] But it is the investments in basic and capital goods industries and in social and economic overheads which build up the foundations of economic development and to which a high priority should be given in the investment plan of an underdeveloped country. Thus in view of these considerations, the criterion of the maximisation of the rate of turnover in the allocation of investment does not appear to be satisfactory.

The criterion of maximising the rate of turnover has also been found inadequate as a guide to policy because "a high rate of turnover may be associated with a high rate of depreciation and the rate of net output may not necessarily be high."[20] This difficulty can be avoided to some extent by stating the criterion in terms of the net rate of turnover. But even then it does not become a satisfactory investment criterion because "it ignores the cost of employing labour in operating the capital. When the cost of employing labour in an economy is zero, a very good case can be made for the criterion of maximum addition to net output from a given amount of capital investment. If, on the other hand, employment of labour involves some

---

[17] *Ibid.*, p. 24.

[18] Harvey Leibenstein, *Economic Backwardness and Economic Growth* (1957).

[19] H. B. Chenery has also expressed identical views. He has pointed out "that when all sectors are taken together, there is if anything a negative correlation between capital turnover and social marginal productivity, because unused resources and the possibility of saving on imports or increasing exports occur predominantly in sectors having low capital turnover," and he maintains that a shift to less capital-intensive sectors would not be desirable. *Quarterly Journal of Economics* (Feb. 1955), p. 87.

[20] A. K. Sen, *op. cit.*, p. 562.

cost to society, we have to take that into account."[21] It has been seen that the adoption of the rate of turnover criterion will be incompatible with the objective of attaining a higher rate of economic growth in the long run. This is because the investment which maximises the rate of turnover will lead to a low rate of capital accumulation.

Thus if the planners in an underdeveloped economy are interested in attaining higher rate of economic growth, they will abandon the rate of turnover criterion in favour of the criterion of reinvestment as suggested by Galenson and Leibenstein.

THE MAXIMISATION OF THE RATIO OF LABOUR TO INVESTMENT

It has also been suggested that those investment projects should be selected which will maximise the ratio of labour to investment. This means that in the allocation of investment those investment projects should be preferred which have the maximum employment potential. Most of the underdeveloped countries, especially those which are densely populated, have a large mass of unemployed labour and this unemployment exists in the form of "disguised unemployment" or structural underemployment. "This is the type of unemployment with Harrod's juxtaposition of the natural and warranted rates of growth implies, and which Joan Robinson has chosen to call Marxian unemployment."[22] It has been maintained that "structural under-employment can appear and persist in an underdeveloped economy whose supply of labour tends to outrun its demand for labour, even if effective demand is high enough to keep the existing capital stock fully utilised and even if technological progress is neutral so as not to diminish the amount of labour required per unit of output."[23]

Those who have advocated the maximisation of the employment of labour as investment criterion in the underdeveloped countries have argued that this mass of unemployed labour has to be maintained by them in any case at a minimum level of subsistence, and as there are limited opportunities for productive employment due to the backwardness of these countries, those investment projects should be preferred which have the largest potential of giving employment to the idle manpower to those which do not possess such potentials.

The idea behind this proposition is that when such manpower would be employed in the investment projects, the real cost of their employment would be less than the expenditure which will have to be incurred in maintaining them at the subsistence level. Thus those who have advocated the maximisation of the ratio of labour to investment as an investment criterion have deduced this corollary from the broader principle of social marginal productivity. But the volume of employment which a particular project of investment generates directly is not an adequate basis for measuring and comparing the social productivity from alternative investment projects. This is because in the estimation of the productivity of an

[21] *Ibid.*
[22] Kurihara, *The Keynesian Theory of Economic Development* (1959), p. 109.
[23] *Ibid.*, p. 113.

investment project the various constituents of cost such as the cost of labour employed, cost of the equipments and raw materials, and the interest paid on the capital have to be set against the value of the product.

An investment project may create three types of employment: the primary employment directly created in the particular investment project, the secondary employment generated by the additional demand resulting from the expenditures of those directly employed, "and the more permanent employment opportunities which are, so to say, sedimented on the completion of each investment."[24] The employment potentials of different investment projects constituted by a combination of these three kinds of employment are bound to be different. Therefore, if "we are concerned with 'the employment potential' of alternative investment schemes (which must take into account all the three types of employment, with the appropriate weightage given to each), it would be obviously not possible to choose one out of the different combinations of these types of employment associated with different investments, unless time and productivity are also made the objects of social evaluation."[25]

The maximisation of the ratio of labour to investment has other implications as well. First, it may mean that the maximisation of the employment of labour rather than that of productivity becomes the objective of development policy. If an investment project is to maximise the employment of labour, it must be highly labour-intensive. This means that such an investment will not be able to make use of the most modern technological innovations, and, as a result, it will not be able to maximise productivity. Considered from this point of view, maximisation of employment and maximisation of productivity as investment criteria are antithetical. Investment projects which maximise productivity do not maximise employment and those which maximise employment do not maximise productivity. Thus if the pattern of investment in an underdeveloped country be geared to the objective of maximising employment, it may not be compatible with the condition of maximum economic growth. Secondly, if an investment project is selected on the basis of the criterion of maximising the ratio of labour to investment, the expansion in demand for consumption goods will be greater in proportion to the increase in output, and, therefore, this will be fraught with inflationary potential. Thirdly, such investments will tend to reduce the volume of investible surplus, as they result in a greater proportion of the increment in output to be consumed. Considered from this point of view, the allocation of investment directed to maximise employment will be incompatible with the condition of an accelerated economic growth of an underdeveloped country in the long run.

The mass of unemployed manpower in the rural sector of an underdeveloped country lives at the subsistence level. But when this unemployed manpower is given employment in investment projects designed to provide maximum employment opportunities, these new entrants to the employment sector tend to increase their propensity to consume. As a result, they tend to spend a considerable pro-

---

[24]K. N. Raj, *op. cit.*, p. 6.
[25]*Ibid.*, p. 7.

portion of the output on consumption. In capital-intensive projects, as the productivity of investment is greater, the resulting surplus in output will be greater.

But in investment projects which are labour-intensive, the resulting surplus available for capital formation will be low. This means that it will lead to a slower rate of growth of output in future. As Walter Galenson and Harvey Leibenstein have pointed out, "there may be situations in which the maximum labour absorption criterion would not maximise the addition to total output."[26]

CONCLUSION

The upshot of the analysis is that it is difficult for the planning authorities of an underdeveloped country to determine the choice of investment projects on the basis of a single criterion. Many of the criteria come in conflict with one another. Investments in social overheads help in the formation of human capital, and the choice of such investments may be made largely on the basis of the criterion of social marginal productivity. But the formation of human capital is an indispensable condition of accelerated economic development. Thus the criterion of social marginal productivity is mixed up with that of economic growth in determining the choice of investments in social overheads. Investments in capital-intensive projects and in basic and heavy industries may be determined mainly on the basis of the criterion of maximising the addition to total output and building up the infrastructure of economic development as well as of maximising the investible surplus and defence potential of an economy. Investment in labour-intensive projects may be determined on the basis of the criterion of maximum labour absorption. Such investments are also compatible with the criterion of social marginal productivity in the special conditions of underdeveloped economies. In the case of such investments, there arises a conflict between the maximum labour absorption criterion and the criterion of maximising the rate of growth in the long run. Thus the planning authorities have to find a compromise between the different investment criteria, and to a large extent investment decisions may be made by purely political considerations.

---

[26]"Investment Criteria, Productivity, and Economic Development," *Quarterly Journal of Economics* (Aug. 1955), p. 348.

Selection **7**

An Appraisal of Investment Projects

H. C. BOS

From: "Discussion Paper," in Walter Isard and John H. Cumberland (eds.), Regional Economic Planning: Techniques of Analysis for Less Developed Areas; Papers and Proceedings of the First Study Conference on Problems of Economic Development, Conference on Regional Economic Development, Bellagio, Italy, 1960 (Paris: European Productivity Agency of the Organisation for European Economic Co-operation, 1961), pp. 369–373. Reprinted by permission of the Organisation for Economic Cooperation and Development, Paris.

I. THE APPRAISAL OF INVESTMENT PROJECTS AND INVESTMENT PLANNING

Benefit-cost analysis is a technique designed for the appraisal of investment projects and, therefore, a tool in the field of investment planning. For this reason it might be useful, before discussing the merits of benefit-cost analysis, to indicate briefly the role which the appraisal of investment projects can play in investment planning.

The questions we have to answer in investment planning can be distinguished as follows.

The choice of the total investment volume (both public and private) for the economy as a whole. This choice is the most basic one to be made. It is the choice between saving and consuming the national income. Taking account of capital imports, this choice determines the rate of growth of the consumption and income levels, especially in countries where capital is the main bottleneck for economic growth.

The distribution of the total investment volume between industrial sectors. This distribution has to be such as to utilize fully the available savings and capital imports and as to increase the production capacities of the different industrial sectors such that the new capacities are just sufficient to meet the total demand, both for final and intermediate products, in each sector.

A third aspect concerns the distribution of the total investments between regions of the country. This question, which is the most neglected aspect of investment planning at present, has to be answered in any economy and not only in economies which are wholly or partially underdeveloped.

The decisions in each of these three stages have to be based on a formulation of the aims of the economic policy and have to consider the many interdependen-

75

cies that exist between the economic phenomena in an economy. The policy aims may include national income, employment, regional income distribution, etc. The interdependencies may be definition relations (social accounts), technological relations (input-output), behaviour relations (consumption, demand and supply functions).

It will be clear that the use of mathematical models will be very helpful, if not indispensable, if we want to make consistent and optimum choices which take account of the factors mentioned.

The choices mentioned so far lead to the formulation of an *investment plan*, i.e., the distribution of the total investment volume between industries and regions. However, this investment plan has to be filled up with concrete investment projects. At this stage of the planning procedure we need a criterion for selecting between alternative projects and, therefore, here the appraisal of individual investment projects has to play its role.

The above is a rough sketch of a procedure for investment planning which seems to give some guarantee for formulating a consistent and optimum investment program.[1]

However, this procedure will only be applicable in countries which have already a developed planning apparatus or which are able to develop such an apparatus in the near future.

At present practical planning work approaches the problem of formulating an investment program in many cases from the other end; i.e., on the basis of concrete investment projects, both private and public, an investment program is built up. The need for a national investment criterion is in this case still more urgent. Here also, a choice between projects has to be made taking account of the aims of the economic policy and the interdependencies between the economic phenomena. Therefore, in principle there is no difference between the two approaches. In underdeveloped countries and regions, which are in the process of structural change, more attention should be given to the sectorial and regional allocation of the investments; in developed countries more emphasis can be given to the appraisal of individual projects. But both aspects have to be considered, because the questions they answer are of a different character.

II. The Appraisal of Investment Projects and Benefit-cost Analysis

In the discussion of the methods of appraising investment projects the following logical stages involved in the appraisal can be distinguished:

The description of the technical and economic characteristics of each project.

The estimation of the influence of the project on the economy, both during the construction period, during which the project is being carried out, as well as during the operational period, when the investment is completed and the newly created productive capacity is in operation. The influences of the project may be direct

---

[1] For a recent exposition of some techniques of investment planning, see U.N. Economic Commission for Asia and the Far East, *Programming Techniques for Economic Development*. Report of the First Group of Experts on Programming Techniques (Bangkok, 1960).

or indirect. The direct effects consist of the immediate contributions to production, within the sector of the project. The indirect effects are those in sectors vertically connected with that sector, either preceding or following, because of direct technological links. Secondary or multiplier effects are all other effects.

The evaluation of the consequences of the project and the formulation of a criterion for the selection of the projects.[2]

The traditional investment criterion is the private profitability of the project. Annual profits, calculated on the basis of monetary revenues and costs to the entrepreneur, are related to the capital invested. Benefit-cost analysis, however, is recommended as a more appropriate method when investments have to appraised from a national point of view. This method includes under the benefits not only the monetary revenues but also the imputed returns, not actually received. The benefits are not related to the capital invested, but to the annual total costs, including both capital and operation costs.

The question whether the benefit-cost criterion is superior to private profitability as a criterion for the selection of investment projects and whether the benefit-cost criterion is an acceptable measure of the economic value of a project from the national point of view cannot be answered without specification of the project to be appraised and of the economic situation in which the project has to operate. The answers to these questions depend also on the definitions of the benefits and the costs which constitute the criterion.

The reason why no simple answers are possible is the fact that the theoretical bases of private profitability and of the benefit-cost analysis as investment criteria are in principle the same. This theoretical basis is the well-known proposition from welfare economics that, roughly formulated, under certain conditions decentralized decision making, and especially decentralized profit maximization, leads to an optimum welfare for the community as a whole. This statement is the justification of the appraisal of investment projects independently of each other and on the basis of the direct effects only.

However, as was mentioned, the proposition is correct only under certain assumptions. The most important assumptions are full utilization of all resources, the absence of production under decreasing cost caused by indivisibilities either in input or output, and the absence of external economies or diseconomies. Under these conditions and some others, perfect competition is the optimum economic system, and profits, calculated on the basis of market prices for output and costs, are a reliable guide in investment decisions.

Naturally, those who accept the profitability or the benefit-cost criterion recognize that reality corresponds imperfectly to the theoretical model described. However, the deviations between theory and reality are considered to be of minor importance. The economic system of perfect competition is accepted as a workable approximation of reality. Some modifications are introduced where the deviations are too apparent, e.g., the inclusion of certain indirect benefits and of imputed returns. However, it remains arbitrary in this method which indirect effects to

---

[2] Details of the different aspects of the appraisal of investment projects are discussed in *U.N. Manual on Economic Development Projects* (New York, 1958).

include and which to exclude. The opposite opinions held in the long discussions on these problems are indicative of the difficulties to which a broader interpretation of the benefit-cost analysis leads.

Professor Otto Eckstein has only modest claims, if any, in defence of benefit-cost analysis. This demonstrates clearly that he is fully aware of the limitations to which a strict application of the benefit-cost analysis is bound. Perhaps he could have stated more explicitly that in underdeveloped countries or regions the fundamental conditions on which the theoretical justification of benefit-cost analysis is based are usually far from realized and, therefore, a strict application of this method of appraising investment projects is not justified. These countries or regions are by definition in a situation of structural economic disequilibrium. In most cases fundamental scarcity of capital and foreign exchanges is combined with large unemployment of labour. Market prices of products and factors of production are not a correct expression of the opportunity costs.

The position which Professor Eckstein seems to take under these circumstances is to renounce the application of benefit-cost analysis and to rely only on macroeconomic planning or programming methods.

From the discussion in section I, it follows that we do not oppose the use of macroeconomic planning methods. However, these methods, when they are at our disposal, cannot help us to choose between individual projects. Further, our experience in using economic planning models in underdeveloped countries is still very young, and, therefore, it is useful to have an alternative approach to the same problem as a check on the results of our macroeconomic methods. In addition, in many cases these last methods cannot be applied due to the lack of the required statistical data.

For these reasons it is necessary to have a method for the appraisal of investment projects which more appropriately takes account of the specific circumstances in underdeveloped countries than benefit-cost analysis as applied in a developed country like the United States does.

III. THE APPRAISAL OF INVESTMENT PROJECTS IN UNDERDEVELOPED COUNTRIES

The following remarks discuss the aspects of the appraisal of investment projects which seem to be of special importance in underdeveloped countries or regions.

> The investment projects should not be appraised individually, but as a combination or a programme of projects. The projects to be included in the programme need not be of the same nature.
>
> The benefits should be measured as the addition to the national product induced by the investment programme. The value of the scarce factors used can be counted as negative benefits.
>
> The benefits should not only include the direct, but also the indirect effects made possible by the existence of unused capacity. If there is no unused capacity, no indirect effects have to be included under the benefits of the project considered.
>
> Secondary or multiplier effects should only be considered in a situation of cyclical depression. These effects, however, cannot be attributed to specific projects.

When market prices are not a correct expression of equilibrium prices (or opportunity costs), *accounting* or *shadow prices* have to be used for the evaluation of the physical influence of the projects on the economy. In underdeveloped countries the market wage for unskilled labour is for social reasons often higher than the opportunity costs of labour. On the other hand, the intrinsic values of capital and foreign exchange are higher than the corresponding market prices. An accounting wage lower than the market wage and an accounting interest and an accounting foreign exchange rate higher than the market prices should be used. The correct determination of the accounting prices is not possible without the use of mathematical models. In many cases some alternative calculations on the basis of more or less intuitively chosen accounting prices can indicate the sensitivity of the value of the benefits to changes in prices.

The costs should include the value of all scarce factors used in the programme. The factors should be valued at accounting prices. If capital is the main scarce factor, the benefits have to be expressed per unit of capital.

It is not sufficient to determine the influence of an investment program on the national product in one year, since the program may influence the rate of savings and, consequently, the rate of growth of the economy as a whole. Therefore, the influence on the development in time of the national product has to be determined.

Not only the influence of the projects on the national product should be measured but also the influence on the other aims of economic policy, such as the employment, the balance of payments, the regional income distribution, etc. Weights can be given to each of these elements in order to be able to reduce these several aspects to one single measure.

Selection **8**

A Long-Term Growth Model
of a Developing Economy

A. QAYUM

From: "Long Term Growth of a Developing Economy," Economia
Internazionale, *Vol. XVII, No. 3 (Aug. 1964), pp. 437–445. Reprinted by
permission of* Economia Internazionale *and the author.*

Most growth models that have recently appeared are based on assumptions
which are more relevant to the developed economies. Two important aspects of
these economies are: (1) savings tend to approach a more or less stable rate,[1] and
(2) the productive structure tends to be settled on a more or less fixed technology.[2]
If there have been any movements in the savings rate and capital-output ratios of
the developed countries, they have been downward. Under these conditions it is
not surprising to find that in most of the models that have appeared, the rate of
savings and the capital-output ratios have been assumed to be constant. And these
assumptions will not be unjustified in the context of the developed economies
with the characteristics mentioned above.

However, the above assumptions by their very nature will be unjustified in the
context of the developing economies. For two things are absolutely necessary for
any economy to be labelled developing. First, capital should accumulate at an
increasing rate, which in turn means that the savings rate should rise; secondly,
there must be, as far as possible, an optimal utilisation of resources, which, taken
in conjunction with the first, means that the techniques of production and hence
the capital-output ratio can be constant only by accident, i.e., the techniques of
production will keep changing. Due to these facts, the usual models of economic
growth are not very useful for the developing economies.

In addition the developing economies have certain characteristics which make
the usual models based on the customary multiplier and accelerator principles
even less satisfactory. This is largely due to the following reasons. First, almost
all developing economies are short in capital. The scarcity of capital is the biggest

---

[1] Cf. N.B.E.R., *Capital Formation and Economic Growth* (Princeton University Press, 1955),
p. 6.
[2] Cf. P. S. Anderson, "The Apparent Decline in Capital-Output Ratios," *Quarterly Journal
of Economics* (Nov. 1961).

impediment in the way of speedy development of these countries and forms the main bottleneck. The role of the accelerator is, thus, very much weakened, if not eliminated, for real investment cannot react to changes in national income in the same manner in a capital-scarce economy as it can do in a developed economy. It cannot exceed the volume of (ex ante) savings, given the international movement of capital, due to the simple fact of nonavailability of additional capital. Similarly, it can hardly fall below the volume of (ex ante) savings in a developing economy, owing to the existence of pent-up demand for consumption goods which ensures a ready market for goods produced and supplied.

In a developing economy, the consumption behaviour of the self-subsistent households particularly in the early stages of development may be significantly different from the rest of the spending units, in that an increase in the household output might not generate the same sequence of increased consumption and investment as it might do normally. This is due to the allegedly negative elasticity of work-effort to output. The influence of these households, however, seems to be limited in the developing economies or (perhaps more correctly) it is insulated from the general functioning of the economy. For the over-all effect in all the countries moving on the path of development has been a general rise in work-effort and consumption at an increasing rate. Moreover, the self-subsistent character of the households weakens as the economy grows, education spreads, and the means of communication and transportation are developed. Nonetheless, it is obvious that the existence of self-subsistent households does modify the multiplier effect by dampening it.

It should be pointed out, however, that the role of the multiplier has not been very dynamising even in the growth models pertaining to the developed countries; it is still less so in models pertaining to the developing countries. In fact it is very much subdued and its dynamising effect is generated through a process which is the reverse of that observed in the case of the developed countries; i.e., the lesser the rate of growth of consumption, the greater the rate of growth of investment and the greater the expansion.

After these preliminary remarks, we proceed to construct a long-term model of economic growth for a developing economy. Let the initial amounts of labour and capital be L_0 and K_0, respectively. We assume that the labour force increases exogenously at a constant rate of λ per year. The rate of capital formation depends upon the rate of savings. We assume the savings rate to increase at a rate of s per year from an initial rate S_0. The total output in the economy in the tth year is

$$P_t = F(L_t, K_t) \tag{1}$$

where L_t is the labour force in the tth year and K_t the amount of capital. We have

$$L_t = L_0 \, e^{\lambda t} \tag{2}$$

$$\dot{K}_t = S_0 \, e^{st} \, P_t \tag{3}$$

We finally assume that the productive activity of the economy is adequately described by the Cobb-Douglas production function, so that

$$\dot{K}_t = S_0 \, e^{st} \, L_t^\alpha \, K_t^\beta$$
$$= S_0 L^\alpha e^{(s+\alpha\lambda)t} \, K_t^\beta \tag{4}$$

the solution[3] of (4) is

$$K_t = \left\{ \frac{S_0 L_0^\alpha (1-\beta)}{s+\alpha\lambda} \, e^{(s+\alpha\lambda)t} + c \right\}^{1/(1-\beta)} \tag{5}$$

where c is the integration constant which can be determined by initial conditions and is given in our case by substitution of (2) and (5) in (1) completes the model.

$$K_0 = \left[\frac{S_0 L_0^\alpha (1-\beta)}{s+\alpha\lambda} + c \right]^{1/(1-\beta)}$$

or $$c = K_0^{1-\beta} - \frac{S_0 L_0^\alpha (1-\beta)}{s+\alpha\lambda}$$

We can compute the future growth of national product for given values of S_0, L_0, K_0, α, β, s, λ. We illustrate the model with figures that are more or less relevant to Indian conditions. As we are interested in percentage changes rather than in absolute values, we take $L_0 = 1 = K_0$, $S_0 = .1$; take the usual values for α and β, i.e., .75 and .25, and stipulate that $s = .005$ and $\lambda = .02$.
  For these values

$$K_t = (3.75 \, e^{.2t} - 2.75)^{4/3} \tag{6}$$

From (2), (6), and (1) we compute Table I tracing the long-term growth of a developing economy.

Table I

SHOWING THE LONG-TERM GROWTH OF NATIONAL PRODUCTION

t	L_t	K_t	P_t	P_t/K_t	P_t/L_t
(1)	(2)	(3)	(4)	(5)	(6)
0	1	1	1	1	1
5	1.105	1.557	1.204	.77	1.0896
10	1.221	2.238	1.421	.63	1.1646
15	1.350	3.059	1.656	.54	1.2266
20	1.492	4.032	1.913	.47	1.2822
25	1.649	5.181	2.196	.42	1.3317

Table I shows that for the values of the parameters the value of national product is doubled in 20 to 25 years (col. 4). This conforms well to the targets fixed in the successive Indian Plans.[4] The Indian planners have been generally thinking in

---

[3] Cf. E. L. Ince, *Integration of Differential Equations* (1946), 4th ed., p. 22.
[4] Cf. *Third Five Year Plan*, Govt. of India, p. 21.

terms of doubling the national product in 25 years. The output-capital ratio (col. 5) keeps falling at a diminishing rate. This again is in keeping with the underlying assumptions of the Indian Plans.[5] The national product per worker shows a much lower rate of increase.[6] It registers a rise of 33 per cent only in 25 years. This is at variance with the assertion of the first two Five-Year Plans that the level of national income in 1950–51 could be doubled by 1970–71 and that of per capita income by 1977–78. The mistake was realised by the Third Five-Year Plan, though no systematic attempt has been made to estimate the rate of per capita growth of income.[7]

It is interesting to study the movement of the consumption level in the framework of the theoretical model we have constructed. The main concern of the people at large in a developing economy is the rise of the per capita consumption level, even though the growth of the national product is important.

It is obvious that the aggregate consumption is equal to the total net product minus the net investment, i.e.,

$$C_t = P_t - \dot{K}_t \tag{7}$$

where C_t is the aggregate consumption in period t. As we have assumed that the initial rate of savings is .1, and our unit of measurement of labour and capital is such that $L_0 = 1 = K_0$ and hence $P_0 = 1$, we must have $C_0 = .9$ (for $C_0 = P_0 - \dot{K}_0 = 1 - .1 = .9$). As $C_t = P_t(1 - S_0\, e^{st})$, putting as before $\lambda = .02$ and $s = .005$, we have the rate of growth of per capita consumption:

$$w = \frac{\log\,[P_t/C_0(1 - S_0\, e^{st})]}{t} - \lambda$$

$$w = \frac{\log\,[P_t/.9(1 - .1\, e^{.005t})]}{t} - .02$$

Table II (p. 84) gives the values of w corresponding to 5, 10, 15, 20, 25 years.

For the assumed initial values of the variables and assumed values of the parameters, Table II, col. 3, gives the magnitude of total consumption. The level of aggregate consumption in the 25th period is more than double of the level in the initial period as is that of the total product (col. 2). The aggregate consumption per annum increases at a simple rate of roughly 4 per cent, but the compound rate reckoned from the initial rate decreases at a diminishing rate from 3.6 to 3.1 per cent roughly. The overall rate of growth of per capita consumption is 1.6 per cent for the first 5 years; it is 1.45 per cent for the first 10 periods, but it goes on decreasing but at a diminishing rate.

---

[5] Cf. *Second Five Year Plan* p. 11. Here the incremental capital-output ratio has been shown as increasing, i.e., the output-capital ratio is falling. Figures in Table I are not real, because of our arbitrary units of measurement of initial values of labour and capital. They, however, purport to show the trend of the output-capital ratios.

[6] If we assume a worker's family of five members, the per capita output will be one-fifth of the per worker output.

[7] Cf. *Third Five Year Plan*, Govt. of India, p. 21.

Table II

SHOWING THE MOVEMENT OF PER CAPITA CONSUMPTION LEVEL FOR THE
ASSUMED VALUES OF VARIABLES

t	Total product	Total consumption	Rate of growth of aggregate consumption per year over the last t years	Rate of growth per capita consumption per year over the last t years
(1)	(2)	(3)	(4)	(5)
0	1	.9	—	—
5	1.209	1.0805	.0365	.0166
10	1.421	1.2715	.0346	.0145
15	1.656	1.4775	.0331	.013
20	1.913	1.6922	.0316	.0118
25	2.196	1.9471	.0309	.0107

Planners and policy makers are more frequently concerned with the inverse of the problem stated above. In what has preceded, we assume a certain annual rate of increase in the rate of savings. But the equally (if not more) important problem is to ensure a certain given increase in the per capita consumption per annum. In this case the rate of savings or investment in each year will be dependent upon magnitudes of output and consumption in each year. In fact, as argued earlier, the volume of investment in each year will be equal to the difference between the volumes of output and consumption, i.e.,

$$\dot{K}_t = P_t - C_t \tag{8}$$

We further envisage that per capita consumption is to be increased by θ per cent. So that

$$C_t = C_0 \, e^{\lambda + \theta}$$

where C_0 is the initial level of consumption and λ is the rate of increase of population as before. Now

$$\dot{K}_t = L_t^\alpha K_t^\beta - C_0 \, e^{(\lambda + \theta)t} \tag{9}$$

Further we have:

$$K_t = K_{t-1} + \dot{K}_{t-1} \tag{10}$$

Equation (10) implies that savings of a period are invested in the succeeding period, or else they are invested in the same period but start to yield output in the succeeding period. It is obvious that if we know $\dot{K}_t$'s for successive t's, we can find K_t's for all t's from (10). $\dot{K}_t$'s can be determined by solving (9). A general solution of (9), however, is not possible; we therefore adopt the pedestrian method[8]

---

[8] The adoption of the pedestrian method is not by choice. Equation (9) as it stands is not amenable to solution.

I tried a solution by linearising it through substituting $f(t)K_t$ for $L_t^\alpha K_t^\beta$, where $f(t)$ is a function giving output-capital ratios for t, so that (9) is transformed into of finding K_t's for given initial values of L and K and assumed values of λ and θ by the iterative process. The following table gives the values of total output, consumption, and investment for the first 10 years under the assumption that the per capita consumption increases at the rate of 1 per cent per annum so that $\theta = .01$. Further as the initial saving is supposed to be .1, $C_0 = .9$; the values of other variables and parameters remaining the same as before.

Table III

SHOWING GROWTH OF NATIONAL PRODUCTION UNDER THE ASSUMPTION OF AN
ANNUAL INCREASE OF 1 PER CENT IN PER CAPITA CONSUMPTION

t	Total capital stock	Total output	Total investment	Total consumption	Capital-output ratio	Rate of savings
(1)	(2)	(3)	(4)	(5)	(6)	(7)
0	1	1	.1	.9	1	.1
1	1.1	1.04	.113	.927	1.057	.109
2	1.213	1.081	.125	.956	1.122	.116
3	1.338	1.125	.140	.985	1.189	.125
4	1.478	1.171	.154	1.017	1.262	.132
5	1.632	1.218	.172	1.046	1.339	.141
6	1.804	1.268	.191	1.0773	1.422	.151
7	1.995	1.323	.212	1.111	1.508	.160
8	2.207	1.374	.230	1.144	1.606	.167
9	2.437	1.430	.251	1.179	1.704	.176
10	2.688	1.488	.273	1.215	1.808	.184

Comparing Tables II and III, we see that total consumption in the latter is lower than that in the former for the first 10 periods (for which figures have been given in Table III). This means that a mere half per cent annual increase in the rate of savings from an initial rate of 10 per cent is compatible with a more than 1 per cent annual increase in the rate of per capita consumption per annum, which is implied in Table III. As column 5 of Table II shows, this incremental rate is more than 1 per cent for all the years, though it is gradually diminishing. The latter, in turn, implies an obvious fact that a constant annual increase in the rate of savings under the type of models we have discussed brings about a diminishing rate of annual increase in the per capita consumption.[9]

The simple model outlined above possesses the general defects of the growth models that have been developed in the recent past. These models take savings

$$\dot{K}_t = K_t f(t) - C_0 \, e^{(\lambda+\theta)t}$$

The solution of this equation is (cf. L. Ince, *op. cit.*, pp. 18–19),

$$K_t \, e^{\int -f(t)} + \int C_0 \, e^{(\lambda+\theta)t} \, e^{\int -f(t)} = \text{some constant.}$$

Unfortunately any decreasing function for $f(t)$ which we can assume makes the second term in the right-hand side of the above equation nonintegrable.

[9] After a few periods, rate of growth of per capita consumption in Table II will become less than 1 per cent. As the rate of savings in Table III increases at a faster rate than that in Tables I and II, both the total output and consumption will be higher under the assumptions of Table III after the critical period and thereafter keep increasing at a faster rate than that will be possible under the assumptions of Tables I and II.

rate, technology, and preferences, as given, and then set up to work out a growth process mostly on the basis of accumulation of capital. The present model too assumes the rate of savings as given, but increasing at a constant rate. We have not gone behind the savings rate to study the forces that are at work in bringing savings rate to the levels assumed. The increases in savings rate may be either induced by deliberate monetary fiscal policies or they may be brought about quite endogenously due to increases in per capita incomes as the development process starts. In any complete model, these forces will have to be thoroughly analysed and integrated.

Although the present model does not assume capital-output ratio or the technology as given, yet it is based on a certain function, i.e., the Cobb-Douglas. In an aggregative model, we do not really have any alternative choice[10]; but this cannot justify our approach as wholly sound. The limitations of the Cobb-Douglas function have been adequately discussed, and a model based on a production function will certainly partake of its weakness. The use of a production function, however, is an improvement over that of a capital-output ratio in that it allows for substitution of factors, choice, or use of alternative technology commensurate with variations in the availability of resources. In the developing countries these two aspects are crucially important; hence the need for introducing a production function.

In an aggregative model of the type outlined here, the changes in the community's preferences can hardly be accounted for. The framers of such models implicitly assume that preferences and so relative prices remain unchanged. This is a major simplification in itself, but when we consider our failure to take into account the intertemporal preferences with which the rate of savings is inalienably connected, the situation becomes grossly oversimplified. It is, therefore, advisable that in the course of a study of aggregative growth models recently developed, and particularly the model presented here, these limitations are kept in mind.

---

[10]An alternative production function has been put forward by Arrow, Chenery, Minhas, and Solow in the *Review of Economics and Statistics* (Aug. 1961). This function is more relevant in case of individual industries than in that of the whole economy. The function, however, is even less amenable to mathematical operations than the Cobb-Douglas.

PART 3

STRATEGY AND POLICY

Once the over-all development goals are established, emphasis then shifts to devising particular strategies and to formulating specific policies. Logic suggests that in view of the political, economic, and social differences among countries, both strategies and policies must match each country's environment. Otherwise, sizable obstacles might arise, scarce investment funds might be dissipated, and the entire development effort might even be jeopardized.

Recent experience of developing countries provides a conclusive demonstration. For instance, it has brought to light that an exclusive emphasis on physical capital is very unlikely to produce desired results if plans fail to stress simultaneously the need to improve the human factor and the need to change the social structure of a country. Experience has also revealed the pitfalls of too great an emphasis on industrial growth and too little stress on development of the agricultural sector and at the same time has drawn attention to the vital role that certain measures, such as monetary and fiscal policies, must play if countries are to achieve their planned objectives.

The selections in Part 3 cover material dealing with some leading issues involved in policy formulation and execution.

Selections 9 and 10 provide a background for the topics covered in the remaining selections.

In Selection 9 MYINT examines the relationship between economic theory and development policy and takes a closer look at the controversy centering on the question of appropriateness of applying economic theories to conditions found in underdeveloped areas. He disassociates himself from those who argue that these theories are inapplicable and provides a few examples to support his position.

In Selection 10 BHATT is concerned with the dispute between the protagonists of balanced and unbalanced growth theories. He concludes that the positions taken on either side of the argument are overstated, that there is not so much a cleavage between those viewpoints as one might think, and that, in fact, both theories complement each other.

In Selections 11 through 15 attention centers on human resources development and social change. Selections 11 and 12 deal with manpower considerations and the role of education, respectively. Selection 13 emphasizes the importance of attitude changes, Selection 14 underscores the need for changing the social structure of underdeveloped countries, and selection 15 deals with demographic aspects of development.

HARBISON maintains that a human resources development strategy demands a careful assessment of manpower requirements. He also underlines the importance of integrating manpower development programs into national plans.

WAINES stresses the contribution that education can make to economic development and emphasizes that developing countries should not imitate educational systems of advanced countries, because the educational process in each developing country should necessarily be based on its specific conditions and should be geared to its individual needs. He underscores the long-run aspects of educational programs and disapproves of crash programs as likely to yield no worthwhile results.

ROSENBERG maintains that undesirable methods of holding assets, low propensity to save, and lack of entrepreneurial talent are among the most important causes of underdevelopment. He then emphasizes that changes in basic human attitudes are imperative if economic activity is to be stimulated and economic development is to be promoted.

MILLIKAN and BLACKMER stress that profound changes within the traditional society must take place before a working modern system can be achieved. This modernization process is normally both painful and time-consuming, since forces of tradition are well entrenched and deeply rooted. However, counteracting these forces, the authors point out, are certain dynamic groups, such as the military, the intellectuals, and the innovating entrepreneurs, who are the moving force in various developing countries.

In Selection 15, COALE analyzes the relationship between the pace of economic development and the rate of population growth, concentrating in particular on the short- and long-run effects of a reduction in fertility.

Selections 16 through 21 concern production techniques and investments in agriculture and industry. Selections 16 and 17 deal with the role of technology as a prime mover in the developmental process, and Selections 18 through 21 deal with selected aspects of agricultural and industrial development.

> ECKAUS stresses the central role that technological change can play in the improvement of economic conditions of the developing countries and, in doing so, points out the difficulties encountered in bringing about such changes. He then proceeds to identify criteria for the selection of suitable technologies.
>
> In the following selection, SHEARER is concerned with the problem of alternative technologies encountered in overpopulated developing countries. He focuses attention on the conflict that exists in those countries between the goals of accelerated capital formation and maximum employment of labor and concludes with a number of very pertinent policy recommendations.

The low level of agricultural productivity, having its source in poor farming practices and in inappropriate systems of land ownership, has repeatedly been singled out as one of the main characteristics of underdevelopment, and it has been suggested that improvements in agriculture are necessary if developing countries are to meet their food requirements, to release manpower to other productive sectors, and to raise their per capita incomes. At the same time, others have strongly advocated industrial development as the main hope for economic advancement, supporting their arguments by citing the role of industrialization in the development of advanced countries.

Problems connected with agricultural development and the issue of land reform are the topics of Selections 18 and 19. On the other hand, selections 20 and 21 are devoted to complex issues of industrial development.

> JOHNSTON and MELLOR deal with the controversy over priorities in the allocation of investment funds and argue for a simultaneous promotion of agricultural and industrial development, expressing strong opposition to the opinions of those writers who have maintained that agricultural development must necessarily precede industrial development.
>
> In Selection 19, LONG introduces several economic and technical considerations concerning the issue of land reform, giving particular attention to the relationship existing between farm size and productivity. He maintains that careful research is needed to weigh the desirability of a land reform program in each developing country.
>
> KREBS presents a systematic approach to formulating an industrial development strategy in which he lists the institutional, procedural, and substantive elements of a successful strategy.
>
> In Selection 21 HIRSCHMAN describes the main features of import-substituting industrialization and stresses its sequential nature. Relating this type of industrialization to the over-all goals of economic development, he pinpoints the main problems that arise when a country pursues this path toward development.

Selections 22 through 24 deal with selected aspects of public financial policy. The stress on this policy is justified on the grounds that monetary and fiscal measures can significantly facilitate economic development. It is a well-known fact that most governments of developing countries have had little success in carrying out these vital measures.

In an attempt to determine whether an inflationary monetary policy promotes or impedes economic development, ELLIS examines the economic literature on the subject. He quotes many well-known writers and demonstrates that a wide difference of opinion exists among them that allows no definite conclusion to be drawn.

URSULA HICKS and KALDOR, the authors of Selections 23 and 24, deal with the desirability of an adequate financial infrastructure and the need for establishing an effective tax system, respectively. As practitioners of development finance, both convey their concern about the ability of governments of developing countries to formulate and to execute financial policies properly.

Selection **9**

Economic Theory
and Development Policy

HLA MYINT

From: Economica, *Vol. 47, No. 134 (May 1967), pp. 117–130. Reprinted
by permission of* Economica *and the author.*

Both economic theory and development economics are getting highly specialised
nowadays. A specialist in a branch of economic theory cannot hope to keep up
with the highly technical development in other branches of economic theory.
Similarly, a specialist in a particular aspect of economic development or on a
particular group of underdeveloped countries cannot hope to keep up with the
vast outpouring of publications in other fields of development economics. The
proliferation and subdivision of development economics is most dramatically
shown by the many periodicals which devote themselves entirely to some particular aspect of the subject, such as development finance, development agriculture,
and so on.

But it seems to me that precisely because of this trend towards specialisation
there is some need, in the universities at least, for a general practitioner to act as
a middleman between different specialised fields of development economics and
also between development economics and general economics. Such an economist
should try to acquire a good working knowledge at least of the broad economic
dimensions and the basic features of the situation in a wide range of underdeveloped countries. His aim should be to try to apply the existing economic theory in
a more realistic and fruitful way to suit the varying conditions of the different
types of underdeveloped country. An equally important part of his job would be
to try to prevent serious misapplications of economic theory, whether of the
orthodox type or the newer modern theories, to the underdeveloped countries.

This way of looking at a general development economist as a middleman
between the tool-makers and the tool-users brings me face to face with the perennial
controversy: how far are the existing tools of economic theory applicable to the
underdeveloped countries? There are many distinguished economists[1] who would

---

[1] For example, G. Myrdal, *Economic Theory and Underdeveloped Regions* (1957); also his
An International Economy (1956); D. Seers, "The Limitations of the Special Case," *Bulletin of the
Oxford Institute of Economics and Statistics* (May 1963).

be impatient with my proposal to start from the existing theoretical framework and try to improve its applicability to the underdeveloped countries in the light of accumulating experience and factual knowledge. They would say that the existing "Western" economic theory is so intimately bound up with the special conditions, problems, and preconceptions of the industrially advanced countries that large portions of it have to be abandoned before we can come to grips with the problem of the underdeveloped countries.

These economists have advanced three main types of criticism against the existing economic theory.

First, they question the "realism" of trying to apply the standard models of theoretical analysis meant for the advanced countries to the different economic and institutional setting of the underdeveloped countries. I have no quarrel with this line of criticism. In fact I shall be giving illustrations of other types of lack of realism in applying economic theory to the underdeveloped countries which are not mentioned by the critics. But it seems to me that this is not an argument for abandoning existing economic theory but merely an argument for trying to improve its applicability.

Second, the critics question the "relevance" of the static neo-classical economics concerned with the problem of allocating given resources within an existing economic framework to the problem of promoting economic development in the underdeveloped countries, which is concerned with increasing the amount of available resources, improving techniques, and, generally, with the introduction of a dynamic self-sustaining process of economic change, disrupting the existing framework. Here again I agree that we do not possess a satisfactory dynamic theory for studying development problems. In fact, I would go further and say that the recent developments in the theory of dynamic economics in terms of the growth models are not very relevant and are not meant to be relevant for the underdeveloped countries.[2] But I do not accept the conclusion which the critics have drawn; viz., that the static theory of efficient allocation of given resources is irrelevant for the underdeveloped countries. I shall come back to this point.

Third, the critics maintain that the orthodox economic theory is inextricably bound up with preconceptions and biases in favour of the orthodox economic policies of laissez-faire, free trade, and conservative fiscal and monetary policies. They believe that these orthodox economic policies are generally inimical to rapid economic growth, which can be promoted only by large-scale government economic planning, widespread protection, import controls, and deficit financing of development programmes, if sufficient external aid is not available. Thus they propose that large chunks of existing economic theory, particularly the orthodox neo-classical theory, should be abandoned to pave the way for the adoption of these new development policies.

There are two questions here. The first is the general question whether the new policies are always more effective than the orthodox policies in promoting economic development in the underdeveloped countries. The second is the more specific question whether there is an unbreakable ideological link between orthodox

---

[2] Cf. Sir John Hicks, *Capital and Growth* (Oxford, 1965), p. 1.

economic theory and orthodox economic policies, so that if we wish to adopt the new development policies, we must necessarily abandon much of the existing theory.

The underdeveloped countries vary widely among themselves, and I, therefore, find it difficult to accept the general presumption that the new policies will always be better for their economic development whatever their particular individual situation. Later, I shall give some examples where the orthodox type of economic policies have in fact been more effective in promoting economic development than the new-style development policies. However, I have chosen as the subject of my lecture today, not the general debate on the rival merits of the orthodox and the new development policies, but the relation between economic theory and development policy. I have done this partly because I feel that such a general debate without reference to a concrete situation generates more heat than light and partly also because it has been rapidly overtaken by events. Whether we like it or not, it is no longer an open question whether the underdeveloped countries should choose the orthodox or the new type of development policies. One after another, they have already made their choice in favour of the new policies which have now become a part of conventional economic wisdom. Accepting this as one of the facts of life, the more immediately relevant question seems to be the second question, viz., whether large parts of orthodox economic theory have now become obsolete because the underdeveloped countries wish to plan for rapid economic development.

I shall argue that this is not so: that on the contrary, the orthodox economic theory assumes a greater significance in the context of the new "progressive" development policies. I shall show that even if development planning is to be regarded as new and radical policy, the *theory* underlying development planning is, technically speaking, quite orthodox and conventional. Similarly, I shall show that the orthodox theory of international trade can be made to support more liberal and generous trade and aid policies towards the underdeveloped countries, if we choose to use it in this way. What I am saying is not new. It is merely a restatement of the familiar doctrine that economic theory is "ethically neutral" and can be made use of in the more efficient pursuit of the economic objectives to be chosen by the "value judgments" of the policy-maker.

However, let us start from a closer look at the question of "realism" in applying existing economic theory to the underdeveloped countries. Some critics speak of "existing theory" as though it were contained in a modern textbook like Samuelson. Properly speaking, it should include the whole corpus of Western economic theory, offering a wide choice of theoretical models, ranging from those of the older economists writing at earlier stages of economic development to the highly complex and abstract models of contemporary economic theory. To my mind, a very important cause of lack of realism arises from the wrong choice of theoretical models to be applied to the underdeveloped countries. In much the same way as the governments of the underdeveloped countries succumb to the lure of the "steel mills" embodying the most advanced and capital-intensive type of Western technology, many development economists have succumbed to the lure of the intellectual "steel mills" represented by the latest and most sophisticated theoretical models. This is where I believe the greatest mischief has been done. This is why I have always maintained that a good development economist should also be something of an applied historian of economic thought.

If it is unrealistic to apply highly sophisticated theoretical models meant for the complex economic structures of the advanced countries to the simpler economic structures of the underdeveloped countries, has this been corrected by the new theories of development and underdevelopment which are specially meant for the underdeveloped countries? Looking at these new theories which became popular during the 1950's, such as the "vicious circle," the "take-off," or the "big push," it does not seem to me that these have stood up any better to the test of realism. The weakness of these new theories is that they try to apply to all the underdeveloped countries a composite model of *the* underdeveloped country, incorporating in it certain special features of some one or other type of underdeveloped country. The "vicious circle" theory assumes poverty and stagnation caused by severe population pressure on resources; the "take-off" theory assumes the pre-existence of a fairly high level of development in the political, social, and institutional framework; the "big push" theory assumes both and also an internal market large enough to support a domestic capital-goods sector. By the time we have incorporated all these special features into a composite model, the number of the underdeveloped countries to which this model might apply becomes severely limited to one or two countries such as India and possibly Pakistan.

The limitations of these new theories of development, particularly the "vicious circle" theory, can be illustrated by looking at the broad dimensions of the economic performance of the underdeveloped countries during the decade 1950–1960. During that decade, compared with the 4 per cent average annual growth rates for the advanced Western countries, the gross domestic product of underdeveloped countries as a group has grown at the average annual rate of 4.4 per cent, giving them a growth in *per capita* incomes of a little over 2 per cent per annum.[3] This may or may not be very much, but the really interesting thing is that some underdeveloped countries have been growing at a faster rate than the average, say between 5 and 6 per cent, while others have been barely able to keep up with their population increase. Thus instead of the earlier *simpliste* view according to which all underdeveloped countries are caught up in a vicious circle of stagnation and population pressure, we are led to the question why some underdeveloped countries grow faster or slower than others.

When we try to answer this question, we become greatly aware of the differences between the underdeveloped countries, in size, in the degree of population pressure on natural resources, in the conditions of world demand for their exports, and in their general level of economic development and political stability. These differences by themselves will explain quite a lot of the differences in the growth rates among different underdeveloped countries. If in addition we want to say something about the influence of development policies, we shall have to choose a fairly uniform group of countries where the basic social and economic differences are small enough for us to isolate the effect of economic policy.

[3] United Nations, *World Economic Survey* (1963), Part I, p. 20.

To illustrate, let me take the concrete example of the postwar economic development of Southeast Asia. This will also serve to illustrate the dangers of generalising about development policies, particularly the danger of assuming that the new "progressive" development policies will always promote faster economic growth than the orthodox economic policies.

The five countries I have chosen, Burma, Thailand, the Philippines, Indonesia, and Malaya, form a fairly homegeneous group. In contrast to India or China, they are not only much smaller, but also do not suffer from any great pressure of population. They do not have to contend with food shortage and have much more elbow room in respect of natural resources to allow for the working of economic incentives. They are also similar in the general level of social and economic development and moreover have common exports such as rice, timber, and rubber. Yet the rapid postwar economic development of Thailand, the Philippines, and Malaya contrasts sharply with the economic stagnation of Burma and Indonesia. By 1960, both Thailand and the Philippines doubled their prewar gross national product (in real terms) combined with a considerable growth in import-substituting industries, while the gross national product of Burma and Indonesia rose by a bare 11 per cent above the prewar level, much slower than their rate of population growth during the same period. Malaya, starting at a somewhat higher per capita level than the others, has also enjoyed economic prosperity which compares favourably not only with Burma and Indonesia, but also with Ceylon to which her economic structure is similar in many aspects.

These large differences in the rates of economic growth are closely related to the rate of expansion in the exports of the two groups of countries, and, since they have common exports sharing the same world market conditions, the differences in their export performance must be traced largely to the domestic economic policies which have affected the supply side of their exports. Here, broadly speaking, the first group of countries with the faster rates of economic growth, viz., Thailand, Malaya, and the Philippines, have pursued the more orthodox type of economic policies with a greater reliance on market forces, private enterprise, and an outward-looking attitude to foreign trade and enterprise; while Burma and Indonesia lean heavily on economic planning and large-scale state intervention in economic life combined with an inward-looking and even hostile attitude towards foreign trade and enterprise.

More specifically we may note the following. (1) Thailand and the Philippines have very successfully used market incentives to encourage their peasants to bring more land under cultivation and expand production both of export and domestic food crops, while the Burmese peasants have been depressed by the operation of the state agricultural marketing board which has used peasant agriculture simply as a milch cow for government investment in state enterprises in manufacturing industry and social overhead capital. (2) Thailand and the Philippines have encouraged their domestic entrepreneurs to set up new manufacturing industries through protection and subsidies, while Burma and Indonesia have tried to do this by state enterprises which have failed, among other reasons, because of a shortage of entrepreneurial ability among the civil servants. Here it may be noted that all these Southeast Asian countries suffer from the fear of being dominated by the Chinese or the Indian entrepreneurs, who are or were prominent in small- or medium-scale enterprises in light manufacturing industries. Thus one may say that Burma and Indonesia have chosen to substitute Indian and Chinese private enterprise by indigenous state enterprise, while Thailand has absorbed the Chinese entrepreneurs into her own business class and the Philippines have successfully substituted Filipino private entrepreneurs for them. This problem has yet to be solved in Malaya. (3) Malaya, Thailand, and the Philippines have offered a stable economic climate to Western enterprises both in the traditional plantation and mining sectors and in the new manufacturing sector and have benefited from a considerable inflow of private foreign capital, while Burma and Indonesia have discouraged fresh inflow of private investment by nationalization and other hostile policies. (4) Malaya and Thailand have pursued conservative monetary and fiscal policies and their currencies have been strong and stable, and the Philippines tackled her balance-of-payments disequilibrium successfully by devaluation in 1962. In contrast Burma and Indonesia have tried to solve their balance-of-payments problems arising out of deficit financing and domestic inflation through an intensification of inefficient and hurtful import controls, which, combined with pervasive state interference at all levels of economic activity, have throttled most of the promising infant industries.[4]

It is not for me to judge the ultimate rightness or wrongness of the economic nationalism and the anti-Western attitude of Burma and Indonesia contrasted with the more pro-Western attitude of Malaya, Thailand, and the Philippines. But at the conventional level at which economists judge development policies, it seems to me that in the case of Southeast Asia at least, the orthodox type of economic policies have resulted in a more rapid rate of economic development during the postwar period than the newer "progressive" development policies. How far is the Southeast Asian experience applicable to other underdeveloped countries outside the region? I think that it may be of some relevance to the other smaller and less densely populated export economies, notably in West Africa. There, also, expansion in the exports of primary products still offers the most promising engine of economic development both as a source of foreign exchange earnings to finance the new import-substituting industries and, even more important, as the method of drawing the under-utilised natural resources of the subsistence sector into the money economy. But these conclusions in favour of the orthodox policies are likely to become weaker as we try to extend them to less similar types of country, particularly to large overpopulated countries like India. But conversely it would be equally unrealistic to try to apply the Indian model to the smaller export economies.

Let me now conclude my remarks on the "realism" of applying economic theory to the underdeveloped countries by drawing attention to the dangers of

---

[4] For a fuller treatment, see my article, "The Inward and the Outward Looking Countries of Southeast Asia and the Economic Future of the Region," Symposium Series II, *Japan's Future in Southeast Asia* (Kyoto University, 1966).

trying to be too different from the standard models of economic analysis. These arise from selecting the "queer cases" in the standard Western models of analysis and in taking it for granted that these exceptions to the standard case must automatically apply to the underdeveloped countries because they are so different from the advanced countries in social values and attitudes and institutional setting. Such, for instance, is the famous case of the "backward-sloping supply curve" of labour attributed to the underdeveloped countries by many writers, who nevertheless speak also of the "demonstration effect" and "the revolution of rising expectations." Such also is the belief that the people of the underdeveloped countries, being more communally minded, will take more easily to co-operative forms of economic organization, despite the fact that writers on the cooperative movement in the underdeveloped countries frequently complain about the lack of cooperative spirit and the excessive individualism of the people. Yet another example is the generalisation that the people of the underdeveloped countries naturally lack entrepreneurial ability, irrespective of the economic policies followed by their governments. Here, if one were to tell the politicians of the underdeveloped countries that their people are lazy, stupid, lacking in initiative and adaptability, one would be branded as an enemy: but if one were to rephrase these prejudices in another way and say that they lack entrepreneurial capacity, one would be welcomed for giving "scientific" support for economic planning. To take just one more example, there is the hoary belief that peasants in the underdeveloped countries do not respond to economic incentives, while agricultural economists have been accumulating abundant evidence to show that peasants do respond to price changes by switching from one crop to another or by bringing more land under cultivation. The real problem is how to introduce new methods of cultivation which will raise productivity: this is a difficult practical problem, but in principle it is little different from, say, the problem of introducing new methods to raise productivity in British industry.

This is where I think that a closer cooperation between economics and other branches of social studies is likely to prove most useful, both in getting rid of questionable sociological generalizations and also in tackling the more intractable problems of analysing social and economic change.

Let me now turn from the "realism" to the "relevance" of the existing economic theory to the underdeveloped countries. The problem of promoting rapid economic development in these countries may ultimately lie in the realm of social and economic dynamics of the sort we do not at present possess; and there is nothing in my argument to prevent anyone from launching into new dynamic theoretical approaches to the underdeveloped countries. But in the meantime it is dangerously easy to underestimate the significance to the underdeveloped countries of the orthodox static theory of the allocation of given resources. The affluent Western economies with their steady rates of increase in productivity may be able to take a tolerant attitude towards misallocation of resources. But the underdeveloped countries are simply too poor to put up with the preventable wasteful use of their given meagre economic resources. In particular, they can ill afford the well-recognised distortions of their price system, such as the excessively high levels of wages and low levels of interest rates in their manufacturing and public sectors compared with those in the agricultural sector and the overvaluation of their currencies at the official rates of exchange. Having to bear the brunt of low earnings and high interest rates discourages the expansion of agricultural output both for export and for domestic consumption, and this in turn slows down the overall rate of growth of the economy. Higher wages attract a large number of people from the countryside to the towns, but only a small proportion of this influx can be absorbed because of the highly capital-intensive methods adopted in the modern import-substituting industries. This aggravates the problem of urban unemployment and the problem of shanty towns which increases the requirements for investment in housing and social welfare. The scarce supply of capital tends to be wastefully used both in the government prestige projects and in private industry because of the artificially low rates of interest. This is aggravated by the overvaluation of currencies and import controls in favour of capital goods which positively encourage the businessmen who are fortunate enough to obtain licences to buy the most expensive and capital-intensive type of machinery from abroad.

These then are some of the glaring sources of waste which can be reduced by a better allocation of resources. Now I should point out that just because the orthodox neo-classical theory is concerned with the efficient allocation of *given* resources, it does not mean that the theory becomes unimportant in the context of aid policies to increase the volume of resources available to the underdeveloped countries. On the contrary, a country which cannot use its already available resources efficiently is not likely to be able to "absorb" additional resources from aid programmes and use them efficiently. That is to say, a country's absorptive capacity for aid must to a large extent depend on its ability to avoid serious misallocation of resources. A similar conclusion can be drawn about an underdeveloped country's ability to make effective use of its opportunities for international trade. If we find that a country is not making effective use of its already available trading opportunities, because of domestic policies discouraging its export production or raising the costs in the export sector, then we should not expect it to benefit in a dramatic way from the new trading opportunities to be obtained through international negotiations.

This is a part of the reason why I have suggested that orthodox economic theory, instead of becoming obsolete, has assumed a greater significance in the context of the new "progressive" policies for promoting economic development in the underdeveloped countries. Let me illustrate this argument further by examples from development planning theory and from recent discussions about the appropriate trade and aid policies.

I think that a great deal of confusion would have been avoided by clearly distinguishing the *policy* of development planning and the economic *theory* which underlies development planning, which is, as we shall see, only an application of the traditional theory of the optimum allocation of the *given* resources. This confusion was introduced during the 1950's when it was the fashion to try to make out the case for development planning mainly by attacking the orthodox equilibrium and optimum theory. At the macroeconomic level, there were theories of deficit financing trying to show how economic development might be accelerated by forced saving and inflation or by making use of "disguised unemployment" for capital formation. More generally, the theories of the "vicious circle," the "big push," or "unbalanced growth" tried to show, in their different ways, the desirability of breaking out of the static equilibrium framework by deliberately introducing imbalances and disequilibria which would start the chain reaction of cumulative movement toward self-sustained economic growth. Ironically enough, when the underdeveloped countries came to accept the need for development planning and asked how this might be done efficiently, it turned out that the economic theory required for this purpose was basically nothing but the traditional equilibrium and optimum theory.

Thus according to the present-day textbooks on development planning,[5] the first task of the planner is to test the feasibility of the plan at the macroeconomic level by making sure that the aggregate amount of resources required to carry out the plan does not exceed the aggregate amount of resources available. That is to say, deficit financing and inflation are to be avoided, and this is to be checked at the sectoral level by seeing to it that the projected rate of expansion of the services sector does not exceed the possible rate of expansion in the output of commodities by a certain critical margin. The next task of the planner is to test the consistency of the plan at the sectoral and microeconomic level to make sure that the demand and supply for particular commodities and services are equated to each other and that there is an equilibrium relationship between the different parts of the economy, not only within any given year, but also between one year and another during the whole of the plan period. Finally, if the plan is found to be both feasible and consistent, the task of the planner is to find out whether the plan adopted is an optimum plan in the sense that there is no alternative way of reallocating the given resources more efficiently to satisfy the given objectives of the plan.

If this standard formulation of development planning is accepted, then there is no fundamental theoretical difference between those who aim to achieve the efficient allocation of the available resources through the market mechanism and those who aim to achieve it through the state mechanism. Both accept the optimum allocation of resources as their theoretical norm and their disagreements are about the *practical* means of fulfilling this norm. In any given situation, they will disagree how far planning should be "indicative" or "imperative," that is to say, how far the task of allocating resources should be left to the decentralised decision making of the market or to the centralised decision making of the state. But technically speaking, they are using the same type of economic theory, viz., the extension of the orthodox neo-classical theory, in the pursuit of their different practical policies.

From a theoretical point of view the great divide is between those who believe

---

[5] See, particularly, W. A. Lewis, *Development Planning* (1966); A. Waterson, *Development Planning: Lessons of Experience* (Oxford, 1966); and W. B. Reddaway, *The Development of the Indian Economy* (1962).

on the one hand that economic development of the underdeveloped countries can be promoted in *an orderly manner* by a more efficient allocation of the available resources which is assumed to be steadily expanding between one period and another through good management of domestic savings and external aid, and those who believe, on the other hand, that only sudden disruptive and *disorderly* changes such as social revolutions and technical innovations can bring about economic development. Now this second revolutionary approach to economic development may well be the correct approach for some underdeveloped countries. But it is difficult to see how this can be incorporated into the planning approach. Development planning is by definition an orderly approach: on the other hand, genuinely far-reaching and disruptive social changes cannot be turned on and turned off in a predictable way and incorporated into the planning framework. Those who advocate the necessity of breaking out of the static equilibrium framework by deliberately introducing imbalances and tensions are in effect advocating at the same time the need to break out of the planning framework. Thus one may advocate social revolution now and planning later, but one may not advocate social revolution and planning at the same time without getting into serious contradictions. Further, it should be pointed out that the revolutionary approach to economic development is by no means the monopoly of the critics of the private enterprise system. The case for *laissez-faire* can be made, not on grounds of static allocative efficiency, but on the ground that it imparts a "dynamism" to the economy by stimulating enterprise, innovation, and savings. Schumpeter's picture of the disruption of the existing productive framework through a process of "creative destruction" by innovating private entrepreneurs is a well-known illustration of this type of revolutionary approach to economic development.

Let me conclude by illustrating how the orthodox theory of international trade may be used in support of more liberal or generous trade and aid policies towards the underdeveloped countries. There is still a considerable amount of prejudice against the export of primary products in the underdeveloped countries. To some extent this has been overlaid by the more pro-trade views which have gained ground since the United Nations Conference on Trade and Development. The views which are now accepted by most underdeveloped countries may be summarised as follows. (1) While the underdeveloped countries should be allowed to protect their domestic manufacturing industries in any way they think fit, they should have preferential treatment or freer access to the markets of the advanced countries for their exports of primary products, semi-processed products, and fully manufactured products. (2) More aid should be given to supplement the trade concessions, but there should be less tying of aid to imports from the donor country and also less tying of aid to the specific projects chosen and managed by the donor country.

Now it is possible to find a variety of opinions among the orthodox-minded economists on the question of giving aid to the underdeveloped countries. There are some who are against aid giving either because they fear that this would lead to a misallocation of the world capital resources or because of the various undesirable political and sociological side effects of aid. For instance, Professor Bauer has recently argued that the material benefits which an underdeveloped country might obtain from aid would be swamped by the deleterious sociological and political effects, such as the development of a beggar mentality and the growth of centralised power which would pauperise the aid-receiving country.[6] On the other hand, not all orthodox economists are against aid giving. In this connection, I should mention the name of the late Professor Frederic Benham, who wrote what I consider to be the best book stating the case for aid-giving.[7] These individual views aside, the standard orthodox economic theory would say something like this on the subject: how much aid the rich countries should give the poor countries should be decided by "value judgements" based on moral and political considerations which are beyond the scope of economic analysis. But once it is agreed that a certain amount of aid, say 1 per cent of the national income of the rich countries, should be given, economic analysis can be used to show how this given policy objective can be carried out in the most efficient way. By a familiar process of reasoning, orthodox theory would say that this could be most efficiently carried out by free trade for both the aid-givers and the aid-receivers. For the aid-givers, the more efficient allocation of their resources through free trade would enable them to spare the 1 per cent of their income they are giving away with the least sacrifice. For the aid-receivers, free importation of goods at cheaper prices than could be produced at home would maximise the value of the aid they received. Further, if the aid resources are to be invested, the more efficient choice of investment opportunities under free trade would raise the returns from investment.

Thus from the point of view of orthodox trade theory the one-way free trade plus aid for which the underdeveloped countries are asking is less efficient than two-way free trade plus the same amount of aid. This is likely to be so even when the need to protect the "infant industries" has been conceded.[8] But if the underdeveloped countries insist on adopting what they consider to be the less advantageous option, then the orthodox trade theory can still say something useful within this restricted framework: and what it has to say is in support of opening the markets of the advanced countries more freely to the products from the underdeveloped countries and in support of the untying of aid.

Take the rather protracted debate about "reciprocity," on the question whether the advanced countries should give trade concessions to the underdeveloped countries without getting back some *quid pro quo*. In support of one-way free trade the champions of the underdeveloped countries usually appeal to moral considerations such as not having the same rule for the lion and the lamb and the

---

6 Barbara Ward and P. T. Bauer, *Two Views on Aid to the Developing Countries*, Institute of Economic Affairs, Occasional Paper 9, 1966.

7 F. Benham, *Economic Aid to Underdeveloped Countries* (1961).

8 For one thing, the import controls practised by the underdeveloped countries are too indiscriminate and bound up with short-run balance-of-payments considerations to give selective protection to the promising infant industries; for another, the correction of the distortions due to the imperfections of the domestic market may require other forms of government intervention than protection. See my paper (Ch. 7) in R. Harrod and D.C. Hague (eds.), *International Trade Theory in a Developing World* (1963); and H. G. Johnson, "Optimum Trade Intervention in the Presence of Domestic Distortions," in *Trade, Growth and the Balance of Payments*, Economic Essays in Honor of Gottfried Haberler (Amsterdam, 1965).

need for a double moral standard when dealing with unequal trading partners. The advanced countries, on the other hand, tend to argue that while they do not expect "reciprocity" from the underdeveloped countries, they would like other advanced countries to give similar concessions to the underdeveloped countries before they commit themselves. Professor Harry Johnson[9] has recently reminded us that these arguments, based on the mercantilistic view of trade, have entirely overlooked the point that according to the theory of comparative costs the gains from trade consist in having cheaper imports. By allowing free imports from the underdeveloped countries, the consumers in the advanced countries already would have gained from trade by being able to buy these imports more cheaply: thus there is no need to ask for a further *quid pro quo*.

Basing himself entirely on the orthodox trade theory, Professor Johnson has argued that the United States would gain by a unilateral removal of trade barriers to the products from the underdeveloped countries without waiting for other advanced countries to follow suit. Similarly, he has shown that the official figures for the United States aid to the underdeveloped countries would be very appreciably reduced if the goods and services given under tied aid, notably aid in the form of agricultural surpluses, were revalued at world market prices under free trade conditions.

These seem to me to be very good illustrations of how orthodox trade theory can be used in support of more liberal trade and aid policies, if we choose to do so. What has given flexibility to the theory is the much-maligned postulate of the "ethical neutrality" of economic theory. The champions of the underdeveloped countries tend to look upon it with great suspicion as a sign of an underdeveloped social conscience on the part of those who adopt it. But I hope that I have shown it to be no more objectionable than the notion of a constrained maximum.

Finally, the question of how far aid should be tied to the specific projects to be chosen and managed by the donor country raises fundamental issues of how far we consider the underdeveloped countries to be competent to run their own affairs without a benevolent supervision from the advanced country. Here we come at last to the "presumptions" and "preconceptions" of the orthodox economists which conflict sharply with those of the planning-minded economists. One important presumption of the liberal orthodox economists which I believe in is that the underdeveloped countries can best educate themselves for economic development by being allowed to make their own mistakes and learning from them, and that without this painful process of self-education and self-discipline they are not likely to acquire the degree of competence required for economic development. I think this runs countrary to the implicit or explicit philosophy of the present-day administrators of aid. They would like to make up for the underdeveloped countries' lack of "absorptive capacity" for aid by insisting upon tighter planning and supervision of their economic affairs by economic and technical experts from the advanced donor countries. Ultimately, then, we have two philosophies about aid giving to the underdeveloped countries. The liberal

9 H. G. Johnson, *U.S. Economic Policy Towards the Less Developed Countries* (Washington, D.C., 1967).

orthodox view is to give an agreed amount of aid to the underdeveloped countries and then to leave it to them to use it freely in any way they think fit, to learn from their mistakes and to take the consequences of their action. According to this view the advanced countries can only guarantee the amount of aid but not the rate of economic development of the underdeveloped countries, which must to a large extent depend on how they use the aid. One further implication of this view is that, since the underdeveloped countries differ so much in their circumstances and capacity to benefit from mistakes, it would be unrealistic to expect an equally fast rate of economic development for all the underdeveloped countries. The alternative view which pervades thinking at present is that the advanced countries should take the responsibility of guaranteeing a politically acceptable target rate of economic growth for all underdeveloped countries, and, if this cannot be achieved by the latter countries' own efforts, the advanced countries should be prepared not only to increase the total volume of aid but also to increase the planning and supervision of the use of this aid so that the peoples of underdeveloped countries may enjoy economic development in spite of themselves.[10] Obviously the underdeveloped countries cannot insist on freedom to use aid in any way they like and at the same time insist that the advanced countries guarantee a minimum target rate of economic growth for them all. Ultimately they will have to choose the one or the other. I, with my orthodox liberal inclinations, hope that they will choose the former.

---

[10] For example, contrast I. M. D. Little and J. M. Clifford, *International Aid* (1965), p. 192, with H. G. Johnson, *op. cit*, Ch. 4.

Selection **10**

Theories of Balanced
and Unbalanced Growth

V. V. BHATT

From: "Theories of Balanced and Unbalanced Growth: A Critical Appraisal," Kyklos, *Vol. XVII, No. 4 (1964), pp. 612–624. Reprinted by permission of* Kyklos.

The nature of the controversy between the protagonists of balanced growth and those of unbalanced growth seems to suggest that the two are mutually exclusive alternative strategies of growth for the underdeveloped countries. However, it is the contention of this paper that the two strategies are complementary to each other and the idea of balance is as much significant for an unbalanced growth strategy as that of unbalance is to the balanced growth strategy.

The basic difference between them, as it generally happens with such alternative formulations, is with regard to their respective assumptions. Balanced growth theories implicitly assume lack of a motivational problem and perfect knowledge with regard to the constraints operating on the growth process. Unbalanced growth protagonists question these assumptions; they argue that because of imperfect knowledge with regard to the constraints as well as the possibility of modifying them through the growth process, it is not possible to formulate a priori any unique maximum development path; it is only by adequately motivating the growth process that the maximum attainable growth can be known as well as realised. A certain unbalance, they argue, is necessary for motivating the process. What they fail to realise is that even to attain this unbalance, a certain balance or consistency among various variables is necessary. Further, since the rationale of creating an unbalance lies in generating forces which can correct this unbalance, it is also necessary to have some idea about the nature of the balance that is sought to be attained by a process of unbalanced growth. Thus, there does not seem to be any basic conflict between these two formulations of the growth strategy; the two can be integrated in operational terms, as is shown later in this paper.

Section I of this paper gives a brief review of these theories, while in Section II the basic differences between the two are discussed. How the two can be integrated in formulating an operational growth strategy is indicated in Section III.

I

Though it is not very clear-cut, a distinction can be drawn with regard to the advocates of balanced as well as unbalanced growth: between those who deal with the problems of initiating development and those who concentrate, once it is initiated, on accelerating its pace, in the developing countries. Both Rosenstein-Rodan[1] and Nurkse,[2] among balanced growth theorists, and Hirschman,[3] who advocates unbalanced growth, are primarily concerned with starting the process of growth, while Lewis[4] and Scitovsky[5] argue for balanced growth and Streeten[6] for unbalanced growth, to accelerate the pace of development, assuming that the development process has already been set in motion.

Rosenstein-Rodan and Nurkse emphasise the lack of adequate markets as a bottleneck for any isolated advance toward industrialisation; basing their argument on the celebrated 1928 article by Allyn Young,[7] they suggest a strategy of balanced growth of mutually supporting industries, which would create the market for each other's products. Rosenstein-Rodan argues that "the whole of the industry to be created" should be "treated and *planned* like one huge firm or trust."[8] Nurkse suggests "a balanced pattern of investment in a number of different industries, so that people working more productively, with more capital and improved techniques, become each other's customers,"[9] "balanced growth is first and foremost a means of getting out of the rut, a means of stepping up the rate of growth when the external forces of advance through trade expansion and foreign capital are sluggish or inoperative."[10] Nurkse thinks that "as a means of creating inducements to invest, balanced growth can be said to be relevant primarily to a private enterprise economy."[11] Later on, he draws a distinction between "balanced growth as a method and balanced growth as an outcome or objective" and also accepts "alternative possibilities: central planning—generally optimistic expectations leading to spontaneous advance on a wide front; or the 'disequilibrium' method of zigzag growth in successive industries or sectors, each tugging the other along by signals given by the price-mechanism."[12] He, however, advocates horizontal balance; with regard to nonimportable social overheads, he is in favour of unbalanced growth, of "building ahead of demand in a dynamic setting of development."[13]

---

[1] Rosenstein-Rodan, "Problems of Industrialisation of Eastern and South-Eastern Europe," *Economic Journal* (June 1943).

[2] R. Nurkse, *Problems of Capital Formation in Underdeveloped Countries* (Oxford, 1953).

[3] Albert O. Hirschman, *The Strategy of Economic Development* (New Haven: Yale University Press, 1958); references unless otherwise specified are to the third printing, 1960.

[4] W. A. Lewis, *The Theory of Economic Growth* (London, 1955).

[5] Tibor Scitovsky, "Two Concepts of External Economies," *Journal of Political Economy* (April 1954).

[6] P. Streeten, "Unbalanced Growth," *Oxford Economic Papers* (June 1959).

[7] Allyn Young, "Increasing Returns and Economic Progress," *Economic Journal* (Dec. 1928).

[8] Rosenstein-Rodan, *op. cit.*

[9] *Equilibrium and Growth in the World Economy, Economic Essays by Ragnar Nurkse*, edited by Gottfried Haberler (Cambridge, Mass.: Harvard University Press, 1961).

[10] *Ibid.*, p. 248.

[11] *Ibid.*

[12] *Ibid.*, pp. 279–280.

[13] *Ibid.*, p. 272.

He does not advocate autarky; balanced growth need not "impinge on the export sector at all."[14] However, since their "exportable primary products face a low rate of expansion in external demand" and since "their exports of manufactured goods encounter obstacles, there remains only a third possible opening: output expansion for home consumption."[15] Balanced growth, further, is to be restricted to the expansion of consumers' goods industries and agriculture "in accordance with domestic income elasticities of demand so as to provide markets for each other locally"[16]; they would "import the greater part of their capital goods requirements."[17] "The international division of labour, which used to be largely 'horizontal,'" would "become more and more vertical."[18] Further, "the case for diversified output growth for domestic consumption cannot be confined to national limits. Manufacturing for home markets in the less developed countries must include also production in those countries for export to *each other's markets*. This is particularly important for the smaller countries, and it constitutes a strong argument for liberalisation of trade policies, leading up to customs unions if possible among groups of countries in the underdeveloped class."[19]

Lewis concentrates his attention largely on the nature and character of the growth process, once it is initiated. He advocates balanced growth in the sense that "the various sectors of the economy must grow in the right relationship to each other, or they cannot grow at all."[20] In this connection he illustrates how the three sectors agriculture, industry, and exports should grow in a balanced way, so as to generate adequate demand and supplies.[21] Only the export sector can grow under its own steam without the other two sectors growing, for the needed supplies can be met by imports. However, external demand may be sluggish and the terms of trade may deteriorate; in this situation, the growth of the export sector may not lead to a cumulative process of growth. Hence "all sectors of the economy should grow simultaneously, so as to keep a proper balance between industry and agriculture, and between production for home consumption and production for export."[22]

Lewis is pragmatic with regard to the role of the State; he, however, recognises that its role would be greater in an underdeveloped country than that in a developed country.[23] In his view, "there is a much better case for piecemeal planning" than for detailed central planning; ". . . planning can be confined to those spheres where it is considered most important to modify the results that market forces acting alone would yield."[24] Even for this purpose, he recognises the need for a production programme, which is balanced in the sense that it is internally consistent and feasible. ". . . however tentative the programme, it ought to be tested for

[14]*Ibid.*, pp. 255–256.
[15]*Ibid.*, p. 314.
[16]*Ibid.*
[17]*Ibid.*, p. 322.
[18]*Ibid.*
[19]*Ibid.*, pp. 318–319.
[20]Lewis, *op. cit.*, p. 276.
[21]*Ibid.*, pp. 277–278.
[22]*Ibid.*, p. 283.
[23]*Ibid.*, pp. 376 and 382.
[24]*Ibid.*, p. 384.

its internal consistency, however tentative the tests, since sectors may otherwise be hopelessly out of balance with each other."[25]

Scitovsky, like Rosenstein-Rodan and Nurkse, argues the case for a "proper coordination of investment decisions" on the basis of the "pecuniary external economies" generated by indivisibilities in the investment process and dynamic interdependence among the various sectors of the economy. Investment in one sector affects the demand and costs relating to the other sectors.[26]

Later on, Scitovsky argues that "it is always desirable to sacrifice balanced output or balanced growth for the sake of economies of scale."[27] This is rather inconsistent with his earlier view, where, on the basis of pecuniary external economies generated by economies of scale, he had argued for coordination of investment decisions.[28]

As early as 1951, I had argued the case for balanced growth. ". . . the process of economic development can become self-sustaining, self-reinforcing and cumulative only if a coordinated, integrated, balanced growth takes place in all the interrelated sectors of the economic system. The underdeveloped economies will face all the problems connected with lack of effective demand if such a coordinated growth is not started. No such problem of lack of effective demand appears if all the mutually interrelated industries move in step."[29]

Hirschman criticises the balanced growth doctrine on two counts: first, with regard to its feasibility; and, second, with regard to its applicability to the problems of the developing countries. He argues that "there are tasks that simply exceed the capabilities of a society, no matter to whom they are being entrusted. Balanced growth in the sense of simultaneous multiple development would seem to be one of them."[30] The basic reason for backwardness in his view is the lack of decision-making ability and growth process can be set in motion by generating "a chain of unbalanced growth sequences"[31] so as to maximise induced or routinised decision making through the deliberate creation of pressures, tensions, and incentives for private entrepreneurs as well as the State.[32] Such a growth sequence and strategy is in fact facilitated by the indivisibilities and complimentarities in the investment process.[33]

Hirschman favours unbalance in the direction of shortage of social overhead facilities in relation to the needs of directly productive investment,[34] and he recommends the strategy of initiating development in those sectors, which are linked, through their input requirements and through the other sectors' demand

[25]*Ibid.*, pp. 384–390.

[26]Scitovsky, *op. cit.*

[27]Tibor Scitovsky, "Growth: Balanced or Unbalanced," in Abramovitz (ed.), *The Allocation of Economic Resources* (Stanford, Calif: Stanford University Press, 1959).

[28]See S. K. Nath, "The Theory of Balanced Growth," *Oxford Economic Papers* (June 1962).

[29]V. V. Bhatt, *Employment and Capital Formation in Underdeveloped Economies* (Bombay: Orient Longmans, 1960), Chap. IV.

[30]Hirschman, *op. cit.*, p. 25.

[31]*Ibid.*, p. 72.

[32]*Ibid.*, p. 27–28.

[33]*Ibid.*, Chap. VI and pp. 40–44.

[34]*Ibid.*, Chap. V.

for their outputs, to the maximum extent with the other sectors.[35] In his view, the State should not only initiate such an unbalanced growth sequence but should also be ready to react to, and to alleviate, the resulting pressures in a variety of areas.[36]

Streeten[37] also maintains that unbalanced growth would result in a higher rate of growth than balanced growth because of indivisibilities and dynamic complementarities in the investment process. Unlike Hirschman, Streeten argues the case, like Nurkse, for building social overheads ahead of demand not only because of economies of scale but also because of "the cluster of complementary investment which it provokes." Further, unbalanced growth, as it has done historically, would motivate innovational investment; scarcities and bottlenecks provide the stimulus for adopting innovations. Balanced development would reduce or eliminate this incentive.

He believes that "unbalanced growth, to be most effective, does require planning and preferably State planning, because no private firms may want or be able to carry the surplus capacity and the losses and because private horizons are too narrow."[38] He recognises that inadequate attention is paid to the "precise composition, direction and timing" of unbalanced growth and the resistances caused by unbalanced growth have not been taken into account.[39]

II

Balanced growth discussion implicitly assumes, as it appears from this brief review, that the basic constraints operating on the growth process, like technical and demand relations, rate of capital accumulation, possibilities relating to foreign trade and assistance, the growth rate of the labour force, and the natural resources endowment, are more or less known;[40] and it is the task of the development strategy to realise the maximum growth potentialities consistent with these constraints. Further, they implicitly assume that once this maximum growth path is known, it would not be necessary to provide any additional inducement to the various actors in the process to move on this path. Given these two assumptions, the development problem becomes a mathematical problem of maximisation of growth under given contraints, as Nath[41] has argued.

However, neither the problem nor the solution is as clear and neat as is made out by the balanced growth doctrine. Both its assumptions are vulnerable. As unbalanced growth theorists argue, it is not possible to have a priori knowledge relating to the nature and intensity of basic constraints; this knowledge grows only during a growth process. Unless, therefore, the economy keeps bumping

---

[35]*Ibid.*, Chap. VI.
[36]*Ibid.*, pp. 202–205.
[37]Streeten, *op. cit.*
[38]P. Streeten, "Unbalanced Growth: A Reply," *Oxford Economic Papers* (March 1963).
[39]*Ibid.*
[40]Lewis, of course, recognises that demand and output relations are apt to alter in unforeseeable ways. See Lewis, *op. cit.*, p. 389.
[41]S. K. Nath, *op. cit.*

against the Hicksian ceiling,[42] it is not possible to know the full potentialities of growth even under existing constraints.

Further, and here lies the basic distinguishing feature of unbalanced growth, the basic constraints are amenable to change, of course within certain limits, which are not known a priori, during a growth process, and it is the *raison d'être* of unbalanced growth to modify the conditioning factors or the external frame of the economy so as to raise the growth rate higher than what can be attained otherwise.[43] Technical change or innovational activity is as much conditioned by the nature of the growth process as the latter is by the former. The nature and volume of innovations, defined in the Schumpeterian sense, are not known in advance and represent a creative as well as an adaptive response of the economy to existing constraints. Similarly, even the rate of capital accumulation, the nature and volume of labour force, the organisational frame, and the magnitude and composition of consumer demand are amenable to change within wide limits and the extent to which they can be modified for accelerating development depend upon the nature of the growth process.

Unbalanced growth provides the inducement mechanism for overcoming the constraints. Imbalances at strategic places motivate the innovational process by generating strains, stresses, pressures, and inducements. These pressures and inducements operate not only on the private sector, but also on the State, and thus lead both to take appropriate corrective action.

Thus the problem of adequately motivating the growth process is basic to the process. It is the function of unbalanced growth strategy to provide this motivation so as to modify the constraints and thus realise much higher growth than can be attained by operating within the constraints as known in advance.

But then, as Streeten argues,[44] the real problem is to find out the nature and magnitude of imbalances and the strategic places at which they should be created so as to generate the necessary pressures and inducements that could modify the constraints. Hirschman attempts to solve this problem through what he calls the backward and forward linkages, obtained from the input-output structure of various economies.[45] These linkages reflect the degree to which the other sectors are dependent on a given sector through technical and demand relations. His strategy would be to start the process by initiating development in such sectors on which the other sectors depend to the maximum extent. The development of these sectors would provide the necessary inducements and pressures to the lagging dependent sectors, and these chain effects would provide the momentum to the process.

His quantification of the linkage effects of various sectors suffer from certain limitations. This is based on data of the advanced countries in which the development of basic facilities, including transport, has already reached a high level. And further, as he recognises, his linkages are calculated only on the basis of

---

[42]See J. R. Hicks, *A Contribution to Theory of the Trade Cycle* (Oxford, 1950).

[43]Albert O. Hirschman, *The Strategy of Economic Development* (New Haven, 1958), Chap. IV.

[44]P. Streeten, "Unbalanced Growth: A Reply," *op. cit.*

[45]Hirschman, *op. cit.*, Chap. VI.

current input requirements and not also on the basis of capital requirements.[46] The value of linkages in the case of basic facilities like transport is low in his calculations because of these reasons. Moreover, the unpredictable but nonetheless massive inducement effects through trade *creation* of the development of basic facilities emphasised by Nurkse[47] have been ignored by him. If these factors are taken into account, he would have emphasised the creation of surplus capacity not only in the intermediate sectors like steel, but also in the sector of social overheads. Surplus in these sectors would reflect shortages in the other sectors, and both these would provide the motivation to correct these imbalances.

Significant thing to note is the reliance of both the doctrines on the dynamic interdependence among the various sectors of the economy. Given the basic assumptions of the balanced growth doctrine, this interdependence becomes an argument for balanced growth; while if these assumptions are modified, dynamic interdependence provides the inducement mechanism for motivating the growth process through the creation of imbalances.

Balanced growth does not imply, as is sometimes suggested,[48] that the pattern of domestic output should be perfectly consistent with the pattern of domestic demand; it merely implies that the growth of the export sector should be adequate to meet the requirements of imports of goods, which cannot be produced or produced in adequate amounts to meet the home demand. Further it is consistent with the creation of surplus capacity in sectors which experience economies of scale and the products of which are nonimportable; from the longer-term point of view, it would be cheaper in such cases either to provide for surplus capacity as in the case of transport, or to provide room for expansion (as in the case of a steel plant), than to create capacity just adequate to meet potential demand. Balanced growth thus tries to exploit fully what Scitovsky calls the pecuniary external economies generated as a result of interdependence within the economic system through consumption as well as production. Price mechanism cannot be a substitute for a balanced growth strategy in an underdeveloped economy when structural change is taking place, as it would give the signals too late in the case of external economies generated through interdependence and would not give the correct signal at all in the case of economies of scale.[49]

But balanced growth does not advocate the deliberate creation of shortages in any sector. That is because it takes the basic constraints as given and does not visualise any modification of these constraints by adequately motivating the growth process. Unbalanced growth provides such motivation through the creation of imbalances at strategic points in the economy; these imbalances imply surpluses in the leading sectors and shortages in the lagging sectors. As with balanced growth, here also, there is no reliance on the price mechanism for initiating the growth strategy. Present prices provide no indication of the relative scarcities

---

[46]*Ibid.*

[47]Nurkse, *op. cit.*, pp. 267–274.

[48]See, for example, Scitovsky, "Growth: Balanced or Unbalanced," *op. cit.*

[49]Hollis B. Chenery, "Interdependence of Investment Decisions," in Abramovitz (ed.), *The Allocation of Economic Resources, op. cit.*

in the future. However, with unbalanced growth, once the growth process is initiated, the new structure of relative prices as well as other nonmarket forces are assumed to provide the necessary inducements and pressures for corrective action. These inducements and pressures would result in a more or less compulsive corrective sequence of investment decisions *because of* the dynamic complimentarities in the investment process. The greater the potential pecuniary external economies generated by the leading sectors, the greater would be the inducements and pressures in the dependent lagging sectors to exploit these to their advantage by trying to overcome the constraints on their outputs.

III

With the unbalanced growth strategy, as Hirschman emphasises, the function of imbalances is to set in motion a corrective process toward the attainment of a balance; this balance may be overreached, but criteria for judging the appropriateness of the nature and magnitude of imbalances relate to the inducements and pressures which they provide to correct them. All imbalances which lead to an explosive result do not thus satisfy these criteria.

For providing a basis for judging the nature and magnitude of imbalances, it is, thus, necessary to have an idea about the nature of the balance that is aimed at. Without such a basis, it would be difficult to judge the direction of the process. This means that the objective of balance needs to be specified. However, it is difficult to specify it because of imperfect knowledge about the constraints and the way in which they would be modified by the growth process. Hence arises the need for judgment on the basis of which, the broad range within which, as an objective, the degree of imbalances should lie, could be indicated. This may never be attained, but then the process should be capable of generating a reverse movement toward a new balance.

This means that at least as an objective of unbalanced growth strategy it is necessary to have a broad idea about the nature of balance that is sought to be realised. Unbalanced growth strategy thus can have justification only to the extent to which it can set in motion, each time that the desired imbalances arise, a cyclical process which corrects them. Unbalanced growth thus is not inconsistent with balanced growth; it provides the necessary motivation which the latter lacks and thereby makes it possible for an economy to widen its horizon with respect to growth potentialities.

In operational terms, an economy can formulate two different balanced development paths: one based on the existing state of knowledge with regard to the basic constraints and the other based on informed judgment (as no a priori knowledge in this matter is possible) about the extent to which the existing constraints can be modified. The former provides the lower limit and the latter the upper limit with regard to growth potentialities. The objective should be to attain the balance indicated by the upper limit. This would inevitably generate imbalances, as it is only through these imbalances that the desired balance can be attained. If the actual movement is toward a balance which is at a level lower than that indicated by the lower limit, it would indicate that the initial judgment about the relation between the nature and magnitude of imbalances and the induced corrective processes was incorrect and should be revised.

The formulation of these development paths is the function of planning. Excepting Nurkse and Hirschman, the protagonists of both the doctrines realise the relevance of planning to their strategies. Without such planning, it is difficult to judge whether the economy is actually pursuing the desired balanced growth path in the case of the balanced growth strategy; Nurkse's approach in fact implies such planning as is realised by the other balanced growth theorists. With respect to unbalanced growth, too, how to judge without planning whether the desired imbalances are actually created and further whether these imbalances set in motion a corrective process toward the desired balance objective. A plan would provide the necessary basis for judging the appropriateness of the path pursued. Further, since Hirschman lays emphasis on induced decision making, planning should be an integral part of his strategy, as it would make it easier for the State as well as the private sector to take appropriate decisions.

Since growth is a social objective, its attainment has to be the responsibility of the entire community. The community in this matter can function only through the State, and hence it is obviously its responsibility to choose a development strategy and ensure its implementation. If the spontaneous forces by themselves, as Nurkse suggests, could generate the desired growth process, all discussion about growth strategies would become irrelevant. The *extent* of the role of the State in the development process and the *nature* of planning would vary from country to country, depending on the special characteristics and problems of each. The State itself may not even formulate a plan, and it may not even participate in the actual implementation process; but it would be its responsibility to ensure that a plan is formulated which is acceptable to it (and that it is implemented) and to take appropriate policy measures for the purpose. If the State does not perform this function, the community would have to devise another institution which can perform it with all the powers of the State given to it.

With the unbalanced growth strategy, there may not be any need for very detailed planning. Once the crucial sectors are identified, and some broad idea about the nature of the movement of the economy toward a balance at a higher level is obtained on the basis of informed judgment, what is necessary is just to plan the crucial projects well. The rest would be taken care of by the inducement mechanism set in motion both with regard to planning as well as growth.

For an underdeveloped economy which does not possess the required technical expertise as well as information for detailed planning, this is probably the only effective course of action. To wait for building up information and technical expertise would delay the whole process and employ scarce technical personnel in the task of planning when their productivity in planning and implementing projects would be much higher. Planning is just an instrument for the rational attainment of growth objectives; what is of paramount importance is growth. Therefore one has to judge the cost of refinement in planning techniques in terms of the growth opportunities to be given up and compare it with its returns. As in other matters, so also in deciding about the nature of planning a rational decision is necessary. Technical expertise as well as information would increase with growth and each stage in the process would indicate the nature of planning that is optimum.

The present trend toward building planning models of increasing complexity may mislead some underdeveloped countries in devoting their scarce resources to an undue extent in the planning effort when they would be much more productive elsewhere. What is required is not an ideal planning model, but a model which is workable in the context of the situation in the underdeveloped countries. As is happening with engineers, the economists engaged in planning work too are probably tending to urge the use of the most up-to-date techniques, when the techniques economically most viable are perhaps less complex and less refined. Underdeveloped countries have to beware not only of the latest production techniques but also of the latest planning techniques; techniques in both these spheres would have to be chosen in the context of their resources endowment and their objectives.

Selection **11**

The Need of Developing
Human Resources

FREDERICK H. HARBISON

From: "Human Resources Development Planning in Modernising Economies," International Labour Review, *Vol. LXXXV (January– June 1962), pp. 435–442 and 454–458. Reprinted by permission of the International Labor Office.*

The newly developing nations of the world are in a state of revolt. They have rejected the notion that poverty, squalor, and disease are preordained. No longer are they disposed to entrust their economic and political future to the forces of the market, the will of God, or the omnipotent judgment of colonial rulers. And, in pressing for high-speed modernisation, they think in terms of leaps rather than mere steps forward. They are hoping and planning for accelerated development.

A country which commits itself to accelerated growth needs a strategy for development. It must increase sharply its rate of savings by one means or another. It must emphasise industrialisation, but at the same time it must modernise agriculture. It must invest wisely in both things and people. And, in so doing, it must develop a sense of priority, so that savings and manpower are directed into the most productive channels.

A strategy for development of human resources—i.e., the building and the effective utilisation of the skills of people—is an essential element of any modern development strategy. The wealth of a nation is as much dependent upon the development of its people as upon the accumulation of material capital, and there is little need to argue which is the more important. Both material and human capital must be accumulated at high rates of speed if rapid growth is to be achieved. And it is essential for politicians and planners to understand that the development of human and physical resources must be integrated carefully in any master plan for growth.

In this article I propose, first, to examine the manpower problems which seem to be emerging in the newly modernising countries, and then to set forth the elements of a strategy of human resources development. And, in a concluding section, I shall advance some suggestions for the integration of manpower development programming with overall economic development planning.

The Manpower Problems of Modernising Economies

Most modernising economies are confronted simultaneously with two persistent, yet seemingly diverse, manpower problems: *the shortage of persons with critical skills* in the modernising sector and *surplus labour* in both the modernising and traditional sectors. Thus, the strategy of human resources development is concerned with the twofold objective of building skills and providing productive employment for unutilised or underutilised manpower. The shortages and surplus of human resources, however, are not separate and distinct problems; they are very intimately related. Both have their roots in the changes which are inherent in the development process. Both are related in part to education. Both are aggravated as the tempo of modernisation is quickened. And, paradoxically, the shortage of persons with critical skills is one of the contributing causes of the surplus of people without jobs. Although the manpower problems of no two countries are exactly alike, there are some shortages and surpluses which appear to be universal in modernising societies.

Manpower Shortages

The manpower shortages of modernising countries are quite easy to identify, and fall into several categories:

1. In all modernising countries there is likely to be a shortage of highly educated professional manpower, such as, for example, scientists, agronomists, veterinarians, engineers, and doctors. Such persons, however, usually prefer to live in the major cities rather than in the rural areas, where in many cases their services are most urgently needed. Thus, their shortage is magnified by their relative immobility. And, ironically, their skills are seldom used effectively. In West Africa and also in many Asian and Latin American countries, for example, graduate engineers may be found managing the routine operation of an electric power substation or doing the work of draughtsmen. Doctors may spend long hours making the most routine medical tests. The reason is obvious.

2. The shortage of technicians, nurses, agricultural assistants, technical supervisors, and other subprofessional personnel is generally even more critical than the shortage of fully qualified professionals. For this there are several explanations. First, the modernising countries usually fail to recognise that the requirements for this category of manpower exceed by many times those for senior professional personnel. Second, the few persons who are qualified to enter a technical institute may also be qualified to enter a university, and they prefer the latter because of the higher status and pay which is accorded the holder of a university degree. Finally, there are often fewer places available in institutions providing intermediate training than in the universities.

3. The shortage of top-level managerial and administrative personnel, in both the private and public sectors, is almost universal, as is the dearth of persons with entrepreneurial talents.

4. Teachers are almost always in short supply, and their turnover is high because they tend to leave the teaching profession if and when more attractive jobs become available in government, politics, or private enterprise. The scarcity is generally most serious in secondary education and particularly acute in the

fields of science and mathematics. This shortage of competent teachers is a "master bottleneck" which retards the entire process of human resources development.

5. In most modernising countries there are also shortages of craftsmen of all kinds as well as senior clerical personnel such as bookkeepers, secretaries, stenographers, and business machine operators.

6. Finally, there are usually in addition several other miscellaneous categories of personnel in short supply, such as, for example, radio and television specialists, airplane pilots, accountants, economists, and statisticians.

I shall use the term "high-level manpower," or, alternatively, "human capital," as a convenient designation for the persons who fall into categories such as those mentioned above. The term "human capital formation," as used in this paper, is the process of acquiring and increasing the numbers of persons who have the skills, education, and experience which are critical for the economic and political development of a country. Human capital formation is thus associated with investment in man and his development as a creative and productive resource. It includes investment by society in education, investment by employers in training, as well as investment by individuals of time and money in their own development. Such investments have both qualitative and quantitative dimensions—i.e., human capital formation includes not only expenditure for education and training, but also the development of attitudes toward productive activity.

As stressed earlier, a central problem of all modernising countries is to accelerate the process of human capital formation. Human capital, or high-level manpower, may be accumulated in several ways. It may be imported from abroad through a variety of means such as technical assistance, expatriate enterprises, hiring of consultants, or immigration. It may be developed in employment through on-the-job training, in-service programmes of formal training, management development seminars, part-time adult education classes, and many other means. It is also developed in employment through better organisation of work, creation of appropriate attitudes and incentives, and better management of people. It is accumulated through formal education in schools, technical training centres, colleges, universities, and other institutions of higher learning. And finally, it may be developed as a by-product of modern military training.

The analysis of human capital formation is thus parallel and complementary to the study of the processes of savings and investment (in the material sense). In designing a strategy for development, one needs to consider the total stock of human capital required, its rates of accumulation, and its commitment to (or investment in) high-priority productive activities.

The rate of modernisation of a country is associated with both its stock and rate of accumulation of human capital. High-level manpower is needed to staff new and expanding government services, to introduce new systems of land use and new methods of agriculture, to develop new means of communication, to carry forward industrialisation, and to build the educational system. In other words, innovation, or the process of change from a static or traditional society, requires very large "doses" of strategic human capital. The countries which are making the most rapid and spectacular innovations are invariably those which are under the greatest pressure to accumulate this kind of human capital at a fast rate. Here we may make two tentative generalisations:

First, the rate of accumulation of strategic human capital must always exceed the rate of increase in the labour force as a whole. In most countries, for example, the rate of increase in scientific and engineering personnel may need to be at least three times that of the labour force. Subprofessional personnel may have to increase even more rapidly. Clerical personnel and craftsmen may have to increase at least twice as fast as the labour force, and top managerial and administrative personnel should normally increase at a comparable rate.

Second, in most cases, the rate of increase in human capital will need to exceed the rate of economic growth. In newly developing countries which already are faced with critical shortages of highly skilled persons, the ratio of the annual increase in high-level manpower to the annual increase in national income may need to be as high as three to one, or even higher in those cases where expatriates are to be replaced by citizens of the developing countries.

The accumulation of high-level manpower to overcome skill bottlenecks is a never-ending process. Advanced industrial societies as well as underdeveloped countries are normally short of critical skills. Indeed, as long as the pace of innovation is rapid, the appetite of any growing country for high-level manpower is almost insatiable.

Labour Surpluses

The overabundance of labour is in most countries as serious a problem as the shortage of skills. Its more common manifestations are the following:

1. In nearly all countries the supply of unskilled and untrained manpower in the urban areas exceeds the available employment opportunities. The reasons are not difficult to find. First, large urban populations are likely to build up prior to rather than as a consequence of the expansion of industrial employment. Second, as industrialisation gains momentum, the productivity of factory labour tends to rise sharply, and this limits the expansion of demand for general industrial labour. Modern industrialisation may even displace labour from cottage and handicraft industries faster than it is absorbed in newly created factories. Third, the government service is able to provide legitimate employment for relatively few people. And, finally, unless development is extremely rapid, trade, commerce, and other services simply do not absorb those who cannot find jobs in other activities. But despite relatively limited employment opportunities and overcrowded conditions, the modernisation process impels people to migrate from the rural areas to the cities. And, as progress is made toward universal primary education, nearly every modernising country is faced with the problem of mounting unemployment of primary school leavers.

2. In overpopulated countries, such as, for example, Egypt or India, the rural areas are also overcrowded, resulting in widespread underemployment and disguised unemployment of human resources. Indeed, in many countries it is evident that total agricultural output could be increased if fewer people were living on the land and the size of agricultural units was increased. Thus, surplus labour in rural areas in most cases is no asset and in some cases is definitely a liability for increasing agricultural output.

3. The "unemployed intellectual" constitutes an entirely different kind of surplus. In many countries, for example, it is reported that there are too many lawyers or too many graduates of the arts and literature faculties. And there may be instances also of unemployed or underemployed engineers, scientists, economists, and even agronomists. The unused intellectual, however, is unemployed only because he is unwilling to accept work which he considers beneath his status or educational level. A university education creates very high employment expectations. In some countries, a university degree may be looked upon almost as a guarantee of a soft and secure job in the government service, and in most it is assumed to be a membership card in the elite class. But, even in rapidly modernising countries, the purely administrative jobs in the government service become filled fairly rapidly; the demand for lawyers, for example, is certainly not as great as the demand for technically trained personnel. And in some societies where large enterprises are owned and managed by members of family dynasties, even the opportunities for professionally trained engineers and technicians may be limited, at least in the early stages of development. Rather than accept work beneath his status, or employment in remote rural areas, the university graduate, and sometimes even the secondary school leaver as well, may join the ranks of the unemployed. A sizeable quantity of unused human capital of this kind reflects a wasteful investment in human resources development and poses a serious threat to a country's social and political stability.

4. There are other miscellaneous kinds of surplus labour. For example, the introduction of new processes and automated machinery may throw skilled labour out of work. Or secondary school leavers, who feel that they should qualify for white collar jobs, may shun manual work of any kind. And, in some countries, immigrants and refugees swell the ranks of the unemployed.

Some labour surpluses, however, can be eliminated and others reduced substantially by a well-conceived and balanced programme of economic growth. A strategy of human resources development, therefore, must include an attack on surpluses as well as shortages.

Manpower Analysis

As indicated above, no two countries have exactly the same manpower problems. Some have unusually serious surpluses, and others have very specialised kinds of skill bottlenecks. Politicians and planners, therefore, need to make a systematic assessment of the human resources problems in their particular countries. Such assessment may be called "manpower analysis."

The objectives of manpower analysis are as follows: (1) the identification of the principal critical shortages of skilled manpower in each major sector of the economy and an analysis of the reasons for such shortages; (2) the identification of surpluses, both of trained manpower as well as unskilled labour, and the reasons for such surpluses; and (3) the setting of forward targets for human resources development based upon reasonable expectations of growth. Such forward targets are best determined by a careful examination and comparison, sector by sector, of the utilisation of manpower in a number of countries which are somewhat more advanced politically, socially, and economically.

Manpower analysis cannot always be based on an elaborate or exhaustive survey. It is seldom possible to calculate precisely the numbers of people needed in every occupation at some future time. But, whether statistics are available or not, the purpose of manpower analysis is to give a reasonably objective picture of a country's major human resources problems, the interrelationships between these problems, and their causes, together with an informed guess as to probable future trends. Manpower analysis is both qualitative and quantitative, and it must be based upon wise judgment as well as upon available statistics. In countries where statistics are either unavailable or clearly unreliable, moreover, the initial manpower analysis may be frankly impressionistic. The methodology of manpower assessments, however, lies beyond the scope of this article, and is to be treated more fully in forthcoming publications of the Inter-University Study.[1]

In conclusion, the major shortages and surpluses of manpower in most countries are easy to identify. Many of them are common to all modernising societies. Manpower analysis, based on relevant comparisons with other countries at different stages of development, is useful in assessing particular problems and probable future trends. To be sure, there is need for research in manpower supply and demand as related to economic growth. But those who are responsible for the planning of accelerated growth cannot and need not wait for the completion of definitive studies before designing a realistic strategy for human resources development.

A MANPOWER PLANNING STRATEGY

Once the manpower problems of a newly developing country are identified, a strategy must be developed to overcome them effectively. The essential components of such a strategy are the following: (1) the building of appropriate incentives; (2) the effective training of employed manpower; and (3) the rational development of formal education. These three elements are interdependent. Progress in one area is dependent upon progress in the other two. The country's leaders should not concentrate on only one or two of them at a time; they must plan an integrated attack on all three fronts at once.

•   •   •

IMPLEMENTING THE STRATEGY

. . . Investments in formal education alone are not likely to solve either critical skill shortages or persistent labour surpluses in modernising societies. Investments in education are likely to contribute effectively to rapid growth only (1) if there are adequate incentives to encourage men and women to engage in the kinds of productive activity which are needed to accelerate the modernisation process, and (2) if appropriate measures are taken to shift a large part of the responsibility

---

[1] International organisations such as the I.L.O., the O.E.C.D., U.N.E.S.C.O. and the planning ministries of several countries have developed a wide variety of techniques for manpower surveys. It is hoped that, with the assistance of the Inter-University Study, progress can be made toward development of a common methodology which will facilitate cross-national comparisons.

for training to the principal employing institutions. The building of incentives and the training of employed manpower, therefore, are necessary both as a means of economising on formal education and as a means of making the investment in it productive.

In the building of incentives, a cardinal principle is that the status and compensation attached to occupations should be related to their relative importance as measured by the high-priority needs of a developing society, and not to arbitrary levels of education, degrees, family status, or political connections. This is essential for the accumulation of human capital and for its most effective utilisation. The surpluses of labour, particularly those connected with rural-urban migration and the unemployment of primary school leavers, may be reduced in part by a far-reaching programme of modernisation of agriculture and rural life as a counterpart to a programme of industrialisation. Because of rapidly increasing populations and the early emphasis on universal primary education, however, there will still be large numbers of unemployed or underemployed persons in most modernising societies.

The potentialities of fully utilising government agencies, private employers, expatriate firms, and technical experts as trainers and developers of manpower, though very great indeed, are seldom exploited fully. Thus, a key element in the strategy of human resources development is to shift as much as possible the responsibility for training to the major employing institutions and to provide the necessary technical guidance to enable these institutions to develop in-service training programmes along modern lines.

The third component of the strategy is wise judgment and prudent investment in building the system of formal education. This calls for giving priority to investment in and development of broad secondary education. It requires that the costs of universal primary education be kept as low as possible by applying new technologies which can make effective use of relatively untrained teachers and which can multiply the contribution of a very small but strategic group of highly trained professionals. Finally, in the area of higher education, the strategy stresses the need for giving priority to investment in intermediate-level training institutions and the scientific and engineering faculties of universities. But this does not mean that the production of liberally educated persons should be neglected.

The three essential components of the strategy are interdependent, and call for a well-designed and integrated attack on all three fronts at once. And it is imperative that the strategy of building and utilising human resources be an integral part of a country's national development programme. The strategy assumes that the politicians of the country are firmly committed to the goal of accelerated development and that they have the will to do the things which are imperative for its attainment.

Some Obstacles To Be Overcome

There are, however, obstacles which lie in the path of implementation of a consistent strategy of human resources development. The most formidable, perhaps, is traditional thinking. For example, those who have experience with traditional methods of elementary education are suspicious of new technologies which might reduce teaching costs. Most of the leaders of the underdeveloped countries are unaware of the great strides made recently in methodology of in-service training in the advanced countries. The thought of overhauling the wage and salary structure of government ministries is frightening. The idea of tampering with higher education to turn out larger proportions of subprofessional personnel is not consistent with the kind of indoctrination one may have had at Oxford, Cambridge, or the Sorbonne. And the very thought that there is a strategic relationship between incentive, in-service training and formal education is strange and difficult to grasp. Yet those who preach the revolutionary doctrine of planned, accelerated growth—more rapid and more sweeping than anything before—must be prepared to reject outworn concepts and employ the most modern techniques available. In their approach to development, they must be more modern in many respects than the advanced nations from which they seek aid and advice.

The governmental structure of the developing countries is another obstacle. Thinking and planning tends to be in compartments. The ministries of education deal only with formal education, and some do not even have jurisdiction over technical education. Ministries of labour are concerned with employment standards and some aspects of training skilled and semi-skilled labour. The ministries of industry, commerce, and agriculture are likely to be preoccupied with technical and financial questions. The economic development ministries or development boards, if they exist at all, are generally concerned with physical capital formation, the balance of payments, and other urgent economic questions. The traditional economic planners are likely to banish human resources development to that "no-man's-land" of social welfare. Thus, no ministry or board is in a position to see the problem as a whole. Each grasps rather blindly for some programme of manpower development and in justification makes wild claims for its indispensable role in promoting rapid growth.

Until recently, moreover, foreign technical experts have added to the confusion and fragmentation of effort in this field. Each has a particular package to sell; each normally deals with only one ministry; each with tireless zeal tries to "educate the top leadership" on the importance of a particular project. There is "competition among the givers." In the developing country offers of help may be forthcoming from the United Nations, U.N.E.S.C.O., the I.L.O., or the I.C.A., as well as from governments, philanthropic foundations, and a host of church missions and other voluntary organisations. Each has an interest or a programme which it may be pushing in particular countries and in most cases offers assistance in a specialised field.

This "competition among givers" is desirable in many respects. It offers the developing countries a range of choice. It puts pressure on the givers to do as good a job as possible. It gives the recipient countries a feeling that many nations and many institutions are concerned with their welfare. And it makes it easier for these countries to maintain a position of neutrality as recipients of assistance. But there are obvious drawbacks. Aid is given in pieces without regard for broader, underlying problems. The energies of the recipient governments are consumed by a proliferation of scattered and unrelated projects. Often the best-qualified local manpower is lured away to foreign countries on fellowships, study tours, and other exciting ventures, leaving virtually no one at home to handle the day-to-day work of project development. And, worst of all, in some countries the politicians are tempted to use some of the givers as scapegoats by asking for "a survey of experts" as a convenient means for postponing action on a thorny problem.

Implementing Machinery

The design of a strategy calls for integrated rather than compartmentalised planning. The implementation of a strategy requires coordinated activity. Assuming that a strategy can be developed, what machinery is necessary for its implementation?

Since manpower problems are the concern of many ministries, the programme of human resources development should be implemented by an interministerial board. In addition to members of the government, this board should normally have representation as well from the nongovernment employing institutions and organised labour. As a general rule, this board should report to the head of state rather than to a particular ministry. It is essential, however, that such a board should have a secretariat. And this board and its secretariat should be integrated with whatever machinery is established for general economic development planning. Among its key functions would be the following:

1. The assessment of human resources problems through periodic manpower analysis.
2. The integration of human resources development strategy with other components of the country's plans of economic and political development.
3. The promotion and stimulation of planning activity on the part of the ministries represented on the board, as well as on the part of employers' and workers' organisations.
4. The coordination of the above planning activities.
5. The determination of priorities in the strategy of human resources development and the continuous reassessment of priorities as the programme progresses.
6. The selection and design of research projects which may be useful for the formulation, implementation, and evaluation of the strategy of human resources development.
7. Coordination and approval at the national level of all requests for external and technical assistance involving manpower and human resources development.
8. The general review of all activity connected with human resources development, and periodic evaluation of the work of the various agencies which assume responsibility for it.

Formal machinery such as that suggested above is not difficult to establish. Its effectiveness, however, will depend upon the people who provide its leadership and the kinds of personnel recruited for its secretariat. Its success will be related also to the effective use of the right kind of foreign experts as consultants. In short, the critical element in the creation of machinery for the implementation of the strategy of human resources development is the right kind of high-level manpower.

A human resources strategy board should be neither a statistical agency, a study commission, nor a long-range planning organisation. Though primarily concerned with policy formulation, it is at the same time involved in certain critical operations. It may have both advisory and executive responsibilities. Its top staff, therefore, should be neither statisticians, professional educators, nor economists as such. Its key personnel should be strategists—persons who combine political insight with a rational understanding of the processes of modernisation. Such strategists of necessity are generalists, in that they must be able to comprehend the interrelationships between the component parts of an intricate programme for accelerated development. And they are difficult to find and to train.

Selection **12**

The Role of Education
in Economic Development

W. J. WAINES

From: "*The Role of Education in the Development of Underdeveloped Countries,*" The Canadian Journal of Economics and Political Science, *Vol. XXIX, No. 4 (November 1963), pp. 437–445. Reprinted by permission of* The Canadian Journal of Economics and Political Science *and the author.*

During the last decade and more there has appeared a vast literature on economic growth, especially with reference to underdeveloped countries. This literature ranges from the sophisticated models of the mathematically inclined to the very practical down-to-earth reflections of the less erudite technical assistance expert with experience in the field. The literature demonstrates that there are many approaches to the problem of economic development and also that there are still areas of controversy to be resolved. In fact, while we have learned much about economic growth and much more about underdeveloped countries, it seems that we are still feeling our way towards devising a satisfactory analytical framework for economic growth.

There has been waste of manpower and capital not only because the processes of economic growth are imperfectly understood, but also because governments of recipient countries have a propensity to ask either for the wrong things or the right things in the wrong order of priority. Waste also results from the failure of assistance agencies, even within the framework of the United Nations, to co-ordinate their activities, from competition amongst the departments of government in the recipient countries for preferred treatment in the matter of aid, and competition amongst assisting countries, agencies, and organizations in giving aid for political and prestige reasons.

Technical assistance agencies have generally regarded the expert as either paving the way for material capital formation by surveys and the like or providing administrative, operational, and maintenance skills. The training function of the technical expert is, of course, recognized. But in practice training falls far short of the desirable level, either because there are no counterparts to train, or because these counterparts are ill-equipped to receive training, or because the expert is fully occupied with other tasks, some of which can hardly be read into his terms of reference.

When I arrived in Africa on a technical assistance mission, I was confronted by most of these limitations and others as well. Public administration was in many cases in the hands of untrained and inexperienced people, and those who were experienced carried an intolerable load of work. Technical manpower was in short supply and inadequately trained. Mechanical equipment was idle or not properly maintained for lack of operating and maintenance crews. Technical assistance personnel often found themselves in effect expatriate administrative officers.

Health and education were not ignored but they took second place. They could not be provided until the country had advanced economically to the point where they could be afforded. The lack of technical personnel was the most obvious but, in the long run, not the most critical area of neglect. The people were illiterate. Only about 5 per cent of the adults had been in school. Cultural patterns which had satisfied the primitive needs of the peoples were often inimical to the transplantation of Western techniques and ideas. While the departments of health and education had extensive plans for the development of their facilities, the lion's share of the development budget went to the departments concerned with agriculture, irrigation, transportation, and communication, with smaller amounts to the development of minerals, forests, and fisheries.

Much of the literature has emphasized the importance of the role of material capital in the process of economic growth, and so have the recipient countries. "What economists have not stressed," says Prof. T. W. Schultz of the University of Chicago, "is the single truth that people invest in themselves and that these investments are very large." It is his contention that "investment in human capital accounts for most of the impressive rise in the real earnings per worker."[1] Schultz and others have argued that increases in the quantity of material capital and in the numbers of the working population do not account for the whole of the economic growth in the United States in recent decades as measured by real income. From studies of the National Bureau of Economic Research, Schultz has shown that between 1919 and 1957 in the United States, with the addition of only 1 per cent in total inputs of tangible capital and in man hours per annum, real income increased at the rate of about 3 per cent per year.[2] He found the difference between measured inputs and measured outputs in Latin America to be substantial, though less than in the United States. Working on research conducted by personnel of the Economic Commission for Latin America, Schultz found for 1945 to 1955 an increase in economic growth of 4.88 per cent per year as compared with an increase in inputs, including land, of 3.12 per cent per annum.[3] Presumably this difference between the United States and Latin America is accounted for in part by the substantial differences in the stock of human capital in the two regions.

---

[1] "Investment in Human Capital," *American Economic Review*, Vol. LI (March 1961), p. 1.

[2] T. W. Schultz, "Education as a Source of Economic Growth," United Nations, Economic and Social Council, a paper prepared for the Conference on Education and Economic and Social Development in Latin America, Santiago, Chile, March 1962, p. 3.

[3] *Ibid.*

Recent research indicates plausibly that the increase in the education and training of workers and the advance of knowledge generally, together with economies of scale, account for a large part of the growth otherwise unexplained. Expenditures on the production of human capital include expenditures other than those on education: for example, medical care, hospitals, and all such expenditures which improve and maintain the health and vigour of the population.

In this paper I am primarily concerned with the production of human capital, which involves expenditures on education and the training of people to enhance not only their manual skills and dexterity but also their ability to comprehend new problems and situations and deal with them in an imaginative fashion. It involves, too, expenditures on education which facilitate changes in the cultural pattern of a community or which may result in improved processes of production and new forms of social and economic organization. Included in the growth of knowledge must be advance in sanitation, medicine, and so on, which can do much to enhance the productive capacities of an economy. Strictly speaking, all forms of educational expenditure should be included but, for practical reasons, the costs of formal schooling at all levels and earnings foregone by students while engaged in formal education are taken as the measure of the investment. "When all is said and done," says Schultz, "the principal resource is labour. . . . It is the *capability* of the labour force that has been improved and these improvements have resulted from a major investment outlay." He estimates that in the United States, between 1929 and 1957, at least 21 per cent of the increase in national income was the contribution of education of the labour force. The real income of the United States rose by $152 billion, of which additional education of the labour force contributed about $32 billion.[4] Denison, using a different approach, finds the contribution of education to growth in the same period amounting to about 23 per cent of the growth rate of the aggregate national product.[5]

Poor countries are prone to think of their rate of development as depending upon the amount of physical capital they can obtain. They consequently search vigorously for outside sources to supplement their own meagre supplies, which are usually derived from budgetary surpluses in the early stages of development and in large part have to be matched by foreign exchange. But ability to use capital effectively depends upon available natural and human resources. The studies to which I have referred emphasize the importance of the quality of human resources as affecting the capital absorptive capacity of the country and of education, in the broad sense, as very largely determining that quality, whether it be engaged in the political, cultural, or economic life of the country. It is just as important to have political leaders and civil servants of high calibre as it is to have qualified and skilled entrepreneurs, professionals, technicians, and tradesmen. The provision

---

[4] T. W. Schultz, "U. S. Endeavours to Assist Low Income Countries Improve Economic Capabilities of their People," *Journal of Farm Economics*, Vol. XLIII (1961), p. 1070; Schultz, *op. cit.*

[5] E. F. Denison, *The Sources of Economic Growth in the United States and the Alternatives before Us*, Supplementary Paper No. 13, Committee for Economic Development (1962). But see Review Article of this publication by Moses Abramovitz, *American Economic Review* (1962), pp. 762–782.

of educational opportunities, therefore, should have top priority in a newly developing country.

The importance of a background of literacy and know-how in economic development is well illustrated by the speed with which Western Europe recovered with Marshall Plan aid. Japan's rapid postwar recovery and present strength must be due in large measure to making effective use of capital with limited natural resources but with human resources of great strength. Israel, too, is a striking modern example of very rapid development. In the eight-year period 1950 to 1958 aggregate gross national product increased at an annual rate of 10 per cent and gross national product per capita grew at an average rate of 5 per cent per year. Even a superficial comparison of the rate of growth in Israel and in other Middle East countries which have had similar financial resources and are similarly or better endowed with natural resources suggests that it was the quality of Israel's human resources that made rapid growth possible. Notwithstanding its location in the Middle East, Israel is culturally a part of the Western world. The early immigrants were mainly Europeans who brought with them the knowledge, skills, and conventions which were necessary to make effective use of the stream of capital. This Western culture provided the base from which economic advances could be made each year. It was receptive to education and to new techniques and skills and highly adaptable to new situations. Above all, the people displayed the energy and initiative which is associated with Western culture.

We turn now to the problem of developing in the poor countries the educational facilities which they require to promote economic growth. First, let us consider the magnitude of the problem. Estimates of the demand for higher and secondary education in the underdeveloped countries of Africa, Asia, and Latin America to 1970 were presented by Tinbergen and Bos at the OECD Conference in Washington in 1961.[6] These estimates were based on the assumption of a desirable increase in per capita income in the underdeveloped countries at the rate of at least 2 per cent per annum, a rate which is probably beyond possibility of achievement. The estimates, then, are target figures expressing desirable levels of educational effort; they are approximations and are tentative. They are startling in what they imply about the amount of effort required of both developed and underdeveloped nations to support an educational program which will result in modest improvements in the standards of living in these countries.

With respect to the number of students, it was estimated that for the underdeveloped regions as a whole an approximate 80 per cent increase would be required in the number of students in secondary education, including both general and vocational, and a twofold increase would be required in higher education between 1958 and 1970. The estimated absolute numbers of students in each year are shown in Table I. The twofold increase of students in vocational training and the threefold increase of those in science and technology are worthy of special notice.

---

[6] J. Tinbergen and H. C. Bos, "The Global Demand for Higher and Secondary Education in the Underdeveloped Countries in the Next Decade," *The Challenge of Aid to Newly Developing Countries*, Vol. III, Policy Conference on Economic Growth and Investment in Education (Washington, D.C.: Organization for Economic Cooperation and Development, 1961), pp. 71–80.

So great an increase in the number of students would obviously put a tremendous strain on facilities for training teachers in both underdeveloped and developed countries. It would be impossible for underdeveloped countries to make the effort without extensive aid. Assuming that the student-teacher ratio is not to be increased

Table I

NUMBERS OF STUDENTS IN 1958 AND NUMBERS REQUIRED IN 1970 IN AFRICA, ASIA, AND LATIN AMERICA

	1958	1970
Secondary education (general and vocational)	16.9 million	30.3 million
General	15.0 ″	26.2 ″
Vocational	1.9 ″	4.0 ″
Higher education (including science and technology)	2.2 ″	4.3 ″
Science and technology	.5 ″	1.4 ″

and that unqualified teachers are not to be employed in universities and colleges, the gross increase, including replacements, from 1958 to 1970 in higher education would be about 124,000 for the whole area. The graduate student ratio is about 10 per cent. "If all university teachers had to come from the body of university graduates in the period 1958–70, the percentage of graduates which would have to go into university teaching would then be 4.5 in Africa, 2.5 in Asia, and 5.5 in Latin America."[7] Less than 1 per cent of university graduates in developed countries become university instructors. To Tinbergen and Bos,

> The conclusion is inescapable that the underdeveloped countries will be unable to increase from their own resources the number of university teachers by 120,000 during the next decade. It is not possible—nor necessary—to make a reliable estimate of the teacher gap: even if the advanced countries had to supply as little as 5 per cent of the increase, this would mean sending 6,000 more university teachers to the underdeveloped countries. This purely quantitative aspect is one that will need the most urgent attention on the part of governments and international organizations concerned.[8]

Taking the teacher-student ratio as 1:30, Tinbergen and Bos have estimated that the secondary schools of the region would require 1,280,000 teachers in 1970 as compared with 840,000 in 1958—an increase of 440,000 or about 50 per cent. However, when replacements of about one-third of those employed in 1958 are added, the gross increase is 730,000 teachers who must come from the universities, teacher-training institutes and colleges, and some general secondary schools. Assuming that teacher-training institutions will supply one-half the gross increase, the number of students at these institutions would have to be increased from about 130,000 to about 470,000. Tinbergen and Bos, therefore, conclude that "in order to raise the number of students in secondary education by about 80 per cent between 1958 and 1970, the facilities for teacher training would have to increase by well over 250 per cent."[9]

---

[7] *Ibid.*, p. 77.
[8] *Ibid.*, p. 78.
[9] *Ibid.*, p. 79.

This, of course, introduces the critical question: how to provide the necessary number of qualified teachers for the training institutions. It was estimated that the number would have to be increased from 7,000 in 1958 to 16,000 in 1965 and to 23,000 in 1970 for Africa, Asia, and Latin America. "As the gross increase during this period will exceed the net increase of 9,000, it follows that the advanced countries will have to provide some 8,000 to 10,000 'teachers' teachers' before 1965—a figure which clearly shows the impact the development of secondary education in the underdeveloped world must have on the advanced countries."[10]

These estimates may simply illustrate the impossible. However, they do indicate that even for a very modest rate of growth, vast resources, both local and foreign, must be channeled into a *continuing* program of educational development, that these resources must be used *as efficiently as possible*, and that every effort must be made by experiment and research to develop more effective methods of teaching and learning. This is a formidable challenge to the various assistance agencies.

While the shortage of qualified teachers is probably the main deterrent to educational development, it is also imperative that the educational requirements of the area be assessed in relation to the development potentialities of the country in order to formulate appropriate priorities for the balanced expansion of education. This involves decisions about the proper balance between primary, secondary, and advanced education, about the proper balance between general education and technical and vocational training, and about the kinds of technical and vocational training most suitable to the circumstances. There is also the problem of the content of the curriculum for general education, having in mind the cultural, social, and political values and conventions of the people. How much and what kinds of research should be initiated and maintained? Deciding what constitutes properly balanced expansion in a particular region is most difficult and no formula is suitable for all situations.

In Latin America, elementary education was given top priority at the Santiago Conference in March, 1962. The aim was to eliminate illiteracy during the next ten years for the population in the appropriate age group. Apart from the fact that six years in school is no guarantee of literacy even in Canada, too rapid increase of primary education can have serious consequences. It will probably accelerate migration from rural to urban communities in search of better-paid clerical jobs in government and private offices. The net result at least in the short run may be a very large volume of unemployment in the towns and cities, as appears to have happened in West Africa. This is a short-run phenomenon. In the long run, a community can absorb any number. Furthermore, as W.A. Lewis remarked: "Where fundamental social change is necessary for development it is possible that by producing educated numbers far in excess of absorptive capacity one may ultimately create a new situation in which a revolutionary increase in absorptive capacity has occurred."[11]

---

10 *Ibid.*
11 W. A. Lewis, "Education and Economic Development," Information Document No. 4, Conference on Education and Economic and Social Development in Latin America, Santiago, March 1962, p. 4.

Primary and secondary education fosters mobility. In many countries there is a bias against primary and secondary education in favor of training for technical and trades positions; for administration, public and private; and for specific areas such as agriculture, public health, and the like. These are preferred because they obviously fill immediate needs, and, of course, it is important that these needs be met. University education is highly regarded in most underdeveloped countries and in some has produced "educated unemployed," as, for example, lawyers in Latin America and engineers in Israel. Also, professional training may raise the sights of the professional to the point where it is beneath his dignity to engage in anything but administration. It has been said that this attitude prevails amongst Indian engineers.

The ultimate goal for elementary education must be the provision for all in the appropriate age group of four to six years in school. However, since the higher levels of education which must go with this extension of elementary education cannot be provided at the same time by poor countries, they should approach the goal slowly. Lewis has pointed out that "those who make compulsory primary education their first priority are asking for trouble, and get it. Their budgets are strained by teachers' salaries, their towns are disordered by the influx of primary school graduates seeking clerical jobs, and their lives are harassed by irate parents demanding secondary, university and other superior training facilities to which similar priority has not been accorded."[12] Lewis suggests for sub-Saharan Africa a first target of 50 per cent of the age group in elementary school, 5 per cent in secondary, and .5 per cent in university, to be increased, after achieving the first target, to 100 per cent, 10 per cent, and 1 per cent. Secondary general education would have to be supplemented by technical and trade training to the extent required. Lewis' suggestion is for Africa. At this stage of development the targets could be higher for India and Latin America. The expansion of education must be preceded by an intensive program of teacher training either at home or abroad, and it is this kind of outside assistance which is most valuable in the early stages of educational expansion.

Underdeveloped countries often have cultural patterns which are inimical to economic growth. Traditional agricultural methods are firmly adhered to. Where animal husbandry consists in following the rains, where shifting agriculture prevails, and where irrigation depends on the "shadouf" or the "sagia," the demonstration of better methods to an illiterate population is not enough. Customs, beliefs, superstitions even, which inhibit economic growth are hard to eradicate. Western-type industrialism requires continuous attention to duty rather than the somewhat casual application of bursts of energy followed by periods of relative inactivity which may be more suitable to primitive agriculture. I think we can agree that cultural and social change are necessary concomitants of economic growth. Not only is this most difficult to achieve, but it involves a grave risk—the risk that the existing cultural pattern may be destroyed without there being put in its place a way of life that will sustain the people in their newly developing economic environment.

---

[12]*Ibid.*, p. 14.

Education can be imported or, within limits, produced at home. Elementary education and most secondary education must be provided in the home country, but at the higher levels of technical education and the university there is a choice between providing it from domestic resources or from such resources as may be made available by assistance agencies without cost to the recipient country.

Imported education may consist in employing foreign administrators, engineers, accountants, economists, and the like, by inviting agencies to send technical experts for a few years—Schultz's "light workhorses"—or by inviting the representatives of financial assistance agencies as a preliminary to obtaining a loan or grant or expert assistance of some kind. Another possibility is to send people abroad for advanced study, professional or technical training, and in-service training in government and industry.

In my view, too much reliance has been placed on imported education by developing countries. This is in part because these countries are in a hurry and in part because of the competition of assistance agencies, governments, and private organizations to provide aid. There has been too much emphasis on crash programs and not enough on long-range programs of education. Wasted effort is often the result. For example, the foreign technical expert is generally expected to train counterparts in the country he is serving. But very frequently there are no counterparts to train, or if there are such, they are insufficiently educated to benefit from the training. The expert, therefore, finds himself struggling with minor assistance in planning, or in implementing a plan, which the natives should be learning to do for themselves.

At the elementary and secondary level the most urgent needs is for trained teachers, and the most significant form of assistance from outside is aid in setting up teacher-training institutions, that is, planning the curriculum, planning the physical plant, and providing qualified teachers. Apart from the prohibitive cost of sending students abroad for teacher training, there is the serious defect that the training abroad would be generally unsuitable for the circumstances within which the teacher must eventually work. The curriculum requires careful planning along lines that are relevant to the culture and to the ultimate economic and social objectives of the country in question. This applies to technical and trade training as well as to general education.

In the universities at the undergraduate level the same general principles apply. The new universities need a great deal of assistance from abroad in planning, organization and administration, and teaching until a sufficient number of the native population have completed graduate work and are ready to join the university staff. I should like to see contiguous countries cooperate in the development of universities rather than dissipate their resources in establishing numbers of institutions in the early stages of development for purposes of prestige. They might establish junior colleges in each of the countries with intercountry cooperation in senior undergraduate work and in graduate work and research. For some time, however, a good part of the graduate work will have to be done in foreign universities. This has the defect that, in the sciences and professions in particular, graduate training tends to be specific to the Western world and remote from the requirements of the poor countries.

Western universities, and foundations, governments, and assistance agencies can perform a significant role in advancing the level of education in poor countries. "Twinning" arrangements such as that of the University of British Columbia with the University of Malaya could be usefully extended. In this instance, the University of British Columbia is assisting the University of Malaya in establishing a School of Commerce by sending UBC instructors to Malaya and by receiving Malayan instructors in Vancouver for training. This could be extended by universities to education, engineering, medicine, and other fields, and in particular to teacher training. Universities, agencies, and foundations could establish centres for research into specific local problems and these centres in themselves could become institutions for training local personnel. The Rockefeller Foundation has established such centres in Mexico and Colombia, and, I understand, they have achieved considerable success.

Newly developing countries are in a hurry. They would like to accomplish in twenty-five years or less what the Western world has accomplished in two hundred years. There are, of course, emergencies, and crash programs are sometimes indicated. But often too much emphasis has been placed on the programs which are expected to yield results quickly. Education, training, and research are strong and relatively cheap sources of economic growth, but they cannot make their full contribution unless planned to fit the social, cultural, and political fabric of the area and the long-run aims and ambitions of its people. To make its full contribution to growth in developing countries, the educational program must be well conceived, well planned, and enduring.

Selection **13**

The Importance of Changing
Behavior Patterns

NATHAN ROSENBERG

From: "Capital Formation in Underdeveloped Countries," American
Economic Review, *Vol. L, No. 4 (Sept. 1960), pp. 706–715. Reprinted
by permission of the* American Economic Review *and the author.*

In the rapidly growing volume of literature on the problems and prospects
for economic development, considerable attention is being devoted to the determinants of net capital formation or, more particularly, to the obstacles to and
limitations upon capital formation in underdeveloped countries. This preoccupation is, without question, well deserved. One need not subscribe to a monocausal
theory of development to argue that an increase in the percentage of annual
output devoted to investment is an urgent and indispensable prerequisite to a
long-term rise in real per capita incomes. Indeed, current attempts at what is now
being called, rather pretentiously, "development programming," often consist
exclusively of measures designed to raise the over-all rate of capital formation
and to exert some centralized guidance over the allocation of investment resources.[1]

A central question in a theory of development, then, is: why are rates of capital
formation as low as they apparently are in most underdeveloped countries?
Economists can hardly be accused of having neglected this question. Indeed, it
will be suggested that we now have too many explanations.

Explanations of capital deficiency are commonly organized in terms of two
separate sets of forces: factors accounting for low saving propensities, on the
one hand, and those responsible for weakness in the inducement to invest, on the
other. However, such an approach leads to a preoccupation with certain phenomena and preference patterns which are commonly treated as independent causal
agents, although there appear to be compelling reasons for regarding them as the
superficial consequences of more fundamental factors.

---

[1] "A programme of economic development is the expression of a simple idea, namely, the
desirability of increasing and judiciously regulating capital investment, so that a stronger impetus and greater order may be given to the growth of the country." U. N. Economic Commission
for Latin America, *Analyses and Projections of Economic Development*, I: An Introduction to the
Technique of Programming (New York, 1955), p. 3.

It is proposed to show that certain preference and behavior patterns which are commonly observed in underdeveloped countries are in fact part of an elaborate adaptive mechanism geared to an economic environment characterized by a generally low marginal efficiency of capital and by a limited spectrum of profit opportunities. It will in fact be suggested that an adequate explanation of the general weakness of investment incentives and of the peculiar distribution of profit prospects in different sectors of underdeveloped economies would, *by itself*, account for many of the other apparent causes of low rates of capital formation. It will be demonstrated that the failure to "shake out the implications" of weak investment incentives has led not only to a double-counting of "causes" of low rates of investment but also to serious analytical errors and highly questionable judgments.

I. LOW AGGREGATE SAVINGS

The most obvious explanation for low rates of capital formation is the present poverty of underdeveloped countries. Their capacity to undertake productive investment appears to be sharply limited by the very low levels of per capita income combined with the frequently extravagant expenditure patterns of the rich and an interest, among virtually all income classes, in the acquisition of certain kinds of durable consumer goods.

What is not so apparent, however, is that individuals in underdeveloped countries may regard the acquisition of certain types of consumer goods as a form of personal saving and investment. This may well be the case for a variety of so-called luxury goods, especially such items as jewelry and precious ornaments which may constitute excellent stores of value in an environment characterized by political insecurity or inflationary pressures. Even where such conditions do not prevail, the absence of well-developed and reputable financial institutions may provide strong inducements for the acquisition of jewelry, gold, or even foreign assets as relatively secure forms of personal saving. To the extent that this is so, our present measures of capital formation may significantly understate the capacity for saving and productive investment in underdeveloped economies. What appear to be low rates of saving in underdeveloped countries may be attributable, in part, to the fact that durable consumer goods are acquired and held not so much as the result of a real taste preference as because these goods are regarded as a form of personal saving in a backward economic environment.

A closely related and much more serious difficulty of a theoretical nature arises over the common practice of explaining low rates of productive investment in terms of the failure of underdeveloped economies to generate a sufficient flow of domestic savings. The low rate of saving is in turn attributed to practices and preferences which squander the "potential economic surplus"—purchases of jewelry and gold, acquisition of foreign currencies and assets, lavish consumption expenditure patterns of the upper income classes, etc. In a certain sense such actions do help to explain the low rates of saving and productive investment, but only in the same sense as the statement "I prefer to stay home and watch television tonight" explains why I do *not* attend the local high school concert. It seems necessary to insist that statements of preference call for an examination and evaluation of the nature and comparative attractiveness of available alternatives. Precisely what is involved here is the unattractiveness of the alternatives, i.e., the unprofitable nature and/or high risk factor attaching to productive investment in underdeveloped countries. Low rates of saving and the absence of attractive investment opportunities are not independent of one another and cannot be treated as entirely separate and unrelated causes of capital deficiency. Rather, the actions referred to above may, to a large extent, be attributed to the "undeveloped" nature of the investment mechanism and to the complex of forces which weaken the inducement to invest.

The problem discussed here cannot be dismissed as of a "Which came first, the chicken or egg?" nature—not, at least, without discarding much of Keynesian economics. That is to say, the same forces which account for the weak inducement to undertake productive investment may also account, in large measure, for the unproductive disposition of potential savings; and policies which have the effect of raising the marginal efficiency of capital schedule and therefore increasing the inducement to invest may reasonably be expected to induce, at the same time, an increased flow of (ex ante as well as ex post) domestic saving.

Implicit in much of the current discussion, however, is the classical assumption that the real limitations upon investment lie in the limited willingness or capacity of the public to save, and that, therefore, an increased propensity to save is all that is needed to generate an increased flow of productive investment activity. Such analysis, however, often not only ignores the current weakness in the inducement to invest, but may also overlook the fact that an increased propensity to save, by its adverse effect upon the marginal efficiency of capital schedule, may weaken the inducement to invest even further.

Moreover, the priority which is usually attached to the need to increase savings as a precondition for raising the rate of capital formation really involves the concealed premise that an increased rate of capital formation ought not to be achieved at the expense of domestic inflation. Obviously, all measures or policies which result in a transfer of resources from the production of consumer goods to the production of investment goods necessarily generate an equivalent amount of ex post savings. This is not to ignore the many cogent reasons for avoiding the inflationary route, but merely to suggest that the currently fashionable way of stating the problem may be seriously misleading.

II. METHODS OF HOLDING ASSETS

The preoccupation with the low level of domestic saving in underdeveloped areas as an independent determinant of low rates of capital formation creates a host of difficulties in attempting to move from the micro- to the macroeconomic level of analysis. The general problem involved here is the macroeconomic consequences of certain kinds of asset preferences on the part of individual savers. It is important that we distinguish between (1) factors which affect the aggregate volume of savings, and (2) the *forms* in which an individual chooses to hold his assets.

It is frequently held, e.g., that when an individual chooses to hold a net increase in his assets in the form of liquid balances (i.e., "hoarding") that this does not result in genuine saving in an aggregative sense, i.e., in the release of resources for nonconsumption purposes.

This argument appears to result partly from the failure to distinguish between the hoarding of cash balances and the "hoarding" of physical assets—jewelry, gold, or other durable commodities—the acquisition of which may involve a drain upon scarce domestic resources (or the supplies of foreign currencies, if imported.)[2]

The hoarding of cash balances, even in the absence of appropriate financial institutions, will nevertheless result in the release of resources which might otherwise have been used for consumption purposes and therefore creates an added potential for capital formation.[3] Obviously, such hoarding does not ensure that resources will be devoted to investment purposes. The deflationary consequences and the unfavorable impact upon interest rates and the inducement to invest may simply result in unemployment and an increase in the volume of unused resources. The point is that hoarding of cash balances in no way absorbs real resources but releases them from consumption uses, just as do other forms of saving. To the extent that savers decide to add to their stocks of liquid assets, the possibilities for raising the rate of capital formation are increased, and may be realized, for example, in a noninflationary fashion by deficit spending on the part of the government. Whether such possibilities *are* realized is not at issue. The essential point is that hoarding of cash balances, in itself, releases rather than absorbs real resources.

Although the hoarding of cash balances does not reduce the volume of savings, it may have an important consequence in limiting the availability of financial resources to certain potential borrowers and therefore influencing the composition of the capital formation which takes place. In this respect the hoarding of cash balances is one aspect of the more general problem of the deficient or inappropriate financial institutions of underdeveloped countries. In spite of the extremely serious nature of the latter problem, however, it needs to be kept conceptually distinct from the forces determining the volume, as opposed to the composition, of investment activity. Much confusion may result from the failure to maintain a clear distinction between the determinants of the volume of saving, on the one hand, and the factors influencing the supply and availability of financial resources, on the other.[4]

---

[2] "Though the potential of capital formation in underdeveloped regions seems considerable when judged by the high share of output retained by the landowner, actual capital formation goes on at low rates. Oriental landlords have been known for generations for their high propensity towards 'unproductive' use of accumulated revenues. Even if the money is not spent in travelling abroad, it is invested largely in hoards of cash, jewellery and gold." A. Bonné, *Studies in Economic Development* (London, 1957), p. 38.

[3] Of course it is possible that the absence of secure financial institutions discourages the saving habit and that individuals would save more readily if they had convenient access to a bank or other saving institution. Moreover, the absence of adequate financial institutions may also partly account for the habit of acquiring and holding goods as a liquid asset.

[4] See A. Bonné, *op. cit.*, esp. pp. 197–203, for an example of such confusion.

As has already been pointed out, hoarding frequently takes the form of the acquisition of physical commodities such as jewelry, gold, or other durable assets which are regarded as highly liquid and which possess the added advantage over cash balances that they may constitute useful hedges against inflation or political uncertainty. Such preferences obviously involve (in a closed economy) the use of domestic resources in their production and may therefore be regarded as absorbing scarce productive agents. However, certain structural features and other peculiarities of underdeveloped economies may play an important role in determining the consequences of such preferences. An increased propensity to hoard commodities whose domestic elasticity of production is very low (as seems to be the case, for example, with gold mining in India) will result almost exclusively in a price effect and virtually no output effect; it will not significantly increase the quantity of the commodities hoarded, nor will it result in an increased use of domestic resources for such purposes. There may, then, be sharply defined limits to the extent to which a preference for hoarding physical goods results in an absorption of domestic resources. If, moreover, there are legal (and adequately enforceable) restrictions upon the importation of a commodity whose domestic elasticity of production is very low, the results of an increased preference for such commodities are formally similar to an increased preference for nonreproducible assets.[5]

III. Preference for Investment in Land

The classic example of nonreproducible assets is, of course, land. It appears to be a widely held belief that one of the reasons for the low rates of capital formation in underdeveloped countries is that upper-income groups employ their savings in the purchase of land. The following statement by Meier and Baldwin [*Economic Development: Theory, History, Policy* (New York, 1957), pp. 307–308] is illustrative[6]: ". . . inequality in the distribution of income does not contribute as much to productive investment as might be expected . . . (because) the group at the top of the income pyramid is composed of landowners and traders who tend to invest in more land, real estate speculation, capital flights, or inventory accumulation rather than long-term industrial investments or public utilities."

Assuming that the purchase of land was financed out of current incomes, such individual savings must have resulted in the release of real resources for nonconsumption purposes. Insofar as a desire for the acquisition of land generates a willingness to abstain from current consumption, it thereby increases the volume of *ex ante* saving and may, indeed, be one of the most important motives for such saving in underdeveloped countries. If we assume that net saving is positive (i.e.,

---

[5] Where such commodities may be legally imported (or where they are successfully smuggled into the country in spite of import restrictions), the result is a drain upon domestic resources because of the increased exports ultimately resulting from such transactions. The effect is the same as if people were acquiring foreign currency or other foreign assets.

[6] Cf. also W. A. Lewis, *The Theory of Economic Growth* (Homewood, Ill.: Richard D. Irwin, Inc., 1955), p. 227; and United Nations, *Processes and Problems of Industrialization in Underdeveloped Countries* (New York: United Nations, 1955), p. 22.

that the savings of some individuals are not offset by the dissavings of others) and that total output does not decline, an equivalent amount of capital formation of some sort must be taking place within the economy.

A "preference for investment in land," whatever it may do to the price of land and the distribution of landholdings, does not, *in itself*, reduce the volume of capital formation by "absorbing" a part of current saving. Nevertheless, the belief that it does so seems to be firmly entrenched in the current literature. It is true, of course, that from the point of view of the individual investor, such a purchase represents a real alternative to the purchase (and creation) of a new capital good. However, the analysis ought not to be terminated, as it typically is, with the purchase of an existing, as opposed to a new, asset. The ultimate impact of the transaction will depend, among other things, upon how the seller chooses to dispose of the revenue received from the sale of his asset. If, as is at least conceivable, the seller of land intends to use the proceeds to acquire a new, reproducible capital good, the ultimate result will be an addition to the community's stock of such goods. It is only where the saving of the buyer is offset by an equivalent amount of dissaving on the part of the seller out of such revenue that real saving (and capital formation) are not increased. Although this is a possible consequence, there seem to be no compelling reasons for regarding it as a necessary consequence of land purchases.

Although a strong preference for land need not, as is commonly asserted, automatically reduce real saving and capital formation, it may have this as well as other important consequences, under certain special circumstances and via a more circuitous mechanism than has yet been specified. For example, in agricultural economies where land is a highly liquid asset, the ease of borrowing, on the part of landowners, by using their land as collateral, may induce a higher level of consumption expenditure and/or the growth of debt for strictly consumption purposes on the part of the owners of land. In such a case aggregate saving will be reduced, not because of the preference for land per se, but rather because such a preference makes possible an upward shift in the consumption expenditures of landowners.[7]

Some such process may, in the past, have played a significant role in reducing aggregate saving in peasant economies. If, to the generally low level of real incomes of small landowners are added the pressures resulting from population growth, occasional crop failure, and a variety of other emergency (as well as ceremonial) occasions, the high liquidity uniquely attaching to land may have been the strategic factor making possible the growth of rural indebtedness for strictly consumption purposes.[8]

Moreover, if the rate of return on money lending to an impoverished peasantry, who borrow on the strength of their small landholdings, is very high (and there

---

[7] This, of course, may cut both ways. The high liquidity attaching to land may facilitate borrowing on the part of landowners for investment rather than consumption. All that is suggested here is a set of circumstances under which a strong attachment to land *may* reduce capital formation.

[8] It is also possible that the bidding up of the price of land may induce owners of land to increase their consumption expenditures or to dissave because of the increase in the market value of their asset.

is much evidence that this is so), we have an important factor accounting for the low level of investment in industrial enterprises in underdeveloped countries. In addition to such well-known deterrents as high degree of risk, limited markets, and absence of external economies attaching to industrial investment in under-developed countries is the decisive consideration that rates of return for rural lending, even after discounting for risk, are extremely high, partly for institutional reasons and partly because of serious market imperfections.[9]

A further possible consequence of a strong preference for holding land is that it may reduce industrial investment by establishing high interest rates on borrowed funds which act as a deterrent to potential industrial entrepreneurs. A strong preference for land means that owners of wealth (potential lenders) can earn high rates of return by lending money for the purchase of land (i.e., buying mortgages). The combination of a small and inelastic supply of funds with a relatively high demand for their use serves to establish unusually high rates of interest. Therefore potential borrowers for industrial investment find that they must compete, in borrowing funds, with people whose preference for land is such that they are willing to pay extremely high rates of interest for such funds. In this respect a strong preference for land acts as a serious deterrent to industrial investment.

This last case is similar to the one which Keynes seems to have regarded as of major importance [J. M. Keynes, *The General Theory of Employment, Interest and Money* (New York, 1936), p. 241]:

> ... it is conceivable that there have been occasions in history in which the desire to hold land has played the same role in keeping up the rate of interest at too high a level which money has played in recent times. ... The high rates of interest from mortgages on land, often exceeding the probable net yield from cultivating the land, have been a familiar feature of many agricultural economies ... in earlier social organizations where long-term bonds in the modern sense were non-existent, the competition of a high interest-rate on mortgages may well have had the same effect in retarding the growth of wealth from current investment in newly produced capital-assets, as high interest rates on long-term debts have had in more recent times.

Thus, statements to the effect that a preference for land on the part of upper-income groups automatically reduces real saving and investment are, at worst, incorrect and, at best, highly elliptic. Where saving and investment are in fact reduced, it is due not to the preference for land by itself, but because of the presence of other important conditions which are often unspecified.

IV. INADEQUACY OF ENTREPRENEURIAL TALENTS

Much attention has been devoted, in recent years, to the apparent shortage of entrepreneurship in underdeveloped countries. It has become fashionable to deplore the absence of Schumpeterian entrepreneurs, and many economists have

---

[9] Evidence on the profitability of rural lending is available from many sources. Among recent works, Reserve Bank of India, *All-India Rural Credit Survey* (Bombay, 1954), esp. Vol. II. Ch. 14, and U Tun Wai, "Interest Rates Outside the Organized Money Markets of Underdeveloped Countries," *International Monetary Fund Staff Papers* (Nov. 1957), pp. 249–278, will be found very illuminating.

dwelt at length upon political, sociological, and historical explanations for this shortage. Although such noneconomic explanations are not to be despised, it is difficult to avoid the conclusion that these people have been led into a faulty line of analysis by excessive preoccupation with their own definitions. Having defined entrepreneurs as those daring and imaginative individuals who undertake risky long-term industrial investments, the observed absence of such investment in underdeveloped countries is then attributed to the absence of entrepreneurs. A more plausible and purely economic explanation, or at least a more fruitful working hypothesis, is that most underdeveloped countries possess a reasonable number of people with entrepreneurial talents, but that these people behave in a subjectively rational fashion when they adopt short economic horizons and avoid long-term commitments in industry. Many of the activities referred to in this paper in fact help to account for the often-lamented "absence" of entrepreneurship in under-developed countries.

To quote from an interesting paper by Henry Aubrey ["Investment Decisions in Underdeveloped Countries," in *Capital Formation and Economic Growth*, a report of the National Bureau of Economic Research, (Princeton, 1955), p. 398]:

> *The acquisition of real estate is often considered as evidence of sentimental attachment to land or of feudal patterns of unproductive investment. This explanation may be perfectly correct in some instances; in others, however, such "investment" may result from preferences well founded in the expectation of profit or, conversely, of security against a danger of depreciation that might face other forms of asset-holding.*

Rather than infer from the absence of long-term industrial investment the nonexistence of entrepreneurs, it seems more reasonable to infer that potential entrepreneurs, in evaluating alternative opportunities (including the purchase of existing assets), usually conclude that personal income maximization is not to be achieved in long-term industrial activities. In so doing, entrepreneurs are not necessarily irrational or behaving in response to considerations of social status, prestige, family honor, or even necessarily lacking in the "capitalist spirit." Considering the special circumstances of many underdeveloped countries, their decisions may constitute a perfectly rational evaluation of the structure of economic opportunities. The notion that there is an extreme scarcity of entrepreneurship in underdeveloped countries usually involves a failure to distinguish between the aggregate supply of entrepreneurship and its distribution. To employ the terminology recently adapted by Leibenstein from Von Neumann and Morgenstern, potential entrepreneurs are behaving in un-Schumpeterian but subjectively rational fashion by selecting to play zero-sum rather than positive-sum games. If adherents of the entrepreneurial school of thought reply that such people are not, by *their* definition, entrepreneurs, they must weigh the serious consideration that such businessmen could conform to their definition only by deliberately failing to employ the calculus of profit maximization.

This question of the determinants of investment decisions in underdeveloped countries deserves more attention than it has so far received. It has, unfortunately, often been lost sight of in the current practice of indiscriminately lumping together a highly heterogeneous combination of factors which are presumed to be responsible for low rates of capital formation and unproductive investment patterns in low-income countries. The following statement by Gunner Myrdal is illustrative [*An International Economy* (New York, 1956), pp. 202–203; italics added].

> It is . . . *highly characteristic of all the underdeveloped countries that their business classes are bent upon earning quick profits not by promoting long-term real investment and production but by buying and selling, moneylending, and other* easier ways *of making money, which also often escape taxation. Profits tend to be invested in land, or else hoarded or transferred abroad, when they are not dissipated in a costly display of wealth and social status. There is a low propensity to save and to invest productively in new enterprises.*

Myrdal's statement seems to imply that the investment pattern which he deplores is somehow connected with certain peculiar features of the "business classes" of underdeveloped countries. Yet, by his own assertion, they are merely pursuing the "easier ways of making money." Surely what is significant in this context is the existence of such opportunities and not the fact that businessmen take advantage of them. Is it at all probable that "Westernized" entrepreneurs would behave differently when confronted with the same spectrum of alternatives?

V. Conclusions

A theory of economic development (which involves, of course, an analysis of why development does *not* take place as well as why it does) must include, above all, an explanation for the existing structure and distribution of market opportunities in underdeveloped countries. The fundamental question in an *economic* theory of economic development is: why is the structure of market opportunities in underdeveloped countries of such a nature that it fails to provide the personal incentive for individuals to undertake those activities which appear to be conducive to economic growth? When this question has been adequately answered, many of the other pieces in our puzzle will fall easily into place as dependent, rather than independent, variables. The low amount of *ex post* savings, the widespread preference for the acquisition of assets which fail to enlarge productive capacity, the apparent malallocation of the small volume of resources which are devoted to investment purposes, the "scarcity" of entrepreneurship, and the propensity to engage in short-term speculative ventures all fall, to a substantial degree, within this category. They represent behavior patterns which may reasonably be expected either to disappear or significantly decline in importance in the face of a drastic outward shift in the marginal efficiency of capital schedule.

Selection **14**

The Desirability
of Social Change

MAX F. MILLIKAN and
DONALD L. M. BLACKMER (eds.)

From: The Emerging Nations: Their Growth and United States
Policy (*Boston: Little, Brown and Company, 1961*), *pp. 27–42. Reprinted
by permission of Little, Brown and Company;* © *1961, Massachusetts
Institute of Technology.*

In the early period of transition, when a society begins to break out of its
traditional structure, the most powerful social class often consists of the men who
own or control the land, a group likely to be deeply conservative in every respect.
Feeling a deep attachment to the old ways of life, and sensing that social and
technological change threatens their hegemony, they tend to resist all efforts to
modernize. In Africa, where communal landholding by the tribe is common, such
resistance is often identified less with distinctions of social class than with a widespread commitment to the tribal way of life as a whole.

Where landowners do exist as a substantial and powerful class, their strategy
has sometimes been to resist by partially adopting new ways; in such cases they
have often retained some of their power as individuals while their power as a class
was waning. Where landowners have resisted all efforts at modernization, the
landed class and its members have generally gone down together. The basic shift
to urban and industrial life, which is the core process of modernization, has always
spelled the end of hegemony by landowners as a class. In tribal societies the
transformation is not in the status of a landowning class but in that of tribal prerog-
atives as a whole.

A traditional society is also characterized by the absence of an indigenous
middle class large enough or strong enough to challenge the landowners' power.
In the early stages of transition, therefore, the decisive challenge to the landlords'
supremacy generally comes not from any one social class but from a coalition,
a group that varies considerably in specific composition from one country to another but whose leadership is almost invariably made up of men deeply affected by
Western ways of thought and action.

In colonial countries those at the forefront of independence movements have

142

often received a university education in the West, sometimes being trained for one of the professions, such as law or medicine. They may also have been introduced to Western patterns of thought and organization through military corps, administration, and industrial and trade union organizations. In countries without colonial histories, such as Turkey, leadership has sometimes been assumed by military officers whose sense of power combined with a strong sense of national pride created in them a desire to lead the way to modernity.

Whatever their particular background, those who lead the fight for independence, or in noncolonial societies the struggle to displace the landowning class, are likely to be more skilled in the political and military tasks of achieving power than in the arts of governing and modernizing a traditional society. Depending on the circumstances and problems of achieving independence, they may become skilled in communicating with and organizing peasants and workers for disruptive activity, in writing revolutionary tracts and editing revolutionary journals, or in conducting guerrilla warfare. Once independence or power is achieved, they often find it difficult to turn their minds and convert their skills to the tasks of modernization. As a result, the first generation of new leaders is often inadequately prepared by experience and training to deal with the problems confronting them when responsibility is attained. Thus progress toward modernization is inevitably slow in the early transitional period. Groups within the governing elite are likely to contend in an erratic and unstable manner, with frequent shifts of power from one to another. Moreover, the elite groups tend to rally around individuals, the substance of whose programs may be ambiguous and unclear even to themselves. Political activity revolves around issues of power and personality rather than around alternative national policies.

Nevertheless, during this period certain dynamic forces are at work in the society which tend to move the social structure and the political debate into a new phase. First, contacts with more modern societies are likely to increase the number of persons trained in the West or otherwise introduced to modern ideas and skills. Second, the very responsibility of managing a national government, even if conducted without great skill and purpose, tends to enlarge the number of men with modern attitudes and commitments. Third, even if sustained economic growth is unlikely at this early stage, commercial activity is likely to increase, cities to grow, and some experiments in industrialization to be undertaken. Finally, because progress is slow and the high hopes and optimistic slogans that accompanied the arrival of independence (or the proclamation of a modern-style government) remain still largely unfulfilled, there is a dynamic created by the sense of frustration on the part of members of the younger generation of the Westernized elite.

A combination of such forces may bring into being a coalition determined to push forward with a more purposeful program of modernization. The balance of the social elements in such a coalition varies widely according to the initial structure of the traditional society and its experience during transition. In some instances, as in Turkey and Egypt, the coalition has contained a large percentage of men from the military; in others (for example, the Congress Party in India) the military has played no significant role. Almost invariably at some stage in the process, though not necessarily at the beginning, intellectuals and professionally trained men have been influential. Occasionally leaders of commerce and industry have played a prominent role, as did Birla in India. In a few places, particularly in Latin America, individual landowners have also played a constructive part, largely as a consequence of a partial shift in their investments out of agriculture and into the industrial sector of the economy. It is in general true that the social basis for the modernizing coalition has lain in the city and in the essentially urban skills of the elite, particularly the military and intellectual elite, who have adopted Western attitudes.

If this modernizing coalition meets with some success, and modernization actually begins to make a dent upon the society, the pace of social change steps up rapidly. New people begin to take over the shaping of public policy, people with the attitudes and technical skills needed to perform the manifold tasks of urbanization, industrialization, and monetization as well as the complex tasks produced by the rationalization of work and the secularization of beliefs.

In general, and with deference to the variety of specific forms that modernization has taken historically and in the contemporary scene, the central tendency of sociological change appears to be the multiplication of key social roles—in part new roles, in part adaptations of old ones. As life becomes more technically oriented, power and prestige shift away from the few dominant men in the traditional structure—the wealthy pasha, the wise priest, the village elder—toward men equipped to perform more specific functions in the modern division of labor. Professional and technical skills are required for the roles associated with the growth of cities and the spread of industries, the technical advances and monetization of agriculture, the growing dependence of public policy upon an informed and participant citizenry. The banker and the economist tend to replace the landowner and moneylender as sources of cash and managers of credit; the industrialist and manager replace the merchant and trader; the civil servant, the engineer, the agronomist, and others take over special functions that earlier were concentrated in village elders and other men of hereditary wealth or wisdom.

We shall deal particularly with three of the groups often found in the modernizing coalition: first, the military, which is playing a decisive role in many transitional societies today; second, the secular intelligentsia, the manipulators of symbols who shape the slogans and doctrines by which the new ways of life are rationalized and justified; third, the innovating entrepreneurs of many sorts who play a crucial role in modernization.

THE MILITARY

With the exception of most parts of Africa, substantial military groups having considerable political and social influence have played a significant role in the modernization process. The likely social origins of the military group in a transitional society, the nature of their profession, and the context in which they operate help explain their potential for leadership.

The top officer group was often traditionally from the landowning class and committed to the preservation of old privileges and social relationships. But lower officers sometimes came from other classes; their social status was not high, and they were consequently not so firmly committed to defend the old social order. Moreover, because the military has recently had to be expanded in many countries, officers have increasingly tended to come from less elite classes—even from craftsmen or peasant groups—and sometimes are dissatisfied with the old order.

In addition, a contemporary military organization is by nature a modern rather than a traditional structure. In concept at least, men are arrayed according to function and advanced according to skill and reliability in the execution of this function. They are judged by individual performance rather than by their connection with other persons, family group, or clan. While these objective norms have by no means been fully and promptly recognized in all the armies that have emerged in transitional societies, they have nevertheless exercised a powerful modernizing influence.

This influence has been strengthened by the care and resources often devoted by professionals from Western societies to the training of the military, and by traditional pride in military prowess, which has made it easy for restless individuals to find satisfaction in a military career. It is no accident that competent and distinguished military units have emerged in transitional societies well ahead of modern institutions in the civil service, politics, or the economy; for example, the Indian army, the Malay Regiments, the Philippine Scouts, the Arab Legion, the Gurkha Regiments, and the King's Own African Rifles. As long as these forces were controlled by foreign powers they were naturally conservative—or at least their feelings of rebellion at colonial policies were suppressed. But once independence was achieved, the military could acquire only through the national government the equipment and the professional stature they sought. It is of the nature of the modern military profession to accept a concept like nationalism with all its implications for modernization.

Finally, the members of the officer corps are likely to face an easier set of problems in the transitional period than their civilian counterparts within the new leadership. They may have to undertake military operations either against the colonial power or against residual traditional elements, but where successful, these exercises arouse confidence in their strength. Aside from combat itself, their tasks are to acquire new equipment, to train men in their use, and to maintain with reasonable efficiency the peacetime round of military life—inherently an easier job than to get political, social, and economic programs organized for the society as a whole. Thus it is possible for the army to develop a group of confident officers with modern attitudes and modern skills, operating within a reasonably orderly modern institution administered on relatively modern lines.

Supplementing these broad influences on the officer corps is the fact that those who are recruited into the army are given with their training a certain minimum technical education for modern life. Historically armies in transitional societies have been a vehicle for expanding literacy; and the handling of motor transport, guns, and other military equipment has tended to spread elements of basic training in industrial skills rather quickly through the army. The Burmese army, for example, in addition to the standard engineer corps and signal corps, has special chemical warfare and psychological warfare sections and even an historical and archaeological section. In all the new armies attempts have been made to introduce specialized training schools and advanced techniques of personnel and procurement. Inevitably, then, a certain number of officers and men are being trained in industrial skills more advanced than those common to the civilian economy.

It is by no means foreordained—as the history of the military in Latin America amply demonstrates—that their potentials for modernization will automatically and constructively harness the military to the modernization process. The military leadership may for long periods build and maintain their modern units in a vacuum, drawing important resources from the society but keeping aloof from its civilian problems and making little contribution to their solution. The officer corps may develop a hypernationalism and throw its inevitably substantial political weight toward external adventure, diverting the society from modernizing tasks. It may exploit its unity and high degree of organization to seize power but bring to power little insight and sympathy for the complex civil tasks of modernization. In some instances its political weight has been used to preserve the status of groups rooted in the traditional society who conceived it to be in their interest to forestall the course of modernization. Or, conversely, an officer corps born in revolution may, as in Cuba, seek irresponsibly to keep alive the perpetual excitement of a fighting horde rather than to preserve peace and order.

But history has also demonstrated numerous times, from the Samurai and the Prussian army of the nineteenth century down through Atatürk and Magsaysay, that the military can indeed play a thoroughly constructive part in modernization.

A striking example is the evolution of the Turkish Republic. Although the military played an important role in founding the Republic, Atatürk succeeded in establishing a clear division between civil and military leadership. This distinction was successfully maintained for 35 years despite the continued importance of the military in many aspects of civilian life. The corps of officers who with Atatürk made the revolution and founded its republican institutions were obliged, like Atatürk himself, to resign their commissions when they took up posts of political authority; as a corollary, no officer who remained in uniform was permitted to be active in political life. This tradition survived until 1960, when significant failures in civil leadership and a strong tendency to revert to autocratic rule led the army to take over. The army has, however, thus far shown a restraint in its practices which reflects the impact of the Atatürk tradition. There is good reason to hope that its intervention will be transient and that the democratic process, including the principle of civilian supremacy, will in the end be strengthened.

The Turkish army recruits some 200,000 young civilians into its training program each year. These young men (and women) are often illiterate villagers, whose induction into the army represents their first sustained exposure to men in other parts of Turkey. They are taught to read and write, to handle tools and equipment; they are taught the fundamentals of personal hygiene and public health; they are taught the symbols and institutions of modern political life in a republic. As they complete their training and return to their villages, these young people become a permanent asset in the modernization of Turkey. They put their new knowledge to work; they teach other villagers at home some of what they have themselves learned; they remain "relay points" for information and opinion emanating from the modernized sector of Turkish society. Thus they speed the process of modernization and help to stabilize it.

In summary, then, the military—the one traditional social order likely to survive the process of social change—may be able to play a key role in promoting mobility while maintaining stability, in facilitating change while preventing chaos. Upon the efficiency with which the military sector can be made to perform this role may hinge the successful outcome of the transition in many societies.

The Secular Intelligentsia

While the military are strong in their capacity to manage violence, in their commitment to rational institutions based on functional criteria and efficient performance, and in their sense of nationhood as a supreme value, they are often weak in other skills and attitudes needed in a modernizing society. Consider, for example, the basic process of economic growth. Military men are not generally sophisticated economists, and their economic programs are likely to be inspirational rather than productive. In the Middle East, where military take-over has been virtually continuous over the past few decades, instances have multiplied in which new military regimes rapidly foundered on their own well-meant land reform programs. Virtually every new regime has made some more or less serious gesture in the direction of land reform which has won it popular plaudits for a time but which has failed to solve the basic problem of raising agricultural productivity.

Military elites are likely to make dangerous errors in framing and administering laws, instituting and operating schools, devising and sustaining a communication network, unless they are guided by people with professional knowledge and experience in these activities. Such people are the "secular intelligentsia"—the economists and engineers and agronomists, the lawyers and administrators, the doctors and public health officers, the deans and professors, the "communicators" who manage the flow of public news and views that no modernizing polity can do without. They are an "intelligentsia" because it is they who acquire and apply modern knowledge to the manifold tasks of running an urban, industrial, participant society efficiently. They are "secular" because their public roles and social functions are independent of, and usually hostile to, the sacred symbols and institutions of the traditional society.

Often their first problem as they emerge is to win pre-eminence over the "sacred" intelligentsia, who traditionally performed most of the legal and judicial, teaching and counseling, healing and helping, soothsaying and certifying functions that the secular intelligentsia now seek to perform. In societies moving toward a modern division of labor with increasing urbanization, industrialization, and participation, the new men of knowledge steadily gain strength. But there are continuous frustrations. The doctor is unhappy when people go to the *shaman* for medical therapy, the lawyer when people go to the *shariya* for adjudication; the teacher when people go to the *imam* for learning, the agronomist when people go to their neighbor for weather forecasts, the communicator when people go to the village elder for guidance on moral judgment of public issues.

These frustrations mount as the number of modern specialists expands in an environment that remains highly traditionalized. The men of the secular intelligentsia become individually impatient and as a group extremist in their views of what must be done. They may form alliances of various sorts—with each other, with foreign agents, even with "deviants" among the traditionalist sectors of landowners and sacred intelligentsia. But ultimately, if they are to make more than a quick splash, the secular intelligentsia ally themselves with the military sector, the bureaucracy, or the business elite.

The historical logic is clear. The other elites have the coercive power and organization needed to maintain stability; the secular intelligentsia have the knowledge needed to effect change. Military, bureaucratic, or business leadership alone usually has foundered because its perspective is too narrow to cope with the variety of problems that arise in modernizing societies; the secular intelligentsia alone usually have failed because their ideas outrun their capacity to develop institutions that are operational. Neither can manage the transition without the other, and so forms the "unholy alliance," which Western social scientists have described (and decried) since Pareto, Mosca, Michels, Lasswell.

The intelligentsia have sometimes been kept from playing a positive part in the process of modernization by becoming isolated and irresponsible critics of their society. Critics they will always be, for discontent is the price of imagination and knowledge. But discontent can also lead to nihilism and fruitless abstentionism. In developing countries it is particularly easy for this to happen. The intellectual knows about the modern world from his reading and study, or sometimes from travel, and he becomes attached to it. He easily becomes a man without roots in his own society. Many college-educated intellectuals do not know a single villager, would rather be unemployed than work in the stink of a mud-hutted rural community, have contempt for the idiocy of tradition. But this contempt is not the fruitful anger of righteous indignation. It is likely to be conflict-ridden guilt and ambivalence. The educated man may see deep inside himself residues of traditional values and attitudes which he is ashamed to admit and which he is afraid to expose to stimulation through participation in the rites of his own traditional culture. Too often the intelligentsia in underdeveloped countries are for all these reasons simultaneously cut off from effective identification with their own people in the villages and from the responsible wielders of power. Such dual irresponsibility may find convenient expression in the shallow platitudes of Fabian socialism or neocommunism, for those doctrines preach modernization while at the same time reassuring their adherents that they are genuine members of the masses and opponents of the newly modernizing elites.

The avoidance of such ideological temptations is not easy. The development of a vigorous intelligentsia is a prerequisite of modernization. Universities, a press, and cultural institutions must be developed, but these are not enough to assure the intelligentsia a responsible attitude. The intelligentsia must be given a constructive image of their potential role. This may be done through the mystique of a democratic development plan. It can be facilitated by programs of international cooperation and intercourse among free intellectuals. It requires also that jobs in adequate numbers be made available for the mobilization of intellectual skills on the problems of development.

THE INNOVATING ENTREPRENEURS

Entrepreneurs are not necessarily engaged in private enterprise. Among the imaginative promoters of new institutions in the West were many who carried the flag of sovereign authority. There were the buccaneers and explorers on the high seas and in new continents, searching for gold as agents of the king. There were the creators of semi-public exploring and development companies of the sixteenth and seventeenth centuries, such as the British and Dutch East India Companies. There were the builders of canals and railroads. When we talk of entrepreneurs, we talk of such men as well as of the imaginative villager who buys a bus for himself to institute a hitherto unknown service, or of the private entrepreneur who raises business capital to build a factory to earn profits for himself. We are not prejudging the forms of entrepreneurship when we say that an aggressive entrepreneurial group, along with a responsible military, an effective bureaucracy, and a secular intelligentsia, is necessary for modernization.

Entrepreneurship is not something that is found in equal portions in all societies. ... Without an environment that breeds a group of men with strong motivation for personal achievement and habits of hard work and economy, the process of modernization may be long delayed. Entrepreneurs are found in different proportions also among sectors of a single society. In Colombia, for example, the bulk of the entrepreneurs have been found to come from a single valley where wealth could not be fruitfully invested in land. That fact, coupled with certain competitive needs of an otherwise disadvantaged leading strata of the population, produced historically a different pattern of motivations from that found elsewhere in the country. Ethnic minorities have often been the source of entrepreneurial innovators.

The innovating entrepreneur is by no means always in the saddle in a developing country. As a man who is ready to struggle for unconventional goals, he, like the intellectual, is likely to be discontented and to feel himself deprived. As an agent of change and as a man who most often gets his modernizing inspiration from association with alien sources, he is likely to be distrusted. He may find himself fighting regulations and restrictions. Still, the society with which he struggles may be on the road to modernization, despite his strictures and complaints, if it provides him with incentives and freedom to seek ways to reorganize and improve life. The sign of stagnation is not that the entrepreneur must struggle but that no one chooses this role.

The Peasants and Urban Workers

Our analysis thus far has focused on narrow elites—on men who acquire certain Western skills and are in a position to contend for power and to direct the course of events within their nation. We turn now to the evolution of attitudes and skills among the people as a whole and to their slow change from a passive to an active role in the modernization process.

Here again the course of events depends substantially on the kind of traditional structure that existed; on whether the society underwent a period of colonial tutelage and on the kind of colonial policy that was pursued; on the particular setting and impulses that led to the overthrow of the traditional society, colonial rule, or both. Without excessive distortion, however, we can draw a general picture of the changing horizons of the peasant and the urban worker as modernization proceeds.

In the traditional society and in the early stages of transition something like 75 per cent of the population live in rural areas and up to 90 per cent of the population may be illiterate. Mass media, if they exist at all, reach only a small number of people. There are no institutions that permit genuine popular participation in the political process. The peasants are likely to appear apathetic, accepting their traditional lot, but their apathy may well conceal extremely complex feelings. They may harbor, for example, a deep hunger to own their own land or to see their children healthy, educated, and advanced, aspirations that find expression only when a realistic opportunity for change presents itself. On the other hand, as we have previously noted, they may simultaneously feel great reluctance to abandon the familiar way of life, which offers psychic security as well as a protection from some of the crushing burdens of poverty.

In the early period of transition, as urban activity increases, the attractions of the city draw men away from the countryside, even though urban life itself is often impoverished and demands an almost revolutionary shift in social and cultural adjustments. In the cities the unskilled worker is generally left on his own, but in the trades of higher skills, unions are organized at a relatively early stage of the modernization process. Literacy and technical training begin to spread. Thus fairly early in the transitional stage the cities often develop a quite modern way of life, standing as advanced enclaves in a society still predominantly rural and primitive.

The coming to power of the modernizing coalition has direct effects on both the urban worker and the peasant. Their political role begins to change, for the new leadership feels impelled to make a direct appeal to the mass of citizens. The legitimacy of the new leadership, which has often won out by revolution against the colonial power or the old order, rests in large measure on a real or pretended commitment to advance the interests of the people as a whole and to achieve for all the citizens of the nation the fruits of modernization. At a minimum, the modernizing coalition is likely to take steps to establish means of communication between the government and the people as a whole. This is the stage at which politicians are likely to take to the air waves and to encourage the creation of a popular press. Whatever the substantive accomplishments of the modernizing coalition in its early period of power, and however deep or shallow its commitment to furthering popular interests, its very existence will probably increase the demand for modernization and for an increasing degree of participation in the society's decisions.

This is a point of maximum danger for the developing society. The mass media, bringing news and views of the world to illiterates in their urban slums and remote villages, introduce a new element into the process of modernization. People learn for the first time about the world outside their immediate environs, and their sense of life's possibilities begins to expand. We recall Nasser's statement: "Radio has changed everything. . . . Leaders cannot govern as they once did. We live in a new world."

One danger is that people will learn the fashions of popular participation long before the institutions of representative government are properly functioning. Then pseudo-participation takes command; that is, plebiscites that offer the form of public election without its substance, mob politics-of-the-street in which "popular will" can destroy people and property without constructing better public policy. When exposure to the mass media overstimulates a people to this point, the leadership is pressed to give radio propaganda primacy over political economy. While oratory resounds, development is likely to be shunted to the side and growth impeded. The result, for people led to impose demands which their transitional society cannot yet supply, may be a potentially explosive and spreading sense of frustration.

Whereas the West achieved a participant society as an outcome of the slow growth of physical, social, and psychic mobility over many centuries (the centuries our history textbooks now summarize as Age of Exploration, Renaissance, Reformation and Counter Reformation, Industrial Revolution, Rise of Democracy), the new societies seek to accomplish this sequence in decades. In their desire for rapid progress lies the danger that the effect of mass media will be to increase popular desires and demands faster than they can be satisfied by economic and social growth. Acute imbalances are likely to be built into the growth process by the government's desire to register rapidly those improvements that will be highly visible to the public eye, without due concern for the durability of these improvements. Health, welfare, and educational improvements—often made possible by foreign aid—are particularly prone to prove less durable than planned because the environing institutions needed to sustain them have not been adequately modernized. The common tendency of such improvements is to equip people for longer, healthier, more productive lives. People who live longer multiply every demand put upon a society—for food, clothing, shelter; for work and recreation; for adolescent opportunity and senescent security. People who acquire skills create new demands for opportunities to use them productively. Those who acquire mechanical skills demand machines to operate; those with professional training demand opportunities to practice their professions. If a society fails to supply these opportunities—to satisfy the demands posed by rising expectations—then it must face a "revolution of rising frustrations." In the decade ahead, the strategic question will be how to sustain the high expectations that have already been created in the modernizing world. In some cases, excessive expectations will have to be reduced or revised. In all cases, stable development will require a significant increase in the supply of both visible improvements and durable opportunities.

To analyze such dangers is easier than to prescribe ways of overcoming them. What the new governments must do is to create institutions through which individual citizens can begin to take part in the decisions of the community. Fully as important as plebiscites, representative assemblies, and other instruments of participation on the national scale—indeed probably a vital prerequisite for the successful operation of national institutions—are local organizations of many sorts which can engage people actively in matters of immediate concern to them, and enable them to see realistically the problems as well as the opportunities that modernization brings.

In the villages, community development and other programs for agricultural cooperation and reform; in the towns, trade unions and other organizations; in both town and country, institutions of local government which engage the interest and support of the people—such activities as these help to bridge the gap between government and people, help to introduce content into the forms of democracy which most of the underdeveloped societies have eagerly accepted.

In terms of social change the problems confronting the transitional societies which are led by modernizing coalitions are those posed by the very nature of democracy. Democracy is not adequately summed up in the formula of universal suffrage; the individual requires something more than a vote to guarantee that his interests will be taken into account in the society's decisions. A sound democracy depends heavily on the strength and number of the institutions that stand between the individual and the national government, defending his individual rights in the process of defending institutional interests. While the process of modernization creates some of the preconditions for democracy, its emergence is by no means foreordained. Democracy is a purposeful human achievement, not in any sense an automatic reflex of modernization.

Selection **15**

The Problem of Rapid
Population Growth

ANSLEY J. COALE

From: "Population and Economic Development," in Philip Hauser (ed.),
The Population Dilemma (*Englewood Cliffs, N.J.: Prentice-Hall,*
Inc., 1963), pp. 46–62. Reprinted by permission of Prentice-Hall, Inc.

Anyone examining estimates of per capita incomes or other indexes of material well-being must be impressed with the wide difference—by a factor of ten or more —between the wealthiest and the poorest countries. The countries with the highest average incomes are those that have undergone industrialization or modernization, and the countries with lowest incomes are those that retain traditional techniques of production and modes of industrial organization (with a predominance of agriculture in most instances) that have persisted without essential change for generations. The disparity between the prosperity of the industrialized countries and the poverty of the pre-industrial countries is an increasing irritant to the pride and ambition of the leaders in the underdeveloped areas and to the conscience of the modernized countries.

It is the purpose here to consider how the demographic characteristics of the low-income countries are related to their poverty, and how their population trends will influence their modernization. . . . Among the demographic characteristics of low income areas today are:

High fertility—Most underdeveloped areas of the world have birth rates of forty per 1,000 or higher and an average number of children born at the end of the fertile period—at age of forty-five or fifty—of at least 5. This fertility contrasts with experience in Europe, where birth rates are, with only two or three exceptions, below twenty per 1,000, and total fertility is two to three children. The fertility of Japan is at the low end of the European scale. Other highly industrialized areas outside of Europe—the United States, the Soviet Union, Australia, New Zealand, and Canada—have birth rates between twenty and twenty-eight per 1,000 and a total fertility of three to four children.

Low or rapidly falling mortality—As a consequence of the invention and application of low cost techniques of public health, underdeveloped areas have recently experienced a fall in mortality more rapid than ever seen before. They have not had to wait while the gradual process of developing medical science took place, nor have they had to depend on the possibly more rapid but still difficult process of constructing major sanitary engineering works and building up of a large inventory of expensive hospitals, public health services, and highly trained doctors. Instead, the underdeveloped areas have been able to import low-cost measures of controlling disease, measures developed for the most part in the highly industrialized countries. The use of residual insecticides to provide effective protection against malaria at no more than twenty-five cents per capita per year is an outstanding example. Other innovations include antibiotics and chemotherapy and extend to the discovery of relatively low-cost ways of providing a safe water supply and adequate environmental sanitation in villages that in other ways remain little touched by modernization.

Accelerating population growth—The result of a precipitous decline in mortality while the birth rate remains essentially unchanged is, of course, a rapid acceleration in population growth, reaching in some instances rates of three to three and one-half per cent per year. The underdeveloped areas with more moderate growth rates of one and one-half to two and one-half per cent per year are typically in the midst of a rapid decline in death rates and are experiencing steep increases in the rate of growth of their populations.

A very young age distribution—The high fertility of low-income countries produces a large proportion of children and a small proportion, in consequence, of adults in the economically most productive ages. The underdeveloped countries have forty to forty-five per cent of their population under age fifteen, in contrast with a maximum of twenty-five to thirty per cent in the highly industrialized countries. Differences in mortality among countries, whether industrialized or not, have only slight effect on the distribution of the population by age, and specifically on the proportion of the population that children constitute. Indeed, the effect of a lower death rate on the proportion of children is in a surprising direction. Mortality is typically reduced the most in infancy and early childhood; and if fertility remains unchanged, a reduction in mortality of the sort usually occurring increases the proportion of children and reduces rather than increases the average age.

Density ranging from low to high—There are great variations in population density from one low-income area to another, with fewer than ten persons per square mile in Bolivia and more than 600 in Korea.

We shall consider how these characteristics of the population affect the process of industrialization or modernization to which the low income areas aspire. Their populations at present suffer from inadequate diets, enjoy at best primitive and overcrowded housing, have a modest education or no formal education at all (if adult) and rarely attend school (if children), and are often productively employed for only a fraction of the year. These populations suffer all of the misery and degradation associated with poverty. They naturally wish to enjoy the universal education, adequate diet, housing equipped with modern amenities, the long and generally healthy life, the opportunity for productive work and extensive voluntary leisure that the highly industrialized countries have shown to be possible. To do so, the underdeveloped countries must modernize their economies.

The changes in social and economic structure that make up the process of modernization or industrialization are many and profound. More productive techniques must displace traditional methods of manufacturing, agriculture, trade, transport, and communications. Economic activity must become more diversified and more specialized. The emphasis in production must shift from extractive industries, especially agriculture, to manufacturing, trade, and communications. The interchange of goods through a monetary medium on widespread markets must replace local consumption of goods produced on the farm or exchanged only in small village markets. The labor force must be transformed from illiteracy to literacy. A sufficient supply must be found and trained of what has become to be known as "high talent manpower"—doctors, lawyers, engineers, entrepreneurs, and managers. Production must shift from small, family-oriented enterprises into large, impersonal, professionally supervised organizations. However, many of these essential changes are related only indirectly to demographic characteristics such as growth and age distribution.

Here only two important aspects of industrialization or modernization will be considered. One aspect is increasing income per person as a consequence (and an index) of industrialization, and the other is the attainment or maintenance of productive employment for the labor force.

POPULATION AND INCOME PER HEAD

Examining the implications of population change for the growth of real income, we shall consider nations rather than areas within nations. The selection of the nation as the unit for analysis implies that gains or losses of population through migration can generally be considered of negligible importance. There are a few exceptions (perhaps four or five small countries that can expect gains or losses from migration of important magnitude compared to natural increase), but for the majority of underdeveloped countries and certainly for the larger ones there is no such realistic likelihood.

For somewhat different reasons, the possibility of alternative courses of mortality can also be ignored, at least for a generation or two. The basis for paying little attention to different possible courses of mortality is that the technical feasibility of reducing mortality to lower levels—of increasing expectation of life at birth at least to some fifty or sixty years—has been widely demonstrated in the underdeveloped areas themselves. Unless the effort to start and continue the process of modernization fails completely, or unless there is a breakdown in world order, the attainment and maintenance, at least for a short time, of low mortality rates seems potentially within the reach of most low-income countries. It does not appear that widespread famine or even severe increases in malnutrition are a necessary consequence in the next few decades, even if the low-income countries experience population growth rates of two to three and one-half per cent.

The agricultural and industrial technology that can be introduced into low-income countries is, in a sense, parallel to the medical technology that can be imported to achieve a rapid reduction in mortality rates. Rates of increase in agricultural output of at least three or four per cent a year appear technically feasible, even in such a densely settled, highly agricultural country as India. If the birth rate in India is not reduced, the population will probably double in the next generation from about 450 million to about 900 million persons. Agricultural experts consider it feasible within achievable limits of capital investment to double Indian agricultural output within the next twenty or twenty-five years. In the short run, then, it can be assumed, provisionally at least, that mortality reduction can be achieved and maintained.

Finally, if sickness can be reduced and death postponed within the resources available to the health authorities in the underdeveloped countries, assisted by the World Health Organization, UNICEF, and directly by the industrialized countries, it is scarcely imaginable that by deliberate policy these opportunities would be foregone. In other words, the only factor that can be realistically considered as variable in causing population change by deliberate policy is fertility. We shall be concerned here with the implications for the growth in per capita income and for the provision of productive employment, of alternative possible future courses of fertility. The specific alternatives to be considered are the maintenance of fertility at its current level (which would involve in almost all underdeveloped countries the continuation of an essentially horizontal trend that has already continued for generations) and, as the contrasting alternative, a rapid reduction in fertility, amounting to fifty per cent of the initial level and occupying a transitional period of about twenty-five years.

We will inquire what effects these contrasting trends in fertility would have on three important population characteristics: first, the burden of dependency, defined as the total number of persons in the population divided by the number in the labor force ages (fifteen to sixty-four); second, the rate of growth of the labor force, or, more precisely, the annual per cent rate of increase of the population fifteen to sixty-four; and third, the density of the population, or, more precisely, the number of persons at labor force age relative to land area and other resources. Then we shall consider how these three characteristics of dependency, rate of growth, and density influence the increase in per capita income.

Alternative Population Projections

It is possible to translate assumptions about the future course of mortality and fertility in a specific population into numerical estimates of the future size and age composition of that population. Table I presents the projection one hundred fifty years into the future of a hypothetical initial population of one million persons with an age distribution and fertility and mortality rates typical of a Latin American country. The current birth rate is about forty-four per 1,000, the current death rate is about fourteen per 1,000, so that the population is growing at three per cent per year. The current expectation of life at birth is about fifty-three years, and the average number of children born by age forty-five is slightly over six. It is assumed that in the next thirty years the expectation of life at birth will rise to approximately seventy years, so that mortality risks at each age become closely

Table I

ILLUSTRATIVE PROJECTIONS OF THE POPULATION OF AN
UNDERDEVELOPED AREA

(Initial population 1,000,000 persons. Initial age distribution, fertility, and mortality typical of Latin America north of Uruguay. Mortality rapidly improving.)
    Projection A—Fertility continues unchanged.
    Projection B—Fertility falls linearly by fifty per cent in twenty-five years, thereafter unchanged.

Population in thousands

	Year	0	10	20	30	40	50	60	150
Projection A	0–14	434	616	870	1,261	1,840	2,655	3,848	110,700
	15–64	534	718	996	1,406	2,003	2,901	4,204	120,800
	65+	32	43	65	90	132	180	245	14,000
	Total	1,000	1,377	1,931	2,757	3,975	5,736	8,297	245,500
Projection B	0–14	434	567	637	676	783	901	994	3,014
	15–64	534	718	985	1,287	1,573	1,869	2,181	6,613
	65+	32	43	65	90	132	180	245	850
	Total	1,000	1,328	1,687	2,053	2,488	2,950	3,420	10,477

comparable to today's experience in the most highly industrialized countries. Once the expectation of life reaches seventy years, no further improvement is assumed. If this projection of one million persons is multiplied by 70.5, it would fit Brazil; by 34.6, it would fit Mexico, starting in 1960.

The initial population and the expected mortality risks at each age in the future are the same for the two projected populations. However, two contrasting assumptions are made with regard to the future course of fertility. In one projection, it is assumed that the current rates of childbearing at each age of women continue indefinitely into the future. In the other projection, it is assumed that fertility rates are reduced each year for twenty-five years by 2 per cent of their initial value, so that in twenty-five years fertility is reduced by a total of 50 per cent. After twenty-five years, this projection is based on a continuation of fertility at 50 per cent of current levels. Note that there is no difference in the first fifteen years in the projected population over age fifteen. Differences in fertility such as are assumed between these alternative projected populations inevitably affect the child population before the adult population is affected. In fact, at the end of twenty-five years, when fertility for one population has fallen by 50 per cent, the population fifteen to sixty-four is only 4 per cent greater in the high fertility projection. It is 9 per cent greater after thirty years. In the more distant future the divergence becomes increasingly rapid. After about sixty-two years the high fertility population would have twice as many people in the labor force ages, and by 150 years it would have eighteen times as many.

The three population characteristics whose implications are to be examined here are of differing relative significance in the short run, over an intermediate period, and in the long run. In the first twenty-five or thirty years the age distribution effect, or the difference in burden of dependency, is almost the sole factor at work. There is a rapidly widening difference between the projected populations in the burden of dependency during the first generation (Figure 1). This difference

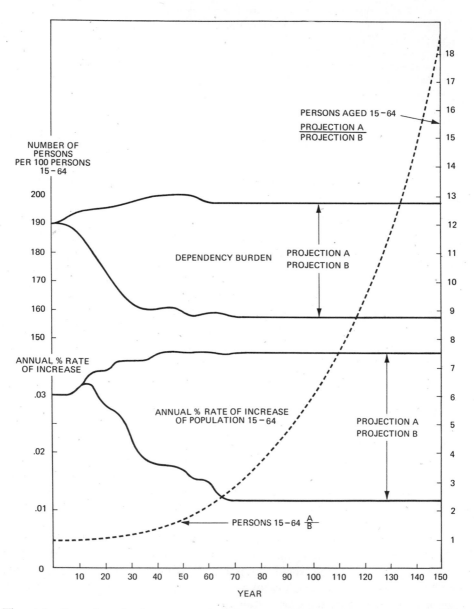

Figure 1   *Dependency burden (total number of persons 15–64); relative size of the population 15–64; and annual rate of increase of population 15–64 in two model projections (projection A, fertility unchanged; projection B, fertility reduced linearly by 50 per cent in twenty-five years, thereafter constant). (Reprinted by courtesy of the Office of Population Research, Princeton University.)*

in dependency once established then continues more or less unchanged. Starting in about twenty years there develops first a slight and then a widening difference in the rate of growth of the population aged fifteen to sixty-four. This difference in rate of increase reaches a maximum value, at which it thereafter remains, in about sixty-five to seventy years (or forty to fifty years after fertility levels off). The period of widening differences in the growth rate will be considered as an intermediate one separating the short and the long run. The two projections have essentially constant differences in age composition and rate of growth in the long run (from sixty-five to seventy-five years on). During the intermediate period there develops an increasingly conspicuous difference in the size of the two labor forces, and therefore in the density of the labor force relative to resources. In the long run the difference in density assumes overwhelming dimensions. For example, in something less than three hundred years the high fertility population would be a thousand times bigger than the low fertility population.

To sum up: in the short run there is a reduction in the burden of dependency in the low fertility relative to the high fertility population. This difference reaches a stable maximum in some thirty years. In addition to this effect there begins to develop in the intermediate period a widening difference in the rate of growth of the population of labor force age. This difference attains a maximum (thereafter maintained) within seventy years. The cumulative effect of differences in rates of growth of the labor force in the long run produce overwhelming differences between the high fertility and low fertility population in the size or density of the labor force.

Economic Development and Demographic Variables

We shall consider primarily the implications of our demographic variables for the capacity of the economy to divert effort and resources from producing for current consumption to producing for the enhancement of future productivity. In other words, it will be assumed that to accelerate the process of modernization an economy must increase its level of net investment. Net investment here means additions to factories, roads, irrigation networks, fertilizer plants, and other productive facilities. It also can include in a broad definition resources and effort devoted to education and training. It is not an intended implication that merely stepping up the rate of new investment automatically insures a major speedup in industrialization or assures the attainment of the fastest possible pace of modernization. Resources mobilized for productive purposes must be wisely allocated. Adequate leadership must be found for the new forms of productive organization that an industrialized society requires. Long-standing customs and traditions must be altered if new and more effective techniques of production are to be employed. In other words, a high level of net investment is a *necessary* but not a *sufficient* condition for a rapid pace of industrialization. In the ensuing analysis it will be assumed that the other crucial elements in modernization are present.

Age Distribution and Investment

At the end of twenty-five years there is only a four per cent difference in the size of the labor force or, more precisely, a four per cent difference in the number of persons fifteen to sixty-four. Let us suppose that productive employment can be found for all males of labor force age seeking employment and for all females who are not bound to housekeeping duties by lack of education, tradition, and the necessity to care for small children and who also are in search of productive employment. Let us assume further that twenty-five years from now the progress toward modernization has included the establishment of virtually universal primary education, so that the effective age of entry in the labor force is not before age fifteen. Let us also make the provisional assumption, which we shall reexamine shortly, that national income is, in the twenty-fifth year, the same for the two projected populations. If the reader objects that this provisional assumption seems unrealistic because the high fertility population would have some four per cent more persons of labor force age, let him consider the offsetting fact that the low fertility population would contain only about half as many young infants and half as many pregnant women. If allowance is made for the greater number of women free to work outside the home, the number of persons actually available for productive employment would not really be four per cent less in the low fertility population but might actually be slightly greater. It is certainly reasonable to disregard the small difference in size of population over age fifteen.

If there were the same total national income to be utilized by the two projected populations, the pressure toward utilizing nearly all of it for consumption would be substantially greater in the high fertility population, as a direct result of the greater burden of dependency that must be borne by the labor force. In the high fertility population after twenty-five years, there would be ninety-six persons in the dependent ages for every one hundred persons in the productive ages, while in the low fertility population there would be only sixty-five dependents for every one hundred persons fifteen to sixty-four.

The pressure to spend a higher fraction of national income on consumption can take many forms in different kinds of economies. In a capitalist economy, where investment is financed out of private savings, the fact that families with a large number of children find it more difficult to save reduces the volume of savings and hence the level of investment. When low-income families are not an important source of savings, higher fertility creates social pressure to increase the share of national income received by the poorest earners (the nonsavers) in order to maintain minimum standards of consumption.

High fertility can depress private savings in two ways: (1) by reducing the volume of savings by individual families when such savings are an important component of the national total; (2) by increasing the proportion of national income that must accrue to nonsavers if standards of consumption play any part in determining the earnings of low-income families.

When it is the government rather than individual entrepreneurs that provides a large proportion of national investment, fertility affects the level of investment through its effect on the capacity of the government to raise money through taxation. Suppose the government attempts to maximize the fund it mobilizes for net investment. For any given level of deprivation that it is prepared to impose, it can raise more taxes from a low fertility population than from a high fertility population with the same national income and the same number of adults in each. Even if the government does not calculate the maximum revenue it can assess, the existence of such factors as exemptions for children would automatically reduce income tax revenues.

After this lengthy review we reach a simple conclusion. Given the same labor force and the same total national income, a low fertility population will achieve a higher level of net investment than a high fertility population. It will therefore be able to make larger additions to the productive capacity of the country and achieve a higher national product in the next year. In addition, the population with a higher burden of child dependency feels a constant pressure to divert investment funds to less productive or at least to less immediately productive uses. To meet given target dates for achieving universal literacy or universal primary education, more funds must be spent on education. In a population of large families rather than small, more construction must be diverted to housing rather than to factories or hydroelectric plants.

During a short-run period of twenty-five to thirty years, the age distribution effect of declining fertility enhances the capacity of the economy to increase its net investment and to utilize investment in more immediately productive ways. The labor force available for productive employment during the short-run period is the same, or perhaps a little larger during the first fifteen years, because persons over fifteen would be the same in number and more women could participate in productive employment. Actual numbers available for employment probably become equal in the two projections some time between twenty-five and thirty years after the decline of fertility starts. The resources available would presumably be identical. In consequence, there emerges a conclusion that may seem paradoxical. During a period of twenty-five or thirty years, at least, after fertility reduction begins, the population reducing its fertility would produce a more rapidly growing national product than a population which kept its fertility unchanged. This more rapid growth would cumulate into a consequentially higher total product at the end of the thirty-year period. In other words, in the short run not only does a population with reduced fertility enjoy the benefit of dividing the national product among a smaller number of consumers, it enjoys the additional benefit of having a larger national product to divide.

Effects of Labor Force Growth

After twenty-five or thirty years declining fertility begins to cause major differences in the growth rate and later on major differences in the size of the adult population. The difference in dependency burden reaches a maximum by about forty years, thereafter remaining unchanged. The high fertility labor force must continue, as in the short run, to share what it produces with a distinctly greater number of dependents, and this necessity continues to impair the capacity of the economy to attain a high level of investment. But after the short run a new element, the different rate of growth of the labor force itself, assumes important dimensions.

The significance of the growth of the labor force for income per head is that higher rates of growth imply a higher level of needed investment to achieve a given per capita output, although there is nothing about faster growth that generates a greater supply of investible resources. A larger labor force requires a larger stock of productive facilities in order to have the same productivity per head. The per cent of national income that must be invested merely to keep productivity from declining is some three times the annual per cent rate of increase of the labor force. In other words, if the labor force were growing by three per cent a year, a level of net investment of nine per cent of national income would be required to prevent declining productivity; while if the rate of growth of the labor force were one per cent a year, the needed level of investment for this purpose would be only three per cent of national income.

This rule of thumb assumes that the stock of capital must increase as much as the labor force to prevent a decline of productivity, and assumes further that the stock of capital is roughly three times as large as the current level of national income. Yet the faster growing labor force has no intrinsic advantages in achieving a high level of savings to finance the needed higher level of investment. It needs more investment but has inherent advantages in achieving more.

Another way of presenting the difference between a rapidly growing and a slowly growing labor force is to consider the effect of net investment at the respectable rate of fifteen per cent of national income. A population with a rate of growth of three per cent in its labor force can with such a level of net investment add about two per cent per year to the endowment of capital per worker. If the labor force were growing at one per cent, the annual increase in the stock of capital per worker would be four per cent.

An economy where additional members of the labor force settle on empty land, a "frontier society," is a partial exception to the above line of reasoning. If frontier settlement provides an outlet for the growth in the labor force, it is possible that new members provide most of their own capital—by clearing land, constructing roads, building log houses, etc. Under these hypothetical circumstances the rate of capital formation might be automatically higher with a more rapidly growing labor force. However, it is uncertain whether there are genuine instances of this kind of frontier settlement in the world today. Indonesia has attempted to resettle families from densely populated and rapidly growing Java to the relatively empty land in Borneo. However, the Indonesian government has felt impelled to make a generous capital investment in the form of tools and equipment for each family, the numbers involved have been at most a trivial fraction of the annual increase in Java's population, and many of the pioneers have returned to Java after a short period.

Most underdeveloped countries find it difficult to invest as much as fifteen per cent of their national incomes and hence will find it necessary for the next generation to utilize more than half of their investment merely to provide capital for the growing labor force. In the short run a reduction of fertility would not affect this necessity. However, even in the short run the age distribution advantages of reduced fertility would increase the level of net investment that would be attained. During the intermediate period, when reduced fertility results in a substantially slower growth of the labor force, the age distribution advantage would continue. A greater capacity to allocate output to investment would be combined with a less imperative necessity to invest merely to keep up with the growth of the labor force.

Effect of Density

The question of population density tends to be the dominant concept in most casual thought about the population problems of underdeveloped areas. The notion of excessive density is certainly implicit in the term "overpopulation." The underlying idea is that when there are too many workers relative to the available resources, per capita output is smaller than it would be with a smaller number of workers. Given gross enough differences in the numbers of workers being compared, it is certainly possible in principle to establish that overpopulation in this sense exists. For example, in 150 years the high fertility population that we projected would be eighteen times as large as the population that would result from fifty per cent reduction in fertility. Even the labor force with reduced fertility would imply a density more than twelve times greater than at present, while the population with sustained fertility would involve a density more than 200 times greater than at present. There is little doubt that in most countries a density 200 times greater would have a depressing effect upon per capita output compared to a density twelve times greater.

There are, however, two reasons for doubting the immediate usefulness of the concept of density in considering population problems of underdeveloped areas. The first is that in this period of human history few countries have any genuine freedom of choice of policy that would have an important effect on population density (or, more specifically, on the density of the labor force) in the short run. There are few areas where realistic alternatives of promoting or retarding international migration would have an important effect upon density. It is unlikely, and I would argue strongly undesirable, that an underdeveloped country should contemplate a deliberate restraint on its public health programs in order to retard the decline of mortality and thus prevent an increase of population density. As is shown in Figure 1, a reduction in fertility does not have an important effect on density for a long time in the future. The difference in the size of the labor force is less than ten per cent thirty years after a rapid and extensive decline and fertility begins. After thirty years, however, the difference in density between sustained and reduced fertility rapidly mounts, reaching a factor of two in about sixty years, a factor of three in seventy-five years, and a factor of eighteen after 150 years. In other words, so far as acceptable and attainable policies are concerned, only in the relatively distant future can the density of the labor force relative to resources be affected. In the meantime the policy that would have a long-run effect on density, namely, one that reduces fertility, would through changes in dependency and differences in the annual rate of growth of the labor force have produced major economic effects.

A second reservation about the relevance of density is that it is of clear-cut importance only in a closed economy—i.e., one that does not trade extensively—or in an economy where the principal industry is extractive. Only in extractive industries—mining, agriculture, and forestry—are resources as related to numbers of workers a dominant element in productivity. For example, if India were compelled to continue to employ seventy per cent of its labor force in agriculture, increasing density would inevitably mean smaller average holdings. The average holding today is only about two acres per person aged fifteen to sixty-four dependent on agriculture, and the possibility of bringing new areas under cultivation is limited.

In nonextractive industries international trade can greatly reduce the effect of limited resources. In all industries, extractive or otherwise, productivity is determined to a large degree by the stock of capital per worker. The underdeveloped areas have in common a small endowment of productive equipment per worker relative to the industrialized countries; in other words, the underdeveloped countries all have a "high density" of workers relative to capital, whether the country appears to be sparsely or densely settled relative to land and other resources.

Two examples indicate the dubious relevance of the concept of overpopulation where nonextractive industries are dominant and a large volume of trade is possible. One is the narrow strip of territory extending from Boston to Washington along the east coast of the United States. There is a 400 mile long line of contiguous counties with an aggregate area of about 14,000 square miles and an aggregate population in 1960 of about 28,000,000, or a population density of more than 2,000 per square mile. There are few if any areas of similar extent in the world with a higher density. The median family income of this strip is $6,660, just a thousand dollars more than the median for the United States as a whole. Is it overpopulated? It would certainly be difficult to demonstrate that per capita output would be greater if the population density were less. Of course this area belongs to a large market—the United States and its territories—where trade is unrestricted. Extractive industries play a trivial role in the output of this area. It can readily import the raw materials and semi-finished products that it requires in exchange for the finished goods and services it produces.

The second example, Hong Kong, shows that the possibility of importing raw materials and semi-finished goods in exchange for finished goods and services is not limited to a region within a country. Hong Kong has a population of 3.1 million on a land area of 398 square miles, with a resultant density of 12,700 persons per square mile. Land for new buildings on Victoria Island is dredged from the harbor. After the war Hong Kong had a very low per capita income, and its density was inflated by an influx of refugees. Nevertheless Hong Kong has achieved increases in national produce of seven to ten per cent per year and has probably doubled its real output in a decade. It obtains its needed imports (including food) on the world market. Mainland China has receded to a minor position in Hong Kong's pattern of trade, providing only seventeen per cent of Hong Kong's imports in 1961. Hong Kong has very important special advantages, especially in terms of human capital, as data from the 1961 census show. The refugees that swarmed into Hong Kong were not illiterate peasants but had an average educational attainment well above what must characterize China as a whole. Among the immigrants were experienced entrepreneurs from Shanghai. In short, Hong Kong was endowed with an energetic, literate, and partially trained labor force and had no scarcity of organizational and entrepreneurial skills. It nevertheless remains a fact that an extraordinarily high density of population relative to resources has not prevented an extraordinarily rapid increase in per capita income.

In the normal course of industrialization the proportion of the population engaged in agriculture and other extractive industries steadily declines. In the history of every highly industrialized area a period was reached during which the number of persons dependent on agriculture was stabilized so that all increases in population of labor force age caused increases only in nonagricultural employment. The period of unchanging numbers engaged in agriculture has typically been followed by a shrinkage in the absolute number. This sequence has been typical both in countries where the initial density of agricultural settlement was very high, such as Japan, or where it was relatively low, as in the United States or New Zealand. The implications of this sequence for employment in industrializing countries will be considered later. Here its relevance is that for countries in the earlier stages of economic development some of the increases in the labor force must seek employment in extractive industries. If the agricultural population is already densely settled (as in India), this necessity undoubtedly constitutes a greater hardship or barrier to rapidly increasing incomes than in a less densely settled country.

As was noted earlier, the underdeveloped countries all suffer from what might be called a high density of population relative to *capital*. Therefore the effects not only of the age distribution but also of the rate of growth of the labor force (with their respective implications for the ease with which capital formation can proceed and for the rate at which it must proceed to attain given objectives in per capita output) operate in sparsely settled as well as in densely settled countries. In very sparsely settled countries the adverse effect upon the possible reduction of density relative to capital of rapid growth of the labor force may be partially offset by an increasingly advantageous relationship between numbers and land area and other resources. A larger population may, when original density is unusually low, permit the use of more efficient large-scale operations. This possibility does not imply, however, that the more rapid the rate of growth the better. Additional capital for the additional labor force is still essential, and rapid growth prevents an increase in the capital/worker rates. Moreover, from a strictly economic point of view the most advantageous way to attain a larger labor force is through immigration, because it is possible by this means to obtain additional labor without incurring the expense of childhood dependency.

Declining Fertility and Per Capita Income: Summary

A reduction in fertility has the immediate effect (during the first generation after the decline begins) of reducing the burden of child dependency without any major effect on the size of the labor force. After twenty or twenty-five years the decline in fertility begins to effect a major reduction in the rate of growth of the labor force. In the more remote future, beginning after forty or fifty years and with increasing importance with the further passage of time, reduced fertility produces a population of lower density—with a smaller labor force relative to the available resources. The age distribution effect of reduced fertility operates to produce during the first generation a larger total national product than would result if fertility had not been reduced. The greater rise in total output results from the fact that the same number of producers—the same number of persons eligible for participation in the labor force—is accompanied by a smaller number of consumers. The smaller number of consumers decreases the fraction of national output that must be allocated to current consumption and thus promotes the mobilization of resources for economic growth. Both private savings and the ability of the government to raise funds for development are increased.

In addition, a smaller number of consumers (especially children) permits the expenditure of savings and tax receipts in ways that raise national output more (or more immediately) than other uses. Less must be spent for primary education, housing, and "social overhead" purposes generally.

Another indirect effect of reduced fertility is that, as a result of larger per capita consumption, the labor force is perhaps more productive because of better nutrition, and because of the effects of rising consumption in combatting apathy, and in providing better work incentives. These effects of a reduced number of consumers relative to the producers in the population caused in the short run by a decline in fertility continue into the future so long as fertility remains below its former level. Starting after twenty-five or thirty years is the additional effect of reduced fertility in slowing down the growth of the labor force. A reduced rate of growth of the labor force means that a given level of net investment can be used to add more to the per capita endowment of the labor force in productive equipment than if the labor force were growing more rapidly.

In the long run the slower rate of growth that reduced fertility brings would result in much lower density of population than with the continuation of high fertility. Even with a fifty per cent reduction in fertility, the population in most underdeveloped areas would grow very substantially during the next two or three generations. For example, in the projection presented earlier showing typical prospects for Latin American countries, with fertility falling by one-half, density would be multiplied by 2.46 in thirty years and by 1.71 in the ensuing thirty years, a total increase of 4.2 times in sixty years. In spite of greatly reduced fertility, the density of workers relative to resources would increase by a factor of something like four in the next two generations.

Brazil is often cited as a country that might derive economic benefits from more dense settlement. Even with a fifty per cent reduction in fertility, the population of Brazil aged fifteen to sixty-four will have increased from 38 million to 161 million in the next sixty years. This would give Brazil a population at these ages sixty years from now forty-two per cent larger than that of the United States today. It is hard to argue that this density would be too small to achieve an efficient exploitation of Brazil's resources, especially since much of Brazil's vast area is of uncertain economic value. Not all underdeveloped areas have as high a current growth potential as Latin America. Current fertility is in many instances below that found in Mexico or Brazil, and in other instances success in reducing mortality is somewhat behind the achievements of the more advanced Latin American countries. In India, for example, where current fertility is probably lower than that of Mexico, Brazil, or Colombia and current mortality higher, the increase in the labor force in the next two generations, if fertility were to be cut in half in the next twenty-five years, would be only two and a half to three times rather than more than four times. It should be added that any increases in density are scarcely advantageous to India's economy.

In sum, the population density that would result from a fifty per cent reduction in fertility in the next twenty-five years would in almost every underdeveloped area be at least adequate for the efficient exploitation of the resources available. The much *higher* density that would result from sustained fertility, a margin of higher density that would increase with ever-greater rapidity the further into the future one looks, might in the most favorable circumstances cause no insuperable difficulties for a few decades. It might be possible, for example, to offset a high density of population in some areas, as Hong Kong has done, by engaging in trade, provided there remain areas of the world prepared to supply agricultural products and raw materials in exchange for finished goods and services. But in all areas, a prolonged continuation of rapid growth would lead to intolerable over-crowding.

Selection **16**

Technological Change in the Less Developed Areas

R. S. ECKAUS

From: Robert E. Asher et al., Development of the Emerging Countries; an Agenda for Research (*Washington, D.C.: Brookings Institution, 1962*), *pp. 120–133. Reprinted by permission of The Brookings Institution.*

The urgency of economic development in the less developed areas of the world is now generally agreed on, even though not so long ago such development was widely regarded as of only marginal concern for United States policy. In any case, the premise having achieved wide acceptance, there need be less distraction from the issues of understanding and implementing economic growth in the less developed areas. There is also general agreement that technological change has a central role in the improvement of the economic conditions of the peoples of the less developed areas. There is less appreciation of the problems of adopting technologies that will use the resources available as effectively as possible to achieve the growth desired. The less developed areas vary in their natural resource endowments, the structure of their economies, their current capabilities, and their future objectives. Unskilled labor is nearly always relatively abundant, while skills and capital equipment are relatively scarce. The degree to which technologies are suited to these different resource availabilities and to the achievement of growth targets determines their aptness for use.

Technological change is important for the less developed areas but is opposed by strong forces of tradition that attempt to forestall the consequent social changes. Thorough study is required in order to decide which technologies will contribute most to economic growth and to find methods of implementation that will facilitate rather than counteract the change.

The discussion that follows will concentrate on technological change in an industrial context; neither related sociological changes nor technological change in agriculture will be considered except insofar as some of the broader generalizations may be applicable.

The Role of Technological Change
in Underdeveloped Areas

Although there is agreement that technological change is important in under-developed areas, there is no unanimity on why it is important or on its most important features. It may not be necessary to decide on its most significant role, but it is necessary to appreciate the various influences it exerts.

The role most commonly assigned to technological change is the achievement of a more rapid rate of economic growth and improvement of the standard of living than would otherwise be possible. The belief is quite widely held that in modern technology there is the means by which the less developed areas can avoid or reduce the sacrifices and the time span required to achieve a satisfactory level and rate of economic development. Certainly there is a substantially larger inventory of technology that can be drawn on now than there was when economic modernization began in the nineteenth century. If this body of knowledge can be made available to the less developed areas, they will undoubtedly progress more rapidly than would otherwise be possible. Although technological transfer will make the tasks easier, it is almost never costless and seldom, if ever, will yield something in the way of output for nothing but a new idea. So the essential economic problems remain of finding the techniques that impose the least sacrifices for achieving specified targets of future output.

Recent economic research on the growth of the United States has reinforced the general impression that, quantitatively, technological change has been a major causal influence. Studies such as those of M. Abramowitz, J. W. Kendrick, and R. M. Solow indicate that ordinary capital accumulation and growth in the labor force can alone account for only 10 to 20 per cent of the economic growth in the United States in the past half century or so.[1] It is by no means clear that all the remainder is due to technological change,[2] but there is a general consensus that it is a substantial factor. These studies, therefore, reinforce the impression of the importance of technological change in the development of the less developed areas.

Technological characteristics have a major role in many of the most widely discussed problems of economic development. The possibilities and the significance of "balanced growth" in economic development depend to a considerable extent on the character of technology. Economic programing, the relative roles of agricultural and industrial development, and significance of "external economies" are

---

[1] Moses Abramowitz, "Resource and Output Trends in the United States since 1870," *American Economic Review, Papers and Proceedings*, Vol. 56 (May 1956), pp. 5–23, reprinted as National Bureau of Economic Research, *Occasional Paper 52* (1956); John W. Kendrick, "Productivity Trends, Capital and Labor," *Review of Economics and Statistics*, Vol. 37 (Aug. 1956), pp. 248–257, reprinted as National Bureau of Economic Research, *Occasional Paper 53* (1956); R. M. Solow, "Technical Change and the Aggregate Production Function," *Review of Economics and Statistics*, Vol. 39 (Aug. 1957), pp. 312–320.

[2] E. Domar refers to it as the "residual." See his as yet unpublished paper, "On the Measurement of Technological Change," which surveys and analyzes the methodology of such measurements.

likewise related to the technology of the various sectors. For such reasons the problem of optimal choice of technology which will be discussed below has been a central theme in development literature.

A less common conception of the role of technological change in the under-developed areas is that it should provide *new* technologies especially adapted to their resources and conditions. This approach recognizes the differences that prevail in the relative availabilities of productive factors in the less developed as compared to the more advanced areas. Most of modern technology has been developed in and for the latter areas and is, therefore, less obviously suited to the conditions of underdeveloped areas. Facilitating technological change in this conception means research to find new production methods suited to the less developed areas and implementing them there.[3]

In a number of analyses the touchstone of a country's prospects for development is its ability to initiate continuing technological change. Professor Everett Hagen makes this the heart of his theory.[4] One has the impression from Professor Hagen that it is both a necessary and sufficient condition for economic development to occur. The rate at which technological change can be implemented is not independent of other economic conditions, to be sure, and there is great scope for all the tools of economic policy. Initiation of technological change is the key, however, and this requires initiators: enterprisers, who play the central role in Professor Hagen's cosmogony. The most important issues in development are, therefore, the emergence of such individuals and the psychological and cultural factors that account for them. These define the crucial areas of research for understanding of the basic problems of development.

Professor Hagen's emphasis is reminiscent of that found in a number of other analysts of economic growth, though none have carried research into the factors which create the entrepreneurial personality so far as he has. Yet the view that the role of the entrepreneur in initiating technological change must certainly be an important factor in development is reinforced by the fact that it has been stressed by Joseph Schumpeter[5] and even earlier historians and analysts of capitalist development.[6]

In addition technological change is regarded by many persons concerned with the advancement of underdeveloped areas as one of the major instruments for necessary changes in the general social structure. There is no doubt that this structure to a considerable extent always reflects former economic and technical patterns. Though these may once have represented an optimal adaptation to the existing conditions, the social patterns that facilitate economic growth are likely to be different. As a result, old adaptations become modern barriers. Technological

---

3 This is an avenue that is being explored at the Massachusetts Institute of Technology by the Center for International Studies and is discussed in the recent staff paper of the Stanford Research Institute, *Scientific Research and Progress in Newly-Developing Countries.*

4 See E. E. Hagen, "How Economic Growth Begins: A General Theory Applied to Japan," *Public Opinion Quarterly*, Vol. 22 (Fall 1958), pp. 373–390.

5 J. Schumpeter, *Business Cycles* (New York: McGraw-Hill Book Company, 1939).

6 The classical references are Max Weber, *The Protestant Ethic and the Spirit of Capitalism* (New York: Charles Scribner's Sons, 1930) and R. H. Tawney, *Religion and the Rise of Capitalism* (New York: Harcourt, Brace, & World, Inc., 1926).

change is undoubtedly powerful in destroying the rationale of old social roles and demanding new ones. A special aspect of this is the effect of technological change on the distribution of income and, therefore, on the division of income between spending and saving. Since capital scarcity is one of the common features of the less developed areas, the effect of a new technology on saving is sometimes regarded as its most significant feature.[7]

The conclusion that technological change has a number of important effects in economic development is hardly challengeable. That does not, however, mean that all types of technological change are equally feasible and desirable in the process of growth or that the underdeveloped areas are intended to become technological facsimiles of the advanced areas. Nor are the means of introducing and disseminating technological change at all obvious. The criteria for technological change and the means of facilitating it must be developed in terms of the influences it is intended to have. All the influences described here are related to growth via increases in the amount of and the productivity of the available resources. Generally, the relation is direct, though in some cases, to be mentioned, it may be inverse.

The first job in discussing technological transfer is to establish a terminology and methodology of measuring technology. These can then be used to address the issues involved in making the optimal choice of technology.

MEASURING TECHNOLOGY AND MAKING AN OPTIMAL CHOICE

It is easy but misleading to assume that everyone knows what is meant by a particular technology. A little experience in discussing technology with engineers and businessmen is enough to show that lack of a common terminology is a major source of confusion. Clearing it up will take us far along the path toward deciding what research is necessary.

The ordinary engineering names or descriptions of technology are usually qualitative and may refer to a set of physical or chemical processes. A technology may be described in terms of some basic physical equations in which the variables are physical quantities such as material weights and volumes or electrical energy or heat inputs. Often a technology will be described and summarized in terms of the name of a particular piece of physical equipment. Thus, an engineer or a businessman or a foreign aid official may discuss the introduction of high-speed automatic lathes in India as a particular technological change. Or they may refer to the Frasch process for sulfur extraction or some particular chemical process for which the equations are well-known.

These are deceptively easy ways of discussing technology. They are easy because they are connotative; they convey a general meaning, at least to people versed in the terminology. But they are deceptive because by themselves they do not convey a precise, quantitative indication of all the inputs and outputs required. It is necessary to *measure* a technology in order to arrive at an appreciation of its

---

[7] Walter Galenson and Harvey Leibenstein, "Investment Criteria, Productivity and Economic Development," *Quarterly Journal of Economics*, Vol. 69 (August 1955). pp. 343–370.

significance. The economist has developed the conceptual tools but has not gone very far in giving them empirical content. The engineer has his own set of concepts, which do have empirical content but are not the most suitable for economic analysis. Therefore, for the means of measurement the skills of the engineer and the economist must be combined.

A technology is defined by an economist by identifying and measuring the various inputs of productive resources that are used to create a certain output.[8] The economist has usually had recourse to such global terms as capital, land (natural resources), and labor, which are not unfamiliar to the businessman as he often discusses his firm in somewhat similar words. These terms do not discriminate sufficiently between alternative types of resources, however, and thus do not match the types of inputs the engineer will ordinarily specify as required for a particular output. Basically, however, the approaches are the same. Though an engineer may sometimes start from the most basic materials, energy, and chemical change concepts, in working through his design procedure he will end up with the values of machinery and material of each type, electrical power, and labor of various skills required for a specified output. What is mainly needed between the engineer and the economist is some reconciliation of vocabularies.

The differences which exist in terminology do not vitiate the main point that ultimately technology is defined both by economists and engineers in terms of the amounts of inputs necessary to achieve a particular output. This permits the comparisons and evaluations that are the necessary basis for the formulation of a policy which must itself be in quantitative terms.

This concept of a technology as something that can be measured and precisely defined will be useful in future discussions. It is not an overstatement to say that it is absolutely necessary if any headway is to be made in attacking the various problems mentioned above of finding, choosing, and transferring appropriate technologies. For example, the quantitative notion of a technology permits the distinction between processes that are physically efficient and those that are not and thus makes it possible to focus on only those processes which might be economically efficient. In comparing any two technologies, one is physically inefficient if it uses more of all productive inputs or even more of any one input, if all its other requirements are the same. There is never any point in using physically inefficient technologies; it amounts to an absolute waste of resources.

When alternative technologies require, for the same level of output, more of some productive factors but less of others, the economic issue arises: which is the best technological process to use in a given situation? This is the problem of making the optimal choice of technology which was referred to previously. Though the problem need not be resolved here, it is important to pose it. As alternative processes are considered in discussing the transfer of technology to underdeveloped areas, the criteria for choice must be kept clearly in mind.

The optimal allocation or combination of resources in production, which is equivalent to the choice of technology, is an old problem in economics and fully discussed in the context of a static economy. In such circumstances the rule for

---

[8] In linear programing terms, this is called an "activity."

choice is, roughly, to use that combination of techniques in the various sectors which, overall, will employ productive factors in proportions as close as possible to the proportions in which the resources are available. This is entirely consistent with using factors in different intensities in different sectors, for optimal allocation requires that resources make the same *relative* contributions to output in the various types of production. Thus, capital-intensive methods in producing electric power in central stations and labor-intensive agricultural methods, for example, may both be optimal for particular countries. The criterion for optimal choice does not involve maximizing either the productivity of the employed labor force, the equipment used, or of any other particular resource input. Its objective is to maximize the total output that can be obtained from *all* the resources *available* to the country. Even with such an optimal allocation, the productivity of any one factor such as the labor employed in some particular line of production can be increased by choosing a different technology which is, say, more capital-intensive. That, however, will always involve a greater loss of output in other sectors. Of course, any costless method of increasing the productivity of labor or any other resource ought always to be seized, but such methods seldom exist. A criterion for choice of technology which is confined to increasing the productivity of the amount used of only one productive factor, such as labor or machines of particular types, is quite misleading.

The criteria for optimal choice of technique in developing economies start from the static criterion and consist of modifications of it that arise from the many problems involving time in an essential way, the statement of different goals, and the imposition of additional constraints. In a dynamic context, for example, differences in the gestation period of production processes and in their durability must also be taken into account in choosing the technology, which in turn determines the relative intensity with which productive factors are used. As between processes with equal input requirements and equal outputs, the one with the quicker payoff is to be preferred. When a faster return requires having more inputs or getting less output, again an economic question arises.[9]

If the goal is to increase the rate of growth, another set of influences related to but not purely technological must be taken into account. Different technologies which use different combinations of labor, capital plant, and equipment and materials will give rise to different distributions of incomes. Each income distribution will have its own savings characteristics and, therefore, will differ in the amounts of resources that will be made available for further investment and economic growth. In this way, there may be a specific savings and investment potential associated with each type of technology. The choice of technology in the context of a developing country must take this feature as well as the immediate contribution to output into account.[10]

---

[9] In this case the best procedure, put briefly, is that which gives the highest present discounted value.

[10] A substantial literature exists on this problem. The recent article by Prof. Hollis B. Chenery, "Comparative Advantage and Development Policy," *American Economic Review*, Vol. 51 (March 1961), pp. 18–51, and the book by A. K. Sen, *Choice of Techniques* (Oxford, 1960), are good guides into this area.

The choice of technology in developing economies involves other features not generally considered in a static context. Economies of scale, which do not fit easily into static economic analysis, may be an essential feature in a developing country. One type of technology may have external effects, as in labor training, which tip the scales in its direction.

These issues may be illustrated and made more concrete by a few examples. The recent Chinese experiment with small iron ore smelting furnaces provides a frequently cited example of a technological revival supposedly more suited to their conditions than the methods now generally in use, as it requires a great deal of the abundant labor, which they have. However, the experiment appears to have been virtually dropped; it is likely that the process was simply physically inefficient. The small furnaces undoubtedly required more fuel per unit of output and possibly more capital also, as well as more labor.

On the other hand, it is not unusual to find plants embodying the most modern technologies in the less developed areas, using a good deal of equipment per worker and relatively little labor with a very high average productivity. This may be justified on several grounds. Sometimes it is argued that such methods are the only physically efficient ones, or, that, even at the low wages prevailing, they are economically more efficient than methods that use more of the abundant labor which is available. Both of these answers, if they were true, would be adequate reasons, but, as stated above, it would be wrong to justify a technology solely on the grounds that it increased the productivity of the workers in the plant.[11] It is, after all, the productivity of the entire labor force and the output of the entire economy which is important for development.

To illustrate the impact of changes in technology on savings patterns, the possible implications of a land reform program can be cited. In some of the less developed areas of the world, land reform programs increase the labor intensity of cultivation by breaking up large landholdings and distributing them in parcels to individual families. This means that a change in technology as well as a change in property relationships is involved. The effect may very well be in such cases to increase output per acre or per hectare and total output, though output per man would fall. A further effect might be that an increased proportion of the total output is consumed as the result of its wider distribution in the hands of the workers of the land, and that total saving is reduced. This in turn would tend to impede further overall progress by reducing the total investment possible.

The problems of measurement are handled best in the context of investigation of the characteristics of particular technologies and so will be discussed in the next section. On the other hand, the principles of optimal choice of technology can be investigated and established before they need to be invested with facts and numbers. The logic of making optimal choices has by no means been completely explored in spite of the extensive literature cited above. More work is needed in order to integrate the rules for optimal choice into an overall programing framework. In the present state of knowledge the choice issue is usually analyzed for

---

[11]As an example of this kind of reasoning, see Richard L. Meier, "Automation and Economic Development," *Bulletin of the Atomic Scientists*, Vol. 10 (April 1954), pp. 129–133.

projects as if they are and could be considered separately from each other and independently of the overall growth pattern of a country.

There are analytical tools which, when given empirical content, can be used to establish the *consistency* of various projects in an overall plan. These are best represented by the input-output approach first developed by Professor Wassily W. Leontief at Harvard University[12] and perhaps most skillfully used in application to underdeveloped areas by Professor Chenery.[13] Where input-output methods cannot be applied, something equivalent has to be developed for the purpose of establishing overall consistency in economic programing. The development of input-output-type information must, therefore, be seriously considered in research plans for any underdeveloped area. However, it would be premature to put such research on the current agenda for every country. In many areas the economic programing currently required is not sufficiently complex or elaborate to require the full input-output apparatus to establish consistency. In these and other cases, the quality of the statistical data available may not warrant the empirical effort involved. Where the data make the project feasible, various methods of constructing input-output tables should be considered. These are by no means completely settled in themselves so that in this, as in other fields, alternative approaches should not be foreclosed by a premature commitment to a particular method.

The problem of optimality is logically and practically distinct from that of consistency. Though input-output tables will help establish the latter, more is required for the former problem. The theoretical framework necessary for forming policy has not yet been completed, though theoretical programing models exist which give useful insights and are of value as partial guides. Relevant work is going on,[14] but much more needs to be done. Again, for some countries, the priorities are so obvious and the opportunities so limited that no highly sophisticated tests of optimality and consistency are necessary. For other areas, with greater scope for choice and action and better data availabilities, the problems of formulating a consistent and optimal development program are pressing ones.

The recent attempts to place United States economic aid on a long-term basis highlight the need. This country may soon be asking recipients of our economic aid to prepare long-term development programs. Yet the means to do this are not fully available. Therefore, more research is necessary just to get a good start.

The problem of optimal choice of technology can be treated with the full generality with which it needs to be treated only in the context of complete, consistent, and optimal programs. Though it will always be necessary to make prag-

---

[12]*Studies in the Structure of the American Economy, Theoretical and Empirical Explorations in Input-Output Analysis*, Harvard Economic Research Project (Oxford University Press, 1953).

[13]For example, "The Role of Industrialization in Investment Programs," *American Economic Review, Papers and Proceedings*, Vol. 45 (May 1955), pp. 40–57.

[14]For example, S. Chakravarty, *The Logic of Investment Planning* (Amsterdam: North-Holland Publishing Co., 1960), and "The Use of Shadow Prices in Programme Evaluation" (unpublished); Hollis B. Chenery, "The Interdependence of Investment Decisions," in Moses Abramowitz *et al.*, *The Allocation of Economic Resources* (Stanford, Calif.: Stanford University Press, 1959); R. S. Eckaus and L. Lefeber, "Capital Formation and Economic Growth: A Theoretical and Empirical Analysis" (unpublished).

matic compromises with inadequate methods and data, the nature of the inadequacies should be recognized.

This conclusion can be illustrated by another type of reference. One of the sectors in which the choice of technology is most important for underdeveloped areas is transportation. Transportation systems can be based on railroads and locomotives and rolling stock of various types, or highways and buses, trucks, and cars, or some combination of the two systems. The choice of methods is a choice of technology. Yet it is obviously not one that can be made in abstraction from the rest of the economy for the choice itself will determine how the rest of the economy develops. That is, it is not legitimate to ask "What is the optimal technology to move so many ton-miles of freight?" and then choose a technology of railroads or highways and buses and leave it at that, because the answer to the question will change the way the question is formulated; specifically it will change the number of ton-miles which have to be transported to achieve the economic development specified.[15]

Lacking a fully general way of treating the problem, partial solutions may have to be accepted, but that does not justify being permanently satisfied with second best. There should be a major effort to improve the ability of countries to take into account the full ramifications of technological choice: to have that choice fully sensitive to the targets specified, on the one hand, and to have the choice feed back and affect the targets to be chosen, on the other hand. The analytical problems are among the most complex faced by economists. Research work in this area may seem far removed from the pressing issues of economic development because of its abstraction. Yet it is only by pursuing the abstractions that models can be formulated which, when given empirical content, will provide concrete guidance in particular circumstances.

There are relatively few individuals working in this area, and nearly all of them are in academic institutions. The nature of the research, which must include tentative theorizing, also suggests that academic institutions or private research organizations are the proper location for such work. It is likely to the done best if the injunction to make a contribution to development programing is clear, though full scope is given for theoretical development.

FINDING TECHNOLOGIES ADAPTED TO THE CONDITIONS OF UNDERDEVELOPED AREAS

There are two aspects to finding technologies adapted to the conditions of underdeveloped areas. The first constitutes searching among already known technologies; the second involves research to find new technical methods especially suited to the unique conditions of underdeveloped areas. Both aspects will be discussed below, but it will help to clarify the issues if another question is discussed first—why the choice of technology is less difficult in advanced than in underdeveloped areas.

---

[15]See Louis Lefeber, *Allocation in Space: Production, Transport, and Industrial Location* (Amsterdam: North-Holland Publishing Co., 1958).

In principle the problems of technological change in advanced countries are not different from those in underdeveloped areas, but practically they are of a different magnitude. The technological changes occurring, or in prospect, are first of all pervasive and profound departures from previously used techniques. These have become imbued with cultural traditions so that a change in production methods requires fundamental adjustments in all aspects of the society. By comparison technological innovations in advanced countries are, for the most part, marginal changes occurring in societies more readily adaptable to change.

Secondly, technological changes in underdeveloped areas are nearly always imported from advanced countries. The characteristic differences in the relative availabilities of the various productive resources in advanced and underdeveloped areas have already been pointed out. As a result, while some of the technological imports may economize on all factors and be physically more efficient than existing techniques, other imported techniques may very well economize on the wrong factors. For example, while it may make good sense to substitute capital equipment for United States labor at three dollars an hour, it may not be sensible in other countries where equivalent labor is, say, three dollars a day, or three dollars for two days, or even less.

Technological change is a more obvious problem in the less developed areas and attracts more attention and greater pressures. It is done more consciously, more publicly, and more often under government control if not under its direction. In advanced countries it occurs regularly with less public attention and seldom with government interference.

Not only do the less developed countries face more difficulties in adopting changes in technology than do the economically more advanced countries, they have much more difficulty in generating new technologies especially suited to their conditions. The overwhelming part of the research and development which is currently going on to develop new technologies is in advanced countries and directed toward their conditions. The amount of technological research directed especially at the problems of underdeveloped countries is virtually negligible.[16]

The research facilities in the less developed countries are themselves quite limited, while research in the advanced areas is directed to their own technical problems. The relative poverty and slow growth rates of the less developed countries mean that they have not constituted a substantial market which has warranted the attention of those private companies that sponsor technical research. Lack of knowledge of the needs and potential requirements in such areas has also contributed to their neglect. Academic research in the advanced countries is preoccupied mainly with problems in the forefront of scientific and engineering sophistication. Rightly or wrongly the applications are directed primarily at the conditions found in the already developed countries.

It should, therefore, not be surprising that finding and implementing appropriate technological changes include some of the most difficult problems in economic development. However, these problems once identified are, themselves, amenable to research.

---

[16]The national scientific research institutes such as those of India and Pakistan do concern themselves with these problems to some extent.

The Case Against Indiscriminate Capital Intensity of Investment in Overpopulated Developing Countries

ERIC B. SHEARER

From: Indian Journal of Economics, *Vol. XLVI, No. 181 (October 1965), pp. 129–130 and 133–146. Reprinted by permission of the* Indian Journal of Economics.

Some recent literature on economic development—though by no means all— has rightly touched on or emphasized what this writer considers to be one of the fundamental problems—perhaps the key problem—in development policy: the apparent conflict between the two principal goals of economic development, accelerated capital formation and maximum employment of labor. This paper is intended as a contribution to a better general understanding of the nature and definition of the problem, which it suggests is perhaps more in need of practical solutions than of theoretical conflict; it also attempts to outline some of the possible solutions as well as the dangers posed by our failure to come to grips with the issue.

In the following discussion, these points are taken for granted:

1. The problem is real only for countries in an early stage of development with a substantial surplus of labor in relation to "horizontal" land resources.[1]

2. Under these conditions, industrialization is the ultimate key to raising labor productivity in agriculture by providing alternative part-time and full-time employment at higher real earnings.

---

[1] The term "horizontal" land resources is meant to reflect land which can be brought into production—or the yields of which can be increased—without an investment of monetary capital per unit of additional productive employment approaching that required for industrial job creation. The mere investment of underemployed rural labor—in any form—to achieve greater land productivity is, of course, not considered "monetary" capital. The implication is that the author agrees completely with those who would place primary emphasis on the development of agriculture under conditions of adequate "horizontal" land resources. (For a masterful exposition of this point of view, see Gunnar Myrdal, *Priorities in the Development Efforts of Underdeveloped Countries and Their Trade and Financial Relations with Rich Countries*, paper presented at the Societa Italiana per 1, l'Organizzazione Internazionale, Rome (March 1964).

Even among the already developed countries there were marked contrasts in the ease with which they adjusted to the comparatively gradual industrial "revolution," depending on the ratio of population to readily accessible natural resources (principally land) at home or in dependent territories or on the possibilities for emigration. But even in those countries where industrialization entailed, at one time or other, serious economic maladjustments and political upheavals, the very gradualness of the process of raising labor productivity, in the then-existing institutional framework, eventually led to economic maturity with a fair degree of social and political equilibrium.

The population explosion and national and international political pressures make a repetition of the industrial evolution of the nineteenth and twentieth centuries unthinkable, even if it were theoretically advisable and practically feasible to re-enact gradual technological progress. But should we not ask ourselves whether the indiscriminate transplanting of equipment and technology from the most advanced nations to backward economies saddled with a low-productivity farm labor force pressing on the land resources can lead to real economic growth without regimentation? Should these countries, in other words, allocate their savings and their borrowed and free foreign resources in a large measure to highly capital-intensive investment, rather than to the type of investment that would create more extra-agricultural jobs while *gradually* raising labor productivity? As imported technology and equipment grow more and more complex and automated, countries with large and rapidly growing low-productivity farm labor forces will find it increasingly difficult to create extra-agricultural jobs as they rush to "catch up."

•   •   •

THE NATURE AND MAGNITUDE OF THE PROBLEM TODAY

The political realities of today make a repetition of the traditional development process, even in its late stages, unthinkable for the overpopulated nations. Labor unions in even the most backward countries are demanding and getting minimum wage standards; labor and social security legislation is at the top of the agenda of the governments of most newly emerging or developing nations; the rivalry between East and West for the allegiance of these same nations, with all its ramifications, has produced great popular expectations for short-term improvements in individual levels of living.

At the same time, there are inevitably arising pressures demanding the creation of new jobs for the armies of unemployed or underemployed in the rural areas and for the additional job-seekers which are entering the labor market each year. In fact, the problem is of huge magnitude precisely because the majority of the countries in early stages of development have a staggering backlog of unemployed or underemployed labor[2] and have currently and for the foreseeable future the greatest rate of increase in population and thus in the potential labor force. This

---

[2] That the bulk of this backlog always weighs on the agricultural sector is thought to be evidence of the point this paper is attempting to make, i.e., that industrial development currently is unable to absorb it.

rate of increase, it should be noted, in an effort to put this problem in historical perspective, is far in excess of that which occurred at any other time in human history. Certainly the countries which earlier experienced the industrial revolution did not (despite Malthus) have to cope with anything comparable. The seriousness of the situation is illustrated by the relative economic growth data for India and Pakistan for 1950–1957. With an average annual growth in aggregate real output of a little less than 3 per cent, their population increase of, respectively, 1.3 and 1.7 per cent (certainly not among the highest in the underdeveloped world today) has kept the growth in per capita real product down to 1.6 and 1.1 per cent per year. In Ecuador, despite a tangible annual growth in aggregate product of 4.7 per cent per year during this same period, the 3 per cent rate of population increase has allowed a per capita economic growth of only 1.7 per cent per year during these same years.

According to the United Nations, the population of the critical areas of the noncommunist world (South America, the Indian subcontinent, and the Middle East and North Africa) in 1960 was nearly 1.1 billion and is expected to grow by about 260 million or 23 per cent during the present decade.[3] Let us assume that, since the sharp rise in the rate of increase is a relatively recent phenomenon, there will be only 80 million new job-seekers during this period. Taking rough averages of a labor force equivalent to one-third of total population, and two-thirds of the labor force engaged in agriculture and related activities, let us also assume that a ten per cent reduction of the existing farm labor force during the decade would be a desirable objective. This would add another 75 million workers for whom productive employment outside of agriculture and services would have to be found (since no significant increase of productive employment in services can be reasonably expected at this stage of economic development).

Only about one-third of these same populations has an average per capita income of $100 or more; all except about 50 million have incomes of less than $300. If all of the 155 million new workers were to be employed in light manufacturing industries, at a modest investment of $2,500 per worker, this would call for a total investment in ten years of nearly $400 billion. This is equivalent to nearly four times the combined estimated national incomes in 1957 of the countries comprised in the "critical regions"; it is $150 billion more than the sum of 15 per cent of their national incomes invested for ten years plus $70 billion from the capital-exporting countries.

A substantial percentage of these 155 million workers will doubtless be employed in activities requiring less capital investment than manufacturing industries, even under the currently pursued investment policies. But most national development plans—to the extent they exist—at least implicitly look to manufacturing industry as the key to employment. Besides, there will necessarily be a great deal of investment, during the early years of development, in intrinsically capital-intensive, basic industry. Hence, it would appear that foreseeable capital resources will be

---

[3] Based on Paul C. Hoffman, *One Hundred Countries, One and One Quarter Billion People*. The population of the some 30 "problem countries" in the sense of this paper is actually closer to 900 million.

insufficient to provide productive employment for all, even at the very modest figure of a $2,500 investment per worker. The problem is aggravated by the current trend toward capital-intensive equipment and technology. The total investment (including plant) per new worker required in U.S. manufacturing industries was estimated in 1950, for instance, at $14,000.[4]

A convincing example of the fallacy of the expectation that industrial development of the conventional type provides new employment—at least in the short run—is cited by Myrdal in the paper referred to in footnote 1. In a study undertaken under his guidance by the ECE in the Central Asian Republic of the USSR, it was found that during the decade 1950–1960 the labor force employed in manufacturing actually decreased, despite heavy industrialization. Likewise, he continues, Indian census figures for this same period show that "industrialization has had hardly any effect at all on the proportion of the labor force that needs to obtain its livelihood from agriculture."

Approached in a more conventional way, the problem looks equally staggering: to raise the mean per capita real income of these populations by only one-fourth (to about $125) in the ten-year period, given a population growth of nearly one-fourth in the same period, would, at a very modest capital-output ratio of 3:1 still call for a capital investment of about $210 billion. If a three-year lag between investment and production is assumed, this would represent an annual investment need of $30 billion during seven years. This is equivalent to 30 per cent of the combined national incomes of these countries in 1960, or at least twice the rate of savings which could reasonably be expected. These figures are not designed to make the job of development appear hopeless; they merely point up the futility of applying "Western"-type capital-output ratios.

A case in point (though in a country with plentiful underused land resources) is the 10-year development plan of Colombia, prepared with conventional CEPAL methodology.[5] While the authors of the plan seem to be unaware of the connection between capital investment and job creation, the figures for the required analysis are provided. In reviewing development during the decade (1951–1960) preceding the plan period, it is stated that employment in the manufacturing industry increased by 82,000, or 50 per cent, while the volume of production rose 95 per cent. Other estimates show that average fixed investment in this sector at the end of the period was in the neighbourhood of 3,000 dollars per worker. The plan then projects an additional fixed investment of 8 billion pesos (at 1958 prices) —with the implicit but unrealistic assumption that the average per worker remains unchanged—for the subsequent decade and (in a separate chapter) the creation of 225,000 more jobs in manufacturing compared with an increase of 2 million in the total labor force.

Most current analysis and planning of basic economic development seems to be concerned essentially with aggregate and per capita increase in the real product.

---

[4] *Capital Goods Review*, No. 3 (Aug. 1950) as quoted in *America's Needs and Resources* (1955 ed.), p. 911.

[5] Consejo Nacional de la Politica Economica y Planeacion, *Plan General de Desarollo Economico y Social* (Bogota, 1962). Primera y Segunda Parte; see also Instituto Colombiano de Reforma Agraria (INCORA), *Informe de Actividades en 1962*, (Bogota, 1963), p. 19.

The "population explosion," of course, plays a large role in these studies, which consider the race between GNP and population as the central problem. What does not seem to enter into the conventional calculation is the maldistribution of the growth in national income which is likely to result from highly capital-intensive industrial investment.

In a rigorously regimented economy, particularly of the communist type, measures can be taken to realize the growth potential from abundant labor resources over long periods without regard to the social and political cost. While, on the one hand, capital-intensive equipment and technology can be introduced at will in manufacturing, extremely labour-intensive methods can be used simultaneously in extractive industries, agriculture, and infrastructure development. Under such a system, at least theoretically, in the absence of a labor "market" and unions, differences in sectoral marginal productivity of labor can be equalized or, at least, disregarded, effectively; in other words, everybody would share equally (though at first in hardly tangible increments) in the greater productivity of isolated sectors or industries. Redundant farm labor used for "nation building" becomes an asset instead of a liability for long-term development, and resources can be channeled exclusively into those basic sectors which the planners consider of the highest priority, rather than being even partially devoted to the satisfaction of demand for "nonessential" goods and services from limited, higher-income sections of the population.

This is roughly the model of the process which took place in the Soviet Union until very recently. But even there social and political pressures are apparently causing important deviations from this model, though great differences continue in labor productivity between agriculture and industry, and among industrial sectors.

Only in Communist China is there a substantial likelihood that this pattern will persist for some time with adjustments only in matters of methodology rather than in substance. If this immense mass of underdeveloped people and area show physical progress in this manner, low-income populations in the noncommunist underdeveloped areas, witnessing at home a lopsided rise of capital-intensive industries accompanied by an unequal distribution of rising national product, may eventually be induced to try the communist recipe, regardless of the cost in human values of which the well-fed statesmen, philosophers, and social scientists of the free world warn—for they may be led to believe that they have nothing to lose but the value of their marginal product.

Today, in the countries desiring to develop under a democratic political system, wages cannot easily be kept low in favor of savings, and national income must be distributed increasingly according to ideas of equity. But this more equal social distribution of the marginal national income is more than a political necessity; it must take place in order to create the demand for the marginal output. Thus, if the benefits of the jump in labor productivity in isolated industrial sectors of a generally low-productivity economy are to be limited essentially to the entrepreneurs and labor in those sectors—as they will tend to be in a democratic setting—the only solution in view would seem to be a siphoning off by the state of the sectoral surplus for redistribution among the rest of the economy, probably in the form of subsidized wages and/or consumption in all other sectors. Otherwise the output of the capital-intensive industries would tend not to be consumed in the long run. An alternative would be a price system (either controlled or under near-perfect competition) largely isolated from international markets which would permit the sale of the output of the new industries at the real costs resulting from the combination of capital-intensive equipment and technology with low wages. Both solutions would entail a high degree of government control and would tend to lead to regimentation.

An illustration of what can happen can be found in the post-World War II developments in Italy. There, despite rapid growth in industrial and agricultural investment in the 1950s—including large-scale land reform—the increase in productivity associated with this investment barely allowed the creation of new jobs for the annual increase in the labor force during the decade. It was not until the end of this decade that a tangible dent was made in the sizeable backlog of unemployed "industrial" workers and a beginning in the farm labor force. Only then did wages—especially in services—rise to a degree which implied a real distribution of the growth in national income. If it took Italy ten years to reach this stage from its relatively high plateau of economic and technological development, with a fair-sized program of social insurance, with substantial emigration outlets, and with a prodigious infusion of foreign assistance and investment, how many centuries would be required for, say, India, if it insisted on investing in the latest capital-intensive equipment of the industrialized world?

In India, the sharp differences between the protagonists of a large role for the "cottage industries" and the "modernists" is an indication that the problem is being felt, though not sufficiently thought through. To follow the cottage industry protagonist all the way would be truly nothing short of a re-enactment of the historical process which took place in the advanced countries. Since it would largely negate even the West's technological advances not primarily directed at labor saving, it would deny India the benefit of this important and relatively cheap resource. Besides, investigation has shown that, in extreme cases, an exaggerated insistence on maximizing hand labor may not only lead to stagnation but can actually be more wasteful of capital than the adoption of more advanced technology. On the other extreme, the proponents of indiscriminate use of "modern" equipment and technology in India's industrialization run the risk of creating islands of local high labor productivity in a sea of subsistence levels of living.[6] Each of the two policies seems hardly designed to produce any real growth of the Indian economy. What is needed here is a middle ground based on social and economic rationality rather than ideological fanaticism or technological infatuation.

---

[6] *The Economist* of March 26, 1960, cites a few interesting and frightening examples in its special section on India (p. 1277), such as the fact that, at that time, six Indian workers at the Tata plant at Jamshedpur equalled the productivity of five Germans at the Daimler Benz works in Stuttgart. It is symptomatic, incidentally, that nowhere in this 14-page section is there any reference to the problem of job-creation.

Insistence by the developing countries to look towards export markets, the pressures of international competition—intensified by the advanced countries' tariff protection against "cheap foreign labor"—will, of course, make it difficult—perhaps even inadvisable—for them to resist the temptation to install the latest labor-saving devices obtainable on the world market in order to take double advantage of their low wage rates. The Indian textile industry's cry for "rationalization" falls into this category. But it should be noted that, whereas Japan, India's chief competitor in foreign textile markets, developed and produced its own high-speed machinery to maintain its competitive lead and thus created new jobs in the process, India needs to import the bulk of its requirements of textile machinery at this time. Thus, in the case of India, foreign exchange and domestic capital, both scarce resources, are being tied up in an effort actually to reduce employment of labor, an over-abundant resource, without, at the same time, creating either jobs for the redundant textile workers (not to speak of reducing the chronic excess of farm labor) or additional domestic demand for textiles, and without necessarily maximizing total profits. Whether the ultramodernization of this industry will bring in sufficient foreign exchange in the long run to compensate for the apparent initial social misallocation of resources should at least have been the subject of serious study.

In the case of industries whose output during the amortization period of the first installation is *prima facie* planned exclusively, or almost exclusively, for the domestic market, there would appear to be little objective justification for choosing to transplant the latest capital-intensive processes into an economy characterized by low wages and by the need for accelerated creation of new jobs and skills (except, of course, in the eyes of the individual entrepreneur). On the contrary, it might be advisable in those sectors to recreate at least the most recent phase of the technological evolution through which the already industrialized countries went, thus raising productivity and wages gradually, while, at the same time, creating a maximum number of new jobs and training workers in the simpler skills.

David Felix touches on the problem in a recent paper, when he states that "while capitalizing on other peoples' scientific and technological pioneering is a major advantage, it also has its undesirable features," and "although in a broad sense the objective of economic development is to economize on labor, that is, to raise labor productivity, methods that pay off socially when wages are $8 a day or more may be optimal when they are $1 a day or less." However, he then abandons the point he started out to make so well when he points out that the techniques of a steel mill do not differ markedly between a developed and an underdeveloped country, and then proceeds on the axiom that "industrial investment in underdeveloped countries . . . involves heavy fixed capital costs, the machinery and equipment component of which must be almost entirely imported."[7]

The pitfall here, which is probably common in much of current thought on this matter, is that the illustration is limited to the steel mill. There are obviously

---

[7] "Agrarian Reform and Industrial Growth," *International Development Review*, Vol. II, No. 2, p. 18.

industries or processes, mostly in the "heavy" fields, and in those others of traditionally slow amortization where a labor-intensive plant or process (even if the equipment could be found) in an underdeveloped country would—if not ridiculous —be neither in the economic nor in the social interest of that country. Steel mills are one example; plants for the production of other metals, of basic chemicals, fertilizer, and electric power are others. But is there any reason this concept needs to be applied across the board by social planners?

CHOICE OF TECHNOLOGY

The problem of technological choice has been intensively treated in at least two recent works, from both theoretical and empirical points of view.[8] Mr. Sen's highly mathematical treatment of the subject is undoubtedly a major (perhaps the only) contribution to theoretical analysis of labor-intensive versus capital-intensive investment in industrial development, though it seems to try too hard to prove that a maximum rate of saving is largely incompatible with maximum labor employment, thus leading to the concomitant, purported dilemma between short-run increase in output and long-term growth. It is characteristic of the nature of the approach to the problem that this study does not suggest any clear-cut answers. Fortunately, Mr. Sen was able to keep his head above his formulae; in fact, he admits that. "It is no use complaining that the real world is not as simple as that of the text-book . . . The solution of our problem in actual cases must necessarily involve a considerable degree of guesswork" (pp. 57–58).

This is illustrated by the at-times diametrically-opposed *ad hoc* recommendations by international experts cited in the first article of the U.N. bulletin entitled "Capital Intensity in Industry in Underdeveloped Countries." But in this instance, too, the author comes to the conclusion that "most experts advocating labor-intensive industrialization policies lay emphasis on short-run rather than long-run aspects" (p. 20). Nevertheless, he, too, finally concedes that "macro-economic tools . . . are inadequate" for the purpose of determining a proper "factor mix" and suggests that only case studies can provide the necessary guidance. Professor Tinbergen's approach in the second paper of the U.N. bulletin "Choice of Technology in Industrial Planning" represents a refreshing pragmatic approach, and his final recommendation to the "technicians, industrialists and governments" in the industrially developed countries to "reorient technological research with a view to meeting the requirements of [the] economics [of the underdeveloped countries] and in particular their need for saving capital" is very noteworthy.

The reluctance on the part of some economists to consider maximization of labor-intensive and capital-saving techniques in industrial development seems to derive for the most part from the assumption (sometimes disguised in the form of a conclusion) that such techniques are incompatible with maximization of further capital formation (see, for instance, Mr. Sen's treatment). This, in turn, is based on the contention that, in an institutional setting which does not permit wage

---

[8] A. K. Sen, *Choice of Techniques* (Oxford, 1960); United Nations, "Industrialization and Productivity," Bulletin No. 1 (New York, April 1958), pp. 5–48.

ceilings, and at subsistence wage rates, the surplus created by higher productivity and distributed in the form of higher labor earnings will tend to go into consumption rather than savings. From a theoretical point of view, this no doubt has a certain validity. But it assumes that the bulk of the compensation of the additional labor will be in the form of wages to factory workers, rather than in increased earnings of family-type or cooperative enterprise where the individual workers may have a stake in saving, and that capitalists in the underdeveloped countries have a high propensity to save and to invest productively. It also does not make any allowance for instruments available to the government for diverting a part of the additional wages (as well as of profits) into savings, through direct and indirect taxation, for instance.

Another, less fundamental objection advanced against labor intensity is the greater cost involved in training greater numbers of workers, which, it is said, also represents a form of capital investment and should not be ignored. This is an unfortunate fallacy evidently springing from minds accustomed to thinking in terms of classical rather than welfare economics and which tend to ignore the great role played by management in productivity. In fact, is not the training of large numbers of workers in relatively simple technology one of the most productive investments in future economic growth and one which, unlike most physical equipment, appreciates rather than depreciates?

Elsewhere the cost of social investment in urbanization of large numbers of redundant agricultural workers is treated as a liability in terms of a hidden "capital cost." This, too, is a result of conditioning to the essentially ethical differentiation of "productive" and "nonproductive" investments. The real point is that these very needs for social infrastructure investments can be an important stimulus to economic activity, particularly since they call, for the most part, for labor-intensive investments. Indeed, a good case can be made for maximizing "social overhead" investments in terms of the "bargain" which they represent for the long run if executed at today's opportunity costs of unemployed labor.

CONCLUSION

The thesis of this paper is that in overpopulated countries and in a nonregimented political system a policy based primarily on the indiscriminate transplantation of equipment and technology from economies with daily factory wages of $8 or $10 or even $20 to those with wages of $1 or less (particularly where factory wages are already substantially above the average per capita earnings of the labor force as a whole) cannot lead to economic growth, except, perhaps, with the aid of exceptional measures hitherto untried in nonregimented underdeveloped nations. Aside from the unnecessary strain on the balance of payments—current and future—and on the limited pool of technicians and skilled workers capable of handling and servicing (or being trained to handle and service) such equipment, it will lead to the superimposition of an artificial facade on economies which, by and large, will continue to be backward. There will continue to be an excess of farm labor—probably a growing excess—whose low productivity will prevent the creation of the demand for the output of the overcapitalized industrial sectors. The ultimate result will be disastrous economically, socially, and politically.

Some aspects of possible reorientations of development policies which come to mind are:

1. Maximum employment of redundant farm labor on infrastructure and "nation building" projects: dams, roads, railroads, schools, soil conservation, housing, reforestation, etc. accompanied by the greatest possible economy of imported equipment. The substitution of human labor with expensive mechanical equipment should not be dictated by moral considerations, nor, in these projects, necessarily by microeconomic calculations of comparative cost. In construction, *as in agriculture*, there must be developed criteria other than that of "greater efficiency" to govern the decisions on mechanization. For we must divest ourselves of the notion that we are doing the underemployed farm laborer a favor, either in the short or in the long run, by substituting mechanical equipment for his labor unless and until we can find alternative, more productive employment for him. Only where the use of mechanical equipment guarantees much more rapid completion of a particular job which should not be delayed for overriding reasons of national interest, or where such equipment can perform tasks which are unattainable for human labor (quantitatively or qualitatively) should there be a *prima facie* case for mechanization. Food grants by surplus producing countries, to be used as part payment of wages, can be an important incentive and support for such a policy if they are guaranteed for a sufficiently long period.

2. The industrialized world's governments, engineers, and enterprises should concentrate on inventing and producing *capital*-saving equipment for industries in the underdeveloped, overpopulated countries and on designing plants which, during their amortization period, would—at each step of the process—represent the optimum combination of modern technology with local labor at prevailing wage rates. Except in the case of inherently capital-intensive processes and export industries, the determining consideration should be whether highly mechanized equipment would result in a substantially better product. What is needed, in other words, is a conscious effort to adapt to equipment and plants specially designed for low-cost labor economies those among the latest technological developments which are not necessarily related to high-cost labor, instead of merely selling and financing plants and equipment designed in scale and degree of mechanization for an entirely different situation of relative input costs.[9]

   While many firms, even in the most advanced nations, could profitably devote themselves to this task, it may be particularly advantageous for some of the more recently industrialized or industrializing countries to specialize in capital-saving equipment. Such countries as Italy, Spain, Greece, Yugoslavia, Japan, and even India, for example, could conceivably base much new industrial capacity on the great potential demand for this type of equipment over a long period; their relatively low labor costs place them in a very competitive position for the production of capital goods.

   It might also be useful to organize a program for supplying to underdeveloped countries partially or wholly reconditioned equipment and plants which have become obsolete in high-wage economies only, or principally, because of the labor input required to run them. Such plants and equipment would have the double advantage of low cost and great labor intensity and would result in

---

[9] *Cf.* A. O. Hirschman, *The Strategy of Economic Development* (New Haven, 1958), pp. 151–152.

important foreign exchange and capital savings to the importing countries. Concessions in terms of customs duties by the importing countries would provide an incentive for this kind of capital saving.[10, 11]

3. The underdeveloped countries should attempt to manufacture domestically as much capital equipment as is practicable and economical for both industry and agriculture. In fact, it might be much more advantageous for them to import certain types of mass-produced consumer goods to meet certain short-run demands. Rather than to set up capital-intensive plants for the output of which there may not be sufficient long-run demand, they might better devote their limited capital resources to the inherently labor-intensive making of producer goods which will foster a gradual industrialization process. (To suggest that these countries give priority to establishing primitive consumer goods industries is nonsense if only because they tend to be wasteful of both capital and labor.)

4. At the same time the underdeveloped nations should undertake studies designed to identify the optimum combination of capital equipment with local labor at prevailing wage rates, from an economic and social point of view, industry by industry and process by process. Such studies could conceivably be carried out cooperatively by countries with similar wage levels and relative population pressure, perhaps under the sponsorship and with the collaboration of the IBRD and the regional U. N. economic commissions. Based on the results of these studies, policies should be developed which would lead to the desired degree of capital intensity, by direct or indirect means (taxation and tariffs come to mind among the latter). Otherwise, it is doubtful that the aims of points 2 and 3 above would be achieved.

POSTSCRIPT

The implementation of economic development policies in the sense outlined here will doubtless entail a great deal of state intervention, certainly much more than during the laissez-faire economic growth of the West, where the by-now socially and politically well-integrated mass-consumption economies make modified "free enterprise" the logical system. Maximization of labor-intensive infrastructure works would require massive organizational and executive programs of a public character. The establishment of criteria and guidelines designed to avoid excessive capital intensity of new investments (as well as of privately financed or executed construction), and thus to spread available capital more widely through the productive structure, would call for thorough government-sponsored studies and planning. Their application would necessitate government controls, incentives, and disincentives for private industrial investment and, in some cases, even direct government investment and operation. Governments would have to shoulder a large portion of the cost of training and urbanizing labor in order to encourage private enterprise to maximize employment.[12]

---

[10]A recent paper by Albert Waterston of the IBRD, entitled "The Use of Second Hand Machinery in Developing Economies," and published by the International Co-operation Administration, makes the point very well and provides some interesting recent examples and proposals.

[11]In many instances, though not always, small scale and decentralization of enterprises can also make a substantial difference. *Cf.* Eugene Staley, "Modern Small Scale Industry," in *International Development Review* (June 1961).

[12]While private enterprise would have to establish a form of "partnership" with labor, in part to avoid excessive government regulation.

Since the urgency of the task requires the forced draft mobilization of all available resources, it is already quite clear that accelerated economic development of the underdeveloped countries entails, in any case, much more public control and intervention than did the gradual process, in a much different national and international political climate, of the advanced countries. Thus, it seems advisable to drop the pseudo-ideological battles over the degree of government intervention and over the pros and cons of the "private" versus the "public" sector, in order to concentrate on finding the most practical measures for assuring private enterprise in conformity with public policy, and the politically least dangerous institutions and most efficient administration for public undertakings. Much damage has already been done around the world by equating "free enterprise capitalism" with democracy, and public controls over and ownership of certain means of production with communism (or doctrinaire socialism). In the underdeveloped countries striving desperately for higher levels of living via the shortest possible route, it is not so-called "creeping socialism" (i.e., forceful and social-minded public planning) which poses a threat to free political institutions. On the contrary, the great danger lies in the probability that uncontrolled private enterprise alone will not be able to meet the expectations of the awakening hundreds of millions. Should their governments also fail them, their most likely reaction will be to turn to the communist panacea, particularly if democracy continues to be identified with types of capitalism and technocracy more appropriate to capital-abundant, labor-scarce economies than to labor-abundant, capital-scarce economies.

Selection **18**

The Role of Agriculture
in Economic Development

B. F. JOHNSTON and J. W. MELLOR

From: American Economic Review, *Vol. LI, No. 4 (September 1961), pp. 566 and 581–591. Reprinted by permission of the* American Economic Review *and the authors.*

The present article deals with issues that have too often been discussed in terms of the false dichotomy of agricultural vs. industrial development. The approach adopted here is to examine the interrelationships between agricultural and industrial development and to analyze the nature of agriculture's role in the process of economic growth.

Diversity among nations in their physical endowment, cultural heritage, and historical context precludes any universally applicable definition of the role that agriculture should play in the process of economic growth. Nevertheless, certain aspects of agriculture's role appear to have a high degree of generality because of special features that characterize the agricultural sector during the course of development. The nature of agriculture's role is, of course, highly relevant to determining the appropriate "balance" between agriculture and other sectors with respect to (1) direct government investment or aids to investment, (2) budget allocations for publicly supported research and education-extension programs, and (3) the burden of taxation levied on different sectors.

·   ·   ·

It has been argued that a substantial rate of increase in agricultural production can be achieved largely through the more effective use of resources already in the agricultural sector and with only modest demands upon the scarce resources of high opportunity cost which are indispensable for industrial development.

The design and implementation of a rational program of agricultural development, however, is by no means a simple task. Although the experience of Japan, Taiwan, Denmark, and other countries that have made notable progress in agriculture throws light on the type of approach that is likely to yield high returns, their experience can only be suggestive. Variations in soil, climate, and human resources are of such importance that many aspects of agricultural development

190

are specific to a particular country, region, district, and, ultimately, to an individual farm. Changes over time in the availability and relative prices of productive factors are also of great importance in influencing decisions concerning the choice of techniques of production and the combination of farm enterprises.

AGRICULTURAL DEVELOPMENT POLICIES

Emphasis is given here to a particular type of strategy for raising the productivity of an existing agricultural economy. The low productivity of farm labor, land, and other resources in the agricultural sector is largely due to the lack of certain complementary inputs of a technical, educational, and institutional nature. Under these circumstances a crucial requirement for devising an appropriate agricultural development program is to identify these complementary inputs, determine in what proportions they should be combined, and establish priorities among programs designed to increase their availability.

Such a policy for agricultural development, emphasizing measures to increase the efficiency of an existing labor-intensive agriculture and with chief reliance on technological innovations rather than large capital investments, is obviously *not* applicable under all conditions. It is therefore convenient, even at the risk of considerable oversimplification, to emphasize the changing position by defining three specific phases of agricultural development. Phase I: development of agricultural preconditions. Phase II: expansion of agricultural production based on labor-intensive, capital-saving techniques, relying heavily on technological innovations. Phase III: expansion of agricultural production based on capital-intensive, labor-saving techniques.

The labor-intensive, capital-saving approach to agricultural development, appropriate to Phase II, requires an environment in which the possibility of change is recognized and accepted, and in which individual farmers see the possibility of personal gain from technological improvement. Phase I is defined as the period in which these preconditions are met.

Improvements in land tenure are likely to be the most essential requirement in Phase I since an unfavorable tenure situation may stifle the incentive for change even though the potential exists for large increases in output.[1] Rural attitudes toward change are also influenced by the attractiveness and availability of consumer goods, awareness of the possibility of technical improvements, availability of market outlets, and many other factors. If traditional group restraints and individual attitudes hostile to change seriously impede agricultural progress, considerable importance attaches to community development programs emphasizing adult literacy, self-help programs directed at the satisfaction of "felt

---

[1] It is impossible to do more than call attention to this complex and important subject of land reform in this general treatment of agricultural development and its relation to overall economic growth. Philip Raup has presented a persuasive statement of the economic importance of land tenure reform. P.M. Raup, "The Contribution of Land Reforms to Agricultural Development: An Analytical Framework," paper prepared for an SSRC Conference on Relations Between Agriculture and Economic Growth, Stanford, Nov. 1960. See also Doreen Warriner, *Land Reform and Economic Development*, 50th Anniversary Commemorative Lectures (Cairo: National Bank of Egypt, 1955).

needs," and similar activities that promote greater receptivity to change. There are probably relatively few underdeveloped areas where agricultural policies should be based on the assumption that the preconditions phase prevails.[2] But certainly there are situations in which deficiencies in the institutional environment or attitudes unfavorable to change are critical limiting factors; and in any event, continuing improvement in institutions and incentives can be expected to facilitate agricultural progress.

At the other end of the spectrum, the capital-intensive, labor-saving technology of Phase III typically represents a fairly late stage of development, especially for countries with a high population density. Japan, for example, is apparently just entering this stage. In this phase, the opportunity costs of most inputs, including labor, are high by past standards and rising. Not only is the use of labor-saving farm machinery increasing, but the use of many other urban-produced inputs is expanding as well. Hence the need for credit facilities becomes acute. Phase III is generally distinguished by the fact that a substantial amount of structural transformation has occurred so that agriculture no longer bulks so large in the economy.

AGRICULTURAL DEVELOPMENT POLICIES IN PHASE II

The emphasis in Phase II on increasing the efficiency of an existing agriculture by heavy reliance on technical innovations associated with labor-intensive, capital-saving techniques, is related to certain distinguishing features of this stage of development: (1) agriculture represents a large proportion of the economy; (2) the demand for agricultural products is increasing substantially, but the "required" increase in output of food for domestic consumption is fixed within fairly narrow limits determined by the rate of increase of population and of per capita incomes; (3) capital for the expanding industrial sector is particularly scarce; and (4) the distinction between resources of high opportunity cost and those which are abundant in agriculture and characterized by low opportunity cost is of considerable importance.

The design of an appropriate strategy for increasing agricultural productivity requires a high degree of judgment and intimate knowledge of the physical resources and agricultural characteristics of a particular region. Precise determination of an optimal production system, including optimal factor-factor and factor-product relations and operation of the various developmental services at optimal

---

[2] With respect to the limitations on development that have been attributed to the allegedly irrational behavior of peasant agricultural producers, there seems to be a growing consensus that this view, espoused particularly by J. H. Boeke, is not borne out by the available evidence. Joosten, whose analysis of rubber exports in Indonesia refutes Boeke's notion of a perverse supply schedule, concludes that: ". . . a scrutiny of the facts shows that the peasant farms his land as rationally as possible under the social and economic conditions affecting him and within the limit of his opportunities as regard labour, land, markets, capital, knowledge and managerial skill." J. H. L. Joosten, "Perverse Supply Curves in Less Developed Economies?", *Netherlands Journal of Agricultural Science* (May 1960), p. 99. Most of those who have given careful study to the problems of peasant agriculture would indorse that view [see, for example, W. O. Jones, "Economic Man in Africa," *Food Research Institute Studies*. (May 1960), pp. 1 and 107–134].

levels, is impossible. There is an inevitable and substantial margin of uncertainty in anticipating the returns likely to accrue from research programs and in forecasting the effectiveness with which knowledge of improved techniques will be disseminated and applied by individual farm operators. Moreover, the importance of innovations developed by individual farmers, an important feature of a progressive agriculture, is even more difficult to anticipate.

The essence of the problem is to identify those factors that are currently limiting increased production and to define a combination of inputs that will yield large returns in increased farm output and productivity. Although general presumptions may be of some value as a guide to research and analysis, there is no substitute for farm-level studies carried out in areas representative of the different types of farming situations that exist within a country or region. Such studies are needed to determine the nature of present input combinations and returns and ways in which efficient decisions and practices at the farm level are hindered by lack of essential inputs.

A number of attempts have been made to inventory the "nonconventional inputs" important for increasing agricultural productivity.[3] Four categories of complementary inputs or developmental services may be listed: (1) research to develop improved production possibilities; (2) extension-education programs; (3) facilities for supplying inputs of new and improved forms, particularly improved seed and fertilizers; (4) institutional facilities for servicing agricultural production, such as credit and marketing agencies, and rural governmental bodies for fostering collective action such as building feeder roads. These complementary inputs have a number of characteristics important to the agricultural development process:

First, they come from outside traditional agriculture. The individual farm operator makes the decision, for example, whether to use fertilizer or improved seed if those inputs are available. But whether the fertilizer or seed is available in a time, place, and form conducive to increased production is in large part determined by influences beyond the control of the individual farmer.

Second, all these nonconventional inputs or developmental services include a large institutional component. Since agricultural research and extension-education programs offer tremendous external economies, these functions are normally performed by governmental agencies. Under the conditions existing in low-income countries, it is also frequently desirable for government to encourage the creation of, or even to provide, the institutional facilities required to supply certain production inputs and credit and to process and market agricultural products.

Third, and most important, is the existence of important complementarities among the various conventional and nonconventional inputs. It is largely because of these complementarities that research and extension programs and making available fertilizers and other critical inputs can yield large returns in increasing productivity of the resources already committed to agriculture. Careful proportioning of the added inputs is also important. The interrelationship between the

---

[3] See, for example, Ministry of Food and Agriculture, *Report on India's Food Crisis and How to Meet It* (New Delhi: Government of India, April 1959), and A. T. Mosher, *Technical Cooperation in Latin-American Agriculture* (Chicago, 1957).

development of improved seed and increased use of fertilizer has already been stressed in reviewing the experience of Japan and Taiwan.

In addition to recognizing the desirability of economizing on resources of high opportunity cost, special attention needs to be given to concentrating resources on programs of the highest priority. Establishing a large number of objectives involves a twofold danger. An attack on items that are not currently of strategic importance obviously increases expenditure and lowers returns on investment. Perhaps even more serious, undue dispersion of effort reduces the effectiveness of critical programs because the shortage of competent administrative personnel imposes a severe limitation on the effectiveness of agricultural development programs.

This last consideration weighs heavily against price support and credit programs which require a considerable amount of high-level administrative talent.[4] The need to concentrate limited resources on priority programs also makes it desirable to identify those geographical regions within a country that have high potential for large increases in production. Ability to supply the food requirements of expanding urban centers or a capacity for low-cost production of export crops with good market prospects are likely to be particularly pertinent considerations.[5]

For many countries the most critical components of an agricultural development program in Phase II are (1) research, (2) programs to make knowledge of improved technology available to farmers, (3) arrangements for supplying certain strategic new types of inputs, and (4) enlarged educational opportunities. Introduction of new crops may offer a potential for large increases in the value of agricultural output and frequently enlarged foreign-exchange proceeds as well. But this is dependent, in part at least, upon research to establish the suitability of possible crops to local conditions, to provide planting material, and to determine appropriate cultural practices.

Agricultural Research

The advances in scientific understanding, particularly during the past century, represent a possible windfall gain for a country launching a program of agricultural development today. It is largely because of the accumulated knowledge in such fields as soil science, plant nutrition, and genetics that there are the potential

---

[4] It is sometimes argued (e.g., Ministry of Food and Agriculture, Government of India, *op. cit.*, pp. 25–28) that it is necessary to shift risk and uncertainty from the innovating farmer to other persons. But the members of the farm population in an underdeveloped country are not at a common level of poverty, and there is usually a group controlling a substantial proportion of the land, with asset and income positions well above the average, that is capable of bearing the risk and uncertainty of innovation and investment. Improved credit institutions become a high priority need as the use of capital equipment becomes more important.

[5] The Swynnerton Plan for accelerated development of African agriculture in Kenya is an important example of a plan and program that have given special attention to "lands of high potential." *A Plan to Intensify the Development of African Agriculture in Kenya* (Nairobi: Colony and Protectorate of Kenya, 1954), pp. 9–15. B. van de Walle's sketch of a plan for agricultural development of the Congo advocates concentration of resources on areas of high potential for export crop production or which possess locational advantages in supplying urban centers; the limited investments in other areas would be justified by social rather than economic considerations. B. Van de Walle, *Essai d'une planification de l'économie agricole congolaise*, INEAC Sér. Tech. No. 61 (Brussels, 1960), p. 48.

increments of productivity which provide the opportunity for taking up slack in a developing economy. Although an underdeveloped country can draw on the fundamental research and understanding that have been accumulated, the identification of promising avenues of progress and the testing and adapting of improved seed and cultural practices to local conditions are indispensable for realizing the gains that are attainable.

Mounting an effective agricultural research program is a long-term project that depends heavily on continuity of personnel. Shortage of qualified agricultural scientists is a critical problem which can be overcome only in part by employment of research workers from abroad.[6] So basic is an effective program of research to the other elements of an agricultural development program that it represents one of the few instances in which plans and budget allocations should err on the side of boldness, provided that this openhandedness applies only within the limits of carefully determined research priorities.

Extension-education Programs

The effectiveness of agricultural research is dependent upon an extension-education program which carries research findings to farmers and carries knowledge of farmers' problems back to the research staff. The extension techniques that have been effective in the United States are not necessarily appropriate in other countries. Japan achieved notable results without an extension service per se; extension-type activities were performed by local experiment stations, village agricultural associations, and in other ways. In Jamaica and Denmark a network of agricultural societies has provided an effective mechanism. Where farmer resistance to change is strong, there may be a need for programs of supervised credit or subsidization of new inputs; and under some circumstances a government tractor-hire service might be justified in part as a technique for securing acceptance of improved practices or more productive farming systems. But the final success of a program to develop agriculture depends on training tradition-bound farmers to make economically sound decisions regarding new alternatives.[7]

A commonly recommended alternative to the slow process of training the mass of farmers to make their own decisions is to institute some form of large-scale farming using specialized management, such as collective farms and various types of cooperative farming. But economies of scale in agriculture do not continue for nearly as far out the scale line as in the case of other forms of production. The high degree of variability in agriculture poses problems of management and decision making which cannot be centralized without considerable duplication of effort. Brewster has stressed particularly the large number of "on-the-spot supervisory decisions" that must be made in agriculture. There is a basic difference

---

[6] The cooperative program of the Rockefeller Foundation and the Ministry of Agriculture in Mexico owes much of its success to the continuity of service of the key scientists and the emphasis given to the training of young Mexican agricultural scientists. J. G. Harrar, "International Collaboration in Food Production," Address before the Agricultural Research Institute, National Academy of Sciences–National Research Council, Washington, D.C., Oct. 4, 1954.

[7] For discussion of the problems and feasibility of a program of management assistance to farmers in low-income countries, see S. E. Johnson, "Management Assistance in Farming," *Indian Journal of Agricultural Economics* (Oct.–Dec. 1959), pp. 14 and 27–32.

between agriculture and industry in this respect because the biological nature of the agricultural production process means that the operations to be performed are separated in time and space. This increases the importance of these on-the-spot supervisory decisions and reduces some of the advantages of mechanization.[8] A further significant economic advantage of decentralized management and decision making arises from the more direct individual interest in the outcome of the farm enterprise with consequent favorable effects on incentives, initiative, and upon what Raup has termed the "accretionary process of capital formation" that are of such importance in agriculture.[9]

Judging from the experience of collective farms and production cooperatives, these considerations are of considerable importance; but they do not rule out the possibility of exceptions. It has been noted, for example, that plantations may facilitate the introduction of new export crops for which the capital and technical requirements are demanding, particularly if integration of production and processing is important for the control of quality. These advantages of large-scale production depend upon a high level of managerial skill, and they are likely to be temporary.[10] Similarly, some form of tractor-hire service or contract plowing provided either by the agricultural department, a cooperative, or private entrepreneurs may be an economical arrangement, particularly if technical considerations such as deep or timely plowing are important.[11]

Supply of Strategic New Types of Inputs

Certain of the complementary inputs of critical importance to increasing agricultural production in Phase II are items such as chemical fertilizers that are

---

[8] An interesting study by G. K. Boon of conditions under which mechanization is economical in the construction of field trenches emphasizes that "labour-intensive methods in construction are characterized by the absence of some of the disadvantages which they usually imply in industrial processes"; for example, "substituting labour for machinery for construction processes does not involve larger factory buildings and other extra capital outlays." G. K. Boon, *Alternative Techniques of Production, A Case Study of a Construction Process—Field Trenches*, Netherlands Economic Institute, Progress Report No. 5, Pub. No. 2060 (Rotterdam, 1960), pp. 11–12. This sort of contrast is, of course, even more evident in the differences between agricultural and industrial processes.

[9] Raup stresses the influence of a suitable tenure situation and of the time-consuming character of production processes upon capital accumulation in agriculture. Both elements are important, for example, in the growth of livestock numbers and quality as a result of slow improvements in feeding levels and better management and disease protection. P. M. Raup, *op. cit.*, p. 14. Likewise, he emphasizes the importance of "periodic unemployment" in agriculture when the opportunity cost of labor is measured only in the reservation price of leisure time. "An incentive system that will maximize the investment of this labor in the firm is one of the basic requirements for agricultural growth. In terms of capital creation that structure is best which creates the maximum likelihood that the farm family will elect to 'exploit' its own labor." *Ibid.*, p. 22.

[10] In past years it was claimed that African smallholders could not produce high-quality Arabica coffee in Kenya; but in the last ten years there has been a spectacular expansion of production by African producers. Problems of quality control have been difficult but by no means insoluble. This development has, of course, been supported by government research and extension programs and loans to facilitate the establishment of cooperative pulping stations.

[11] The highly successful Gezira Scheme in the Sudan exemplifies an interesting combination of labor-intensive and capital-intensive techniques. A. Gaitskell, *Gezira, A Story of Development in the Sudan* (London, 1959), pp. 230–234.

new and must be supplied from outside the traditional village economy. Fertilizers and pesticides depend upon the establishment of new productive capacity or upon foreign exchange for imports; thus they compete directly for scarce resources of high opportunity cost. The returns on investment in those inputs, however, can be extremely high, provided that the full range of complementary inputs is available—notably improved seed, knowledge of fertilizer response under various soil and cropping situations, and an extension organization capable of disseminating information to farmers.

The new inputs also require new institutional facilities to make them available at the farm level. In some countries fertilizer manufacturers have done this job effectively, but frequently in the earlier stages of development it is necessary for the government agricultural service or cooperatives to perform this function. To make available supplies of improved seed requires intricate institutional arrangements for seed multiplication and distribution so as to insure a pure supply; and here again governmental initiative is likely to be essential.

Improvement of transportation facilities may also be crucial to farmer utilization of purchased inputs. Improved transportation also increases production incentives through higher farm prices and speeds the spread of innovation through improved communication.

Education and Agricultural Development

Virtually all aspects of agricultural development hinge on developing a broad range of educational institutions. The critical problems concern the use of the small nucleus of trained personnel to staff training programs and the financial burden arising from enlarged expenditures for education.

Despite difficulties of finance and lack of trained teachers, many underdeveloped countries today are committed to large-scale expansion of educational facilities. This increased supply of trained people can be turned to good account in agriculture since trained manpower is needed to remove the bottleneck to efficient utilization of the labor and land resources that are already abundant in this sector. This is in marked contrast to the situation in industry where the large requirements for capital equipment to be combined with labor constitute a bottleneck to rapidly expanding the utilization of trained labor.

Efforts aimed at developing local government institutions, increasing literacy, and instituting rural social changes by community development or other techniques can be commenced by personnel with slight initial training supplemented by continuing in-service training. Even in the case of agricultural extension, programs at the early stages can emphasize relatively simple production innovations such as fertilizer-seed combinations, introduction of improved tools, and efforts to raise the general standard of husbandry nearer to that of the better farmers. The spread of education among the farm population broadens horizons, provides necessary skills for keeping records and accounts, and strengthens the capacity of farmers to make rational decisions.

Agricultural development in Phase II is potentially a dynamic process characterized by continuing increase in agricultural productivity.[12] This is so in part because of differential rates of adoption of new technology, but it is also a consequence of the continuing stream of innovations generated by an effective research program. This continuing growth of farm productivity depends on a large number of changes which individually give relatively small response but collectively add up to a large response. It requires continued improvement in incentives and in the institutions serving agriculture, including further refinement in the operation of the research and extension organizations, and the establishment or strengthening of institutions of higher education to provide the needed professional and administrative personnel.

CONCLUSIONS

In this examination of agriculture's role in the process of economic development, an attempt has been made to emphasize features that have a high degree of generality. But diversity among nations and the variety that is so characteristic of agriculture inevitably limits the validity of a condensed, general treatment. The density of the rural population and the stage of economic development that has been reached stand out as having a particularly significant bearing on the importance of some of the factors examined in this paper.

Despite these qualifications, it is believed that the general thesis advanced has wide relevance: rural welfare as well as overall economic growth demand a transformation of a country's economic structure, involving relative decline of the agricultural sector, and a net flow of capital and other resources from agriculture to the industrial sector of the economy. Agriculture's contribution to the requirements for development capital is especially significant in the earlier stages of the process of growth; it will not be so crucial in countries which have the possibility of securing a sizeable fraction of their capital requirements by export of mineral products or in the form of foreign loans or grants.

Policies that take account of this process of secular transformation and its implications are in the long-run interest of the farm population as well as the country as a whole. Reduction of the farm labor force is a necessary condition for establishing factor proportions that yield returns to labor in agriculture that are more or less in accord with returns to labor in other sectors. More concretely, insufficient movement out of agriculture will perpetuate, or lead to, excessively small farms and serious underemployment of labor as the proximate causes of substandard farm incomes.

Although this paper has stressed the importance of agriculture's role in development, we part company with those who draw the inference that agricultural devel-

---

[12]Higgins argues incorrectly that "with the labor-intensive techniques of small-scale peasant agriculture the opportunities for technological improvement are extremely limited." B. Higgins, *Economic Development, Principles, Problems, and Policies* (New York, 1959), p. 422. His assertion seems to be based on the erroneous view that agricultural development at this stage is a one-shot proposition—shifting from "bad" seed and practices to "good" seed and practices—and that a dynamic process of agricultural development is impossible until "the discontinuous jump to more extensive and more mechanized agriculture" can be made. *Ibid.*

opment should precede or take priority over industrial expansion. Sayigh, who can be taken as representative of that view, asserts that "deep progress cannot be achieved on both these fronts simultaneously" [Y. A. Sayigh, "The Place of Agriculture in Economic Development," *Agricultural Situation in India*, 14, Annual Number (1959), p. 448.] It is our contention that "balanced growth" is needed in the sense of simultaneous efforts to promote agricultural and industrial development. We recognize that there are severe limitations on the capacity of an underdeveloped country to do everything at once. But it is precisely this consideration which underscores the importance of developing agriculture in such a way as to both minimize its demands upon resources most needed for industrial development and maximize its net contribution to the capital required for general economic growth.

Selection **19**

The Economic Basis of Land Reform
in Underdeveloped Economies

ERVEN J. LONG

From: Land Economics, *Vol. XXXVII, No. 2 (May 1961), pp. 113–123.*
Reprinted by permission of Land Economics; © *held by The Regents of the University of Wisconsin.*

I

Land reform is one of the cornerstones of agricultural policy in most under-developed countries. These reform programs or proposals usually have three basic objectives—mixed in different combinations depending upon political and historical circumstances. These are (1) turning over ownership and management of the farms to those who actually "till the soil," (2) dividing up large holdings into smaller, more evenly distributed holdings, and (3) combining small opera-tional units into larger, group units, i.e., "cooperative farms," "collective farms," "paysannat," "state farms."

Even cursory examination of these objectives will show that they may be—and in many cases are—in conflict with each other. Steps taken to implement one objective may very effectively counteract steps taken to implement another. For example, many of the farms which could best serve as examples of realizations of objective one, i.e., farms fully managed and operated by the owner and his family, exceed the acreage ceiling and so would be broken up in effecting objective two. Furthermore, the achieving of objective three almost inevitably involves sur-render, or at least radical change in the character, of objectives one and two. Paradoxically, local protagonists of "land reform" usually support all three objec-tives, while opponents resist all three. This testifies to the fact that progress on such reform has not been far enough to bring their divergencies into active conflict with each other.

Four years' experience in India has brought me to the conclusion that most proponents and opponents of land reform are honestly concerned with the prob-lems of their country and believe their particular ideas on the subject to be sound. It has brought me even more firmly to the conviction that virtually none of the argument, for or against such reform, is built upon a solid, analytical, factual base. I suspect that this is true in most such countries where land reform is a burning social and political issue. If this were not true, surely both proponents and opponents would be more discriminating in their arguments, selecting certain types of reforms for their fervid support and other types for their equally fervid opposition.

It is at this point where I feel the so-called "foreign expert" can be most helpful in helping set up research and in relating available data to provide a reliable, factual basis for decision in the matter. What is lacking is not ideas but information; what is needed from us is not nostrums but evidence.

II

Behind all the political discussion of land tenure reform is an honest groping for a system which will satisfy two deep and basic needs: (1) a much more productive agriculture as a base for national economic development, and (2) a sense of security (and participation) among the peasantry as a basis for needed political stability. Unfortunately these also are often inconsistent ends; economic progress itself is frequently a powerful catalyst of social turbulence and political instability. At best, many measures to achieve economic progress have very disrupting side-effects. Political generalship of the highest order is required to resolve or compromise these issues. Surely the political leaders require and deserve the best possible supply of reliable evidence, relating actions to their probable consequences, as a basis for forming these difficult judgments.

Evidence regarding the second issue—relating land reform proposals to their probable consequences for social and political stability or instability—is obviously hard to come by. People's social responses to given stimuli vary greatly from place to place and from moment to moment. People are highly capricious in this respect; any overt step taken by government is but one event in a long historical continuum. Its results will depend almost entirely upon its historical antecedents. Failure of a government to take a specific action might cause a social flare-up now which that action itself would have caused a decade or two ago. A healing social ointment in one setting may prove a blistering caustic in another. Social scientists might well be excused for not having provided highly definitive evidence on this issue.

And yet, quite a little has been done. Many, many articles and books have dealt directly or indirectly with various aspects of the problem. Historical examples—and in a few cases even studies—have been extensively cited from which inferences were drawn regarding the effects of various land reform measures upon social stability. Such inferences are almost inevitably gross in character. Many causes interact to bring about the consequences noted and usually little is done analytically to disentangle these causes so as to assess their individual net contributions to the observed effects. Such gross inferences give full and free play to the analyst's preconceptions and personal convictions, which often provide him with the major premise of his ultimate judgment. Nevertheless, such studies (dare I call them such?) are useful, though probably in providing insights rather than reliable evidence. I have a hunch that, if all such studies were collated, a core of agreed-upon basic relationships might be discovered.[1] If so, this would be highly useful; and would be a very good place to begin an effort by social scientists to provide really meaningful evidence on this fundamental issue.

It is rather on the first issue—the effects of various types of land reform activities upon agricultural productivity—that social science has most seriously failed its responsibilities. This is where the agricultural economists' help is most badly needed and where they should be most able to provide it. The agricultural economics profession possesses the necessary analytical tools to do the job, to throw direct light upon the implications of various aspects of land reform for agricultural productivity. The principal shortcoming appears to be that research has not focused sharply enough on the issue. Such evidence as can be assembled is often oblique to the problem, having been developed with other purposes in mind and thus not interpreted with reference to this problem to which public policy attaches so much importance. In consequence, land reform legislation operates largely in an informational vacuum regarding its economic bases; political leaders are obliged to substitute surmise for evidence and hence preconception for judgment.

The core relationship in this entire problem is that between size of operating unit and productivity. Much of the local argument in favor of cooperative or other forms of group farming, for example, is premised upon the assumption that there is a tremendous efficiency advantage in large-scale operations. Opponents of land reform base their arguments against the establishment of acreage ceilings upon the same premise—that agricultural productivity will be reduced by the reduction in farm size. Persons who might be favorably disposed toward a more equitable division of landholdings, and who would oppose cooperative farming, feel obliged to take the opposite stand in the interest of economic development because they assume that there are tremendous positive returns to size-of-operations in agriculture. Political reasoning about land reform, somewhat subconsciously perhaps, appears to follow some such process as this: (1) Political requirements (and perhaps "social justice") demand the breaking up of larger into smaller holdings. (2) Because of the high man-land ratio, this involves setting acreage ceilings at levels far below optimum efficiency levels. (3) Since the economy cannot stand the strain of reduced productivity, these small units must somehow be recombined into larger group-units, or cooperative farms; or at least a large number of such cooperative farms are necessary to offset the reduced productivity potentials of the small owner-operated farms.

It can be seen that this reasoning process is premised throughout on the assumption of a highly positive relationship between size of farm operations and agricultural productivity. But this is by no means an established fact. The assumption is based upon a misinterpretation of the economics of so-called "western" agriculture and I fear even more so upon a misinterpretation of American farm management studies. The problem is simply different in the developed than in most of the underdeveloped countries. More specifically, the measures of agri-

---

[1] From his own observations and study of this issue, the writer would use for such an inquiry, as his key hypothesis, that a system of owner-operated farms of such size as to require family labor only would contribute the maximum toward political and social stability.

cultural efficiency appropriate to the developed countries are inappropriate to most of the underdeveloped countries. This statement requires some explanation.

III

Literally hundreds of American studies have confirmed that larger farms normally have correspondingly higher operator incomes, i.e., higher returns to the managerial and labor contributions of the farm operator and his family. In common usage this has erroneously been too often taken to be synonymous with greater "efficiency," leading to the conclusion that large farms are more "efficient" than small farms. They are! But only with reference to management and labor, i.e., with reference to returns to the human agent. They are not necessarily the most "efficient" in the use of other (nonhuman) resources. In the United States and similarly developed economies, this error creates little difficulty because the human agent is from a social viewpoint the most scarce factor of production. Much more importantly, in the United States maximum returns to the human agent in agriculture, which is obviously the economic goal of the individual farmer, is also roughly congruent with the broad objectives of public agricultural policy. And since management and labor are usually supplied by the same social unit, the individual farm family operator's net income is the most relevant measure of the relative efficiency of farms of different sizes. Maximum operator's income serves as an adequate criterion of both private and public policy action. The situation in India and similar countries is very different.

Faced with an imperative need to increase agricultural production, most underdeveloped countries find almost all production factors limiting, *except* labor.[2] From the public or aggregate social viewpoint, the marginal cost of labor approaches zero. In fact, in the judgment of many leaders it is negative—that is, there is a positive social value in employing additional labor, even worth sacrificing some production to accomplish. Prime Minister Nehru makes a telling point that "cottage industries," though inefficient, are justified in that they give larger proportions of the population a sense of participation in the developmentary efforts of the country and hence a more widely spread personal identification with the success of these efforts. In any event, rural unemployment and underemployment being what they are—and with the certain prospect of even much greater pressure of population upon employment opportunities—labor is, from the social standpoint, essentially a noncost element at any foreseeable levels of increased agricultural productivity. In direct contrast to the case in highly developed economies, therefore, any measure of relative efficiency of farms of different sizes must be in terms of returns to nonlabor resources to be relevant to problems in India and similar countries. *Probably a simple measure of gross value productivity per*

---

[2] Much of this paper relates only to so-called "overpopulated" underdeveloped economies. Throughout the paper, India is used as an example of such an economy. There are, of course, several important countries which are extremely underdeveloped yet have extensive unexploited potential farming areas, to which the principal arguments of this paper would not apply. The land reform problem in these countries is, however, much more simple.

acre, above variable capital costs, is as relevant to policy decisions under Indian conditions as is net operator-income under American conditions.

If, for India and similar countries, the measure of agricultural efficiency relevant for public policy is simply gross value productivity per acre above variable capital costs, then how is this related to size of farm? Stated more simply, are the returns to nonlabor resources higher on the larger or on the smaller farms? This is the question pertaining to the economics of farm size which is really relevant to land reform policy.

A relook at American data from this point of view might yield some rather startling results. In a study made by the writer,[3] although size of farm was, conventionally, highly related to operator-income, productivity per acre of land was inversely related to size of farm. Many other studies reveal the same thing. Even Dr. Warren's pioneer study of Tompkins County, New York, published in 1911, though making a strong case for larger farms as necessary to high operator income, nonetheless found value productivity per acre to be inversely related to size of farm.[4]

In India, crude observation does not suggest that the level of farming practices is higher on the larger than on the smaller farms. Even most of the very large state-owned farms in India, with their obvious "hidden subsidies," produce little if any more per acre than the small farms in the area. With the exception of the highly specialized case of some of the plantation crops, productivity per acre would appear to be about the same for all sizes of farms or perhaps to diminish as size of farm increases.

Thanks to the work of the Farm Management Research Centers in India some data are available to corroborate these observations. Data are available for samples of one hundred to two hundred farms per state in selected areas of West Bengal, Uttar Pradesh, Punjab, Orissa, Andhra Pradesh, Bombay (2 districts), and Madras. The data cover three years in four cases, two years in three cases, and one year in two cases. Because for each state a different size-range was used for computing the frequency distributions, it is impossible to set up a simple table directly from the state data. A composite tabulation, using four size-groups into which

AVERAGE GROSS OUTPUT PER ACRE BY SIZE OF FARM
(IN RUPEES PER ACRE)

Size of farm (acres)	Gross output per acre (rupees)
0– 4.9	240
5– 9.9	213
10–19.9	171
20 and over	103

---

[3] Erven J. Long and Kenneth H. Parsons, "How Family Labor Affects Wisconsin Farming," *Wisconsin Research Bulletin 167*, May 1950; also Erven J. Long, "Return to scale in family farming: Is the case over-stated?" *The Journal of Political Economy* (Dec. 1949).

[4] George F. Warren and K. C. Livermore, "An Agricultural Survey, Township of Ithaca, Tompkin County, New York," *Cornell Memoirs No. 295* (Ithaca, New York: Cornell University Press, 1911).

all the data could be fitted, shows the following relationships between size of farm and productivity per acre as measured in value of output.[5]

The preceding table shows a very decided inverse relationship between the size of farm and value of output per acre. However, it has the defect, for analytical purposes, that some of this relationship is caused by the fact that the areas of lower productivity per acre tend to be characterized by larger farm units. To overcome this difficulty, the frequency distributions for individual states were recombined and classified into four groups: the smallest size-group of farms, the second smallest size-group, the second largest size-group, and the largest size-group. This has the effect of holding differences between states constant in the analysis. Since the sample area studied within each state was chosen to be quite homogeneous, this classification enables us to determine reasonably well the net effect of size of farm upon value of output per acre. (A somewhat more refined analysis could have been made by recourse to original data, but the technique here employed is adequate to the purpose.)

Because of the relatively small sample for each individual state, the relationships revealed are somewhat erratic but a general inverse relationship between size of farm and value of output per acre can be noted. These irregularities disappear when data from all nine states are combined, as shown in the last column of Table 1. This column may be taken as a fair suggestion of the relationship between size of farm and gross value of output per acre in India. It clearly calls into question the supposition in much land reform discussion that large farms are more "efficient" than small farms.

Table 1

RELATIONSHIP BETWEEN RELATIVE SIZE OF FARM AND RUPEE VALUE OF GROSS
OUTPUT PER ACRE FROM SAMPLE AREAS OF EIGHT STATES: INDIA

	Madhya Pradesh	West Bengal	Uttar Pradesh	Punjab	Orissa*	Andhra Pradesh	Bombay	Madras	Average: eight states
Smallest group	87	239	292	201	161 (89)	433	117	209	219
Second smallest group	88	217	267	186	141 (79)	352	82	171	188
Second largest group	84	229	227	173	150 (88)	369	51	75	170
Largest group	93	169	232	143	126 (71)	380	53	75	159

*Figures in parentheses refer to output per acre above variable capital costs. See text.

Additional evidence on the relationship between size of farm and productivity per acre has been obtained from a study of 225 farms in three villages of Bihar State, as shown in Table 2. These data have the advantage that they relate separately to three villages within which there is great homogeneity with respect to soil characteristics and water resources. It can be seen that, in spite of the rather small number of cases for each village, there is a quite constant inverse relationship between size of farm and gross productivity per acre. The last column, showing

[5] Data supplied by G. D. Agrawal, Production Economist, Directorate of Economics and Statistics, Ministry of Food and Agriculture, Government of India, from Farm Management Center Reports from the referenced States.

the averages for the three villages, evens out such minor irregularities as appear for the individual villages.[6]

As indicated earlier, the measure of efficiency most relevant to land reform policies in India is value productivity per acre above variable capital cost. This would be a somewhat better measure than gross value productivity per acre as used in the above tables as it minimizes distortions due to possible differences in amount of variable capital used by farms of different sizes. Investigation of this point reveals, however, that empirically gross value of productivity per acre is equally adequate under Indian conditions. Variable capital inputs, in the form of seeds, fertilizer, insecticides, etc., are so small as not to affect comparisons, even if there were some consistent bias in relation to farm size—which there appears not to be. The same is true for investment in tillage and other equipment. Bullock power for farm operations is the largest item of variable capital expenditure. However, because of the tremendous numbers of such cattle in India and the social and religious sanctions requiring their maintenance, these can be considered in virtually the same fashion and for the same reasons as human labor—as a fixed cost input from the social standpoint. To the extent that amount of feed consumed

Table 2

GROSS OUTPUT PER ACRE AS RELATED TO SIZE OF FARMS FOR 225
FARMS IN THREE VILLAGES, BIHAR STATE: 1955–1956

Size of farm (acres)	Village A, 92 farms (rupees)	Village B, 100 farms (rupees)	Village C, 33 farms (rupees)	Average: three villages
0– 4.9	206	384	315	302
5– 9.9	193	337	306	279
10–14.9	178	329	308	272
15 and above	173	331	278	261

by bullocks is a function of the work they do, such feed is a variable capital input. There is little reason to believe that this is significantly related to size of farm. Value of output per acre above capital costs follows the same pattern as does gross value of output per acre as is shown in the case of Orissa State, where these figures are given in Table 1 in parentheses alongside the gross output figures. Hence, for our purposes, gross value of output per acre as used in the tables would appear to be from the public policy viewpoint an adequate measure of the relative "efficiency" of farms of various sizes.

IV

It is now necessary for the writer to state some disclaimers. It is not his intention to claim that data displayed thus far in any way *prove* an inverse relationship between size of farm and productivity per acre. They are cited merely to

[6] Data supplied by P. Ray, Principal, H. D. Jain College, Arrah, Bihar State, from a study to be submitted as a thesis to the London School of Economics. Analysis is being conducted under direction of the writer and M. B. Badenhop and supported by a fellowship grant from the Council of Economic and Cultural Affairs Inc., New York.

prove that the general presumption of a highly positive relationship which underlies most land reform discussions is extremely suspect. This presumption is equally evident in the arguments for cooperative farming and in the argument that little can be done to increase the agricultural productivity of a nation of very small farms. Though the data do not prove an inverse relationship between size-of-farm and productivity, nor perhaps even that the opposite may not be true, they certainly throw the burden of proof on the common presumption of a strongly positive relationship. This paper is, therefore, an earnest plea for more and better research on this relationship necessarily so central to all land reform proposals.

A primary limitation of the analysis thus far is that it has been cast in a purely "static" context.[7] The real problems of land reform are those of dynamics. Stated simply, what may be the effects of size of farm upon the rate at which productivity may be increased? It is conceivable that even if size of farm were inversely related to productivity in the static sense, it might yet be positively related to the process of increasing productivity. This is a question upon which the data cited cannot throw direct light.

As a matter of fact, it is precisely in this context that the presumption of a positive relationship between size and productivity had its origin. What Western agricultural adviser in India—or what Western-educated Indian agriculturist—looking at expanses of Indian land chopped up into tiny holdings and, resurrecting in his mind's eye the image of Iowa's corn fields stretching endlessly toward the horizon, has not revelled in the thought of what he could do to increase productivity if he could but combine all this land into one large unit? The modus operandi he visualizes for the realization of this dream will depend upon his experiences, his biases, and perhaps his political commitments. But, as John Dewey says: "Existence is existence; and facts about it are stubborn." And the stubborn fact in this case is that land will probably respond as well, or better, to the direct ministration of human hands using simple tools as to huge machines designed to meet the requirements of a different situation. And whereas labor is, from a public point of view, cost-free, the machines are very costly indeed.

Although the data as analyzed are static, the relationships revealed are the end products of such dynamics as have existed in the society. Therefore, data from societies whose agriculture have had more dynamics might be even more relevant. It is for this reason that the writer suggested that an examination of (even) American data from this point of view would be informative. Even more useful, perhaps, would be examination of similar relationships in Japan. If data for such countries reveal a negative relationship between size-of-farm and gross value productivity per acre above variable capital costs as the end result of a highly dynamic agricultural development process, then indeed the presuppositions of most land reform discussions—and also of much technical assistance work—need intense reexamination. Again, this paper is a plea for this type of re-examination of American and other farm management data.

The agricultural productivity problem of underdeveloped economies is, at heart,

---

[7] A crime for which the author would never forgive himself. See, "Some Theoretical Issues in Economic Development," *Journal of Farm Economics* (Dec. 1952), pp. 723–731.

that of the allocation of capital. If the large farms are operationally nothing but agglomerations of small farms, the productivity of farm size is nil. If only managerial responsibilities are affected, the outcome is the net result of two forces working in opposite directions: on one side the presumed advantage of centralized and hence improved management decision making; on the other side the paired forces of cost of overhead supervision and the reduction of individual incentives. Data cited above give no direct clue to the outcome of this contest. True "diseconomies of scale" could not have begun to operate on farms of the sizes referred to above. In these cases smaller farms produced more per acre than larger farms probably because they used their labor more effectively or used more of it per acre. Overhead costs of supervision and management could not have reached the increasing phase on the larger farms. But successful management of truly large-scale farms (of the cooperative farm or state farm type) is an extremely complex undertaking, much more so than management of comparable size industries.[8] On very large farms great costs of supervision are encountered. True diseconomy of scale, due to overhead costs of supervision and management on such farms, takes a heavy efficiency toll. In private undertakings the incentive to gain directly from one's own effort serves as a powerful spur to work. In a shared-gain enterprise this incentive disappears and must be replaced by other incentives (such as appeals to patriotism) or by compulsions requiring heavy expenditure on overhead supervisory and enforcement staff.

But from the economic standpoint the greatest practical disadvantage from any kind of shift to large-scale farming would be that it would tie up in relatively unproductive uses capital which would otherwise be highly productive. This would be the very probable result of such a shift as its justification is that it makes possible the introduction of "modern technology." Indian agriculture is desperately starved for capital, to be invested in such uses as minor irrigation systems, soil building systems requiring better seeds, etc., and especially in chemical fertilizers. Small amounts of capital invested in such forms and properly mixed with large amounts of the superabundant labor could produce marvelous results. But capital invested in essentially labor-saving machinery, such as one tends to find on very large farms everywhere, would add little to total production.

Virtually all American agricultural economists, as well as specialists in other fields of agriculture who have been in India a couple of years or more, are impressed with the low level of husbandry practices on the great majority of Indian farms. Our commonly preconceived image of Indian agriculture as teeming with people squeezing every last bit of productivity out of almost hopelessly limited physical resources is inaccurate; it becomes quickly replaced by the ever-present sight of extremely poorly used land. Fields are often very weedy; planting is haphazard with respect to timing, spacing, depth, and plant species combinations. Seed bed preparation is usually poor. Such soil- and water-conserving practices as contour plowing and planting, terracing, etc., are very rare. Though virtually all the land is extremely deficient in nitrogen, very little use is made on unirrigated

---

[8] John M. Brewster, "The Machine Process in Industry and Agriculture," *Journal of Farm Economics* (Feb. 1950); also, John C. Ellickson and John M. Brewster, "Technological Advance and the Structure of American Agriculture," *op. cit.* (Nov. 1947).

lands of legumes in a fertility-building crop rotation system. In areas where water, rather than land, is the principal limiting factor, such water as is available is very inefficiently allocated, usually wastefully squandered on the over-irrigation of a few acres of high water requiring crops. These and other circumstances combine to result in yields ranging perhaps from 50 per cent down to 20 per cent or less of those which would be obtained from the same physical resources by ordinary "good farming." Small amounts of capital, mixed with large amounts of human effort, invested in overcoming these and similar shortcomings would far outweigh any improvements in productivity which might be achieved through land reform measures—except those which help assure that the farm operator benefits from, and hence has an incentive to bring about, these improvements.

From the standpoint of land reform policy the most important type of very-large-scale farm is the cooperative farm. Apart from the presumption of an advantage due to economy of size (a highly questionable presumption as we have seen) the principal advantage claimed for it is that it provides an effective channel for technological knowledge and mechanism for technological change.[9] How effective it is in either capacity has yet to be determined. So-called "experiments" with a few such farms are of highly dubious value as any favorable results can be attributed to the mere fact of concentration of technical knowledge (and often other resources). In an agriculture operating at 20–30 per cent its reasonable production capacity, such a concentration could be expected to produce highly favorable results almost regardless of the mechanism or channel used. Such a concentration would, of course, be completely impossible were such group farming introduced as a general agricultural policy.

Thus viewed, group farming might best be considered as an alternative to other "extension" techniques and in full view of long-range economic consequences. This recognition might lead to a more energetic quest for more effective extension techniques, applicable under an owner-operatorship mode of farm organization,

---

[9] The most impressive case of these "successful" group-farms which I have seen are the so-called "paysannat" of the Belgian Congo. These huge undertakings with 20,000 or so families each are actually not cooperative farms but combination state-and-private farms. They combine in a unique way advantages of large-scale handling of certain key operations, such as plowing and spraying, with an almost unimpaired system of incentives to the individual family to do its work well. Individual farms are lined up in such a way that state-owned large machines can be used for certain key operations, while, at the same time, each farmer's produce is sold individually and the family permitted to keep the money left after paying its share (prorated on an acreage basis) of these machinery operation costs. Thus, the farm family's income depends entirely upon its own efforts. Undoubtedly, the unquestionable increases in yields that resulted from the establishment of these "paysannat" were actually due to the rapid introduction of improved technology on these farms *and not, apparently, to any inherent advantages in large-scale operations* as such. One could say with a good deal of accuracy that the remarkable success of these farms is attributable to the fact that this proved to be a highly effective way to do "extension" work. Also, and this is extremely relevant, these farms are in a labor-scarce area. Most of their advantages (such as better insect control) could be achieved in India by hand labor, whereas in the Belgian Congo labor is too scarce for such use. And the problem lying ahead for the paysannat, when existing populations on the farms press too tightly against the rather rigidly set land allotments, would be aggravated manyfold in a country like India with an approximately 1,500 per cent greater agrarian population density. The central point is that in Central Africa as in India tremendous productivity increases can be achieved by any device which rapidly upgrades the level of farming practices. The question is whether this device is any better than a good extension program to individual owner-operators and, if so, what are its likely long-run economic consequences.

which should be able to accomplish even more than group farming on the productivity front without the serious long-range economic inefficiency implications. It is the judgment of this writer that the potentials of a virile research-extention organization under owner-operator conditions has by no means been tested in India. At present, agricultural research is still too remote from the everyday problems of farmers, and agricultural extension work is too new, too sporadic, and especially too loosely connected with research to accomplish much. But the potentialities are tremendous as can be observed here and there where genuinely science-based agricultural extension programs are being carried out.[10] As Rainer Schickele states:

> The challenge really is: what can be done to accelerate the rate of adoption of better techniques within a predominantly family-type agrarian structure? . . . I would suggest that if the same people, who could be made available as the managers and technical officers under a system of cooperative farms, would be made available to the same physical area as county agents, along with whatever financial help would be channelled through the cooperatives, the rate of adoption of better production techniques under the present farm-size patterns would not lag behind by many years. Beyond that transitional period the harnessing of the individual initiatives and incentives, and the preservation of the craftsmanship attitude of farmers toward their job, in contrast to an employer-employee relationship, could be expected to surpass, in production performance, the cooperative alternative.[11]

There is one final consideration. This is that massive land reform may be a kind of shock treatment which may cause rural people, in their new found uncertainty, to be more receptive to new knowledge. A somnolent agriculture, heavily encrusted with centuries-old customary practices, may be jarred loose by the simple *fact* of radical reorganization. But this is basically the cynic's view. Peasant people, at least Indian cultivators, are extremely responsive to suggestions which will really improve their economic lot. As one Indian government worker put it to me: "The cultivator is far more ready to receive good advice than we are to give it to him; he is much more prepared to follow than we are to lead."

In summation, therefore, we are brought to the conclusion that much careful research is needed on the relations of farm size to productivity in both its static and dynamic dimensions and in terms truly relevant to underdeveloped, over-populated societies. Research is also needed into the most effective means of introducing technological changes which will capitalize on abundant labor. To the writer the weight of the evidence thus far is in favor of an effective research-extension program, supplemented by a set of government or cooperative services, in support of a flexible system of small scale, owner-operated farms as the proper goal of land reform policy.

---

[10]One factor needing serious consideration—but lying outside the scope of this paper—is that decision making in a village society is a different process from that in countries characterized by family-farm agriculture. Intense study of the decision-making process in village societies is needed as a prerequisite to the designing of effective extension procedures.

[11]From a letter to the author in review of an earlier draft of this paper.

Selection **20**

The Strategy
of Industrial Development

WILLIAM A. W. KREBS

From: Science, Technology and Development; United States Papers Prepared for the United Nations Conference on the Application of Science and Technology for the Benefit of the Less Developed Areas, Vol. IV: Industrial Development (*Washington, D.C.: U.S. Government Printing Office, 1963*), *pp. 12–21.*

INTRODUCTION

1. In the perspective of history the belief that man can remake his economic environment to the image that he desires is a new idea. That he can do so without sacrificing the political freedom of individual citizens is controversial. Combining these notions in a program of action is an act of faith and daring. The remarkable fact is that so many of the nations of the world have embarked on such an adventurous course in this generation.

2. The battle for economic development thus joined is fought on many fronts of which the industrial is only one and, in most nations at this stage of the battle, statistically the least significant. In this decade the greatest advance in per capita income in most of the developing nations will arise from increasing the productivity of agriculture. The symbolic importance of industry is so great, however, that progress in industry is a political necessity in the development battle, quite apart from the important role that the processing and supply industries play in supporting the growth of agriculture everywhere and the promise of rapid industrial advance on a broad front in certain countries.

3. Industrial development, in appropriate balance with other development effort, is thus indispensable, and a strategy especially designed for the industrial sector must be a part of each country's larger strategy of economic development. The design of such a strategy, however, must remain for many years to come more art than science. Industrial-development programs in enterprise economies outside the continental United States or Western Europe are of recent origin, with the notable exception of Puerto Rico, whose 20 years of intensive industrial development provide a rich store of experience. Facts about such programs are

211

inadequately available; analysis of their meaning has scarcely begun. Twenty years from today, one may hope a social science of industrial development may have emerged. For the present, we must work with much less—but work we must.

4. Fortunately it is possible to distill from even such limited experience a body of principles which may be regarded as the elements of a strategy for industrial development having general applicability to the needs of the less developed areas of the world. These elements may be classified as institutional, procedural, and substantive.

INSTITUTIONAL ELEMENTS OF AN INDUSTRIAL DEVELOPMENT STRATEGY

5. The key institutional element in successful industrial-development strategy is a central executive organization having high professional competence and political power. In some less developed countries such an institution already exists; in others, its functions are present but are being exercised in a variety of political and economic organizations scattered through the governmental structure or the private economy. Successful programming requires that these functions be centralized, placed in competent hands, and backed to the hilt with political power.

6. The mere establishment of such an institution—whether it is called an Industrial Development Corporation, an Industrial Development Center, or by some other name—has symbolic importance inside and outside its country. It demonstrates that the country is serious about industrial development. It shows that the acceleration of industrial development is recognized as something that is not expected to happen without major, concentrated effort, that it is seen as a key task which ministries which have their normal work to do cannot be expected to perform adequately, and something which a few key individuals, no matter how highly placed cannot do without adequate budget, technical staff, and capacity to follow through.

7. The role of the industrial development organization is primarily to give leadership in mobilizing the resources of the country for industrial development. This means working closely with both government agencies and representatives of the private sector. It also means making full use of the increasingly wide range of resources available from outside the country from international agencies, from foreign governments, from foreign industries and investment organizations. Another major task is to act as the government's advisor on a wide variety of important policy questions affecting industrial development, including taxation, tariffs, labor laws, education, and financial policy. The organization must monitor the economic climate from the point of view of industrial development to identify the barriers which are holding development back and to take action to see that something is done about them. Many such barriers can be broken but often only after months or years of study, of steady and intelligently applied pressure, and long campaigns. The organization should also be the center for information of interest to potential investors in industry, both foreign and local. This involves

maintaining adequate statistics and library reference material and carrying on research to obtain information not readily available. Publication of basic information of interest to prospective investors is usually also necessary.

8. The conditions which are essential to the success of the key executive organization for industrial development include continuity of basic personnel and policy, strong leadership, highly qualified staff, full support of the key ministries, and the respect of the private sector. Continuity can often best be achieved by establishing such an organization at a position midway between government and the private economy, with a mixed government-private board or governing body. It can then better survive the changing tides of political fortune while remaining responsive to the changes of policy which must come with changes in government.

9. Strong leadership requires that the head of the organization be a person who commands the respect of the ministries of the government, of the bankers and industrialists, of foreign businessmen and government officials, and—in many countries—of labor leaders and the press. This is a large order in any country, but failure to meet it is likely to lead to failure of the program.

10. Backing such an individual with highly qualified staff is equally essential and perhaps even more difficult in view of the shortage of such persons in most developing economies. Fortunately, if the policies of the country will permit it, the use of expatriate specialists, either as individuals or through contract with the increasingly large number of foreign organizations—both public and private—which now operate in this field can fill the gap while nationals are being trained to execute the duties of staff.

11. Full support of the key ministries is important because industrial development depends so heavily on preconditions and services which are the responsibility of government almost everywhere in the world. For example, the design of highway systems can have a stimulating or stultifying effect on regional dispersion of industry; decisions on tariff policy spell for many industrial projects the difference between survival or failure; labor laws vitally affect competitive position.

12. The same conditions which lead to continuity and strong leadership are likely to earn for the organization the other essential ingredient for its success— the respect of the private sector of the economy, without which, in the mixed economy characteristic of so much of the developing world, little can be done. Winning the confidence of those with the private investment resources and managerial skills necessary for industrial development, like winning the confidence of the ministries, is an essential prerequisite for success of the executive organization in building strong industrial development programs.

13. Around or within the key executive organization for industrial development must be clustered a range of ancillary specialized institutions. Like the concept of the central organization itself, the ideas expressed in many of these have emerged only recently. As tools of industrial development, they are still experimental and evolving. They include development banks, technical assistance institutes, industrial development consulting centers, and managed industrial districts. Each of them has a unique contribution to make to a program of industrial development. If institutions of these kinds do not exist in a developing economy, one of

the first tasks of the central industrial development organization is likely to be to create them or bring about their creation.

14. The development bank in one form or another, normally a quasi-governmental corporation charged with responsibility for mobilizing capital for economic development programs, is by now a common phenomenon in the developing economies. The number of such institutions around the world today numbers close to a hundred and more are appearing as new programs of development are launched. Historical studies have shown that such institutions in various forms, normally operating as private investment banks, have been an essential component of economic development in Western Europe and the United States since the beginning of the industrial revolution. The basic difference between a development bank and a commercial bank is that, while the latter engages in financing trade and commerce through loans usually limited to one year, a development bank provides medium- and long-term "soft" loans and, more importantly, invests in equity securities of new enterprises. This is normally the least easily available form of capital in a developing economy. Of almost equal importance in contributing to the success of new industrial projects is the practice of the better-run development banks of making careful technical and financial analyses of new ventures as well as rendering consulting assistance to management during early stages of operations. Fortunately, there are relatively plentiful sources of capital for development banks today from international institutions, from the foreign assistance programs of the industrialized countries, and from the governments of developing countries themselves.

15. A further contribution that a well-managed development bank can make is to stimulate the creation of a capital market for securities of industrial enterprises, thus channeling local capital away from relatively unproductive uses into the mainstream of industrial development. If such a bank also participates actively in cooperation with the central executive organization for industrial development in searching out and analysing the merits of investible industrial projects, it can effectively catalyze the growth of industry. In economies where this kind of institution is not present, or where its effectiveness has been limited for any of a variety of reasons, early attention to strengthening it is an element of industrial development strategy that will pay dividends.

16. The technical assistance institute is another specialized institution for the support of industrial development, which may have to be created or enlarged to accelerate industrial growth. Such an organization ideally will provide at least the following services at a high level of skill and a low level of cost relative to value: management counsel, product and process development, market research, technical trouble-shooting, and applied research and development. In at least a portion of its program, such an institute must be in a position to maintain proprietary confidences of its industrial clientele. It follows that, although it must almost always be subsidized by government in its early stages, it must be so organized as to give it substantial independence of government at the earliest practicable date.

17. Somewhat like the technical assistance institute, and overlapping it in

function in the management field, is the industrial development consulting center. Of particular value in those economies with a thin layer of trained business management or with poorly developed small- and medium-scale enterprises, this institution—of which increasing numbers of prototypes have recently been appearing—concentrates its services on the business management problems of industrial enterprise, and extends in effect a subsidized management-consulting service. In some forms this service has been coupled with provision of a wide range of training programs, both at the headquarters of the institution and on the job, and with an information service designed to bring to the attention of industrial managers the most useful and current knowledge of their professional field and the industry within which they function.

18. The planned and managed industrial district represents still another institutional device called into being by the special needs of industrial development programs. Experience with the industrial district—variously called industrial estate and industrial park—goes back to the nineteenth century in both the United Kingdom and the United States, in both of which it has been spectacularly successful. More recently Puerto Rico and India have experimented in the field with good results. Fundamentally, an industrial district is an area prepared with sites, roads, utilities, a communications network, service facilities, and, in some cases, shell buildings or even completed simple factories, ready for occupancy, with internally consistent legal and management arrangements specialized to meet the needs of industrial tenants or cooperative owners. Prearranged financing for equipment or even working capital is sometimes provided, together with advisory services, assistance in meshing into the community, and other amenities designed to ease the entrance onto the scene of foreign or new indigenous industrial enterprises. Economies of scale in planning and construction and the immense value of "readiness" are the significant advantages offered by this approach to expanding enterprise. Recently, the planned industrial district has been experimentally used in an effort to make national policies for decentralization and regionalization of industrial development more effective.

19. Another group of ancillary institutions must be of concern to the central executive organization responsible for industrial development—those necessary in the creation of the intellectual infrastructure of an industrial society: the vocational-training schools, the centers for management education, and the universities which supply the leaders of the service professions of law, accounting, and finance. Obviously the techniques for stimulating activity in this quarter must be more subtle, more indirect, and in some ways more imaginative than those applicable to other parts of the institutional problem. In the long term, however, the quality of these independent institutions will govern the quality of the development program. In many developing countries the pattern of education has been classical or oriented to the supply of civil servants rather than industrialists, engineers, and businessmen. Redressing this imbalance, consistent with the limitations of the culture and the economy, requires long and costly effort, but it must be made. One technique which has proved effective is fostering linkages between indigenous centers of learning and foreign institutions prominent in technology,

management education, and vocational training. In some countries, ambitious experiments are under way which include the creation of new institutions of learning which emphasize these aspects of education, sponsored by foreign institutions and sharing their faculties during the early years.

20. Each of the ancillary institutions described must be designed for the special circumstances of each national or regional setting into which it is to be fitted. Fortunately, however, experience with all of them is accumulating, and in recent years the literature of experience is becoming more widely available. A successful strategy for industrial development will draw heavily on such experience while adapting it flexibly to local requirement.

PROCEDURAL ELEMENTS OF AN INDUSTRIAL DEVELOPMENT STRATEGY

21. So far as experience may be relied upon as a guide, it suggests the importance of four procedural elements in a successful industrial development strategy:

   (a) Early formulation and use of quantitative objectives,
   (b) Adherence to a system of priorities for development,
   (c) Reliance on sound economic research to illuminate decisions of policy,
   (d) Energetic promotion of investment.

22. That finite goals are important means for mobilizing effort is a fact of human nature. An industrial development program requires a timetable and quantitative objectives. In the most successful programs these have been expressed in the number of industrial jobs to be added to the economy in some fixed period of time, in units of production of key commodities, in numbers of industrial establishments to be created, and in monetary wages. Experience suggests that the danger is greater of setting too modest a target than of unrealistically reaching beyond reasonable capacity. The most successful programs of industrialization have been dramatized in terms which caught the imagination and awakened the enthusiasm of the whole community and, often by contagion, of industrialists and investors in foreign countries.

23. Since industrial development is most effective when carried out in the context of a broad and comprehensive economic development plan for all sectors, sound strategy requires consistency between industrial plans and those for the other parts of the economy. The recent emphasis on intermediate-range national economic planning for development in many countries is a welcome phenomenon and permits industrial development to be both more orderly and more realistic. Critics of planning who express concern that it leads to destruction of private initiative in economic affairs miss the point. On the contrary, a well-defined set of objectives and realistic procedures for moving toward them is evocative of the best efforts of the entrepreneur, as experience in Puerto Rico—certainly an enterprise economy—testifies.

24. Of nearly equal importance to quantitative objectives is adherence to a system of priorities in making the key decisions. Everything cannot be done at

once with limited resources. An explicit framework of priorities for development, honestly constructed and consistently adhered to, will take the heat out of difficult decisions which will otherwise be made on grounds of political expediency, thoughtless enthusiasm, or other unsound bases.

25. Both objectives and priorities can only arise—if they are to be sound—out of careful and conscientious economic and sometimes technical research. The time and money spent in obtaining a clear and complete view of the circumstances within which the development program is to proceed is the least costly investment that can be made, even though it may require hundreds of thousands of dollars and months of painstaking effort. Nor is research something to be done once and filed away. The pace and complexity of change mean that every decision must be regarded as open to revision in the light of changed circumstances, so that a strong economic research staff must be continuously addressing itself to the production of new information and insights into the continuing process.

26. In danger of being overlooked, but critically important for success, is the use of investment promotion in industrial development. Fundamentally, promotion of investment is required because of the imperfect knowledge about opportunity and risk which exists in even the most sophisticated investment community. In the case of a developing economy the imperfections are enormously greater. Promotion is the communications function which connects investor with opportunity and gives him the knowledge and the confidence to risk capital in industrial development. For most developing economies, promotion of investment from abroad is the most critical task. Foreign investors usually have little knowledge of the developing country, its laws, and its people. Accordingly they lack confidence in their ability to enter successfully, even if their attention has been attracted by general favorable publicity. A system must therefore be devised to overcome this lack of confidence and lead the desirable prospective investor virtually by the hand through the stages of early investigation to decision making and later through start-up and early stages of operations. The most highly successful investment promotion programs, like the most highly successful industrial development programs (and they have to date been largely the same ones), have been both massive and highly personalized, with great emphasis on research and the communication of accurate factual data to carefully selected prospects. A failure to budget adequate funds or plan sufficient effort for the promotional phases of development can waste all the other expensive gains of a fine industrial development program.

Substantive Elements of an Industrial Development Strategy

27. The substantive elements of an industrial development strategy are the most diverse, specialized to each situation and controversial. Even here, however, experience has begun to yield lessons which validate principles of general applicability.

The Importance of Market Analysis

28. It is likely that more waste has been caused in industrial development programs from decisions made with inadequate knowledge of the market for production than from any other single cause. This is a particularly common phenomenon where a substantial portion of the capital for the project comes from public agencies or from a large number of private investors, no one of whom has actual experience in the operation of the particular industry. On the other hand, a careful examination of present and potential markets for the products of industry, and the selection of projects on this basis, can be the touchstone of success. Like so many other aspects of management "science," market research has developed methodology and principles which can best be applied by experienced professionals. At the same time, no specialist in marketing can possibly be sufficiently familiar with all sectors of industry and factors affecting markets for a wide range of products. Thus, a successful program of market research requires both the marketing expert and the industry specialist. The selection for emphasis in an industrial development program of those industrial sectors in which market analysis indicates opportunity, not only for the present but through the foreseeable future, can be a key substantive element for success.

A Policy of Integrated Development

29. The extent to which the selection of industrial projects to be emphasized in a development program can be guided through analysis of the degree to which they mutually support and stimulate one another is a controversial matter. It is clear, at least, that industrial projects can be linked to one another in the sense that one provides the raw material or the market for the other. There is a growing body of theory which suggests that certain types of industry tend to induce or stimulate complementary industrial activity to a higher degree than others. Thus, the much-maligned iron and steel industry is seen as having a high degree of interdependence with other sectors both in terms of purchases from them and sales to them, while such activities as fishing, transport, services, and trade have relatively low interdependence characteristics and therefore presumably low priority in development programs, at least for that reason. Of course, the importance of such an activity as fishing for supply of protein in low-protein diets represents the kind of qualification for such a priority selection that illustrates its basic complexity. To the extent that analysis can carry the load, however, it appears important that attention be paid in formulating development strategy to the stimulus-creating aspects of new projects or, in other terms, how well they will "mesh into" the growing economy.

Application of the Test of National Benefit

30. The analysis of an industrial project to test the costs it will place upon the economy as well as the benefits it can be expected to produce is an essential but

sometimes neglected step of industrial development programming. While in many cases an industrial project which is sufficiently promising to attract investment capital will without question represent a net gain to the national economy, there are also situations in which there may be a great difference between the value of a project to its private owners and its value to the economy as a whole. For example, because a project may use labor which is unemployed otherwise, it may be more valuable to the national economy than a simple tabulation of the wages to be paid, for purposes of private analysis of the soundness of the investment, would show. Similarly a project using natural resources which would otherwise be wasted, such as forest products, may have a greater value to the economy than to the private company which must pay for the resources at regular prices. A project which can make a valuable contribution through training labor or in providing services or goods needed by other new industries, thus serving as a stepping stone in the process of industrialization, may have a surplus of value to the economy that will not show up in the entrepreneur's calculation of commercial profitability.

31. The converse may also be true. A project to substitute local production for imports may be commercially profitable only because, through tariff protection, it can sell its product to the local market at protected higher prices. The difference between the protected price and the price at which the competitive import would be available represents a cost to the economy which should be made explicit by analysis.

32. To show such national costs and benefits separately from commercial profitability is not to answer the questions of policy to which they are related, such as: "How much tariff protection is justified?" But to fail to break them out for consideration is to run the risk of making decisions which will later prove to have been faulty for failure to recognize and consider all of their consequences.

Application of the Test of Commercial Viability

33. Strange as it may seem, industrial projects sometimes receive the benefits of national subsidy, tax concessions, and even investment of public funds when careful analysis would have shown that, for technical or commercial reasons, they can never be financially successful. There are many interested parties whose return from the initiation of a project will be secured before the early years of operation have passed and whose support of the project is given without concern for its long-term success. Protecting the program from the influence of such special interests can be achieved only through painstaking analysis of the commercial feasibility of each significant industrial project at a high level of competence. One way of securing such analysis is by arranging for the participation of substantial industrial or banking interests under terms that will make certain that the investment is not fully paid out until commercial viability has been demonstrated. Another is to provide the technically qualified staff directly or through securing competent independent advisors. Regardless of method, the function is an indispensable substantive element of successful industrial development strategy.

Creative Use of Technology

34. It is hard to imagine a successful industrial development program which does not make use of a wide range of technical analysis. Even in the preliminary screening of an economy for identification of sectors of industrial opportunity, the insights of an experienced team of industrial specialists, trained in the engineering and management sciences, can enrich and illuminate the judgments of administrators, economists, and managers. The possibilities for adaptation of processes practiced in the earlier stages of the more advanced economies for application under current and usually more limiting requirements of scale and complexity in a developing economy can best be analysed by the experienced technologist. Furthermore, the wide range of industrial operations and processes to be analysed in the course of project-feasibility studies demands the availability of a similarly wide range of technically qualified industrial specialists. Fortunately, conditions of transportation and communication in today's world make available such services from the resources of the more highly industrialized economies through a variety of institutions and firms. Wise use of such resources is another key to a successful industrial development program.

Respect for the Capacity of Research and Recognition of Its Limitations

35. Most successful industrial development programs put great reliance on both economic and technical research to illuminate problems which must be resolved by the decision maker. Experienced managers and administrators, whether in industry or government, know the value of a cold shower of facts in a heated controversy over plant location, level of subsidy, competition among suppliers, or project selection. The countervailing principle—that all technical analysis falls short of the subtle but overwhelmingly important intangibles of politics, human relations, taste, and "hunch"—is of at least equal importance and perhaps in more danger of being overlooked in the increasingly professionalized field of industrial development. A nice balance is of the essence of success.

A Climate for Enterprise

36. Finally, an industrial development strategy for an enterprise economy will most certainly fail unless it provides the preconditions which evoke enterprise: civil order and good government, reasonable economic stability, laws which encourage risk-taking, and a physical infrastructure—transportation and utilities— capable of supporting an industrial effort. More subtle, but more far-reaching and fundamental than any of these, is the creation and sustenance of an attitude in society which sees in the man of enterprise a symbol of what the society values. To the extent that this occurs, all other measures will be facilitated.

37. To catalogue the institutional, the procedural, and the substantive elements which comprise a successful industrial development strategy is not equivalent to designing it. Designing a strategy is not equivalent to executing it. As in all human affairs, the link in the chain of circumstance supplied by the administrator is indispensable if desire is to culminate in achievement. Nonetheless, sound theory maximizes potential and minimizes risk. It can be disregarded only at peril.

Selection **21**

An Appraisal of
Import-Substituting Industrialization

ALBERT O. HIRSCHMAN

From: "The Political Economy of Import-Substituting Industrialization in Latin America," Quarterly Journal of Economics, *Vol. LXXXII, No. 1 (February 1968), pp. 1–12. Reprinted by permission of Harvard University Press and the author;* © *1968, by the President and Fellows of Harvard College.*

INTRODUCTION: DISENCHANTMENT WITH
INDUSTRIALIZATION IN LATIN AMERICA

Not long ago, industrialization ranked high among the policy prescriptions which were expected to lead Latin America and other underdeveloped areas out of their state of economic, social, and political backwardness. In the last few years, however, considerable disenchantment with this particular solution of the development problem has set in. The present paper will survey some characteristics of "import-substituting industrialization" (ISI) in an attempt to appraise its evolution and the principal difficulties it has encountered. . . .

To set the stage for our inquiry it is useful to illustrate, through quotes from Latin America's most prominent economists, the change in attitude toward industrialization as a cure of the area's ills. In his well-known "manifesto" of 1949 Raúl Prebisch said:

> *Formerly, before the great depression, development in the Latin American countries was stimulated from abroad by the constant increase of exports. There is no reason to suppose, at least at present, that this will again occur to the same extent, except under very exceptional circumstances. These countries no longer have an alternative between vigorous growth along those lines and internal expansion through industrialization. Industrialization has become the most important means of expansion.*[1]

Thirteen years later, Prebisch wrote another basic paper on Latin America, in a sense his farewell message to his Latin American friends upon assuming his

---

[1] R. Prebisch, *The Economic Development of Latin America and Its Principal Problems* (New York: United Nations, 1950), p. 6.

new post as Secretary-General of the United Nations Conference on Trade and Development. Here industrialization is presented in a rather different light:

> *An industrial structure virtually isolated from the outside world thus grew up in our countries. . . . The criterion by which the choice was determined was based not on considerations of economic expediency, but on immediate feasibility, whatever the cost of production . . . tariffs have been carried to such a pitch that they are undoubtedly—on an average—the highest in the world. It is not uncommon to find tariff duties of over 500 per cent.*
>
> *As is well known, the proliferation of industries of every kind in a closed market has deprived the Latin American countries of the advantages of specialization and economies of scale, and owing to the protection afforded by excessive tariff duties and restrictions, a healthy form of internal competition has failed to develop, to the detriment of efficient production.*[2]

If we take a look at the writings of Celso Furtado, the shift in the climate of opinion stands out even more starkly. In 1960, after a decade or more of rapid industrial advance, Furtado celebrated the resulting "transfer of decision centers" from abroad to Brazil in almost lyrical terms:

> *By now the Brazilian economy could count on its own dynamic element: industrial investments supported by the internal market. Growth quickly became two-dimensional. Each new impulse forward would mean an increasing structural diversification, higher productivity levels, a larger mass of resources for investment, a quicker expansion of the internal market, and the possibility of such impulses being permanently surpassed.*[3]

Only six years later, after Brazil had suffered a series of political and economic setbacks, a disillusioned Furtado wrote:

> *In Latin America . . . there is a general consciousness of living through a period of decline. . . . The phase of "easy" development, through increasing exports of primary products* or through import substitution *has everywhere been exhausted.*[4]

Considering these two pairs of quotes one could easily conclude that we have here an instance of the acceleration of history. The phase of export-propelled growth (*crecimiento hacia afuera*) in Latin America lasted roughly from the middle of the nineteenth century until the Great Depression; and it took another twenty years, from 1929 to the Prebisch manifesto of 1949, before the end-of-

---

[2] R. Prebisch, *Towards a Dynamic Development Policy for Latin America* (New York: United Nations, 1963) p. 71.

[3] Celso Furtado, "The Brazilian Economy in the Middle of the Twentieth Century," Industrial Conference on Science in the Advancement of New States, Israel, 1960 (mimeo), p. 5.

[4] Celso Furtado, "U.S. Hegemony and the Future of Latin America," *The World Today*, Vol. 22 (Sept. 1966), p. 375. My italics.—Detailed critiques of the ISI process in Latin America can be found in two influential articles: "The Growth and Decline of Import Substitution in Brazil," and Santiago Macario, "Protectionism and Industrialization in Latin America," both in *Economic Bulletin for Latin America, Vol. IX* (Mar. 1964), pp. 1–61 and 62–102.

export-propelled-growth became official Latin American doctrine. Then came the next phase of Latin American growth, *crecimiento hacia adentro* or growth via the domestic market. It gathered strength during the Depression and World War II, flourished briefly in both theory and practice during the fifties and was pronounced either dead or a dud in the sixties. It looks, therefore, as though the acceleration of technical progress in the developed countries were matched in the underdeveloped ones by an increasingly rapid accumulation of failures in growth experiences!

As will be seen, there may be considerable exaggeration in the announced failure of import-substituting industrialization just as, in spite of the supposed demise of export-propelled growth, Venezuela, Ecuador, Peru, and Central America achieved notable economic gains in the two postwar decades through rapidly growing exports of petroleum, bananas, fishmeal, and cotton, respectively. While *fracasomania*, or the insistence on having experienced yet another failure, certainly has its share in the severity of the recent judgments on industrialization, the widespread criticism of ISI—in Pakistan and India very similar problems are being discussed—indicates that there is real substance to the concern that is being expressed. But the rapidity of the reversal in the climate of opinion makes one rather suspect that ISI had, *from its very onset*, both positive and negative aspects, with the latter simply coming into view a few years after the former. Our inquiry will therefore start out with a brief survey of the principal characteristics which set off ISI from other types of industrialization.

FOUR IMPULSES OF IMPORT-SUBSTITUTING INDUSTRIALIZATION (ISI)

Wars and depressions have historically no doubt been most important in bringing industries to countries of the "periphery" which up to then had firmly remained in the nonindustrial category. The crucial role of the two World Wars and of the Great Depression in undermining acceptance of traditional ideas about the international division of labor between advanced and backward countries is well known.[5] But industrialization has not only been the response to sudden deprivation of imports; it has taken place in many erstwhile nonindustrial countries as a result of the gradual expansion of an economy that grows along the export-propelled path. As incomes and markets expand in such a country and some thresholds at which domestic production becomes profitable are crossed, industries come into being without the need of external shocks or governmental intervention —a process I have described as "import-swallowing"[6] and which has been perhaps

---

[5] Apparently even earlier crises had positive effects on industrial growth in Latin America. The following quote is instructive: "There is no ill wind that does not blow some good . . . the crisis the country is going through is tremendous—and yet this is a perfect wind for national industry. Many of our industries have had a more or less vigorous protection through customs duties. But all of this would not have been enough had it not been for the crisis of 1875 which gave the impulse to industry and for that of 1890 which strengthened and diffused it." Quoted from *El Nacional* in Adolfo Dorfman, *Desarrollo industrial en la Argentina* (Rosario, 1941), p. 11. My translation.

[6] *The Strategy of Economic Development* (New Haven, Conn.: Yale University Press, 1958), Chap. 7.

more aptly termed industrialization through "final demand linkage," as distinct from the continuation of the process via backward and forward linkage effects.[7] Gradual import substitution in response to the growth of domestic markets accounts for the widespread establishment of industries which have substantial locational advantages because of the weightiness of the product (cement, beer) and of those whose market is large even at low per capita incomes such as textiles.

Over the past two decades import-substituting industrialization has, of course, no longer been exclusively a matter of natural market forces reacting to either gradual growth of income or to cataclysmic events, such as wars and depressions. It has been undertaken in many countries as a matter of deliberate development policy, carried out no longer just by means of protective duties, but through a wide array of credit and fiscal policy devices, through pressures on foreign importing firms to set up manufacturing operations as well as through direct action: the establishment of state-owned industries or, increasingly, of development corporations or banks which are then entrusted with the promotion of specific ventures.

It is useful to keep in mind these distinct origins of ISI—wars, balance-of-payments difficulties, growth of the domestic market (as a result of export growth), and official development policy—in focusing on the distinctive characteristics of the process.

Clearly, there is not just *one* ISI process. An industrialization that takes place in the midst and as a result of export growth has a wholly different *Gestalt* from one that feeds on foreign exchange deprivation. For example, in the latter situation it seems much more likely that inflationary developments will accompany the industrialization process than in the former. Or, to proceed to one of the alleged—and often criticized—characteristics of the industrialization process itself, namely, its tendency to concentrate on nonessential, luxury-type goods. This tendency to give importance to what is unimportant will be present only when the primary impulse to industrialization arises out of unexpected balance-of-payments difficulties which are fought routinely by the imposition of quantitative import controls. The controls will aim at permitting continued supply of the more essential goods traditionally imported at the cost of shutting out nonessentials and will thus cause domestic production of the latter to become especially profitable.

It is easy, however, to make too much of this situation. Of the four motive forces behind ISI—balance-of-payments difficulties, wars, gradual growth of income, and deliberate development policy—only the first leads to a bias in favor of nonessential industries. The last, deliberate development policy, is likely to produce exactly the opposite bias; and the remaining two causes are neutral with respect to the luxury character of the industry. Wars cause interruption of, or hazards for, *all* international commodity flows, essential or nonessential, and

---

[7] See Melville H. Watkins, "A Staple Theory of Economic Growth," *Canadian Journal of Economics and Political Science*, Vol. 29 (May 1963), pp. 141–158, and Richard E. Caves, "Vent-for-Surplus Models of Trade and Growth" in *Trade, Growth and the Balance of Payments*, Essays in honor of Gottfried Haberler (Skokie, Ill.: Rand-McNally Co., 1965), pp. 95–115.

therefore provide a general unbiased stimulus to domestic production of previously imported goods. The same is true for the stimulus emanating from the gradual growth of markets. It seems likely, therefore, that the role of nonessential goods within the total ISI process has been exaggerated by the "new" critics who, in stressing this role, sound almost like the old-line Latin American laissez-faire advocates who were forever inveighing against the introduction of "exotic" industries into their countries.

CHARACTERISTICS OF THE INITIAL PHASE OF ISI

Industrialization by Tightly Separated Stages

No matter what its original impulse, ISI starts predominantly with the manufacture of finished consumer goods that were previously imported and then moves on, more or less rapidly and successfully, to the "higher stages" of manufacture, that is, to intermediate goods and machinery, through backward linkage effects. The process can and does start here and there with capital or even intermediate goods insofar as such goods are imported prior to any industrialization because they are needed in connection with agricultural or transportation activities. Machetes, coffee hulling machines, trucks, and fertilizers are examples. In the textile industry, the crushing superiority of machine spinning over hand spinning, combined with a lesser advantage of machinery in weaving, has made sometimes for the installation of spinning mills ahead of weaving mills, especially in countries where a strong handweaving tradition had not been previously destroyed by textile imports from the industrial leaders.

But the bulk of new industries are in the consumer goods sector and as they are undertaken in accordance with known processes, on the basis of imported inputs and machines, industrialization via import substitution becomes a *highly sequential*, or *tightly staged*, affair. Herein lies perhaps its principal difference from industrialization in the advanced countries. This aspect is so familiar and seemingly inevitable that it has not received quite the attention it deserves. It is the basic reason for which the ISI process is far smoother, less disruptive, but also far less learning-intensive than had been the case for industrialization in Europe, North America, and Japan.

This is not the place for renewing the discussion over the advantages or drawbacks of an early or late start in industrialization. Suffice it to point out, however, that those who have stressed the advantages of a late start have often had in mind the ability of newcomers to jump with both feet into a newly emerging dynamic industrial sector (as Germany did with chemicals) instead of remaining bogged down in sectors that had long passed their prime (as England in textiles and railways construction). But the "late latecomers" with whom we are concerned here are not apt to jump in this fashion. Industrialization is here at first wholly a matter of imitation and importation of tried and tested processes. Consider by way of contrast the following description of the establishment of new industries in advanced countries:

Young industries are often strangers to the established economic system. They require new kinds or qualities of materials and hence make their own; they must overcome technical problems in the use of their products and cannot wait for potential users to overcome them; they must persuade customers to abandon other commodities and find specialized merchants to undertake the task. These young industries must design their specialized equipment and often manufacture it. . . .[8]

Not much of this travail occurs when a new industry is introduced into the "late late" starting countries. It is in this connection that one must be on guard against studies purporting to show that the history of industrialization is substantially the same in all countries, working its way from light consumer goods industries, to heavy and capital goods industries, and eventually to consumer durables. The apparently similar pattern of the earlier and "late late" industrializers in this respect conceal an essential qualitative difference. Even when the earlier industrializers were predominantly in the light consumer goods stage (from the point of view of labor force or value added), they were already producing *their own* capital goods, if only by artisan methods. As Marx wrote: "There were mules and steam-engines before there were any labourers whose exclusive occupation it was to make mules and steam-engines; just as men wore clothes before there were tailors."[9] But the "late late" industrializers will *import*, rather than make, their clothes until such time as they are able to set up a tailor in business all by himself. This situation forecloses, of course, for a considerable time any fundamental adaptation of technology to the characteristics of the importing countries, such as the relative abundance of labor in relation to capital. Whether and to what extent such an adaptation is desirable is an idle question under these circumstances; given the sequential pattern of industrialization, there is remarkably little choice. ISI thus brings in complex technology, but without the sustained technological experimentation and concomitant training in innovation which are characteristic of the pioneer industrial countries.

"Late" vs. "Late Late" Industrialization

The "late late" industrialization sketched so far may be contrasted not only with that of the presently advanced industrial countries in general, but particularly with that of the so-called latecomers among them. The "late" industrialization of countries like Germany, Italy, and Russia has been depicted by Gerschenkron through the following propositions:

1. The more backward a country's economy, the more likely was its industrialization to start discontinuously as a sudden great spurt proceeding at a relatively high rate of growth of manufacturing output.
2. The more backward a country's economy, the more pronounced was the stress in its industrialization on bigness of both plant and enterprise.

---

[8] George Stigler, "The Division of Labor is Limited by the Extent of the Market," *Journal of Policitical Economy*, Vol. LIX (June 1951), p. 190.

[9] K. Marx, *Kapital*, Vol. I (Wien-Berlin, 1932), p. 399. This passage and the previous one by Stigler were brought to my attention by Nathan Rosenberg's article "Capital Goods, Technology, and Economic Growth," *Oxford Economic Papers*, Vol. 15 (Nov. 1963), pp. 223–224.

3. The more backward a country's economy, the greater was the stress upon producers' goods as against consumers' goods.

4. The more backward a country's economy, the heavier was the pressure upon the levels of consumption of the population.

5. The more backward a country's economy, the greater was the part played by special institutional factors designed to increase the supply of capital to the nascent industries and, in addition, to provide them with less decentralized and better informed entrepreneurial guidance; the more backward the country, the more pronounced was the coerciveness and comprehensiveness of those factors.

6. The more backward a country, the less likely was its agriculture to play any active role by offering to the growing industries the advantages of an expanding industrial market based in turn on the rising productivity of agricultural labor.[10]

Of these six characteristics only the last one applies unconditionally to the late late industrializers. Special institutions designed to supply capital and entrepreneurial guidance (point 5), became important in most of Latin America after the ISI process had already been underway as a result of private, decentralized initiative for a considerable time. As to the remaining four points, almost the opposite could be said to hold for our late latecomers. Their industrialization started with relatively small plants administering "last touches" to a host of imported inputs, concentrated on consumer rather than producer goods, and often was specifically designed to improve the levels of consumption of populations who were suddenly cut off, as a result of war or balance-of-payments crises, from imported consumer goods to which they had become accustomed. Even though the rates at which new plants were built and at which their output expanded were often respectable, the process thus lacked some of the essential characteristics of Gerschenkron's "great spurt."

As a result, late late industrialization shows little of the inspiring, if convulsive *élan* that was characteristic of the late industrializers such as Germany, Russia, and Japan. This is perhaps the basic reason for the feelings of disappointment experienced by Latin American observers who had looked to industrialization for a thorough transformation and modernization of their societies.

Naturally, the difference between the two types of industrialization must not be overdrawn. At least one experience in Latin America, that of Brazil during the fifties, came fairly close to the picture drawn by Gerschenkron: sustained and rapid progress of steel, chemical, and capital goods industries during this decade was here combined with a "special institutional factor designed to increase supply of capital," namely, inflation, and even with the flowering of a "developmentalist" (*desenvolvimentista*) ideology.[11] But what looked like the hopeful beginning of a

---

[10]Alexander Gerschenkron, *Economic Backwardness in Historical Perspective* (Cambridge, Mass.: Harvard University Press, 1962), pp. 343–344.

[11]While not included in the six points cited above, support by a vigorous movement of ideas has been stressed elsewhere by Gerschenkron as a characteristic of late industrialization. See, for example, *op. cit.*, pp. 22–26. For a survey of developmentalist-nationalist ideas in Brazil during the fifties, see Frank Bonilla, "A National Ideology for Development: Brazil" in K. H. Silvert (ed.), *Expectant Peoples: Nationalism and Development* (New York: Random House, Inc., 1963), pp. 232–264.

"Brazilian economic miracle" was thrown into disarray by the political crises and related economic and social setbacks of the sixties. The gloom that pervades the Latin American mood at present stems precisely from the convergence of frustrations over the unexciting character of late late industrialization in *most* Latin American countries with the despair felt over the stumblings of the *one* country whose advance had assumed the more inspiring characteristics of the "great spurt."

The Sources of Entrepreneurship

A number of important characteristics of late late industrialization remain to be surveyed. What has been said so far permits, first of all, some discussion of the sources of entrepreneurship. As industry is started primarily to substitute imports, those engaged in the foreign trade sector are likely to play a substantial role in the process. This is the reason for the industrial prominence of (1) the former importers of Lebanese, Jewish, Italian, German, etc. origin, and (2) of the large foreign firms intent on maintaining their market and therefore turning from exporters into manufacturers. Once again, however, it is useful to distinguish between an industrialization which is brought underway under conditions of expanding income from exports and one that is ignited by deprivation of previously available imports (due to war or balance-of-payments troubles). Only in the latter situation are local importers and foreign exporting firms likely to be the main promoters of industrial enterprise. When foreign exchange income is expanding, one may rather expect industrial opportunities to be exploited by indigenous entrepreneurship. Under such conditions, the importing interests are apt to be well satisfied with their lot and activity; industrial development will run clearly counter to their short-run interests, especially when it requires the imposition of even a moderate level of protection. Some evidence in support of our distinction may be cited: in both Brazil and Colombia, coffee booms in the late nineteenth and early twentieth centuries, respectively, gave rise to periods of industrial expansion led by domestic entrepreneurs who were in no way tied to the importing interests.[12] The latter, on the other hand, were prominent in these and other Latin American countries during the high pressure drives toward import substitution which marked the World Wars and the Great Depression.

The importance of foreigners, of minorities or generally speaking, of non-elite-status groups in the total industrialization process has on occasion been held responsible for the fact that industrial interests do not wield in Latin America the political influence and social prestige which have been theirs in the older industrial countries. Insofar as the phenomenon is real, it can also be explained by the *kind* of industries most characteristic of the first phases of import-substituting industrialization: opinions of the owners of soft-drink bottling plants or of cosmetic or pharmaceutical industries are unlikely to command as much attention as those

---

[12]Warren Dean, "The Planter as Entrepreneur: The Case of São Paulo," *The Hispanic American Historical Review*, Vol. XLVI (May 1966), pp. 138–152; Luis Ospina Vásquez, *Industria y próteccion en Colombia (1810–1930)* (Medellín: E.S.F., 1955), Chap. 8.

of steel and machinery manufacturers. In addition, the industrialists of the leading industrial countries always gained considerable influence by virtue of being exporters; as such they achieved prestige abord, acquired contacts, and gathered information—all accomplishments that were highly prized by their governments. This source of influence is quite unavailable to the import-substituting industrialists who are usually aiming only at supplying the domestic market.[13]

The Exuberant Phase of ISI and Its Political Consequences

A final characteristic of the early phases of import-substituting industrialization is the growth pattern of the newly established industries. It has been suggested that

> output curves in newly established import-substituting industries have tended to be kinked, rising rapidly when exports are being replaced, but flattening out when further growth of demand has been grounded in the growth of domestic income. Profits have also followed this kinked pattern. Thus industries have moved rapidly from high profit and growth to precocious maturity, at which point they fall back to monopolistic quiescence with lower profit rates, a reduced level of investment, and aging plant and equipment.[14]

The extent to which the kinked pattern of output growth is really a fact rather than an inference from the nature of import-substitution remains to be established. After all, newly established industries have to overcome initial production and organization problems, they encounter some sales resistance due to preference for the imported product so that the early portion of their sales data may still approximate the logistic curve which has given a good fit for the time shape of the expansion of many industries in the advanced countries.[15] Nevertheless, it is probably legitimate to speak of a particularly "easy" phase of import substitution when the manufacturing process is entirely based on imported materials and machinery while importation of the article is firmly and effectively shut out by controls. Under such conditions, the early experience of the new manufacturers is likely to be most gratifying. It is this phase of import substitution that gives rise to the often noted exuberance and boom atmosphere during which demand is easily overestimated. In any event, low duties or preferential exchange rates for machinery

---

[13]The proposition that the comparative *lack* of political power of the industrialists can be explanined by the *lack* of industrial exports becomes perhaps more convincing when one states its positive counterpart: namely, that the continuing political influence of the land-owning interests throughout the period of industrialization in Latin America is explained by the continuing almost total dependence of the capacity to import on exports of primary products. This point is made for Brazil in Francisco C. Weffort, "Estado y masas en el Brasil," *Revista Latinoamericana de Sociologia*, Vol. I (Mar. 1965), pp. 53–71.

[14]David Felix, "Monetarists, Structuralists and Import-Substituting Industrialization," in W. Baer and I. Kerstenetzky (eds.), *Inflation and Growth in Latin America* (Homewood, Ill.: Richard D. Irwin, Inc., 1964), p. 384.

[15]Simon S. Kuznets, *Secular Movements in Production and Prices* (Boston: Houghton Mifflin Company, 1930). Arthur F. Burns, *Production Trends in the United States since 1870* (New York: National Bureau of Economic Research, 1934).

imports make for lavish orders. As a result, the new industry is likely to find itself saddled with excess capacity as soon as it reaches the kink.[16]

[In subsequent sections of the article, the author argues that current pessimism about "exhaustion" of opportunities for import-substitution is excessive and that import-substituting industrialization is not rigidly limited by either market size or foreign exchange earnings. Instead, he draws attention to some neglected economic, political, sociological, and technological determinants of continued industrialization and discusses the prospects that the process will eventually lead to exports of manufactures.]

---

[16]Even if expansion plans of competing firms are known all around and there is no excessive optimism, demand tends to be overestimated for two special reasons: with protection the price of the domestically produced product is going to be higher than that of the imported one; and market studies based on import statistics often overestimate the domestic market for the new domestic industry also because the statistics usually include a fair volume of specialty products which the domestic industry is unable to supply.

Selection **22**

The Importance of Price Stability

HOWARD S. ELLIS

From: "Price Stability: The Conflict Between Growth and Control of Inflation," in Kenneth Berrill (ed.), Economic Development With Special Reference to East Asia; Proceedings of a Conference Held by the International Economic Association (New York: St. Martin's Press, Inc., 1965), pp. 255–269. Reprinted by permission of St. Martin's Press, Inc.

It is the purpose of the ensuing analysis to consider the connexion, which may be positive or negative, between money creation and economic growth. The focus is upon conditions in underdeveloped countries, both in the general a priori analysis and in the presentation of concrete evidence. Economists have expressed divergent convictions upon this issue, it scarcely needs to be said. Perhaps the most profitable first step in seeking a solution is a careful review of the opposing positions.

First let us consider the general abstract case against inflation. Of course, there are myriads of arguments, but the case may be organized around five or six main considerations. There is, in the first place, the ethical angle—that inflation levies the costs of progress in an arbitrary way. It is regarded as particularly harsh upon the middle class who are, as capitalists, not extensive owners of physical plant, and who, as labourers, are not organized into unions to resist the impact of inflation.

High in the list of its economic costs are the various distortions which attend inflation: the distortion of the price system, the obscuring of economic calculation, the misdirection of investment. Some of this biasing of investment is particularly adverse to growth. Permissible charges for the services of public utilities generally lag behind other prices, and "social overhead" investment is penalized. On the other hand, luxury types of consumer durables, fancy apartments and commercial structures, and real estate are apt to get the lion's share of investment from inflationary profits. Of course, the mere appreciation of urban or agricultural land is in itself not a use of real resources; but when property changes hands the recipient of windfall capital gains may increase his consumption, and conceivably even a rise in "book value" without actual sale may induce a feeling of prosperity and thus lead to lavish expenditures.

Another set of objections pertains to saving. Inflation may indeed for a time cause forced savings for those whose money incomes lag behind the advance of commodity prices, particularly behind the cost of living. But the victims of the forcing eventually revolt and discover means of escape. Forced saving thus declines and, even while it persists, may entail an offsetting loss of voluntary saving. Some economic groups experience an "easy come, easy go" situation during the inflationary process. Frequently the accounting practices of firms do not adequately allow for the rise of prices, depreciation allowances are inadequate, and business dissaves.

Economic motivation suffers under inflation. Speculative profits divert man-power from production into mere trading; the incentive to economic efficiency is dulled; and managerial effort must be sacrificed to inventing ways in which to dodge the costs or reap the windfalls of differential price developments. Closely allied to these wastes is the general impairment of economic morale: labour has to strike to keep up with the game, or may be induced to try to keep a jump ahead; savers of money . . . are penalized; competitive excellence counts less. In general, a system of free private enterprise suffers. Lenin was right in saying that inflation sounds the death knell of capitalism.

Far short of this extremity, inflation generally means—in the contemporary setting of relatively fixed exchange rates—a reduction of exports and consequent difficulties with the balance of payments. Generally these difficulties are met with some sort of exchange control. Sometimes exchange controls interfere with the flow of imports which are desirable for economic development. But even if not, exchange controls almost always put obstacles to the withdrawal of interest and profits on foreign investments and thus interpose an obstacle to the inflow of private capital. At the same time domestic inflation, coupled with the artificially low price given to foreign currencies by the exchange control, induces an outward flight of domestic capital, which cripples development.

These constitute the main charges against inflation from the angle of the possibility of economic growth. In addition it is frequently maintained that the mild rise of prices which some economists defend in this context cannot be achieved; it will inevitably deteriorate into excessive inflation.

A retrospect over the a priori case against inflation reveals two points which can in effect, I believe, be eliminated from further discussion. The first is the unethical character of the redistribution of wealth and income which is entailed by inflation. This is scarcely a matter of dispute, except in the communist ethics which justify any means for attaining certain ends. The second point to be elimi-nated from debate is the argument that creeping inflation more or less inevitably passes over into a galloping rate. Sometimes this has happened, but there is nothing inevitable about it. Professor Don Patinkin has found with reference to the economy of Israel that, though money supply and prices rose over the six years 1953 through 1958 by 5 per cent annually, velocity remained about constant.[1] Professor Siegel also discovered that even with an average price rise of 10 per cent per annum in

---

[1] Don Patinkin, in Falk Project for Economic Research in Israel, *Fourth Report, 1957 and 1958* (Jerusalem, 1959), pp. 113, 115.

Mexico, 1935–55, no domestic flight from the currency developed.[2] Siegel has carried on an investigation of the inflation experience of 29 countries in the period since the last war and finds that moderate inflation has seldom provoked a self-generating price spiral through velocity.[3]

Now let us turn to the arguments which have been advanced in favour of inflation as an instrument of economic progress in underdeveloped countries. It has been said that inflation is a device for getting unemployed resources into productive use. Several other arguments seem to rely upon "forced saving" from one source or another. Thus government deficit finance for development purposes, coupled with money creation, bids away factors from consumption. The lag of money wages behind profits shifts income, it is said, from labourers to entrepreneurs who save and invest. W. Arthur Lewis has argued that this shift of real income is bound in the course of time, through the increase of income following investment, to convert the initial forced savings into voluntary savings.[4] With regard to economic motivation in general, it is believed in some quarters that gradual or gentle inflation creates an atmosphere favourable to progress, and that it mildly penalizes the settled conventional part of the economy, correspondingly stimulating the new, pioneering, and progressive sectors.

Somewhat less general cases for inflation have been built upon particular circumstances. The fact that inflation necessitates exchange control if the old rate of exchange is retained has been said to be advantageous in permitting selective import control in favour of capital goods or in favour of development projects. It is said that underdeveloped countries are generally "export economies"—incomes are determined more by the balance of trade than by domestic monetary policy. In this situation, boom times and inflation are the only setting in which incomes are sufficiently in excess of subsistence to admit investment for development.

A retrospect over these arguments for inflation reveals two arguments which can probably be ruled out from serious discussion. In the first place the absorption of unemployed or underemployed labour is not furthered by inflation in most underdeveloped countries. The situation differs fundamentally from cyclical unemployment in an advanced economy, where an increase of monetary (or "effective") demand can put idle manpower into use with the existing unused plant capacity. But where the plant does not exist and where capital needed to create the plant is forthcoming only slowly and laboriously, increasing monetary demand runs into immediate limits. Structural unemployment has to be cured by other devices; indeed inflation may only intensify it. This is so generally admitted that I believe the case need not be argued further.

Similarly, the plausibility of the last argument reviewed above, depending

[2] Barry N. Siegel, *Inflation and Economic Development: Studies in the Mexican Experience*, Ph. D. dissertation, University of California, 1957; published by CEMLA (Mexico City, 1960).

[3] Barry N. Siegel, "Hyper-Inflation—The Velocity Mechanism," *Proceedings of the 33rd Annual Conference of the Western Economic Association*, 1958.

[4] W. Arthur Lewis, "Economic Development with Unlimited Supplies of Labour," *The Manchester School* (May 1954), pp. 162–165.

upon the supposed efficacy of a "spurt" of forced saving, investment, and output, has been fairly conclusively refuted by John H. Adler.[5] Intended savings, he argues, tend to vary inversely with expected prices, intended investment directly. Under inflationary conditions, the inequality of *ex ante* savings and investment will be bridged by drawing down exchange reserves or by borrowing from abroad. Under plausible elasticity assumptions for savings and investment *ex ante*, a price increase per annum of 10 per cent will cause the loss of one-half of a country's foreign exchange reserves if they originally equalled three months' imports, where imports amount to 15 per cent of national product. But the "spurt" theory relies for its efficacy on a supposed shifting of the rate of investment to a *sustainable* higher level by virtue of the spurt. During this longer run, to prevent inflation, restore exchange reserves, and service the foreign debt, savings *ex ante* must exceed investment *ex ante*. But on reasonable assumptions regarding capital-output and savings ratios, this excess is practically unattainable. Consequently, Adler concludes that any special merit in the *spurt* of investment and inflation disappears.

We are left, however, with the more general case for inflation not resting upon unused resources or upon the efficacy of a sudden spurt. And here the adequacy of a priori argument ends. On the one hand are several "compelling" arguments concerning the wastage or the fleeting character of gains from inflation, and on the other hand there are several "not implausible" arguments favourable to inflation. The advocate of inflation for development simply says that he recognizes the possible costs or losses from inflation, but believes the gains outweigh the costs, while the foe of inflation maintains the opposite. Thus an appeal to empiric evidence becomes indispensable. However, there are very narrow limits upon the statistical evidence which can be brought to bear upon the problem. As E. M. Bernstein says, "There are no data covering an extended period on saving in any underdeveloped country. It is not possible, for this reason, to show what the relation to G.N.P. has been in periods of stability with periods of inflation."[6] And statistics relevant to other impacts of inflation are also limited and not easy to interpret. Fortunately, however, statistical information is not the only kind of empiric evidence: there is the evidence yielded to the economic expert by observation and experience. The balance of the present paper is devoted to a survey of this type of evidence. Naturally, such a survey cannot pretend to exhaustiveness, but it may lay claim to absence of bias in the sampling of countries and writers.

The display begins with expressions of judgment adverse to inflation from the angle of the economic development of specific countries. Latin American countries are considered first. Dr. Roberto de Oliveira Campos, President of the Industrial Fomento of Brazil, ascribes the following difficulties to inflation in that country: (1) wage and salary groups organize to defend their real incomes; (2) forced transfers by inflation to entrepreneurs are largely wasted in luxury consumption,

    [5] J. H. Adler, "Nota sobre la inflación 'momentánea' y el desarrollo económico," *El Trimestre Económico* (Oct.–Dec. 1958), special 25th Anniversary Issue on the Problems of Economic Development, pp. 674–684.
    [6] E. M. Bernstein, "Financing Economic Growth in Underdeveloped Economies," in W. W. Heller (ed.), *Savings in the Modern Economy* (Minneapolis, 1953), p. 283.

unproductive investments, hoards, etc.; (3) investment in overhead capital, which embraces several controlled price sectors, is discouraged; (4) balance-of-payments difficulties emerge; (5) there develops a lack of interest in increased productivity and efficiency.[7]

Also speaking about Brazil, Prof. Gudin (former Finance Minister) points to *inverse* relations between inflation and increments to real product in 1952–1953, 1955–1956, and 1956–1957. He believes that forced savings equal to 7 per cent of GNP have been extracted each year from holders of demand deposits by an annual inflation of 20 per cent. But the forced saving has been more than offset, in effects on GNP, by a reduction in voluntary saving, by failure to adjust money amounts of depreciation upward to allow for higher reproduction costs of equipment, and by inflationary consumption. An indicator of the bias of inflation toward mere trading is afforded by the number of bank offices, which increased by threefold, 1940–1956, and by the number of bank employees, which increased nearly fourfold.[8] The inflation has, furthermore, induced a flight of capital from Brazil, has biased investment away from public utilities with their fixed prices, and has induced an excess of investment in buildings and land.

E. M. Bernstein presents figures for Brazil over the years 1941 through 1949, showing that during these years construction first rose (through 1946) under the impact of inflation, and then played out. This happens because the public adjusted to inflation and the forced transfer from consuming to saving groups was ended. "Even after prolonged inflation ceases to affect the volume of investment, it remains a powerful factor distorting the direction of investment." An abnormal amount of financial management must be devoted to avoiding the impact of inflation.[9]

"In a recent lecture, the Dean of the Economics Faculty in the University of Chile, Sr. Luís Escobar Cerda, drew attention to the co-existence in Chile of an annual rate of inflation of at least 30 per cent with unemployment of approximately 8 per cent. In addition, the economy was practically stationary, despite the annual 2.5 per cent growth in population."[10]

In a study covering the period 1945–1951 for Chile, Colombia, and Cuba, Felipe Pazos, a former Governor of the Bank of Cuba, presents annual figures on capital formation, which show lower values for Chile, where inflation was rampant, than for Colombia, where inflation was mild, and still lower for Cuba, where prices were stable. The discouragement to voluntary saving more than outweighed the volume of forced saving.[11]

Barry N. Siegel directs his enquiry of the Mexican economy to the question

---

[7] Paul D. Zook (ed.), *Economic Development and International Trade* (Dallas, 1959), pp. 116–117.

[8] Eugenio Gudin, "Inflation in Latin America," paper presented at the Elsinore (Sept. 2–10, 1959) meeting of the International Economic Association (mimeographed).

[9] E. M. Bernstein, *Inflation in Brazil* (mimeographed), International Monetary Fund (Washington, D. C., March 24, 1952), pp. 116–117. See also his "Financing Economic Growth in Under-developed Economies," *op. cit.*, p. 285.

[10] Intergovernmental Committee for European Migration, *Research Digest* (Geneva, Nov.–Dec. 1959), p. 29.

[11] Felipe Pazos, "Economic Development and Financial Stability," International Monetary Fund, *Staff Papers* (Oct. 1953), pp. 228–253.

as to whether "moderate" inflation has actually promoted development there.[12] During the two decades following 1935 inflation averaged 10 per cent per annum and drastically redistributed national income in favour of profits (a phenomenon observed by a number of other economists). But this marked redistribution failed to increase the aggregate private propensity to save; indeed, in some years capital formation declined. Siegel explains this adverse outcome by the fact that inflation increases the incomes of the unprogressive and the unthrifty entrepreneurs as well as the incomes of those endowed with the opposite characteristics. Furthermore, the wealthy are large spenders on consumption. Inflation in Mexico, he concludes, has probably retarded development.

Taking a perspective over the whole of Latin America, Jorge del Canto, director of the Western Hemisphere Department of the International Monetary Fund, comes to a similar conclusion for the entire continent. For the decade 1947–1957, six countries—Argentina, Bolivia, Brazil, Chile, Paraguay, and Peru—experienced annual average inflation rates exceeding (sometimes very greatly) 10 per cent. The remaining thirteen South and Central American states with "moderate" rates of inflation (under 10 per cent per annum) have in general enjoyed stability of their economies and convertibility of their currencies. ". . . Inflation and exchange control are not necessarily a price that must be paid to achieve economic development."[13]

Outside Latin America, observations pertaining to inflation and development are more scattered. Ragnar Nurkse refers to Latvia during the 1920's and Japan in the 1870's and 1880's as countries which financed remarkable rates of economic growth by government expenditures financed through taxation, without much inflation.[14] Lockwood's monumental study of Japan tends to confirm this judgment, though the author speaks cautiously of a policy of credit expansion which refrained from reckless abuse but also from "excessive regard for the canons of orthodoxy."[15] But he roundly emphasizes that the threefold increases in prices from 1868 to 1938 occasioned social costs through the loss of purchasing power of the masses and the chronic waste of capital resources through speculation and ill-considered investment.

An outstanding authority on the economic history of Indonesia believes that the effects of inflation have been adverse to both stability and progress.[16] Various unpublished studies of the Research Division of the Board of Governors of the Federal Reserve System refer to the costs of inflation or the gains of monetary stability in the cases of the Philippines, Hong Kong, Indonesia, and India. With reference specifically to India, Prof. B. R. Shenoy argues that ". . . it is over-investment that would cause inflation, not economic growth. What is natural under rapid economic growth is a functional rise in prices whereby productive resources

---

[12]B. N. Siegel, *Inflation and Economic Development: Studies in the Mexican Experience.*

[13]J. del Canto, in P. D. Zook (ed.), *op. cit.* pp. 118–119.

[14]Ragnar Nurkse, *Problems of Capital Formation in Underdeveloped Countries* (Oxford, 1953), pp. 148–149.

[15]W. W. Lockwood, *The Economic Development of Japan* (London, 1955), pp. 519–520.

[16]Douglas S. Paauw, "Financing Economic Development in Indonesia," *Economic Development and Cultural Change* (Jan. 1956), pp. 171–185.

are canalized into desired trades and industries. Such relative price changes need not cause a general uptrend in prices."[17]

Speaking with special reference to the Asian scene, Dr. H. W. Singer says that it is a great fallacy to believe that development can be financed by inflation.[18] The proper viewpoint is a span of five, ten, or fifteen years, or even longer. From this perspective, inflation is a very strong discouragement to saving; it causes people to save the wrong things, hoarding commodities and gold; it upsets the cost-price calculation; and it ushers in balance-of-payments difficulties.

Professor Carl Iversen concludes from his study of the economy of Iraq that inflation is to be combated by all possible means, partly because of the social unrest it sets afoot through distorting the distribution of incomes, partly because of its biasing of investment, and partly because of the "unfavorable long-run effects on Iraq's position vis-à-vis foreign countries."[19] Furthermore, the transition to a monetary economy is impeded. Professor Patinkin likewise finds that inflation is inimical to progress, with especial reference to the economy of Israel and the effect of inflation on saving.[20] Finally, we may note that the Governor of the Bank of Greece believes, on the basis of his observation of the Greek economy, that "Monetary stability constitutes a basic prerequisite for an effective solution of the problem of economic development in an underdeveloped economy."[21]

Thus, first and last, a very substantial amount of empiric evidence from statistics and expert testimony exists regarding the adverse operation of inflation for particular countries in the less developed regions. In addition there exists a considerable amount of evidence of a general sort, pertaining to no country specifically but still oriented toward the underdeveloped world as a whole. The International Bank for Reconstruction and Development has conducted studies of the economies of a score or more countries with low *per capita* incomes. The authors of these reports are drawn from many nations and from many professions. Diligent research in these volumes fails to reveal a single case where inflation is recommended as a vehicle of development or even accepted as a necessary price of progress.[22]

There is also the general testimony of scholars and other experts. Nowhere have the drawbacks of inflation for economic development been more eloquently stated than by Professor Haberler.[23] He quotes the testimony of Professor Theodore Schultz in a hearing of the U.S. Congress that Chile operates from 20 to 25 per cent below its normal output because it tries to live with chronic inflation.

[17]B. R. Shenoy, "The Indian Economic Scene—Some Aspects," *The Indian Economic Journal* (April 1958), p. 332.

[18]H. W. Singer, "Development Projects as Part of National Development Programmes" in *Formulation and Economic Appraisal of Development Projects*, Lahore Meeting (United Nations, 1951), Book I, pp. 48–53.

[19]Carl Iversen, *A Report on Monetary Policy in Iraq* (National Bank of Iraq, 1954), p. 162.

[20]Don Patinkin, "The Israel Economy: The First Decade," the Falk Project for Economic Research in Israel, *Fourth Report, 1957 and 1958*, (Jerusalem, 1959), pp. 125, 139.

[21]Xenophon Zolotas, *Monetary Stability and Economic Development* (Bank of Greece, 1958), pp. 21ff.

[22]A possible exception is the report on Mexico.

[23]Gottfried Haberler, "Inflation and Economic Development," in *Contribuições a análise do desenvolvimento econômico, escritos em homenagem a Eugênio Gudin* (Rio de Janeiro, 1957), pp. 177–187.

David L. Grove, economist of the Bank of America, points to the effect of excessive money creation in distorting investment and in making exporting more difficult.[24] David Felix believes it doubtful if inflation is a "successful means of circumventing institutional resistances to development." Inflation may shift the exchange ratio favourably to agriculture but the ones who gain from this—landlords and middlemen—are not those in underdeveloped countries most likely to invest their gains productively. The inflow of imported equipment, raw materials, and fuels necessary to development is hindered rather than helped by inflation.[25]

Evidence in a similar sense has been offered also by officials of public organizations. Dr. E. DeVries, of the staff of the International Bank for Reconstruction and Development, has stated categorically: "A sound budget is the first duty of a government in economic development to give the people in the country confidence to increase saving and investment harmoniously."[26] Senor del Canto, a director of the International Monetary Fund, says that that organization, after twelve years of experience, concludes that inflation is inimical to development[27]. Dr. Karl Brandt, a member of the President's Council of Economic Advisers, cites the evidence presented by the UN Department of Economic and Social Affairs that, of 40 primary producing countries, in the period 1954–1957, 16 had experienced increases in the cost of living between 6 and 26 per cent, 18 between 1 and 5 per cent, and only 6 had no increase. Brandt then proceeds to argue that it is precisely with respect to economic development that these price increases are most injurious.[28] This position is urged with great emphasis by Arthur W. Marget, Director of the Division of International Finance of the Board of Governors of the Federal Reserve System,[29] who also adds the point that, in any country in which the national debt reaches a significant magnitude, even creeping inflation undermines the marketing of long-dated debt, favours correspondingly the issue of short maturities, and thus threatens the efficacy of monetary control over developments in the price level.[30]

What, now, is the evidence as to favourable effects of inflation on economic growth? Apology for inflation in this context rarely takes the form just stated—that there is a genuine positive influence—but instead rests most frequently upon (1) a sort of fatalistic acceptance of inflation as one of the costs of progress, or upon (2) some rather vague a priori grounds. The former is clearly the position

[24]David L. Grove, "Monetary Policy in Relation to Economic Development," lecture at Stanford University, Program on Overseas Development, 12 August 1955 (mimeographed).

[25]David Felix, *Industrialization and Chronic Inflation in Underdeveloped Countries*, doctoral dissertation, University of California, Berkeley, 1955.

[26]E. DeVries, "Financial Aspects of Economic Development," in United Nations, *Formulation and Economic Appraisal of Development Projects*, Book I, p. 320.

[27]P. D. Zook (ed.), *loc. cit.* p. 116ff.

[28]Karl Brandt, *The Threat of Inflation in the Underdeveloped World.*

[29]A. W. Marget, "The Applicability of 'Orthodox Monetary Remedies' to Developed and Underdeveloped Countries," Round Table Meeting of the International Economic Association, Elsinore, Denmark, 2–9 September 1959 (mimeographed).

[30]A. W. Marget, "Inflation: Some Lessons of Recent Foreign Experience," Paper presented to a joint meeting of the American Economic Association and Econometric Society, 28 December 1959 (mimeographed).

of Stacy May with regard to Costa Rica, who, however, immediately launches into a discussion of the ways of lessening inflation in this setting.[31] One finds examples of rather tautological statements, such as this: "So long as the inflation contributes to more activity and higher real incomes, it may be helpful rather than harmful."[32] And Professor Silcock has simply expressed the belief that a 2 or 3 per cent per annum inflation probably stimulates enterprise.[33]

Somewhat more explicitly, Kenneth Boulding found a useful function for inflation in the transfer of resources from "idle owners to enterprising nonowners." But in the long run, he says, the shift to profits may penalize some of the essential government undertakings such as transportation, education, etc. Trying, then, to secure the short-run benefits of inflation with the long-run benefits of stability, he concluded: "The only answer seems to be to have some sort of a cycle."[34] It may be recalled that W. Arthur Lewis, who originally seemed to argue that forced saving involved in the shift to profits automatically passes over into voluntary saving,[35] later abandoned this position in favour of the idea that "if inflation is to be used for capital formation, it is best done in small doses at a time, rather than continuously."[36]

The "shift to profit" argument may also be implicit in the contention made in the International Bank study of Mexico, where, it is said, "the savings of the postward period, which rose greatly over those of the war years, were largely stimulated by deficit financing and credit expansion." The report does advert to the "stagnation of private investment," but on balance seems to hold that credit expansion, even to an inflationary extent, increased saving and investment in Mexico.[37] In passing, it may be noted that the shift to profit defence of inflation was the basis of Professor Hamilton's analysis of the economic history of Western Europe from the sixteenth to the eighteenth centuries.[38]

Other grounds for a favourable view of inflation in the process of economic growth are sporadic in their occurrence. David Rowan has argued that for a "dependent economy" (where incomes depend heavily on foreign trade) "inflation is the process through which the gain in real income resulting from an improvement in the terms of trade is spread throughout the economy." While he does not

---

[31]Stacy May, *Costa Rica: A Study in Economic Development* (New York, 1952), pp. 289–290.

[32]M. R. Benedict and Elizabeth K. Bauer, *Farm Surpluses and Foreign Markets*, Chap. 7, p. 18 (mimeographed).

[33]T. H. Silcock, *The Commonwealth Economy in South-East Asia* (Durham, N.C., 1959), p. 208.

[34]K. E. Boulding, "Some Reflections on Inflation and Economic Development," in *Contribuições a análise do desenvolvimento econômico*, pp. 61–67.

[35]W. Arthur Lewis, "Economic Development with Unlimited Supplies of Labour," *The Manchester School*. (May 1954), pp. 139–191, especially pp. 162–170.

[36]W. Arthur Lewis, *The Theory of Economic Growth* (London, 1955), p. 224; cf. also pp. 217–225, 404–406.

[37]International Bank for Reconstruction and Development, *The Economic Development of Mexico* (Baltimore, 1953), p. 150. The report does not explicitly justify inflation, but does accept the credit expansion which in fact was inflationary.

[38]Earl J. Hamilton, various works including "Prices and Progress," *Journal of Economic History* (Fall 1952), pp. 325–349.

offer a defence of inflation *per se*, he does seem to regard domestic price increases indulgently if they do not interfere with "continuity of essential development projects and the full employment of resources."[39] In somewhat similar vein, Mr. Gunasekera, writing concerning Ceylon as an "export economy" with 40 per cent of its national income coming from tea, rubber, and coconut exports, says that domestic monetary policy cannot cope with a boom coming from foreign trade. Indeed it is only in a boom that an underdeveloped economy of this character can develop out of its own strength. Direct controls of expenditure, bank loans, and foreign payments can be used to cope with rising prices, but not general central-bank restriction of credit.[40] Another line of mild apology for inflation is offered by Professor Hirschman because of its association with the "supply imbalances that are characteristic of the growth process." But inflation is a *pis-aller*, and Hirschman seems merely to want to show that controlling it is more difficult in an economy breaking away from old processes than in a more settled economic scene.[41]

Account should be taken, finally, of the argument evolved by Nicholas Kaldor in favour of a "gently rising price-level" as a generally necessary adjunct to development.[42] His fundamental thesis is that the rate of growth of an economy depends primarily upon the rate of investment, and that this in turn depends on the rate of growth of incomes, and more particularly upon the growth of profits because saving takes place chiefly from profits. To induce net investment, returns must cover the interest cost, plus taxation, plus a payment for illiquidity risk, plus an excess margin to induce growth—for example 2, plus 5, plus 5, plus 4–6 per cent, or 16–18 per cent in total. Unless the expansive factors in the economy are very strong, it may be necessary to reduce the net interest return to zero or negative values through price inflation in order to induce net investment. Indeed, this has actually been the case in the United Kingdom since 1946.

CONCLUSION

Highly plausible lines of argument can be developed to prove that inflation is necessary or favourable to economic growth, as well as for the opposite proposition that inflation obstructs progress. The character of the arguments must, in any event, be understood in order to look for actual evidence as to the workings of inflation. To this end, the present paper first reviewed the abstract or a priori cases, eliminating both on the affirmative and the negative sides some arguments, such as the unethical character of inflationary redistribution, which it seemed unnecessary to debate. The analysis then proceeded to a review of evidence. The

[39]David Rowan, "The Monetary Problems of a Dependent Economy," Banca Nazionale del Lavoro, *Quarterly Review* (Dec. 1954), p. 201.

[40]H. A. de S. Gunasekera, "The Money Supply and Balance of Payments in Ceylon," Banca Nazionale del Lavoro, *Quarterly Review* (Sept. 1954), pp. 146–157.

[41]Albert O. Hirschman, *The Strategy of Economic Development* (New Haven, Conn., 1959), pp. 156–163.

[42]Nicholas Kaldor, "Economic Growth and the Problem of Inflation," *Economica*, Parts I and II (Aug. and Nov. 1959), pp. 212–226, 287–298.

evidence adduced was only occasionally statistical, because statistics of savings and investment in the underdeveloped world are rare, unreliable, and inconclusive. Nor was the reader asked to rely upon the present writer's judgment. Instead the evidence has been chiefly the experience and informed judgment of economists whose professional activities have brought them into contact with the phenomena in question: economic progress or the absence of growth on the one hand and price-level developments on the other. What conclusions can we draw from this evidence?

In the first place, the number of economists who had, according to their own account, observed unfavourable effects of inflation upon development very greatly exceeded—perhaps by 5 or 6 multiples in the sample covered by these pages—the number of persons who held the contrary view. Those whose findings were adverse to inflation in the growth process included numerous representatives from Latin American countries, where experience with inflation has been most extended in time and number of cases. Included among these observers were representatives of international agencies, national development, finance and banking institutions, as well as academic economists. The same breadth of the sample of observers marks the experience with inflation outside Latin America.

In the second place, among those who have spoken favourably of inflation in the context of economic development a considerable number represent the view that inflation is an inevitable accompaniment of growth, without the contention that inflation itself has a positive (i.e., beneficial) function. For this position it is of course legitimate to say that these observers are not presenting a favourable case for inflation but rather a case for practical policies which would make for the attainment of development without the costs and disadvantages of inflation.

In the third place, in the small remaining number of persons who actually ascribe a definable positive function to inflation, nearly all have made the argument general; they have not asserted its validity for a given country and a given time. Thus, Lewis and Boulding, in arguing for "spurt" inflation, did not specify economies where this would be advisable nor did they adduce cases or evidence as to when or where in the past it had proven its merits over stable price conditions. The incompatibility of "spurt" inflation as a vehicle of economic growth with "gently rising prices," designed for the same end, would scarcely require comment. But the specific case for the "spurt" seems to have been effectively destroyed by Adler in any event.

The International Bank study of Mexico is among the few cases in the evidence reviewed here in which an expansion of credit, which was in fact inflationary, was cited as a cause of increased saving in a specific context. Against this, there must be weighed the finding of a later investigator that, despite the marked shift to profits in Mexico in this period, aggregate private savings decreased.[43] In passing it is of interest that Professor Hamilton's association of economic growth in the seventeenth, eighteenth, and nineteenth centuries with inflation in Spain, France, and England has been categorically rejected by David Felix for all of these coun-

---

[43]Cf. p. 239 above.

tries.[44] Professor Rostow's study of England in the nineteenth century led to the conclusion that "periods of falling or stagnant prices were, normally, the intervals when the largest increases in production occurred and the greatest decline in unemployment."[45]

So far as concerns the apologetic attitude of Rowan and of Gunasekera regarding inflationary pressures on domestic prices or incomes arising from the advance of export prices for "dependent" or "export" economies, it would—I believe—be generally thought very difficult to insulate the domestic economy completely from price developments abroad. A difficult compromise has generally to be struck between complete withdrawal from the international price system and complete subordination to it. But it would be difficult to recast this fact into a defence of inflation per se any more than deflation. Both represent the price, partly unavoidable, for something less than complete autarky.

So far as concerns Kaldor's argument, it may very well be the case that generally, though perhaps not invariably, "a higher ratio of investment to output is [therefore] an essential precondition for stepping up the rate of growth of the economy."[46] It is conceivable that a reduction of the rate of interest to zero or less by inflation may in some cases, particularly in the short run, have given an upward fillip to investment. But Kaldor's own suggestion of alternative ways of encouraging investment (p. 298) shows that inflation is not a *sine qua non*. On the contrary, the evidence adduced by many economists for most situations seems to show that for a longer run it would be fatal to a sustained high rate of investment. In Latin America the countries with the most stable price levels have experienced the largest growth rates. On the other hand, in Chile from 1936 to 1951 the rate of interest because of inflation averaged minus 4.8 per cent, and the economy remained stagnant.[47]

Discussion of the connexion, positive or negative, between inflation and economic growth has probably suffered because of completely categoric arguments on one side or the other, and because of a high-handed impatience or indisposition to review the available evidence. There can be little doubt that inflation has sometimes and for short periods supplied a forward thrust to saving and investment. There is also little doubt, on the basis of statistical fact and the evidence of expert observers, that in most cases and over the long run inflation impedes growth.

---

[44]David Felix, "Profit Inflation and Industrial Growth," Cf. p. 238 above.

[45]W. W. Rostow, *British Economy in the 19th Century* (New York: Oxford University Press, Inc., 1948), Chap. 1.

[46]Kaldor, *op. cit.*, p. 297.

[47]Cf. David L. Grove, "The Role of the Banking System in the Chilean Inflation," International Monetary Fund, *Staff Papers* (Sept. 1951).

Selection **23**

The Need of an Adequate
Financial Infrastructure

URSULA K. HICKS

From: Development Finance: Planning and Control (*New York: Oxford University Press, 1965*), *pp. 51–60. Reprinted by permission of the Clarendon Press, Oxford.*

BUILDING THE FINANCIAL INFRASTRUCTURE

The answer to the problem of increasing home savings and harnessing them to development lies in creating an effective financial infrastructure.[1] This is not something that the development countries can afford just to let grow, as it did in England and the United States; they have not time to wait for this to happen. Nor is it necessary that they should do so; there has been enough experimentation and accumulated knowledge to lay down with fair confidence both what is required and what is feasible. Broadly, a financial infrastructure comprises four elements, each of which can become a source of additional savings. These four elements are, first, the currency; second, a central bank; third, an effective commercial banking system (including savings institutions); and fourth, a foundation for the growth of developed monetary institutions, including a market for short-term funds and a stock exchange.

The establishment of an adequate financial infrastructure inevitably takes time. But it will take less time and be more effective if it is undertaken as a deliberate and integrated policy. In some countries primitive habits of investment—in cattle, regardless of quality, or in gold and jewelry—have to be overcome before savings can be made available for development. Again some development countries had central banks during the interwar period. Their experience over the years should be useful in respect of such things as forecasting seasonal movements. In other directions, however, it may not be of much present relevance. In the interwar period banking operations were carried on in a world where there was no conscious push for development. The central banks' preoccupations were with primary

---

[1] Cf. on all this E. T. Nevin, *Capital Funds in Underdeveloped Countries* (New York: The Macmillan Company, 1961).

product prices, the objective being international stability rather than growth. Relations between the central bank and the government tended to be much less intimate than is required in a development country. Thus, even where a country possesses an established central bank, its outlook and possibly also its constitution will require adjustment to the idea that its main task must be to support develop- ment policy.

The most obvious source of funds that can be mobilised for development is the unnecessarily large reserves with which many countries emerged into indepen- dence, particularly those countries where Currency Boards had been in operation. The essence of the Currency Board system is that its operation is virtually auto- matic. The supply of currency in a country depends on the flow of foreign exchange into and out of it. An outflow automatically reduces the money supply (credit money being of negligible importance); a favourable balance-of-payments has the opposite effect. Thus there is absolute security against a balance-of-payments crisis, but none against violent income changes within the country. Traditionally sterling Currency Boards operated with 100 per cent backing, but since 1954 the Bank of England has agreed that 80 per cent provides sufficient cover in most circumstances. This has constituted a welcome, although once for all, addition to development funds. What has now taken place is the change over to an exchange standard, based, so far as Commonwealth countries are concerned, on sterling. (But since sterling is tied to the U.S. dollar, and the dollar to gold, the formal base is not of very great importance.)

The fundamental differences implied in this change is that an exchange standard requires a conscious monetary policy. The exchanges will fluctuate with all the economic winds that blow. The experience of one country will differ from another's according to such things as the natural strength of its balance of payments, and the extent to which its major exports fluctuate, both on the supply side (depending mainly on the vagaries of its climate) and on the demand side (depending on the extent to which they are tied to the level of activity in the advanced countries). A further factor is the extent to which the central bank will itself have to bear the whole burden of protecting the currency or to which overseas-owned commer- cial banks will be prepared to lend a hand by offsetting fluctuations, for instance, by bringing in funds when a temporary outflow occurs.[2]

On the other side is the problem of keeping the internal money supply adjusted to social and economic change. For instance, as the subsistence sector comes into the money economy, more currency will be required. On the other hand, the spread of banking habits will economise in currency, a tendency which the general limbering up of the economy will carry further through an increase in the velocity of circulation.

These are difficult matters which the monetary authorities will have to watch carefully, learning by experience to take the correct decisions. It will be advisable at the start to keep detailed records of currency issues and withdrawals, month

---

[2] If and when a country joins the International Monetary Fund, a new world of advice and assistance (but perhaps subject to stringent conditions) will be open to it. It would take us too far afield to enter into a discussion of these relations.

by month. If it so happens that one particular foreign country is predominantly important to the development country in question, movements into and out of its exchange should be specially carefully watched. It may well be desirable to hold an ample reserve of its securities. Only experience will show what magnitude of reserves it is desirable for the bank to carry. It will almost certainly be substantially lower than that required by even the modified Currency Board system, and a greater proportion of it can safely be held in local assets where it can directly assist development.

In most countries the foreign exchange held as currency backing is by no means the only reserve that can be mobilised for development. Some primary producing countries, for instance, still have Marketing Board reserves invested overseas, but are reluctant to withdraw them, since, as they were invested when interest rates were very low, there would now be a substantial capital loss on realisation. These funds are now urgently needed for development, and there is no point in leaving them overseas, since interest rates are most unlikely to return to the low levels of the middle 1940's in the foreseeable future.

CENTRAL BANKING IN DEVELOPMENT COUNTRIES

The main agency for the mobilisation of savings will be the central bank. Traditionally, as we have seen, the main objective of central bank policy was to preserve economic stability. Indeed (as in nineteenth-century England) when the public sector was still small, and consequently fiscal policy ineffective, the bank was the only stabilising agency. Stability is still an important objective of central bank policy; but in a development country, where the financial infrastructure is only in course of erection and where banking habits only touch a minor part of the economy, the contribution that a central bank can make to development is more important and immediate than what it can do in the way of stabilisation.

There is no difficulty in persuading development countries that they need a central bank, for it has become something of a prestige symbol. Once the true role of the bank is grasped, it will be seen that it need not be a costly affair, with a magnificent building and an army of research officers (who would be better employed in the Planning Department). Hence even a small country can afford its own central bank, although it would be foolish to launch one if there were neighbouring territories with similar development interests with which it could join.[3] Generally speaking, the larger the jurisdiction, the greater and more regular the funds that the bank will have at its disposal, and so the greater the assistance it can give.

It is important, however, that the bank should be strong enough to wield a moral force that will command respect at home and inspire confidence abroad. Inclusion in the bank's statutes of provisions limiting the amount and length of loans to the government will help in this respect. For the sake of reassuring the

---

[3] Thus there is no reason why the smaller Caribbean islands should not have their own central bank, apart from Jamaica or Trinidad, although a joint organisation with Trinidad would have greater opportunities. The similar economies of the East African countries (Kenya, Uganda, and Tanzania) suggest that they might cooperate in a central bank, even without formal federation. Cf. W. T. Newlyn, "Monetary Systems and Integration," *E. A. Economic Review* (June 1964).

established commercial banks it will also be well to announce that the central bank will not compete in commercial banking in any way. (It has been found by experience that the two functions do not go well together.) It will also help to inspire confidence if the bank establishes a separate "Currency" Department, distinct from the Banking Department, the sole business of which would be to look after the soundness of the currency. In fact this provision has no compelling economic or financial rationale, but it follows the precedent of most well-established and successful central banks.

Although the central bank's staff need not be large, it must be of the highest calibre. In a development country the bank will have to be set up almost wholly out of government funds, since no other source will be immediately available. This by no means implies that it should, or need, be the government's creature (or "milch cow" as it is sometimes expressed). Its operations can, and should, be entirely unfettered. It should be in a position to give independent advice and to state its views firmly to the government, on the basis of its own economic and statistical research, although in the last analysis it will have to conform to the government's general economic policy. The idea current in the 1920's, when a number of central banks were set up, that central banks should be entirely independent of governments, has been realised to be impracticable in the face of the growth of public economic policy (dating from the depression of the 1930's[4]). On the other hand there is an important sense in which a well-established central bank can never be "nationalised." Thus it can do much to maintain confidence among the business community at home and abroad, when governments act in a manner which is clearly not in the long-run interests of the economy.

What then should be the main function of a central bank in a development country? It will naturally be the government banker both on current and capital account and will have responsibility for national debt transactions. Thus it will be in very close contact with the government's economic policy. By acting as a channel for savings from public reserves, and also from the general public's purchase of savings certificates and similar securities, it can directly aid the finance of development.[5]

The central bank will probably not be able to do very much to regulate the activities of foreign owned banks; but it can begin at once to require them to keep reserves with it, related (in some way) to their transactions in the country. [Professor Nevin[6] makes the useful point that these should be prescribed in terms of sums of money rather than in ratios: first, because the appropriate ratios for such local transactions would be hard to determine, and second, because a multiple credit expansion (or contraction) cannot be expected in the early stages of develop-

---

[4] It can be argued that from the Bank Act of 1844 the Bank of England was not fully independent of the government, since it could not expand the currency to reflate a crisis without the authorisation of a "Treasury Letter."

[5] According to circumstances it may or may not be useful to set up a separate "Development Bank" to look after this channeling process. The alternative is for the central bank to operate directly through such agencies as an Industrial Development Corporation and an Agricultural Credit Corporation.

[6] *Op. cit.*

ment. The crude quantity theory will operate much more nearly than in a developed credit economy.] Some of these bank reserves can safely be invested in development by the bank itself, as they are not likely to fluctuate very violently.

From the beginning the central bank must be given powers to change the reserve requirements of the commercial banks according to the needs of stability policy. The withdrawal of definite sums from circulation should have an immediate anti-inflationary effect on the economy. On the other side it should be given powers to encourage investment in particular lines by selective credit controls through the banks and through such financial institutions as insurance companies and building societies. In all these ways[7] the central bank can channel savings into the development process while doing what it can to see that stability is observed.

The central bank's second task will be to watch over the establishment of a sound commercial banking system throughout the country. Long-established branches of foreign-owned banks have rendered a very useful service in promoting overseas trade and in establishing a tradition of sound banking. But they have normally taken more out of these countries than they have put in. Some few of these banks are now prepared to re-orientate their policy and to take an active part in providing credit for development, but this does not seem to be general.

The central bank may consequently find that it has to build up an internal banking structure almost from the bottom. One way of doing this is to establish a commercial bank with public funds, which will follow an aggressive policy of "selling" banking even in remote rural areas.[8] In some countries private enterprise is willing to come forward and set up local branch banking. It will be the central bank's responsibility to see that adequate legislation is ready in advance to look after these.[9] The legislation should stipulate such things as the minimum subscribed capital, the minimum ratio of deposits to capital, acceptable qualifications for directors, and the assets which the bank is permitted (or forbidden) to hold. Even if the promotors are sound and solid men (which by no means follows), they will be very inexperienced in financial matters and will need both protection and guidance in the early years.

In respect of old established banks, whether foreign-owned or not, the central bank will be wise to proceed very tactfully. They have to be convinced that in the long run the setting up of the central bank will be to their advantage. In fact this is true[10] in several ways. Its existence will directly enlarge the field in which they can operate. It can simplify transactions by giving assistance with clearings and other services. The establishment of financial markets, especially a money market, will be a great convenience to the banks as a means of investing short-term balances.

---

[7] It would take us too far into the field of technicalities to discuss the use of multiple exchange rates as a means of selective credit controls and export stimulators. Experience seems to indicate that they are mainly of use as short-run devices when the situation has got too involved for more orthodox methods to be successful.

[8] This was successful in Ceylon.

[9] As was not the case in Nigeria, though no fault of the government.

[10] In Canada in the 1920's an international recommendation that a central bank should be established was greeted with scant favour by the well-established and responsible commercial banks. It was not long before they discovered the advantages of having one. Cf. A. F. W. Plumptre, *Central Banking in the British Dominions* (Toronto, 1947).

On the other hand, the central bank would be wise not to force too high a block of reserves to be held locally. The objective should be not to hinder the banks in their business but to lead them into either holding cash (which would help to restrain inflationary pressures) or, better, to activate them to look for new forms of productive investment. The established banks will also be grateful to find that the central bank's control over inexperienced bankers will protect them from bad banking.

In an advanced country the commercial banks are far from being the only sources of credit or depositories for savings. Over the years many other institutions, such as insurance companies and building societies, have developed spontaneously. In a development country such institutions are needed here and now, and so must be deliberately created. In a development country lending risks are so high that without the intermediary of government backed agencies savings will either tend not to be made or will merely be hoarded. The answer to this is a government organisation or savings banks and savings certificates.[11] The central bank can offer invaluable advice on the lending policy of the agencies. The way in which it will be convenient to organise them, however, depends very much on the types of credit demand in the country. The provision of credit for private enterprise is vital to development. It is important to realise that the problem breaks down into three separate compartments: credit for (relatively) large-scale enterprise, credit for agriculture, and credit for small business.

Industrial and hotel credit (representing large business) should be on a strictly commercial basis. It would naturally be handled by an Industrial Development Corporation and a Tourist Board, respectively. It would be their responsibility to make the necessary enquiries into the antecedents of the applicants and into their capital position. These agencies would naturally work closely with the Revenue Department operating the tax concession legislation.

Credit for agriculture (other than plantations), and for small-scale enterprise, is on a different footing. It has to be recognised that it is partly a social service in which an element of subsidy will be necessary. In respect of agriculture the administration of credit can usefully be combined with other agricultural services and advisory organisations. If producers' cooperatives can be effectively organised for particular products (especially for tree crops where continuity of tenure can be taken for granted), credit can most conveniently be organised on the advice of the primary societies. In respect of credit for the little man there is considerable danger that a government may entangle itself in bad debts and open-ended subsidies which contribute little to development. It is consequently important that the conditions under which credit will be given should carefully be laid down and that the administration of grants and collection of interest should be strictly regular and without political favour. The actual terms can then be generous.

The final task of a central bank in building the financial infrastructure should be to lay the foundations of markets for short- and long-term securities.[12] In this

---

[11]Japan has been remarkably successful in the mobilisation of small savings, considering her poverty. India has also done creditably.

[12]"The encouragement of rudimentary markets in long- and short-term loans is a task of first importance." E. T. Nevin, *op. cit.*, p. 85.

exercise there must clearly be very close cooperation between the bank and the government. The bank can help as regards the short-term market by accepting and encouraging the use of familiar types of credit, not excluding bills of lading. But the best stock in trade for the market will be Treasury Bills. The bank should encourage the government to make regular, fairly uniform, short-term issues of these, at reasonably attractive (tender) rates and carrying rediscount facilities. The objective is not so much the convenience of the government as the convenience of investors: "to establish a regular and acceptable channel by which private investors may obtain suitable assets within the economy, and local enterprises may obtain access to funds which would otherwise be lost to investment within the country."[13]

Some development countries have already long-established stock exchanges, but for those who have not, the nucleus of a market in long-term loans will be, to start with (and perhaps for a considerable time), trading in government debt. For success in this field again, the wishes of investors rather than the special interests of the government should have the first claim. The government can arrange its borrowing so that loans are issued fairly frequently and regularly. They should be planned to have the widest possible appeal to private investors, not merely to the banks and insurance companies. Experience shows that government debt is a perfectly good foundation for security trading.[14] In a development country the central bank can cooperate in the establishment of a stock exchange, for instance, by organising (perhaps to start with on the bank's premises) weekly meetings of those interested in buying and selling government debt. Besides arranging its borrowing with a view to the interests of investors, the government can help by giving sufficient support to bond prices to prevent wide fluctuations.

Building up an effective central bank, and still more, establishing a complete financial infrastructure, are long-term operations and patience is necessary. Nevertheless in some development countries where structures of a new type have been set up (for instance, Jamaica and Nigeria), considerable progress has been made even within a few years. As money and credit institutions develop, monetary policy will become increasingly available to assist fiscal policy to make the course of development as smooth and as rapid as the resources of the country will allow. Nevertheless in most development countries today, and for the immediate future, fiscal policy will continue to be the senior partner.

------

[13]E. T. Nevin, *op. cit.*, p. 95.

[14]In pre-1914 England, apart from the railways, almost the whole of the home stock in trade of the London Stock Exchange was Government debt.

Selection **24**

Will Underdeveloped
Countries Learn to Tax?

NICHOLAS KALDOR

From: Foreign Affairs, *Vol. 41, No. 2 (Jan. 1963), pp. 410–419. Reprinted
by special permission of* Foreign Affairs; © *held by the Council on
Foreign Relations, Inc., New York.*

I

The importance of public revenue to the underdeveloped countries can hardly
be exaggerated if they are to achieve their hopes of accelerated economic progress.
Whatever the prevailing ideology or political color of a particular government,
it must steadily expand a whole host of non-revenue-yielding services—education,
health, communication systems, and so on—as a prerequisite for the country's
economic and cultural development. These services must be financed out of
government revenue. Besides meeting these needs, taxes and other compulsory
levies provide the most appropriate instruments for increasing savings for capital
formation out of domestic sources. By providing a surplus over recurrent expenditure, they make it possible to devote a higher proportion of resources to building
up capital assets.

This is not to say that poor countries could or should finance their development
programs entirely by their own effort. The advanced countries with high incomes
have an obligation to assist in the process by providing aid, and this obligation
has been amply recognized—if not adequately implemented—in recent years.
However, foreign aid is likely to be fruitful only when it is a complement to domestic effort, not when it is treated as a substitute for it.

The fact is that in relation to gross national product the tax revenue of the underdeveloped countries is typically much smaller than in the advanced countries.
Whereas the "developed" countries collect 25 to 30 per cent of their GNP in
taxation, the underdeveloped countries typically collect only 8 to 15 per cent.

Is this an ineluctable consequence of their poverty? Since taxation can be paid
only out of the surplus of income over the minimum subsistence needs of the
population, most people believe that the proportion of the national income which
a poor country can divert to communal purposes through taxation—without

250

setting up intolerable social tensions—is much smaller than in a rich country. Two considerations show, however, that this is not the whole, or the main, explanation.

In the first place, though underdeveloped countries show enormous diversity in their economic and social set-up, they all—excepting the more primitive countries of Africa or Polynesia—show a degree of inequality in the distribution of income comparable to, if not greater than, that of the "developed" countries of Western Europe or North America. The statistical evidence is sketchy and not very reliable; yet such as there is all tends to show that the degree of concentration in the ownership of property is quite as great in the poor or semi-developed countries of the Middle East, Asia, or Latin America as in the countries of advanced capitalism. The share of the national income which accrues to property-owners of all kinds is probably appreciably larger in countries like Mexico, Chile, India, Turkey, or Persia than in the United States or in Britain.

Hence, while their average income per head is low, the fraction of their national income which accrues to a small minority of individuals is frequently greater than in the rich countries, and a much higher proportion of that income is devoted to personal consumption and a lower proportion to savings. This is partly a reflection of the failure of their taxation systems, but partly it follows from the fact that—depending on the degree of underdevelopment and the pressure of population on the land—a considerably greater part of wealth comes from the ownership of land, and a smaller proportion from industrial or commercial capital; and the owners of land, unlike the owners of industrial or commercial enterprises, are high spenders, not high savers. In a study which I made of Chile some years ago (one of the countries for which detailed national income statistics are available), I found that the proportion of the GNP which is "taken up" by the consumption of property owners was over 20 per cent—probably three times as high a proportion as that of the United States. This shows that the *level* of the national income per head is not a good indicator of taxable capacity; a poor country may have a high taxation potential if a relatively large part of its resources is nevertheless devoted to unessential or luxury consumption.

The second important consideration is that the incidence of taxation in most underdeveloped countries is regressive—far more regressive (or far less progressive) than that of the developed countries. Indirect taxes, the bulk of which normally falls on articles of mass consumption, make up a much higher share of the total revenue, and far more of the income tax revenue falls on salaries and wages, which is collected by the deduction-at-source method and often operates with a very low exemption limit.[1] As far as the mass of the people are concerned, the burden of taxation as measured by the percentage of income taken in tax is probably just as large in the low-income countries (at least in the urban sectors) as in the rich countries.

The shortfall in revenue is thus largely a reflection of failure to tax the wealthier sectors of the community effectively. Though progressive income taxes and in-

---

[1] In Turkey, for example, the exemption limit for income tax is around $100 a year for a single person.

heritance taxes exist on paper in most of the underdeveloped or semi-developed countries—sometimes imposed at high nominal rates, mounting to 80 per cent or more on the highest incomes—there are few cases in which such taxes are effective in practice. This is evinced by the glaring discrepancy between the amount of incomes of various types—profits, rents, etc.—that can be presumed to exist, judging from national output statistics, and the incomes declared in tax returns or computed on the basis of tax receipts. In the developed countries, the national income estimates based on the "income" and the "output" methods of computation are more easily reconciled and do not reveal such glaring differences. It is probably not an exaggeration to say that the typical underdeveloped country collects in direct taxation (excluding the taxation of wages and salaries) no more than one-fifth, possibly only one-tenth, of what is due—or rather what would be due if the tax laws themselves did not accord wide legal loopholes through exemptions and omissions of various kinds.

This broad generalization requires, of course, a great deal of qualification when applied to individual countries or regions. There are some countries which have been conspicuously unsuccessful in imposing taxes on the wealthy classes—chiefly, I think, the countries of Latin America—for whom the above picture may even be an understatement. There are others, chiefly the ex-colonies of the British Empire, which have only recently gained independence but inherited relatively high standards of tax administration from their colonial days; for these it may be an exaggeration. Some countries have made notable efforts in recent years to improve both their legislation and their tax administration. In others the situation is deteriorating, owing to the paralyzing effect of corruption or the steady erosion of ancient taxes; there the weight of direct taxation may be less now than it was 50 or 100 years ago.

II

Another source of untapped taxable capacity in many underdeveloped countries is to be found on the land. The agricultural or "subsistence" sector, which typically accounts for one-half or more of the national output, virtually escapes taxation at present,[2] owing to the "erosion" of the ancient land taxes of the countries of the Middle East and Asia. It is true that the peasantry is poor everywhere and its capacity to pay is limited. It is also true, however, that in most places—at least in most of the overpopulated regions—only a proportion of the produce accrues to the cultivator; the rest accrues to the owner of the land, or to some intermediary tenant; and as has been known since the time of Ricardo, the incidence of land taxes necessarily falls on the landlord. Despite recent measures of land reform in countries like India, the distribution of landholdings remains very uneven, with no more than one-half, or possibly two-thirds, of the land in the hands of genuine owner-cultivators.

---

[2] This is not meant to apply, of course, to plantation agriculture or to the production of cash crops for export by native farmers who may be heavily taxed through export levies or through the price policy of a marketing board.

The land tax is one of the most ancient forms of taxation in both Europe and Asia, and up to the early part of this century it still provided the principal source of revenue in the countries of the Middle East, India, and Japan. Since that time, however, political pressures combined with monetary changes have succeeded in virtually eliminating it; the tax continues to be collected in most places but on the basis of completely out-of-date valuations. Its rehabilitation now faces heavy political and administrative obstacles. Traditionally, the land tax was one-tenth of the value of the produce of the land. But its current yield in India is only about 1.5 per cent; in Turkey only 0.2 per cent. Yet, as the economic history of Japan demonstrates, the taxation of land can be a very potent engine of economic development, though its importance cannot be measured adequately by its money yield. This is because the land tax yields not just revenue but the right kind of revenue; it enlarges the supply of foodstuffs to urban areas and thus the amount of employment that can be offered outside agriculture without creating inflation. It also promotes agricultural efficiency. It encourages the more efficient use of the land as well as the transfer of ownership from relatively inefficient to efficient cultivators.

It is possible, moreover, to "streamline" this tax in accordance with more modern notions of equity by making it a progressive tax, graduated according to the total value of the land held by an individual and his family, so that the burden is concentrated on the large landowners. A scheme recently proposed in Turkey by the State Planning Organization would have exempted holdings of less than 2 hectares altogether, while larger holdings would have borne a graduated charge rising from 5 per cent on holdings of less than 10 hectares to 15 per cent on holdings of 50 hectares or more. Since the top 1.5 per cent of agricultural families own more than 21 per cent of the land (and a further 14 per cent of families another 31 per cent), this scheme would have made it possible to collect the revenue needed for the new five-year development plan by a levy which, without being exorbitant, would have avoided the anti-social features of the old land tax. However, the Cabinet, which approved the development plan, has refused to sanction the scheme for financing it, and recently it was reported that all the top officials of the Planning Organization have resigned in protest. In countries where a powerful landowning class exists, the prospects for effective land taxation do not appear more promising than the prospects for land reform.

III

When countries pass to a higher stage of development, as the more advanced regions of Latin America have done, industrial and commercial wealth (which is less tangible) assumes increasing importance. The taxation of that wealth raises more complicated problems, while any genuine measure of reform designed to tap it meets with the same kind of political resistance.

The effective administration of income tax on individuals or corporations requires a carefully thought-out legal code and a corps of capable and honest administrators. It is often argued that these taxes are really too difficult for the less developed countries to cope with, and it would be better if they concentrated on simpler forms of taxation. But the fact is that there is no suitable alternative. A graduated system of commodity taxation can never succeed in mitigating growing economic inequalities (and the political and social tensions which are associated with this process), or in reducing the resources devoted to socially unnecessary luxury consumption, in the same manner as progressive taxes on income and wealth. The same commodities are bought by people of very different means—the richer people buying more kinds of goods and services, and not just more luxurious goods; and many of the things on which wealthy individuals spend money cannot be effectively taxed—for example, domestic service, foreign travel, antiques, and so on.

It is also argued that the progressive taxation of industrial and commercial wealth, unlike that of landed wealth, slows down the rate of development by reducing both the means and the incentives to accumulation. In the United States or in Britain, the argument runs, progressive taxation was imposed only after the process of industrialization was largely completed—not in the middle of the industrial revolution. It does not follow, however, that if the system of progressive taxation had been imposed earlier, the course of economic development would have been very different. It is true that profits have always been the main source of industrial and commercial capital accumulation. But experience has shown that taxes on profits affect consumption out of profits far more than business savings. The reason for this is that for a successful businessman or corporation (in developed or undeveloped countries alike) the requirements of business expansion take precedence over the desire for higher consumption; the money that the owners take out of a business is generally no more than what is left after the business' own needs are satisfied. Otherwise it would be difficult to explain why fast-growing businesses should invariably plough back so much more of their profits than slow-growing businesses, or why the proportion of profits distributed as dividends should be so much less in countries where the taxation of profits is high than where it is low.

If the effects of increased public spending are taken into account, and not only the reduction in private spending, and if public money is wisely spent (admittedly this is not something that can be taken for granted), it is difficult to maintain that the reduction in inequality through progressive taxation puts a brake on economic development. It may do the very opposite. For in countries where luxury spending is not effectively curbed, the pattern of investment gets distorted. Too much of the capital accumulation is taken up by the expansion of industries and services which mainly cater to the rich. This kind of "growth" merely serves to make the rich even richer; it does not improve the standard of living of the masses of the population.

There are basic differences in the way capitalism developed in North America and the way it is now developing in the countries of Latin America. They cannot be explained merely by the differences in fiscal systems. Long before progressive taxation was invented, a whole set of attitudes and circumstances forced American business to concentrate on developing products for the mass market; the Woolworths and the Fords made their fortunes by providing goods within the reach of the many and not for the better satisfaction of the few. In Latin America development takes a different course. I know of no Latin American millionaire who made his fortune in the five-and-ten business. But vast fortunes were made in providing luxuries for a class whose members prospered largely by catering to each other. Whatever the true cause of such differences, it becomes vastly more important to apply progressive taxation, as a deliberate corrective to spontaneous economic forces which produce steadily growing inequality.

IV

Nor would it be correct to say that an effective system of progressive taxation cannot work because of the lack of administrative competence or honesty of officials, or the lack of a sense of social obligation of taxpayers. It is true that in most underdeveloped countries—though conditions vary a good deal—revenue officials are grossly underpaid, revenue departments are frequently understaffed and are short of men of ability and training. Straightforward corruption must be widespread. However, it is impossible to find out how much of the shortfall in revenue is due to this, as against sheer inefficiency or incompetence, or a laxity in the enforcement of the law which is tolerated, if not inspired, in higher quarters.

But the experience of many countries which suffered from much the same evils in the past shows that corruption and inefficiency *can* be eradicated if sufficient attention is given to the creation of corps of permanent officials[3] whose pay, status, and prospects of promotion are high enough to attract the best talent, and also high enough to establish the professional standards and etiquette associated with a public service that enjoys a privileged social status. The example of the Chinese Maritime Customs has shown what the creation of a well-paid body of permanent officials could accomplish, even in a country where corruption was as deeply ingrained as it was in Imperial China. Of course no underdeveloped country has the manpower resources or the money to create a high-grade civil service overnight. But it is not sufficiently recognized that the revenue service is the "point of entry"; if they concentrated on this, they would secure the means for the rest.

It is true that the prevailing systems of income taxation in the United States, Britain, or Canada rely heavily on the voluntary compliance of the taxpayer; for important categories of income the revenue authorities mainly depend on the taxpayers themselves to supply information, the accuracy and completeness of which is not automatically or systematically checked. But there is no technical necessity for this. One could conceive of a system in which transactions in capital assets and income payments of all kinds are systematically reported, in the same way as wage and salary payments are now reported. With the aid of modern business machines it would be possible to keep a record of the ownership of all property—land and houses and stocks and shares—and to keep a running check on changes in the personal balance sheet of all wealthy individuals. Each taxpayer

---

[3] In many Latin American countries the top-ranking officials of the tax administration—including district commissioners or even their deputies—are not permanent civil servants at all, but are appointed on the spoils system, changing with each administration.

could be asked to give a statement of his net worth each year, and not only of his income, and the return on this wealth could be independently checked if all property were registered and all changes in property registration were automatically reported in the name and the tax-code number of the beneficial owner. Tax administrators know that the discovery of changes in an individual's net worth over a period is the most effective method of bringing to light concealment of income. In advanced countries such investigations are made sporadically as a spot-check on returns or in cases where fraud is suspected; there is no reason why they should not be made systematically in countries where taxpayers are less honest or compliant.

V

It would be wrong to assume, therefore, that there are insuperable technical obstacles to the introduction of any effective system of progressive taxation. It is not beyond the wit of man to devise laws and administrative procedures which would oblige even the most recalcitrant (or cunning) Latin American or Middle East millionaire to surrender a reasonable share of his income or wealth to the state in taxation. But that is not to say that in the countries where such reforms are most needed they have much chance of acceptance. The secrecy and anonymity of property is regarded as sacred and is safeguarded by the system of "bearer" shares which effectively hides the identity of the shareholders of companies and which enables even the ownership of real property to be concealed through holding companies. Any suggestion that ownership should be disclosed and regularly reported to the government—as is done, for example, in the Scandinavian countries —would be unthinkable.[4] No doubt secrecy of property ownership is a far more valuable safeguard in countries which are politically unstable than in the settled democracies of Western Europe or North America. But political instability is itself a consequence of economic and social conditions which result from the unbridled greed of an oligarchical ruling class.

To the detached observer, fiscal reform undoubtedly appears as the most appropriate instrument for transforming the feudal or quasi-feudal régimes which inhibit the healthy evolution of so many of the underdeveloped countries and prevent them from following the path toward the kind of mass-prosperity civilization which has evolved in Western Europe and North America. But the advocacy of fiscal reform is not some magic potion that is capable of altering the balance of political power by stealth. No doubt, expert advice on tax reform can be very useful in making men of good will—ministers or officials—conscious of the precise

---

[4] In Turkey, one of the achievements of the military dictatorship that followed the Menderes régime was to introduce a measure for a single compulsory declaration of personal wealth. But Parliament insisted that these declarations should be deposited in sealed envelopes with public notaries and should not be opened for at least two years. There is now strong pressure in Parliament for a further provision to the effect that after two years have elapsed, the envelopes should be returned unopened to the taxpayers. In Mexico when it was suggested that some similar provision would be needed for the proper enforcement of inheritance taxes, the Congress responded by abolishing the inheritance tax altogether.

nature of the legislative and administrative changes that are required. But what can actually be accomplished does not depend merely on the individual good will of ministers or on the correct intellectual appreciation of the technical problems involved. It is predominantly a matter of political power.

In a successfully functioning democracy the balance of political power is itself a reflection of a continuous social compromise between the conflicting interests of particular groups and classes, which shift automatically in response to varying pressures. But experience has shown that in underdeveloped countries with a predominantly ignorant and illiterate electorate parliamentary institutions do not, in general, work in this way. Periodic elections and multiparty systems are not instrumental in securing continuous or peaceful social adjustment. Power remains in the hands of certain dominant groups, irrespective of whether one party or another is in office or whether there is an elected government or a dictatorship of some kind. The history of the last ten years produced plenty of examples—in Asia or in Latin America—of dictatorships replacing parliamentary systems, or vice versa, without significantly altering the underlying balance of power in society.

In many areas of the Middle East and of Latin America revolutionary pressure continues to build up, as a result of blind opposition to overdue social reforms. Ostensibly it is motivated by fear of communism: in reality it serves to bring communism nearer. The problem which has to be solved and to which no one has yet found a satisfactory answer is how to bring about that change in the balance of power which is needed to avert revolutions without *having* a revolution. Can it be brought about by outside pressure—by making internal social and economic reforms the *quid pro quo* for external aid, as in the Alliance for Progress? Or can it be brought about by some organized attempt at the political re-education of backward ruling classes—a kind of Westernized version of Chinese brainwashing? History does provide cases—nineteenth-century England is an obvious one—of a ruling class voluntarily relinquishing privileges for the sake of social stability. It did so in an instinctive appreciation of its long-run interests. But when ruling classes evince no signs of such instinct, can they be made to acquire it?

PART 4

TRADE OR AID

It is universally recognized that international trade plays a vital role in the economic life of most developing countries and that, as Alfred Marshall has pointed out, "The causes which determine the economic progress of nations belong to the study of international trade." This is even truer today than in his time.

There is not, however, complete agreement as to whether international trade is still the engine of growth in the twentieth century that it was a century ago. Those who argue in the affirmative stress the advantages that accrue to each country from international division of labor and specialization. Others maintain that international trade has, in fact, retarded growth in developing areas, and they cite the continued concentration of those countries on a few primary commodities as well as adverse long-term shifts of demand in the advanced countries.

> CAIRNCROSS is one of those who take the affirmative position, stressing, as he expresses it, the uniqueness of the contribution that foreign trade can make to economic development.
>
> KEESING also favors international trade and recommends that developing countries adopt outward-looking policies. He analyzes these policies against the background of over-all economic planning and touches upon the presently much-discussed topic, namely, the need to export manufactured goods by developing countries.

A great number of conditions must be fulfilled if economic development is to be fostered through trade; some conditions would need

to be resolved internally and others through international cooperation. Selections 27 and 28 deal with two types of internal policies.

> VARTIKAR stresses the importance of commercial policy,
> claiming that it can serve as a useful tool for furthering development,
> provided it is skillfully employed by the administrators and is made
> a part of their long-range strategy.

> MARSHALL, on the other hand, emphasizes the advantages
> and limitations of exchange controls as an instrument for fostering
> economic development.

Selections 29 through 33 are devoted to the issue of joint international economic policy for development. They deal with the role
that industrial countries can play in promoting economic development
in developing areas.

> MEADE stresses the need for price compensation agreements as a
> means to alleviate the developing countries' balance-of-payments
> difficulties, stemming from declining foreign demand and wide
> price fluctuations of primary products.

> JOHNSON, in turn, contrasts advantages and disadvantages of
> trade preferences for manufactured goods. In the author's opinion,
> trade preferences deserve serious consideration as a means of pro-
> moting exports of these goods from developing countries.

The remaining selections, 31 through 33, are devoted to ramifications of foreign assistance, a topic that is both widely discussed and
highly controversial.

> The articles of SINGER and CARLIN, dealing with forms of aid,
> are good examples of such a controversy.

> In Selection 33 LITTLE and CLIFFORD are concerned with the
> (often neglected) role that technical assistance can play in economic
> development and underscore the dependence of the form and func-
> tion of that type of assistance on each country's absorptive capacity.

Selection **25**

The Contribution of International Trade to Economic Development

A. K. CAIRNCROSS

From: *"International Trade and Economic Development,"* Econòmica, *Vol. XXVIII, No. 111 (August 1961), pp. 235–251. Reprinted by permission of* Economica *and the author.*

Economists have singled out, at one time or another, a great variety of causes of the wealth of nations. Among them are three that have been accorded particular emphasis: the growth of markets, the accumulation of capital, and the progress of technology. All three, like everything else that economists write about, interact with one another, so that the influence of any one of them makes itself felt as much through its repercussions on the other two as by its direct impact. A high level of capital investment, for example, allows new techniques to be exploited more quickly and at the same time helps to speed up the improvement of these techniques and the discovery of still newer ones by providing opportunities of experimentation on a commercial scale. Investment widens markets by enlarging the community's productive powers and contributes to the progress of technology by ensuring an outlet for innovations in technique. Nor is this the end of the matter: the resulting widening of markets and progress in technology react on one another and both create scope for yet more investment. Interactions so complex and far-reaching make it difficult to isolate the consequences of any single element in economic growth and development. They permit economists, indulging an individualism that is at once the charm and the reproach of our science, to pick their own thread to guide them through the maze, and set up their own signposts to prosperity.

The fashionable route today is by way of higher investment—except perhaps on the Continent where investment is already relatively high and the appeal of a larger market is correspondingly greater. In Britain it has also become fashionable to look in the direction of technological education and heavier expenditure on research and development for a short-cut to higher productivity. I have no quarrel with putting up these signposts, provided they are not represented as the only ones to follow. No one can fail to be conscious in the modern world of the enormous dependence of economic progress on advances in technology and on the investment that is necessary in order to give them effect. But there is a danger, particularly in the underdeveloped countries, that the third major influence on development, the widening of markets, may be allowed less than its due. This influence is now regarded with scepticism and distrust. I propose to consider how far this attitude is justified in underdeveloped countries and how international markets affect their economies.

Everyone knows what an electric effect a change in market opportunities can have on a firm or an industry. A sustained pressure of demand can overcome, in course of time, all kinds of obstacles to an increase in output. Whatever the qualifications necessary in mining or in agriculture, the normal experience in industry is, surely, that if market obstacles to expansion are removed, the other obstacles are rarely insurmountable. The production problem is relatively simple if the marketing problem can be disregarded. The same often applies to a whole community. There are rural areas in underdeveloped countries that for centuries have followed an almost unchanging routine and seem quite unresponsive to economic forces. Yet when the international market offers new and tempting opportunities, it often happens that old attitudes yield, the social framework adapts itself, unsuspected energies are released, and output responds on a scale that far surpasses initial expectations.

Equally, no one doubts the propulsive role of foreign trade in the development of the countries that we now think of as advanced. Whether one thinks of Britain at the outset of the industrial revolution or of the United States in the nineteenth century or of Japan in the twentieth, the expansion of exports gave a conspicuous momentum to the economy and helped it on its way to industrialization. Over the past century and a half the growth of international trade has continued to open up new opportunities of specialization and development for all the countries engaging in it. These opportunities were particularly apparent in the primary-producing countries overseas that were still in process of settlement, since trade enabled them to bring into use their great unexploited natural resources and freed them from the limitations of their own domestic markets. The international division of labour that resulted simultaneously helped the importing countries to meet their expanding requirements of materials and foodstuffs from low-cost sources of supply and afforded their export industries the double advantage of a larger scale of operations at lower real cost and the further economies that normally accompany a rapid rate of industrial growth.

In spite of the contribution that it has made to world economic development, international trade is not a popular engine of growth. The reasons for this are well known.

First of all it carries with it dependence on external forces. This means that the pace of development cannot be set by domestic policy but is set by forces that are not within the control of the indigenous authorities nor indeed of any authority, indigenous or foreign. The further exports rise, the higher this dependence mounts. More resources become tied to export requirements and less are left to meet the needs of the domestic market, so that there is less room for manoeuvre in organizing an economic structure adapted to those needs. In the underdeveloped countries dependence on external forces is particularly resented since it is associated with colonialism and loss of status and with the sense of inequality that always accompanies the dependence of the poor on the rich. Whether these attitudes are justifiable in terms of history or not, and whether they are harmful or otherwise to the countries where they prevail, their very existence itself limits the scope for foreign trade and the use that can be made in the future of patterns of development that were important in the past.[1]

A second source of objection is that foreign demand impinges only on a limited sector of the economy. The underdeveloped countries include a large number of what have misleadingly been christened monocultures. Whatever the variety of their agriculture many of them—thirty, to be exact—depend upon a single product for at least half their export earnings. Between them these thirty countries accounted in 1953 for 40 per cent of total exports from the underdeveloped countries, and the number of countries showing this degree of dependence on one export shows no long-term tendency to fall.[2]

It is a further source of disquiet that the export sector in such economies is rarely the vehicle of rapid innovation in other sectors. If the exports are agricultural, agriculture is damned as hidebound and incapable of imparting momentum to the rest of the economy; while if they are mineral, any gains are alleged to accrue to foreigners or to be confined within an enclave that is only loosely tacked on to the rest of the economy. Worst of all, to ship out oil is to part with the nation's patrimony. Mines and plantations supplying foreign markets are only too likely to be run by foreign managers and immigrant workers on behalf of foreign shareholders and with the help of imported equipment and materials, so that they form an intrusion from some other economy rather than an integral part of the economy of the underdeveloped country. The gains may flow abroad while the long-term costs, in the shape of a colony of unskilled and unassimilable alien workers, remain behind indefinitely.

Not only does foreign demand bear on a limited sector of the economy but it tends also to be highly variable. Most of the demand assumes the character of an overspill from the industrial countries of the world and fluctuates accordingly with the level of industrial activity. These fluctuations are not easily offset by parallel changes on the side of supply, for supply is highly inelastic over the short period of a cyclical swing and the result is a violent fluctuation in prices whenever demand and supply diverge.

The average prices received for exports are also thought to be unfair. In some versions they are so attractive that they encourage a kind of Gadarene specialization, resources rushing down the line of least resistance to the lowest possible level of utilization from which there is later found to be no way back. In the more usual version, prices are thought to be unfair for the opposite reason—that they sink lower and lower, the impoverished producer having no option but to submit

---

[1] Cf. B. C. Swerling, *Some Inter-relationships between Agricultural Trade and Economic Development* (Nov. 1960), p. 30 (mimeographed).
[2] F. Lamartine Yates, *Forty Years of Foreign Trade* (1959), p. 180.

to greater and greater exploitation by the lucky countries that have chosen to specialize in industry. The two versions may even be combined—as I have heard them combined—in a single woeful account of betrayal by higher prices followed by repentance throughout a secular slide in the terms of trade.

There is a more recent and more sophisticated argument against putting one's faith in foreign trade. While that may have worked in the past, we are told, it is not working now and will not work in the future. Foreign trade no longer operates as in the nineteenth century so as to allow the primary producing countries to make full use of their expanding resources. The growth that takes place in the centres of industrial development is still transmitted to less advanced countries through a steadily rising demand for imports of primary commodities. But the process works more and more feebly because the intake of materials is not keeping pace with industrial output and more of the materials are obtained without importation from underdeveloped countries. The export markets of these countries are consequently sluggish. On the other hand, they have a growing population to employ and may be losing an opportunity of developing other assets through sheer stagnation of demand. In such circumstances, it is urged, they have no option but to adopt a new pattern of advance and make deliberate efforts to develop their home market. The transmission of growth from foreign markets through foreign trade has ceased to be a sufficiently powerful engine of development.

I shall not attempt to discuss all these arguments. There are some with which I find myself in sympathy: for example, the prices of primary products are notoriously volatile, and the damaging effects of this volatility on the economies of the exporting countries are beyond question. With other arguments I find myself almost entirely out of sympathy: the world economy is not so constructed that primary-producing countries are doomed to a *dégringolade* in their terms of trade with industrial countries. In any event the terms of trade of a group of countries are of very little interest to individual members of the group unless they are all affected in roughly the same way—an assumption far removed from everyday experience. These are not matters on which I have anything to contribute that is not already well known. I shall refer to them only insofar as they help to explain the current pessimism about long-term trends in world trade and its impact on the development of the less advanced countries.

Let me begin, in considering the pessimistic attitude that I have outlined, by emphasizing the importance—indeed, the uniqueness—of the contribution that foreign trade can make to economic development. There is nothing necessarily regrettable about dependence on foreign trade. It is true that in engaging in trade a country puts itself at the mercy of external events: this is the price that any international division of labour exacts. But a country that seeks development must invite foreign influences if it is to succeed. It needs foreign equipment, foreign capital, and foreign ideas. How can it pay for this equipment without earning foreign currency by exporting? Or arrange a transfer of capital, in or out, without those other transactions in goods and services that give effect to the transfer? Or allow the economy to be permeated with the ideas that are the seed of true development without the kind of contacts with foreigners that trade automatically produces? Trade is no mere exchange of goods, least of all when it takes place between economies at different stages of development. As often as not, it is trade that gives birth to the urge to develop, the knowledge and experience that make development possible, and the means to accomplish it.

The importance of foreign trade is particularly great in countries that lack an engineering industry and are obliged to import almost all their machinery. In such countries exports may easily become the limiting factor on productive investment and on the successful development of the economy. The common experience in underdeveloped countries is not that exports are already a dangerously large element but that they are not large enough to give adequate elbow room in the financing of new investment. A high level of exports enlarges the volume of imports of equipment that can be financed without endangering the balance of payments, and this greater degree of freedom makes it easier to take a long view and plan domestic investment without the constant interruption that destroys half its value.

There is nothing particularly surprising when external demand bears on a narrow sector of the economy. This presumably reflects the much higher productivity of resources, especially land, in some specialized use, such as the growing of coffee, than in any less-specialized alternative use. Foreign trade opens up large possibilities of immediate gain by concentrating on a product that foreigners will buy and for which they will pay a relatively attractive price. It helps to transform subsistence into monetary economies by providing a market for cash crops and raises the standard of living of monetary economies by bringing a higher return for the same effort. But it does not and cannot by itself do more than this. It does not, for example, result in an automatic modernization of agricultural methods; nor does it guarantee that the domestic market which it creates or widens will nurse local industry to factory-scale volume. The attitudes, practices, and tenures of peasant cultivators may be little altered and they may buy their manufactures not from the towns but from abroad. Development may be blocked by a social structure that keeps the response to economic forces within narrow channels and itself withstands transformation by those forces. An expanding foreign demand will not be translated into a self-sustaining process of development in every sector of the economy unless many other conditions are fulfilled simultaneously. But the chances are that if these conditions are not fulfilled, the same obstacles will stultify development so long as the forces of change are purely economic.

I confess to some scepticism about the supposed ineffectiveness of foreign trade in producing innovation and development. It does not strike me as entirely plausible to speak as if foreign trade could be contained within an enclave without transmitting its dynamic influences to the rest of the economy. How can one contain the so-called demonstration effects? By what magic is a steel mill supposed to revolutionize an economy while a railway or a copper smelter leaves it essentially unchanged? Every new departure is initially an enclave and it takes time for all innovations to work through and be absorbed. The influence of foreign trade may also make itself felt slowly. Sometimes the influence is bound to be indirect; there is not much in an oil refinery that will transform the agriculture of an Arab country. But indirect influences are not to be discounted: they may embrace half the profits of the oil companies and a good deal of free technical education for the local staff. As Prof. Swerling has pointed out, "the tax machinery can remove much economic remoteness even from mineral enclaves."[3]

Most of the countries that we now think of as advanced have been at one time or another dependent on just as narrow a range of exports. Japan in the early stages of industrialization was heavily dependent on exports of silk, the United States and Canada on exports of grain, Britain on exports of wool, or, at a later stage, on textile manufactures which once supplied over 70 per cent of her export earnings. If you want to make a start, you must use what you have, not lament that the other fellow who is ahead of you is less highly specialized. The more foreign exchange is felt to be a bottleneck, the more important it is to foster in every possible way the limited range of activities from which foreign exchange can be derived.

Yet the risks of specializing on a narrow front are very real. In the long run there is the danger of a substitute produced at lower cost by factory methods; in the short run there is the danger of wide fluctuations in price. Of these two the long-run danger is the more alarming even if, so far, it has been rare for a natural product to be superseded by a synthetic one. The world's consumption of cotton, rubber, jute, butter, and other products threatened by substitutes is higher than ever before in spite of the rise of synthetics. The function of the synthetic product has generally been to supplement an inelastic natural supply and meet rapidly expanding industrial requirements rather than to displace the natural products altogether.

Far too much emphasis is put in current literature on the forces operating to limit or diminish the demand for primary produce and far too little on the constant opening up of new requirements throughout the world as the standard of living rises. It is a useful exercise to list the major raw materials in use today and consider how many of them were available, even a hundred years ago. Steel and petroleum are barely a hundred years old. In 1860 aluminium was a precious metal used like platinum in royal gifts. Rubber, newsprint, synthetic fibres are for all practical purposes twentieth-century creations. Nor is it only the advanced countries that benefit when new materials emerge. The less advanced countries, with luck, can shift from one crop to another or find within their borders the mineral products that technological change brings to the front. If there are losers through the obsolescence of materials, there are gainers as well.

There are, it is true, limitations on the range of produce that the underdeveloped countries can supply. It is perhaps significant that most of them—particularly those in Asia and Africa—lie in the tropical latitudes and are highly dependent on the world market for tropical produce. This means that they are partly screened from competition with the advanced countries except when science produces a

---

[3] B. C. Swerling, *op. cit.*, p. 31.

substitute or when high prices make the development of substitutes commercially attractive. They are not screened, however, from competition with one another. They have between them an enormous population—Asia alone has half the world's population—and the competition is correspondingly intense. Any one country may have advantages of climate or soil that give it some shelter in its chosen field, but among all the tropical countries there are sure to be some that are almost equally well placed. Thus, so long as they keep within the usual round, they are not likely to do much better than their neighbours. They may, for a time, enjoy a run of luck as producers of bananas or coffee or rubber; but if they do, other tropical countries will soon join in and put an end to any exceptional gains. Indeed, if they export tree crops (which form about one-quarter of total exports from this group of countries), the gains are only too likely to be followed by exceptional losses once new plantings have had time to come into production either at home or in competing countries. In minerals, on the other hand, the competition of other tropical countries is without special significance, the success of individual countries being governed largely by geological factors peculiar to each.

The situation confronting agriculture in an underdeveloped tropical country is thus essentially different from the situation faced in the countries settled from Europe during the nineteenth century. The latter were all or nearly all in temperate latitudes and could supply the industrial centres of Europe with foodstuffs in *replacement* of the higher-cost foodstuffs produced there. The specialization between the old world and the new was on a basis that brought low-cost farmers overseas into competition with high-cost farmers in Europe and gave to the development of the newer countries all the leverage of a large cost-differential. The new countries were in a very real sense the frontiers of an older economy. But the underdeveloped countries of today are selling in a more inelastic market.

This is so for two reasons. In the first place such elasticity as there is derives from competition with other products, not from substitution for a similar, home-produced commodity. The Canadian wheat-farmer found it easier to sell his wheat in the British market because British farmers were able to switch from grain to grass, but the only kind of substitution that Brazilian coffee-producers can profit from is substitution on the part of consumers. Secondly, exports of tropical produce bear a much higher relation to world output than exports of primary produce from temperate latitudes. The principal consumers of coffee, rubber, sugar, and so on, lie outside the producing countries so that domestic demand is largely unaffected by changes in output and price. Canadian wheat is a very small fraction of the world crop, but Brazil produces nearly half the world's coffee. A given increase in the Canadian wheat crop or in Canada's exports of wheat involves, therefore, far less disruption in the world market than an equal proportionate increase in the cultivation or exportation of Brazilian coffee.

This brings me to what seems to be the central issue. Is the market for the exports of the underdeveloped countries so inelastic that it no longer provides a satisfactory engine of growth? Is their development being cramped by stagnation of world demand for their traditional exports?

That the nineteenth-century process of growth transmission works rather differently nowadays is not in dispute. The underdeveloped countries are no longer the frontiers of an expanding world economy and the division of labour between them and the individual countries of North America and Western Europe does not involve those vast territorial shifts in primary production that lie behind the rapid growth of world trade in the nineteenth century. In the middle of the nineteenth century that growth averaged about 13 per cent annually, the total volume trebling within thirty years largely as a result of the inflow into Europe of primary produce from countries overseas.[4] Since the scope for similar displacements is now far more limited and the industrial countries are less willing to see their agriculture contract further, it is unlikely that trade will ever grow so fast again over so long a period. To the extent that the underdeveloped countries have to rely on exports of tropical produce, there can be very little displacement of production and the rate of expansion is bound to be limited by the growth of world demand. For other products, however, notably base metals and petroleum, this limitation does not apply.

It is an illusion to suppose that, even in the nineteenth century, mere pressure of demand was sufficient to transmit development from one country to another. It certainly did not by itself ensure the *industrial* development of primary-producing regions. The fact that the United States ultimately became the leading industrial nation should not blind us to the failure of the Southern States, from which came a high proportion of American exports of primary produce, to undergo industrialization or to enjoy the rapid growth experienced in the north. Latin America remained comparatively underdeveloped. Australia and New Zealand, although enjoying a high standard of living and far from negligible as producers of manufactured goods, remain, as exporters, almost exclusively dependent on primary produce.

Again, the countries to which European growth was most successfully transmitted were already comparatively rich countries. Although their development was geared to the supply of export markets, they already had a sufficiently high standard of living to provide an opening for domestic manufacturers. The countries that remain underdeveloped started from a much lower level so that their domestic market is narrower and far less favourable to the building up of local industries. The example of Japan, however, shows that there is no insuperable difficulty in starting from a low level, provided the industries that take root are not confined within the limits of the domestic market.

It was possible in nineteenth-century development for a growing foreign trade to accompany a still more rapidly growing domestic market. This was certainly true, for example, of the United States after the Civil War. There was nothing inconsistent between reliance on exports of primary produce to open up new investment opportunities and a shift in the sources of consumer goods in favour of indigenous producers. This shift might come about through the unassisted operation of market forces or it might be induced or accelerated by protective policies. The important point is that foreign trade could remain the driving force behind an

---

[4] A. H. Imlah, *Economic Elements in the Pax Britannica*, pp. 96–97, 190.

economy even when exports were a diminishing fraction of total production. A demonstration that exports are being outpaced by production does not prove that the motor force which exports provide is running down. On the contrary, it is more likely to mean that the process of growth transmission is really working, that the domestic market is being transformed, and that an industrial structure is taking shape within a hitherto nonindustrial economy.

It is true that in the nineteenth century the dominant pattern was a different one. Trade grew faster than production, both in the industrial and the nonindustrial countries. World trade in the early years of the century grew at 7 per cent per annum, in the mid-century at 13 per cent, and at the end of the century at 7 per cent. World industrial production may latterly have reached 7 per cent and equalled the rate of expansion of trade, but *total* world production never equalled it. It is legitimate to argue, therefore, that in the nineteenth century foreign markets were growing faster than domestic markets and that the external impulse to growth not only took causal priority over the domestic impulse but was operating more powerfully.

In this sense, twentieth-century experience has not followed the nineteenth-century pattern. There was a long period when trade showed no net growth at all, while world production registered a large expansion. Between 1926–1930 and 1948–1950, for example, the volume of trade both in primary produce and manufactures contracted slightly, while world output of primary produce grew by over one-quarter and of manufactures by over two-thirds.[5] Since the war the growth in trade has returned to the normal pre-1914 rate of 7 per cent and is again roughly in line with the growth in world industrial production. But this has not restored the nineteenth-century pattern. For in recent years it has been the trade of industrial countries with one another that has grown fastest, not their trade with nonindustrial countries. In the nineteenth century, the latter were dominated by the newly settled countries, including the United States, which were then the growing points of the world economy. These countries are no longer nonindustrial, and those that remain underdeveloped are a much smaller element in the world economy. They cannot complain that world trade is not expanding rapidly: it is expanding as fast as it ever has done at any time except in the thirty years following the repeal of the Corn Laws. The countries that were drawn along by world markets in the nineteenth century enjoyed no better fortune if rate of growth of trade is the test to be applied. If the engine of development has lost power, it is not because the demands of industrial countries have ceased to overflow national boundaries. It must be because those demands have changed in character or because the underdeveloped countries are less well placed to meet them. For one reason or the other, their share of world trade has begun to diminish.

Now in some ways it is odd that this should have happened in the 1950's. In that decade the world was in one of those recurring situations in which a high level of industrial activity presses on the supply of primary produce and makes it necessary to develop fresh supplies. Such a situation arose, for example, in the 1850's,

---

[5] These estimates are derived from unpublished calculations of Mr. A. Maizels of the National Institute of Economic and Social Research.

and again in the twenty years before the First World War. It is a situation that is normally accompanied by inflation because raw material costs are pushed up, and it is also a situation that generates inflation because capacity to produce raw materials (including fuel and power) tends to make far heavier demands on capital than capacity at later stages of manufacture. In the nineteenth century, when marginal supplies of primary produce could most readily be drawn from overseas, the rise in investment tended to be concentrated abroad and to be financed to a large extent through foreign loans. Hence the coincidence, on which economists have frequently commented, of rising costs and profits, higher foreign investments, and relatively favourable prices for foodstuffs and materials.

Something of all this we can recognize in the 1950's: for example, the rapid development of petroleum in many parts of the underdeveloped world with the aid of foreign capital and in relief of a shortage of fuel in the industrial countries of Western Europe. But in general the industrial countries have not met an increasing proportion of their requirements from supplies from underdeveloped countries and with some exceptions have not sought to open up new sources of supply there through heavy investment. Since the early 1950's, moreover, there has been a drift downward in the price of many important materials, the United Nations index for primary products (excluding petroleum) showing a fall in the six years 1953–1959 of 7 per cent. The past decade has been exceptional, therefore, in that a rapid growth in production and trade has been accompanied by a marked change in the terms of trade *against* primary produce.

It is possible to put a pessimistic construction on these facts and conclude that the underdeveloped countries can neither count on an expanding market nor on reasonably stable terms of trade for their exports. Economies in the use of materials, the development of synthetics, agricultural protectionism, and other forces damping down the demand for imports of primary produce can be cited as evidence that the trend against the underdeveloped countries will continue. This evidence, however, is not conclusive, and a quite different interpretation of the facts is possible.

In the first place the trend in the past decade has to be seen in the light of what went before. The war disorganized the normal sources of supply for many primary products and at the same time raised the level of demand discontinuously. This lack of balance continued into the postwar period, especially after the changeover to production against peacetime requirements, and it was aggravated by the stock-building rush in 1950–1951 at the outset of the Korean war. By 1951 there had been a very pronounced swing in the price of primary products and in the terms on which they were exchanged against manufactures. What took place after 1951 was a return toward more normal price relationships as the supply of the scarcer materials was expanded. If one takes the early 1950's as a starting point, therefore, we are accepting as normal prices which, in the light of history, were anything but normal and interpreting as a trend what was to some extent no more than a return to more durable price relationships.

There seems to me a particularly strong case for this view in relation to tropical produce. As I have already suggested, the products exported by the underdeveloped countries are heavily concentrated in a limited group, of which tropical produce forms a large part. A general price index for primary products may, therefore, convey a misleading impression of what is happening to the export prices of the underdeveloped countries. Mr. Maizels has estimated that while primary products exported by industrial countries doubled in unit value between 1937 and 1950, primary products exported from other (mainly underdeveloped) countries more than trebled. Similarly, it has been calculated that over the same period tropical foods rose by 235 per cent in unit value, while nontropical foods rose by only 135 per cent.[6] There is plenty of evidence that in the postwar years many of the underdeveloped countries started out with unusually favourable export prices.

If we abstract from the trend in prices and consider only the change in the volume of exports, it would seem that the underdeveloped countries found a quite rapidly expanding market for their exports of primary produce. Between 1950 and 1957, for example, these exports rose by 50 per cent or 6 per cent per annum. This was certainly below the rate at which trade in manufactures was growing, but not by very much. It would seem, therefore, that the *main* cause of the divergence in trend between manufactures and primary produce lay in a divergent movement in prices.

Moreover, if we take a longer view and, rather than accept the past decade as the touchstone of future prospects, look back as far as 1913, we do not find any conspicuous lag in exports from the underdeveloped countries. Each of the poorest continents in the world—Africa, Asia, and Latin America—had a larger share of world exports in 1953 than in 1913. In both years they had a quite negligible share of world exports of manufactures, but their exports of primary produce had by 1953 overhauled those from the three richest continents—North America, Europe, and Australasia. Forty years earlier they had differed in the ratio of 1:2; by 1953 the difference had almost disappeared.

Whether one takes a long view or a short, these aggregates are of limited value in interpreting what is going on in the underdeveloped countries. Every underdeveloped country is unique and is affected by the market conditions and prices for its own products and not by the movement of index numbers. To aggregate or average the experience of the group of countries that we think of as underdeveloped is to presume common elements that may have no real existence.

Nevertheless, it may help to give some concreteness to my argument if I turn at this point to consider just what the underdeveloped countries as a group do export and what part trade plays in their economy. For simplicity I shall divide the world into the three poorest and the three richest continents, the first group being made up of Africa, Asia, and Latin America and the second of Europe, North America, and Oceania. This means that one or two advanced countries such as South Africa and Japan will be included in the group of poor countries, but their exclusion would make little difference to the results. At times I have been obliged to use a grouping prepared by GATT which adds Australasia to the three poorer continents and labels the mixture "nonindustrial areas." The communist bloc of countries is excluded throughout, unless otherwise indicated.

The so-called nonindustrial areas, on examination, turn out to be very far

---

[6] Based on GATT, *International Trade 1957–58* (1959), Table 4, p. 15.

from nonindustrial. According to GATT, they import only about one-third of their consumption of manufactures, and this proportion is falling.[7] The remaining two-thirds of their consumption of manufactures is produced at home. Many of them already have a flourishing textile industry and some of them are net exporters of textiles. Of the manufactured goods which they import, a high proportion consists of capital goods, base metals, and so on, while manufactured consumption goods are relatively small, constituting not much more than 10 per cent of total imports. Nor are they by any means entirely dependent on foreign markets for the sale of their primary produce. This is particularly true of food and feeding stuffs; nine-tenths of the output is consumed at home, while only the remaining tenth is exported. Many of the foodstuffs that form their staple diet are quite unimportant in foreign trade. Exports of fuel and raw materials (including materials of agricultural origin) take a higher proportion of total production—on the average, about two-fifths,[8] and sometimes, as in the oil countries, nearly 100 per cent.

Just as it is a mistake to think that underdeveloped countries have no industries, so it is a mistake to think of them as the major sources of primary produce. Every country is a primary producer, and the more advanced it is, the larger, broadly speaking, is its output of primary produce. There can be few countries that fail to grow at least half their food supply or to produce a wide range of raw materials. It is true that some advanced countries employ very little of their manpower in agriculture and that their raw materials are often manufactured rather than mined or grown. But the fact remains that the advanced countries produce more food and more raw materials than the less advanced countries. What they import from the less advanced countries meets only one-tenth of their requirements of food and one-quarter of their requirements of raw materials.[9] Nor are they all net importers. Some of them are large exporters, and the three richer continents account for roughly half of world exports of primary produce. They are in fact larger exporters, just as they are larger producers, of primary products than the so-called primary-producing countries.[10]

The less advanced countries, in the same way, are importers as well as exporters of primary produce: indeed, their imports are half as large as their exports. Thus it is quite wrong to think of the world as if it could be divided into two sets of countries, the advanced and the less advanced, with primary produce flowing exclusively in one direction. On the contrary, international trade brings the primary producers of every country into competition with one another, and the margin of advantage does not necessarily shift steadily in one direction.

Seven items or groups make up nearly three-quarters of the total exports of primary produce from the underdeveloped countries. Listed in order of size they are petroleum, beverages, textile fibres, base metals, sugar, oilseeds and fats, and rubber. The same group of items make up less than 40 per cent of the exports of primary produce from the developed countries. But what is perhaps of more

---

[7] GATT, *International Trade 1959* (1960), p. 14.

[8] *Ibid.*, p. 13.

[9] *Ibid.*, p. 14.

[10] This is true only if we exclude Australasia from the primary-producing countries. See my "International Trade and Economic Development," *Kyklos*, Vol. XIII (1960), p. 549.

significance is the change that has taken place over the past century. For the seven items selected the share of the underdeveloped countries in world trade has risen from 43 to 64 per cent. For all other items, representing nearly half the total volume of world trade in primary products, the share of the underdeveloped countries has remained a little below 30 per cent. It has been where their share was already high that it expanded most.[11]

On the other hand, there has been an unmistakable tendency toward a contraction in their exports of cereals and livestock produce. Exports from the developed countries, especially those in North America and Australasia, have shown a corresponding expansion. The three underdeveloped continents supplied 31 per cent of world exports in 1913 and only 21 per cent in 1953. No doubt this trend is partly associated with American aid. But by itself this is far from adequate to account for it, and it seems to have a deeper origin in the pressure on available land in some underdeveloped countries and the efforts at industrialization in others.

Exports of cereals and livestock products are a comparatively small proportion (about 7 per cent) of total exports from the underdeveloped countries. Exports of other foodstuffs are much larger—over one-third of the total. Of these exports, tea, cocoa, and coffee, in which they come near to having a monopoly of foreign trade, form nearly half, and other tropical produce, such as sugar, oilseeds and fats, and tobacco make up most of the other half. Thus within the food group there is a large tract over which competition is limited. In food that can be grown in temperate latitudes the underdeveloped countries have either contracted or show little expansion. But in tropical foodstuffs they have enjoyed a rapid growth. For example, they were supplying 73 per cent of world exports of sugar in 1953 compared with 64 per cent in 1913. For the group of foodstuffs other than cereals and livestock products (in which their share contracted) and beverages (in which their share was virtually 100 per cent) they improved their share of the world market quite perceptibly.

Foodstuffs, however, account for less than half the total exports of primary produce from the three poorer continents. Petroleum, crude and refined, accounts for about one-quarter (depending upon how the exports are valued) and raw materials, including those of agricultural as well as of mineral origin, unwrought metals, and crude fertilizers, for nearly one-third. For materials as for foodstuffs there is some tendency for the exports of the developed and underdeveloped continents to be in noncompeting groups. Nearly all the world's output of rubber and jute, over 40 per cent of its petroleum, and a high proportion of its hides and skins, mineral ores, and crude fertilizers come from the underdeveloped areas. But in other textile fibres and in base metals they are in direct competition over a wide area.

From this analysis of the trade of the underdeveloped countries I draw four conclusions.

First of all they are highly dependent on a very narrow range of exports. A large proportion of these exports consists of gifts of nature: petroleum, mineral

---

[11]The estimates in this and the succeeding page are drawn from F. Lamartine Yates, *op. cit.*

ores, crude fertilizers. How much a country can earn from exports of this kind is largely a matter of luck and of willingness to make use of foreign capital. Other exports suffer from great variability in supply and low elasticity of supply. The source of these exports tends to be either foreign-owned plantations or peasants who may lack the means, the knowledge, or the incentives to adopt modern methods of production. On top of all this nearly all capital equipment has to be imported, and a shortage of foreign exchange frequently sets a sharp limit to the scale and firmness of any forward planning of investment. These facts point strongly to the desirability of widening the range of exports wherever possible and developing domestic sources of the simpler types of imported manufactures.

Secondly, it would seem that exports from the underdeveloped countries are governed less closely by the level of world demand than is usually supposed. Where they are in direct competition with the more advanced countries, their share of the market depends also on the terms on which they are able to compete: on the movement of their costs and in the alternatives which they can choose. If their exports have lagged behind the exports of the more advanced countries, this is partly because they have been running a large external deficit (now of the order of $5,000–$6,000 m. a year) and this necessarily implies some downward drag on their exports compared with the exports of the countries from which they buy. Other, but not unrelated, factors tending to hold back their exports have been inflation, relatively high prices, and the encouragement of other sectors of their economies.

Thirdly, since agriculture is by far the most important activity and is usually directed more toward domestic than export markets, there is everything to be gained by trying to expand agricultural production. Without a general improvement in agricultural production and incomes, the mass of the population will remain hungry and poor and domestic industry will be stifled for lack of markets. Such an improvement is not dependent on some precise rate of growth of exports. An expanding foreign market can, however, contribute, both by putting more cash in the hands of the cultivators and by introducing a competitive element that may make technical change in agriculture more acceptable.

But what, fourthly, if agriculture proves unresponsive and the government has to think of industrialization without any expansion in foodstuffs? The fact that underdeveloped countries produce about two-thirds of the manufactured goods which they consume shows that some progress towards industrialization has already been made. Industrial development *is* occurring, assisted by higher export earnings and foreign investment and loans. But the industries that have grown up are not, as a rule, very efficient. It is curious, for example, that Latin American countries meet nearly all their own textile requirements but have a negligible share in each other's markets or, indeed, in any foreign market.

One of the principal obstacles to more rapid industrialization is the limited scale of operations in a manufacturing plant supplying only the domestic market of an underdeveloped country. It is precisely this limitation which international trade can remove. If, therefore, we are anxious to encourage development in the poorer countries and doubt whether agricultural expansion will clear the way for industry, might we not turn to a new model of the traditional engine of development and see what could be done through freer trade in manufactured goods?

I see no reason, looking at the experience of Hong Kong, Puerto Rico, and similar countries, why the engine should not be a powerful one. There are countries where costs would still be too high even if new market possibilities were opened. But in general my expectation would be that if there were complete confidence that the markets of the industrial countries would remain open, the supply of the simpler manufactured goods from underdeveloped countries would increase by leaps and bounds. No doubt sufficient people share this view to make it certain that the markets will not be opened and that no one will ever be quite sure that, if opened, they will remain opened.

My object is not to argue the matter. But I think it right in a country that used to plead for "Trade not Aid" to recall that slogan and to suggest that one of our chief economic obligations to the underdeveloped countries is to offer them a market. We should be asking ourselves not whether market forces work, but whether we are allowing them to work so as to reinforce such aid as we can offer. We should also remember that the industrial countries have learned in the 1950's to conduct a much greater volume of trade in manufactures with one another without conspicuous injury and indeed with great mutual advantage.

I have no wish to exaggerate the contribution that trade can make to economic development. Development is not governed in any country by economic forces alone, and the more backward the country, the more this is true. The key to development lies in men's minds, in the institutions in which their thinking finds expression, and in the play of opportunity on ideas and institutions. It happens that the opportunities trade opens up in underdeveloped economies are in a sector where outlook and institutions are alike highly conservative and in which external impulses tend to be dampened rather than amplified before they are transmitted to the rest of the economy. It is true also that the effort of grasping these opportunities may prove too great for a poor and backward country. But this does not justify us in minimizing the opportunities that trade affords or in pretending that they are losing an effectiveness that they once possessed.

Selection **26**

Outward-looking Policies
and Economic Development

D. B. KEESING

From: the Economic Journal, *Vol. LXXVII, No. 306 (June 1967), pp. 303–320. Reprinted by permission of the* Economic Journal *and the author.*

Contemporary experiences of less developed countries in the realm of trade policy have shifted a considerable body of influential opinion away from an inward-looking strategy that relies exclusively on the home market for manufactures toward what may be called an outward-looking strategy of trying to export manufactures early in the process of industrial development.[1] A strategy built entirely around import substitution has encountered discouraging results in Latin America and elsewhere.[2] More satisfactory effects have been obtained where the growth of manufactures has been at least somewhat export-oriented—for example, in Taiwan, Hong Kong, South Korea, Pakistan, Israel, Mexico, and Puerto Rico.[3] This paper seeks to explain the advantages of outward-looking over inward-looking development in terms of such recent concerns of growth theory as improvement of human factors and advances and lags in technology.

Let me start by explaining what I mean by outward-looking development. I am not making a case against import substitution. That is a process that will

---

[1] The strategies will be described further in a moment. Particularly significant has been a subtle but perceptible shift in the outlook of United Nations experts. Compare, for example, United Nations, *The Economic Development of Latin America and its Principal Problems* (New York, 1950), with the United Nations Conference on Trade and Development, Report by the Secretary-General, *Towards a New Trade Policy for Development* (Geneva, 1964), both written by R. Prebisch. The former document emphasises the need for import substitution; the latter stresses the value of manufactured exports.

[2] As Prebisch succinctly puts it, "recourse to very high protective tariffs . . . has had unfavourable effects on the industrial structure because it has encouraged the establishment of small uneconomical plants, weakened the incentives to introduce modern techniques, and slowed down the rise in productivity. . . ." (*Towards a New Trade Policy for Development, op. cit.,* p. 22).

[3] These countries have not all followed an outward-looking policy in all the respects described below, and in this sense the description offered here is an abstraction from reality. Further research is badly needed on the trade policy measures and surrounding conditions that have led to export success. The arguments offered here are intended as hypotheses and ideas around which research can be designed.

occur whether policies are inward- or outward-looking, and indeed, whether import substitution is fostered deliberately or not. To some extent I *am* concerned with the intensity, breadth, and frequency of government intervention. Reliance only on the domestic market permits a high degree of government intervention, whether in Soviet or Latin American fashion. By contrast, an outward-looking strategy compels moderation. If governments are serious about exporting manufactures, their freedom to intervene is restricted by the exigencies of keeping manufactures internationally competitive, and by trade conventions and sanctions that limit permissible methods of trade promotion.[4] An outward-looking, like an inward-looking strategy, however, may be characterised by a mistrust of *laissez-faire* and free trade. Divergences between private and social costs, after all, help to explain the widening economic role of government even in the Western world.

I do *not* mean by an outward-looking strategy that a country places heavy reliance on exports of manufactures, either as an engine of growth or as a means of obtaining the imports essential to development. Rather, exports of manufactures are promoted at an early stage in the process of industrial growth largely for the sake of indirect benefits to be explained here. These gains are not highly dependent on the volume of export sales. Direct gains in income and foreign exchange may remain modest until industrialisation becomes far advanced. If the country is forced to rely on exports of manufactures because it is unable to export anything else, it may be condemned to prolonged miserable living conditions.

Again, I am not suggesting that nations should contort themselves to export manufactures without regard to the paucity of local resources. A complex of highly market-oriented, small-scale industry proliferates in every country or region, even without benefit of government intervention, because of the powerful effects of transport cost protection. A very backward country has its hands full responding to this opportunity, the needs of primary production, and the requirements for infrastructure and essential government services.

The phrase "outward-looking" is deliberately chosen to signify a constant and deliberate attention to industrial and trade happenings outside the country. One ingredient in the policy is a strong effort to remain in touch, absorb the latest technology, catch up and become competitive with the most advanced industrial countries. The government subsidises activities serving these ends.

When preconditions prevail so that ambitious industrial projects lose their absurdity, instead of promoting new industries aimed only at the home market, an outward-looking strategy calls for intervening in such a way as to build up an export-oriented industrial complex. This means that, even where the initial markets are found mainly at home, the physical layout of manufactures is designed to permit an easy transition into export markets. From the first intervention, moreover, incentives to industry create pressures to export rather than simply to supplant imports.

Instruments used to stimulate the early export of manufactures include lowering

---

[4] This is a crucial assumption and is basic to the discussion that follows. I believe it to be historically correct and expect that extreme abuse of export subsidies will continue to be intolerable to importing nations.

the exchange rate, and keeping it low, and a variety of familiar subsidy and tax measures—for example, tax-holidays and liberal depreciation allowances for industry, government-furnished low-cost loans and industrial estates, government-subsidised export credit and export promotion, internal turnover taxes not applied to exports, and the deliberate design of social overhead facilities, education, and research projects to aid export industries in the long run.

If tariffs are required for revenue purposes, a non-discriminatory rate may be applied to most imports, except insofar as tariffs on producer goods are avoided to keep down the costs of inputs required by export industries.[5] To make local prices and wages appear cheap, anti-inflationary monetary and fiscal policies are pursued. These policies, in turn, restrict the size of the subsidies and tax exemptions that the country can afford, providing a built-in check against excessive intervention. Export promotion goes hand in hand with efforts to conquer and defend the home market, but a degree of foreign competition is tolerated at home to toughen the competitive fibre of local industries. A low exchange rate, after all, combines with transport cost protection to reduce the need for tariff protection of local consumer-goods industries.

In short, an outward-looking strategy calls for a direct transition from a simple, open trade policy to vigorous promotion of manufactured exports by all internationally tolerated means, without going through an in-between phase of high protection. The strategy is perhaps best exemplified in Japanese development.

By contrast, an inward-looking strategy is taken here to be one that relies on the home market for manufactured products to the point of abandoning efforts toward an early conquest of foreign markets. Import substitution becomes the keystone of trade policy and is promoted through tariffs, subsidies, quantitative restrictions, exchange controls, licensing, and/or other measures. Protection may be carried to extremes. Inflationary domestic policies may be followed with only peripheral concern for their impact on international trade.[6]

Needless to say, the case for outward-looking development is weakened by the deplorable barriers imposed against manufactured imports in the industrial countries, and this case would be strengthened by a removal of these barriers. I do not intend to discuss this aspect of the subject, since it has received much attention of late and since the case for outward-looking policies does not rest primarily on the quantitative impact of manufactured exports.

In the discussion that follows reasons for preferring an outward-looking strategy will be sought under the following headings:

1. Learning effects and improvement of human resources;
2. The value of competition and close communication with advanced countries, in view of dependence on technology and ideas from abroad;

---

[5] I am thinking of something like the 25 per cent across-the-board tariff, with selected exceptions, that has long prevailed in East Africa. Such a tariff has an effect akin to an import bounty on favoured producer goods. A cost is involved, in that some distortionary effects are almost certain to occur favouring industries and processes with a large input of tariff-exempt imported producer goods.

[6] An inward-looking strategy can also, but need not, involve central planning in physical terms and bilateral barter trade agreements.

3. Increasing returns connected with economies of scale and market size;
4. Authorities' limited knowledge of when and how to intervene;
5. The inapplicability of terms of trade and underemployed labour arguments for protection in relation to less developed countries;
6. Foreign exchange and import constraints in development;

The paper will pay most attention to the first two considerations.

No attempt will be made to discuss the political problems of implementing an outward-looking strategy. Mistakes of the past have created formidable obstacles to correcting the trade strategy of countries already committed in an inward-looking direction. Reversing strategies may prove hard or even impossible. This is, in fact, one of the misfortunes of an inward-looking strategy. But this paper will concentrate on economic aspects of the two strategies, on the optimistic assumption that a country has the political flexibility to set and change its own course.

LEARNING EFFECTS AND IMPROVEMENT OF HUMAN RESOURCES

Economic theorists are coming to recognise that the central process of economic growth is not so much accumulation of material resources as upgrading of human resources along with technology.[7] People must acquire modern horizons, working habits and, above all, technical skills. As they do, the economy increases its productive capacity and flexibility.

New human resources must be created in part through industrial experience.[8] This need for learning by doing stands at the core of the classic infant-industry argument and constitutes perhaps the most important argument for protection.[9] Protecting or subsidising industries for their training effects would repay the community as a whole, when the investment in training would not appear privately

---

[7] This view of economic development, popular—though not among economists—in the eighteenth and nineteenth centuries, has surged back to the fore in recent years. Along with empirical studies of the causes of economic growth, this resurgence owes much to the intellectual leadership of T. W. Schultz and some of his disciples. See particularly his "Investment in Human Capital," *American Economic Review*, Vol. 51 (March 1961), pp. 1–17.

[8] See, for example, K. J. Arrow, "The Economic Implications of Learning by Doing," *Review of Economic Studies*, Vol. 29, No. 80 (June 1962), pp. 155–173, and G. S. Becker, *Human Capital: A Theoretical and Empirical Analysis, with Special Reference to Education* (New York: Columbia University Press and National Bureau of Economic Research, 1964). F. H. Hahn and R. C. O. Matthews, in "The Theory of Economic Growth: A Survey," *Economic Journal*, No. 296 (Dec. 1964), pp. 779–902, postulate that ". . . the division between formal models that do and do not take account of learning by doing, seems to us to be perhaps the most important dichotomisation which could be made" (p. 889).

[9] This point is recognised in a number of recent surveys of international trade theory. To quote H. B. Chenery, "The possibility of rising efficiency as labour and management acquire increasing experience has long been recognised, and forms the basis for the infant-industry argument. This argument has been generalised to include the effects of increasing production in any industry on the supply of skilled labour and management available to other industries. Since manufacturing is thought to have more important training effects than primary production, the fact that improvements in factor supply are not reflected in the market mechanism may introduce a bias against manufacturing." H. B. Chenery, "Comparative Advantage and Development Policy," *American Economic Review*, Vol. 51 (March 1961), p. 24. In this passage he refers to the writings of J. H. Williams, H. Myint, and R. Prebisch.

profitable to the individual entrepreneur because he could not be assured of continuing in his employment the people whom he trained.[10] The need for protection or subsidy to foster on-the-job training may be highest in an early phase of industrial development when the economic value of training is especially high, and when trained workers are especially difficult to obtain to offset those lost.[11] In these terms, sacrifices by developing countries to promote "modern" industrial activities may be perfectly rational wherever the industries in question generate "modern" skills, if world demand and technology can be expected to shift over time toward products and processes requiring these skills.[12]

The above argument contains nothing new, yet it is disappointing that despite the central importance of learning effects to trade and development policy, very little empirical effort has been devoted to finding out which industries actually generate valuable human resources in industrially backward countries, and in what circumstances. This would appear to be an important subject for inquiry.

Thinking about the empirical problems involved, one is struck by the point that the training value to society of an industry cannot be inferred at all from the skill requirements of the industry. All manufacturing industries require skilled labour in greater or smaller proportion to the labour force of the industry; that is, each industry requires managers, engineers, machinists, electricians, and other skilled occupations. The fact that these workers are required, however, has a double-edged impact on the skill supplies available to the economy. On the one hand, the industry subtracts from the skills available to the rest of the economy by employing scarce skilled workers. On the other hand, the industry adds to the human resources of the economy by on-the-job training. Thus, in every industry there is an input and an output of skill, as in any other activity devoted wholly or partly to training. Moreover, as a rule skilled practitioners are required to train

---

[10]Becker, *op. cit.*, argues that in a purely competitive market employers could not afford to pay for on-the-job training, except insofar as the skills were specific to the firm. The cost would otherwise have to be borne by the workers themselves. Under many plausible assumptions, workers would underinvest in their own training, contributing to a divergence between private and social cost.

[11]Becker's point notwithstanding, in an advanced country business may well pay a portion of the cost of on-the-job training by adhering to an institutionally rigid wage structure, because of monopoly positions and expectations that the trained workers they lose will be compensated by workers that they gain, if everyone plays by the same rules. In other words, there may be a socially useful, systematic divergence from purely competitive pricing. Another possibility, following Becker, is that in an advanced industrial society workers may be better able to appreciate and afford an investment in their own training. But it is certainly interesting that this and other component explanations of the infant-industry argument involve divergences between private and social costs that are not necessarily temporary, and that are not restricted to the "infancy" of a single new industry.

[12]The ideas that follow relate to theories and empirical findings that I have advanced in previous papers. See "Labour Skills and Comparative Advantage," *American Economic Review, Proceedings*, Vol. 56 (May 1966), pp. 249–258, and "Labor Skills and International Trade: Evaluating Many Trade Flows with a Single Measuring Device," *Review of Economics and Statistics*, Vol. 47, No. 3 (Aug. 1966), pp. 287–294. "Modern" skills that I have in mind here include, for example, scientists, engineers, technicians, draftsmen, machinists, electricians, and tool- and diemakers. Such skilled workers appear in the labour force of every American manufacturing industry but are especially plentiful in the industries that have been growing most rapidly (not least in world trade) in recent decades.

newcomers in any particular occupation. The employment pattern of the skilled labour force at any one time can therefore be viewed as a deployment to meet at once the training needs and the current production needs of the society.

What counts in every industry, evidently, is not the absolute skill requirements but the productivities of skilled workers in training and in production. There is no a priori way of knowing what is the training-productivity of machinist skills in a turbo-generator plant as opposed to a textile plant or an automobile repair shop. As a policy matter, therefore, it would appear sensible to try to adjust business incentives in all industries, and within each industry, in order to subsidise on-the-job training and penalise a lack of it. But in an absence of special information on the training effects of each industry, there can be no training reason to diminish the current output of the economy by favouring one manufacturing industry over another. Rather, the objective of maximising output would seem to call for a domestic price structure as free of arbitrary distortions as possible.[13]

There are, however, two important qualifications to this argument. First, it would appear advantageous to attract foreign firms by subsidy or protection, if the result would be to induce them to come in with *foreign* skills and train local workers. The benefits would have to be balanced, of course, against the costs. This objective need not involve strongly protective measures if local input costs are kept reasonable by outward-looking policies, and if the potential local market is large enough to lure foreign investment. Second, to maximise the training effects of manufacturing activities, it would appear highly desirable to stimulate the local (or export) demand for scarce skills expected to be needed in industrialisation, to the point where the skilled labour force becomes and stays fully employed and pressure builds up to increase the skill supply.

At first glance, if "modern" skills are really scarce, getting them fully employed should present no difficulty; but this reckons without the impact of lags in technology. "Modern" skills may be redundant or unneeded if the local level of technology is so backward that no one knows how to employ skilled people. This situation would appear to call for a strenuous effort to encourage local absorption of modern technology, as well as a judicious attraction of foreign enterprise into local manufacturing and training ventures.

A high level of aggregate demand for manufactures might conceivably stimulate on-the-job training. This favourable effect could be achieved by the protective effect of a low exchange rate, as an alternative to tariffs and quotas. Conceivably, exchange-rate policy might be so constrained that inflation would be essential; but this would appear to be an extremely costly second-best approach, and one perhaps incompatible with accelerating the absorption of foreign technology.

Up to now, I have talked about the problem as if all the important effects were quantitative, but it must be emphasised that skills are a qualitative phenomenon. While it may often be analytically convenient to reduce skills to a quantitative dimension, the "output" of education and training must ultimately be

---

[13] By "arbitrary distortions," I mean here any restructuring of incentives away from a *laissez-faire*, free-trade direction *not* occasioned by one or another of the well-known shortcomings of the private profit system.

perceived as the quality and character of the human resources created. In learning by doing, the quality of the "output" may depend on the intensity of the surrounding pressures to do the job right, more than on the pressures for quantitative performance. Hence, even if an industry or other activity were known potentially to yield a high output of skill relative to the requisite input, this would not necessarily make heavy protection or subsidy of that industry a desirable policy. The industry might provide more valuable training effects if it operated at a lower volume of production but under greater pressure for high-quality performance.[14]

In this connection, it would seem from the results of heavy protection in various countries that, in terms of an appropriate index of the quality and quantity of human resources created, too much government intervention can easily be worse than no intervention at all.

Consider the human-resource impact of excessive protection. Government officials, from the customs service to the exchange-control authorities to the people who give licences and dole out subsidies, acquire experience in the finer arts of corruption and graft. Managers learn to worry about their political connections and spend much of their energy trying to manipulate officials to improve their protection and assure their supplies.[15] Cutting costs of production, raising the quality of the product, or marketing it more effectively become difficult and secondary ways of making a profit—if indeed they are profitable at all in view of captive markets, uncertain supplies, and the fact that lowered costs may bring about reduced protection. Skilled professionals such as engineers pick up the listless and careless ways of their fellows in a stifling bureaucracy and learn to avoid technical suggestions and decisions. There is little call for their expertise, and it would frequently prove more dangerous to their careers to point out what is being done wrong than to go along and say nothing. Workers learn lackadaisical ways, not being pressed to raise their productivity. Thus, *the wrong skills are learned.* People are also disinclined to work hard (and thus improve their skills) because there is little in the stores for them to buy if they do work hard—only shoddy goods, and those are in short supply. Agriculturists and primary export producers, who are usually discriminated against in favour of manufacturing, also experience negative human resource effects. They fail to introduce new technology or apply themselves to raising their productivity, because it is not worth

---

[14]The beneficial "dynamic" effects of competitive pressures have often been stressed by great economists, notably Smith, Mill, and Schumpeter. In recent years economists' flagging attention has been redirected to this subject by practical discussions surrounding the emergence of the European Economic Community.

[15]G. Myrdal furnishes a vivid description; to quote only a few excerpts: "In many underdeveloped countries . . . the damaging effect [of quantitative controls] have been serious. The system tends easily to create cancerous tumors of partiality and corruption in the very center of the administration, where the sickness is continuously nurtured by the favors distributed and the grafts realized. Industrialists and business men are tempted to go in for shady deals instead of steady regular business. Individuals who might have performed useful tasks in the economic development of their country become idle hangers-on, watching for loopholes in the decrees and dishonesty in their implementation. . . . I believe that this is a very important problem. . . . It can easily . . . destroy the psychological foundation for development planning and its efficient and economic execution." G. Myrdal, *An International Economy* (New York: Harper & Row, 1956), p. 283.

their trouble, given the adverse terms of trade which they face in dealings with the rest of the economy. Indeed, individual farmers tend to withdraw their output and participation from the cash market.[16]

Defects in the quality and character of the industrial experience being acquired are especially grave, because the industrial and professional skills learned by small numbers of people early in the industrialisation process tend to be communicated to workers subsequently trained by the skilled personnel of the society.[17] Creation of inferior skills and habits early in the process of industrial growth casts a long shadow over the future of the economy. It is an investment that must eventually be remodelled at heavy expense, or else it will exert a continuing drag on the performance of the economy, not unlike a badly designed system of transport or education.

The long-run costs of excessive protection, of course, extend beyond the poor quality of the human resources created and the real income lost, because the resulting loss of real output and export earnings may retard processes of accumulation. But it is the failure to create suitable human resources, along with a lack of any rapid improvement of production methods, that can condemn an economy to stagnation as well as sacrifice in the wake of policies intended to stimulate industrialisation. If human resources and techniques could be improved, the resulting increases in output would enable a cycle of growth to get under way that would gradually free the economy from the hardship and ills to which it had been subjected,[18] even though this might not be an efficient growth path compared with the available alternatives. If suitable new resources are not forthcoming, the sacrifices will merely continue pointlessly.

Under an outward-looking strategy, the structure of incentives bearing on the quality of industrial experience comes closer to resembling the situation in industrial countries. Managers, for example, are forced to worry mainly about cutting costs, keeping their facilities and methods up to date, improving the product, and marketing to suit (and shape) consumer taste at home and abroad. Supplies of inputs, and assistance from the government, become comparatively minor concerns. Skilled workers find themselves subjected to greater pressures to perform and to train others, and so on.

So far, I have advanced arguments that do not call for a particular emphasis on exports, but the export of manufactures, even on a small scale, itself teaches valuable industrial and commercial lessons. Generally, I believe, a less developed country gains more valuable experience, and undergoes greater pressure for quality performance, in selling the same value of output abroad rather than at home.

---

[16]This is the "scissors" effect noted in Russia in the 1920's, but seemingly common in less developed countries today.

[17]For models that spell out other implications of the need for skilled workers to train skilled workers, see my "Labor Skills and Comparative Advantage," *loc. cit.*

[18]For example, in the manner implied by Say's Law, increased output would create new income. Expanded markets would, in turn, permit industries to take advantage of increasing returns to scale. The declining scarcity of needed human resources would lower costs, creating demand that would further stimulate output; new human resources would be trained to supply this output; etc.

Exports in turn open the way to further exports, by learning effects both at home and abroad; and successful export performance contributes to successful head-to-head competition on home ground. The technology and the skills of the local industry receive an acid test. If the outcome is a success, the morale-boosting effects may cause local industries to redouble their efforts. After all, one key turning-point in industrial development is the switch from a defensive into an aggressive attitude about local industrial abilities.

In short, an outward-looking strategy produces high-quality industrial experience and thus creates human resources suitable for sustained growth.

Technology, Communications, and Dependence on Advanced Countries

Perhaps it is not surprising that the case for outward-looking development, in terms of its impact on technology, has much in common with the case in terms of human resources. Even drawing an operational line between improvements in skills and in technology, complementary as they are, is an intriguing theoretical and empirical challenge. Clearly, however, the mere existence of skilled labour in a country does not assure an availability of up-to-date technology, and the creation and lagged spread of new technology, though not fully understood, appear a central explanation of observed phenomena of growth and trade.

Countries at any level of development must rely on international exchanges for the resources that they themselves lack. Trade must bridge gaps not only in natural resources but also in technological know-how and skills, and in the case of the less developed countries these latter gaps are immense and growing.[19] Of course, interdependence of nations, in matters of capital goods, technology, and skills, has also been increasing in the advanced countries. Today every nation must depend on the outside world for an enlivening flow of new ideas, techniques, and products. But in backward and peripheral nations this dependence is particularly acute. Without an inflow of machinery, equipment, other goods, services, and, even more particularly, technological and organisational ideas, economic development in the poor countries could be expected to come to nothing. Communications and trade connecting these countries with the outside world represent the vital umbilical cord nurturing their growth.

The goods component of this essential link gives rise to the foreign exchange argument for outward-looking development, to be discussed shortly; but the idea component deserves separate attention. Unfortunately, it is extremely difficult for people in a remote society with a low concentration of skilled people to master the lessons and keep up with the changes that pulse in from the industrial and scientific world. This difficulty in communications is rendered worse by political independence. Customs barriers, migration checks, independent currencies, separate laws, and the power to change them that accompany independence tend to constrict and impede the life-giving inflow of ideas as well as goods and services,

---

[19]For a rough quantitative indication of the labour skills being indirectly commanded by primary-producing nations through their imports of manufactures, see my "Labor Skills and Comparative Advantage," *loc. cit.*

increasing the risks and costs to foreigners who might bring them. These unfortunate hazards can be greatly increased, however, through a nationalistic, inward-looking strategy of development. Both the spirit behind such a strategy and its local focus of attention weaken effective communications with the outside world. In contrast, an outward-looking strategy requires a constant eye on the changes and challenges that appear abroad and keeps communications open through competition, which is neglected under an inward-looking strategy.

Though not always recognised, a close link exists between communication and competition. Whether someone receives a signal intended for him and whether he acts upon it depend in part on his attention and motivation. He will tend to pay close attention and spring into action if his survival, advancement, and success depend on this behaviour. The observation that competitive pressures enhance communications and thus speed learning processes is familiar in the classroom. Examinations against first-rate competition are better in this respect than those against third-rate competition. Inward-looking development has, alas, the same sort of abstract appeal and practical failings as an educational system that simply hands out free library passes, supplies optional lectures, and then grants automatic degrees.

The close analogy with arguments previously advanced in connection with the improvement of human resources extends further. Technological improvement, at bottom, is mainly a matter of the quality of a nation's performance. Absorption of foreign technology can probably be encouraged by specially designed measures and programmes that apply to all industries, and within each industry. Special inducements to foreign firms may be justified. Pressure to innovate can possibly be created and reinforced by increasing aggregate demand, but negative sanctions may be a more powerful stimulus to action. Competition is at least highly desirable. But in a small and poor nation adequate competitive pressure can be achieved only by opening the economy to some competition from abroad. Conversely, "to each a subsidy according to his technological backwardness," though perhaps a caricature of the distributive principle under hyper-protection, is not a formula guaranteed to eliminate backwardness!

INCREASING RETURNS, SCALE, AND MARKET SIZE

Scale or size effects, at the level of the plant, firm, industry, industrial complex, and national market, strew difficult obstacles in the way of small and poor countries seeking to industrialise.[20] These scale considerations can only be partly disentangled from the subjects just discussed, since internal and external economies derive in part from competition, learning, training, innovation, and technological diffusion, while prominent scale effects appear in education, research, and development.

---

[20]The empirical literature that has grown up around scale economies of all kinds is bewildering in variety of methods, findings, and conclusions; yet, in the main, economists still lack the empirical tools to disaggregate and weigh the causes of observed scale or size phenomena. Perhaps the most striking evidence of country-size effects can be found in H. B. Chenery, "Patterns of Industrial Growth," *American Economic Review*, Vol. 50 (Sept. 1960), pp. 624–654.

In many industries a small country must accept either a reliance on imports or an enterprise of such suboptimal size as to saddle the economy with heavy overhead and operating costs.[21] In marketing as well as production, the relevant cost curve (which may be a "learning" curve) may descend only after a high and indivisible cost of entry. In this case, foreign firms can be induced to license up-to-date techniques or train local production staffs only in countries with sizeable prospective markets. Local enterprises may face unacceptable risks and costs in trying to break into competitive export markets.

Moreover, even if the local market suffices to support one or more plants of economical dimensions, economies of scale may effectively perpetuate a local monopoly or oligopoly situation, so that only foreign competition can ensure adequate pressures for cost-cutting and product-improvement.[22] Transport costs may make foreign competition ineffective in any case, so that cost disadvantages of industries supplying key inputs will extend to other industries through technological interdependence, even under the most open trade policies.

The severe handicap of smallness cannot be abolished; but it can be minimised under an outward-looking strategy. A well-situated small country, by exporting manufactures, can take advantage of increasing returns.[23] Through the workings of international competition, the country can hope to share the gains from increasing returns around the world wherever conditions are most favourable. Perhaps most important, by tying its price system to international prices at a realistic exchange rate, a country can avoid inappropriate attempts at import substitution in activities marked by economies of scale. Not squandering the country's scarce resources may mean more than a chance for aggrandisement in other people's markets.

The advantages of widening the market—and the economic disadvantages of autarkic policies in small political units—have been recognised by practical men for centuries. It is only necessary to recall the views of the makers of the Constitution of the United States or the architects of the German Zollverein, not to speak of the builders of earlier nation-states and ancient empires. In recent decades major improvements have taken place in techniques of mass production and transport, so that in many industries larger plants are being built than ever before. Meanwhile, local nationalisms have hurled less developed regions into economic and political fragmentation. Today only six less developed countries have total

---

[21] The choice is not necessarily obvious because of the effects of transport costs in cancelling out increasing returns.

[22] Alexander Hamilton, widely acclaimed for justifying infant-industry protection, but nevertheless an advocate of outward-looking development (witness his federalism), agreed with Adam Smith that "monopoly . . . is a great enemy to good management, which can never be universally established, but in consequence to that free and universal competition, which forces everybody to have recourse to it for the sake of self-defense." *Report on Manufactures* (1791); W. Letwin (ed.), *A Documentary History of American Foreign Policy* (New York: Anchor Books and Doubleday, 1961), p. 26.

[23] Some locations are better situated for large-scale plants than others, however, and transport considerations condemn many a small country to a permanent disadvantage in industries marked by economies of scale.

incomes larger than that of the tiny American state of Connecticut.[24] The resulting dilemma is widely recognised, but leaders are not always ready to accept the full logic of their countries' positions. For example, while it is often noticed that privileged access to someone else's markets could permit plants to be fully utilised that now stand half-idle, little enthusiasm can be found for open-ended competition, unless competitors with strong advantages in large-scale production can be excluded.[25]

Actually, if several countries pursued outward-looking policies at once, international competition could be expected to establish a fairly rational division of labour with respect to economies of scale. The countries "winning" the large-scale industries would be forced by competition to share with their customers most of the gains from increasing returns. Specialisation by some countries in large-scale plants would uncover opportunities for other countries to export items produced in small-scale plants. Such an international rationalisation of production cannot be achieved, however, by one country acting by itself.[26]

Unfortunately, as in the acquisition of skills, many countries have already committed mistakes that they must now live with or undo, in either case at considerable cost. As it is, to cite a common example, the existence of excess capacity to produce steel is being used to justify heavy protection of the local production of automobile parts. Under outward-looking policies it would be less difficult to identify cases where an early abandonment of uneconomical plants would revitalise a country's economic growth.

THE IMPLICATIONS OF LIMITED KNOWLEDGE OF
WHEN, HOW, AND HOW MUCH TO INTERVENE

I have already pointed out that the widening role of government in Western countries can be justified in terms of a multitude of divergences between private and social costs. Public activity inevitably spills over into trade—the government itself imports goods and services, and it prohibits the importation of undesirable items. It deliberately alters incentives that affect trade, if not directly, then through domestic measures such as taxes, subsidies, regulation, and planning. The sectors

---

[24]At prevailing exhange rates. The six countries are India, Mexico, Brazil, Spain, Argentina, and Pakistan. Computed from *Statistical Abstract of the United States 1964* and *U.N. Monthly Bulletin of Statistics* (Dec. 1964). No current income figures were available for Indonesia, but only a very generous valuation of Indonesian subsistence production would push that country into the same class. For that matter, of course, comparisons based on total income overstate poor countries' markets for many goods involving economies of scale.

[25]Even prospective economic integration schemes among less developed countries are not large, in terms of markets; and insofar as they lack in scale, technology, and resources, they must pay careful heed to their external trade policies.

[26]The qualification is fairly serious. If large and well-located countries all erect protective barriers or otherwise exploit their monopoly power, they may turn the terms of trade against hapless smaller countries and thus impoverish them. A surrounding array of tariffs, particularly against simple manufactured products, could force small and ill-located countries into import substitution in the industries marked by economies of scale (or for that matter, skill-intensity), even if the victimised countries pursued outward-looking policies.

that account for the bulk of world trade—manufacturing, agriculture, mining, tourism, long-distance transport, finance—are certainly not free of commonly recognised divergences between private and social costs. Government intervention is required, just, for example, to overcome underinvestment in research, desecration of the natural environment, misdirected responses to temporary false signals from the price mechanism, lack of appreciation of opportunities that lie around the corner, and conspiracies against the rest of the economy. The interdependence of investment decisions is well known, and social and private costs (or information) may diverge to a point where a socially profitable investment can only be undertaken by the government.[27]

Even where arguments favouring government intervention are well understood, however, relevant computations as to when, where, how, and how much to intervene are notoriously difficult and uncertain. One argument for an outward-looking strategy is that price corrections and cost-benefit analyses can be made using more reliable values than under heavy protection. Equally important, however, may be an inability of economists or other technical experts to supply trustworthy quantitative prescriptions in any circumstances. In an absence of adequate technical guidance, it would be insanely optimistic to rest much confidence in the self-correcting nature of the political process or the good intentions and common sense of public officials, though these assets are hopefully better than nothing.

Given the lowly state of present knowledge in many matters of growth and public policy, it is still possible in theory to rationalise almost any level of intervention. But in practice, the art of managing the development of a backward economy still requires not so much a search for perfection as an effort to avoid gigantic and costly errors.

As a result, a case for moderation in the use of protection and subsidy is valid, as it has been for a long time, based on the demonstrable dangers of a wide departure from allocation through the free market. Some of these dangers have already been discussed, but others are also worth mention. A major danger, in getting far away from a reliance on market prices, is that policy-makers will deny priority to an economic activity or product whose role and value they do not understand, and in the process will unhinge some important economic mechanism that they have overlooked. Oversights may range from a lack of appreciation of the value of spare parts or middlemen or interest rates to a lack of recognition that consumer goods represent indirect inputs into production in their role of sustaining and motivating human beings.[28]

---

[27]This theoretical framework clearly contains niches for most of the arguments for government intervention that have captured special attention in the theory of growth and trade. For example, the government may be better equipped than an individual to estimate (or get experts to estimate) the long-range market prospects of various export products. It can then employ taxes and subsidies as well as information policies to correct, in the social interest, the price signals being sent out by the world economy. Similarly, it can correct systematic distortions in other prices and incentives—including underinvestment in on-the-job training, technological improvement, and exporting.

[28]Even the Soviets, who have been experimenting for decades, are still plagued by serious systematic distortions; yet in skill in structuring incentives to spur people to work hard in priority tasks, and in getting a complex economy to function under detailed central management, the Soviets would appear to range far ahead of any non-Communist country.

Ubiquitous employment of protective devices involves special hazards. Resulting unpredictability in supplies and business incentives can lead to frustration-reactions that sharply reduce people's performance as producers. Miscalculation of the level of effective protection of any particular activity is all too easy, given the structure of inter-activity relationships.[29] Spreading protection over more and more activities erodes the relative position of the activities that were set up early in the sequence, bidding away resources until the industries may wind up as unintended victims of discrimination. By raising the price of inputs and spreading managerial and skill resources thinly, a massive application of protection effectively precludes any possibility of a poor country's manufacturing industries, or any other "marginal" export industries, breaking into world markets.

Not least important, once protection is accepted as a legitimate major instrument to promote industrialisation, it has a built-in tendency to overshoot the mark. Every industry is spurred to demonstrate its need to be sheltered from the cruelties of foreign competition; and the consumer, primary producer, and trader who must bear the burden are usually under-represented and their interests are under-rated, if only as a result of prevailing myths and prejudices.

Under an outward-looking strategy of development, mistakes will be made in the application of subsidies and tax exemptions, and pressures that encourage correction of these errors may discourage other intervention that might be useful. But the cost of such errors, since their size will be kept moderate, is likely to be smaller than the cost of massive over-intervention or unintended intervention in the wrong direction.

TWO MISLEADING ARGUMENTS FOR PROTECTION

Two frequently heard arguments for protection, or policies similar to protection, would seem to possess little validity for developing countries. The first is the contention that developing countries would want tariffs to improve their terms of trade. In fact, with few exceptions, these countries are too small for their purchases and sales to exert a perceptible influence on the prices at which they export and import. Moreover, these countries frequently appear to suffer from underemployed and unemployed resources, including unskilled labour, underutilised land and natural resources, underutilised plant and equipment, and even underutilised managerial, commercial, and professional skills.[30] In these circumstances it might make sense for countries to regard low export prices of manufactures as an investment in gaining industrial experience and employment.[31]

---

[29]See, for example, H. G. Johnson, "The Theory of Tariff Structure, with Special Reference to World Trade and Development," in H. G. Johnson and P. B. Kenen (eds.), *Trade and Development* (Geneva: Etudes et Travaux de l'Institut Universitaire des Hautes Etudes, 1965).

[30]These unused resources reflect imperfect and restricted domestic markets as well as specific bottlenecks in production. The extent of underutilised plant and equipment in less developed countries, in particular, certainly deserves more empirical attention than it has received to date. Excess capacity appears common, and because of the inexperience of cooperating human resources, the productivity of capital equipment can be very low.

[31]That is not to say, however, that less developed countries should abandon efforts to improve their terms of trade through collective bargaining.

A second argument often advanced is that because of the near-zero marginal productivity of labour in agriculture—the unemployed unskilled labour just mentioned—protection of manufacturing will put resources to work that would otherwise stand idle, and thus increase total output. The main flaw in this reasoning is that for the most part these resources are unemployed because they are redundant—factor substitution possibilities are not appealing, and the marginal product of unskilled labour is very low in manufacturing as well as agriculture. Putting unskilled labour to work would require managerial talent and complementary inputs of skills, foreign exchange, and other scarce resources. Thus, while increases in employment might prove socially desirable, they must generally be accomplished at a cost in income and growth, because complementary scarce resources must be shifted to lower-productivity roles.

The Implications of Foreign Exchange (Import) Constraints

Rigorous analysis has now confirmed that the ability to pay for needed imports can represent a stringent limitation on economic growth.[32] A foreign exchange or import constraint can occur as a result of the growth needs of less developed countries for machinery, equipment, and other goods and services from abroad. The basic explanation is the lack of substitutability of local resources for foreign-supplied resources.[33] Foreign goods reflect locally unattainable natural resources, skills, technology, and scale of production. Largely as a result of a well-documented sluggishness and inelasticity of world demand for primary exports, less developed countries experience serious difficulties in expanding their foreign exchange earnings to meet their import needs. Thus, what is sometimes described as a foreign exchange gap or bottleneck plagues their development programmes.

Whether imports represent an *effective* constraint on growth depends, of course, on the circumstances. When foreign aid is lavished on a country or export earnings soar, problems of absorption soon appear that bespeak the existence of other stringent constraints connected with human resources and savings. Nonetheless, it is easy to see how a push towards industrial development would generate new import requirements that outrun the economising effects of substituting local production for previous imports.[34] If the available supply of foreign exchange

---

[32]See especially H. B. Chenery and M. Bruno, "Developmental Activities in an Open Economy: The Case of Israel," *Economic Journal* (March 1962), pp. 79–103; and R. I. McKinnon, "Foreign Exchange Constraints in Economic Development and Efficient Aid Allocation," *Economic Journal* (June 1964), pp. 388–409.

[33]Besides lack of substitution in production, there is an unwillingness of consumers to substitute domestically produceable products for those with a direct or indirect import component. Striking evidences of lack of substitution in production between imports and domestic output, especially in machinery, have been found by G. Eleish, "The Input-Output Model in a Developing Economy: Egypt," in T. Barna (ed.), *Structural Interdependence and Economic Development;* and by C. Michalopoulos, *Trade and Development in Light of the Greek Experience*, Ph. D. dissertation, Columbia University, 1966.

[34]Not only does each new industry require imported machinery and equipment, but after it comes into operation, it needs an inflow of intermediate products, raw materials, energy, and spare parts, also involving imports. In addition, the growth process enlarges the demand for

does not rise rapidly, the scarcity value of foreign exchange will be pushed up and up.

If the pre-industrialisation exchange rate is adhered to, these pressures tend to assume the guise of an inflation caused by an ambitious development programme taking place behind a rising wall of import restrictions and exchange controls. The same dilemma can be better solved, however, through a deliberate large devaluation or even successive devaluations.[35]

This solution will achieve the same basic purpose of allocating scarce foreign exchange, and at the same time will reflect the value to the economy of export- and import-substitution activities of all kinds. Devaluation will also encourage tourism and foreign investment.[36] Of course, such an exchange-rate policy can only be made effective if it is combined with anti-inflationary fiscal and monetary policies, which, in turn, presuppose that the basic responsibilities of government can be met and taxes can be collected.[37]

Special efforts to export manufactures, insofar as they are successful, will further relieve the foreign exchange constraint.

CONCLUSION

This paper argues that a country seeking industrial development should strive to export manufactures very early in the process and should orient its industrial complex outward from the start. Both exports and import substitution should be encouraged by the choice of exchange rate and by subsidies and tax exemptions,

---

foodstuffs, consumer goods to serve as incentives, and inputs into agriculture and services. Many of these needs, too, must be met from abroad. This point is widely understood; see, for example, C. F. Diaz-Alejandro, "On the Import Intensity of Import Substitution," *Kyklos*, Vol. 18 (1965), pp. 495–511.

[35] One large devaluation may be preferable, in view of the destabilising impact of exchange-rate instability, which creates disincentives to the international economic exchanges so essential for growth.

[36] While it is not possible to be confident about effects on foreign aid, deliberately aggravating a foreign exchange gap may be losing its appeal in the face of increasing scepticism in donor countries.

[37] If it appears impossible to reach a balanced budget and still subsidise export-oriented industries, the situation may have to be interpreted as meaning that either the economy or the political system is not ready to move into a policy of attracting new industries. Perhaps the need for infrastructure and basic government activities is too pressing to permit a simultaneous effort to stimulate industrialisation; available skills and managerial resources will not stretch that far. Or perhaps, since taxes cannot be collected, the community is not yet sufficiently politically mature to undertake a major industrialisation drive without such a corrupt misallocation of resources as to make the results fairly worthless. Of course, advanced countries are not (nor were they at one time) paragons of political maturity and fiscal discipline; every nation is constrained by areas of political weakness where misallocation of resources must be expected. In any case, it is generally an illusion to suppose that large-scale deficit spending will mobilise valuable new resources compared with a more conservative fiscal policy, especially in view of "costs" (and distortions of incentives) already discussed. Given fiscal stability, monetary stringency under an outward-looking policy does not penalise growth, compared with the available alternatives, because effective rates of interest are normally lower, and private credit is more easily available under conservative fiscal policies than under inflationary policies. Besides, as already noted, outward-looking policies call for generous loans and export credit to export-oriented manufacturing industries.

with only moderate recourse to differential tariffs. A major effort should be made to absorb and catch up with foreign technology.

An outward-looking strategy emphasises the quality and direction rather than the absolute magnitude of industrial development. Human resources and other investments generated early in the process will exert a lasting influence over the character of subsequent growth. New high-quality human resources will be created through industrial experience that could not be obtained under heavy protection. Outside competition will spur adoption of new technology and efficient methods. A more rational and efficient allocation of scarce resources will emerge than under inward-looking policies, and gross errors will be avoided. Foreign exchange constraints on growth will be eased. The result will be to sow the seeds for a flourishing growth of industry that will soon far outstrip the blighted product of an inward-looking strategy.

Selection **27**

The Role of Commercial Policy
in Economic Development

V. S. VARTIKAR

From: "The Role of Commercial Policy in the Development of a Subsistence Economy," Weltwirtschaftliches Archiv, *Vol. 95, No. 1 (1965), pp. 102–122. Reprinted by permission of* Weltwirtschaftliches Archiv.

(1) In the planned development of a backward economy commercial policy is generally given a crucial role to play. It is considered to be useful for furthering economic development in many ways, for example, by protecting import-substituting industries, by subsidizing exports to create a "leading sector," by creating large and sheltered markets by promoting regional economic unions, or by exploiting monopolistic situations in the export market. In most cases development effort starts with the control of commercial policy. Especially the newly independent countries have acquired a complete mistrust of the free trade policy which is almost exclusively blamed for the destruction of handicrafts without replacing them with modern industries; due to a policy of uncontrolled free trade, even technical progress led to the "immiserization of growth"[1] in backward economies. The control of commercial policy is considered essential not only by the backward countries but also it is conceded to be so even by advanced countries and GATT.[2] Backward countries of today are allowed to manage their own imports and exports, choose and vary their exchange rates as they like, follow discriminatory policies, enter into bilateral agreements, control the inflow and outflow of foreign capital, and in general follow any other policy that disregards the interest of the advanced countries without fear of any retaliation. Advanced countries have conceded this double standard of morality for quickening the economic development of backward regions. This change of world opinion itself gives commercial policy a crucial role in economic development.

---

[1] "Economic expansion increases *output* which, however, might lead to a sufficient deterioration in the terms of trade to offset the beneficial effect of expansion and reduce the *real income* of the growing country." Jagdish Bhagwati, "Immiserizing Growth: A Geometrical Note," *The Review of Economic Studies*, Vol. XXV (Cambridge, June 1958), p. 201.

[2] Cf. *The General Agreement on Tariffs and Trade*, Article XVIII: "Governmental Assistance to Economic Development," U.S. Department of State, Publication 7182, Commercial Policy Series 178 (Washington, D.C., June 1961).

(2) There are at least two good reasons commercial policy rightly acquires importance in the strategy of economic development. First, foreign trade and in general all relations with foreign countries can be almost completely controlled by the government as no other field of economic activity could be. People generally acquiesce in such controls perhaps because traditionally it is supposed to be a government prerogative to manage foreign relations. Moreover, trade controls can be managed without frequent confrontation of authorities with the affected people and also without much administrative paraphernalia. Foreign trade controls are indirect and impersonal and, in backward countries, beyond the understanding of the masses. Excise tax or expenditure tax to reduce consumption would be resented by the people but export promotion or import control can achieve the same result without much protest. To control prices of certain necessities produced by innumerable small industries spread all over the country is almost an impossible task, but to a certain extent this could be silently managed by proper manipulation of the export and import of such items. Investment can be channelled in socially desirable direction just by the discreet use of import licensing of capital goods. The larger is the import and export trade of the country, the larger the potential impact of commercial policy on economic development.

(3) Secondly, some necessary flexibility can be introduced in the planned economic development by the proper use of commercial policy. To build the whole industrial structure is a work of generations, and even if unlimited investment is possible, all the industries with all their accessories could rarely be built in a short span of time in any economy. When possible investment at any one time is limited, gaps and bottlenecks in the industrial structure are almost inevitable, and they can be bridged and widened, respectively, by the proper use of commercial policy. With the possibility of subsidizing exports, large-scale indivisible investment can be made even before the home market is sufficiently expanded. By importing complex components, advanced industries can be started even before the whole process of production is mastered in the country. Mistakes and errors in planning can be corrected with the help of commercial policy without much delay and cost. A fine balancing that is needed among various innumerable industries can emerge only slowly; a continuous balanced growth in this sense can only be achieved, if at all, under watertight planning and extensive control of the whole economic and social structure. In a more or less democratic society an obvious alternative to autarky and dictatorial planning is the intelligent use of commercial policy.[3]

(4) There are at least two difficulties in the way of using commercial policy for economic development. First, the very ease with which it can be manipulated creates a temptation to change it too frequently and too abruptly. Tariffs can be changed every year and quantitative restrictions can be varied almost from month to month. This can inject an extra amount of uncertainty in the economic structure. A weak government and inefficient planners may avoid to evolve proper economic priorities, putting the whole burden on commercial policy. More importantly mismanagement or over-manipulation of foreign trade can attract public attention

---

[3] Cf. Tibor Scitovsky, "Growth-Balanced or Unbalanced?" in *The Allocation of Economic Resources*, Essays in Honor of Bernard Francis Haley (Stanford, Calif., 1959), p. 207ff.

to such an extent that its main source of strength, its impersonal and silent character, can be destroyed and then various vested interests or organized and vocal
groups in the population may try to influence it in their own narrow interests.
The secret of the effective use of a commercial policy is either to keep it inconspic-
uous or to evolve a "national" commercial policy; and for a backward country
the former course appears to be more feasible.[4]

(5) Secondly, commercial policy by itself cannot do miracles; to be effective,
it has to be devised as a part of a long-term strategy of economic development.
Just abandoning free trade policy is not enough to help development efforts.
What sort of industries to start and in what sequence, what technique is suitable
in different industries, what sort of economic structure ultimately to be evolved,
consumption of which goods is to be discouraged and which goods are to be
produced in abundance, which saving potential in the society is to be tapped and
with what means, and a host of such decisions have to be integrated in a long-
term plan before commercial policy can be put to work. Otherwise, import controls
can saddle the country with inefficient industries and export promotion can turn
out to be an expensive mistake. Commercial policy is a delicate and a beautiful
tool but it can be effectively used only in the context of a long-term, detailed plan.

(6) The simplest commercial policy that is generally followed by many developing countries today can be roughly summarized as follows: (a) To promote exports
of as many goods as is possible, (b) To encourage imports of capital goods for
building up whatever industries that can be started in the country, (c) To keep
artificially the external value of the currency at a high level, and (d) To maintain
and widen the inflow of foreign capital. It is proposed here to question these
policies and to suggest new ones that are likely to quicken and strengthen the
process of economic development.

(7) A developing country today will certainly have to control its imports for three
interdependent reasons. First, the composition of imports has to be changed;
imports of capital goods have to be relatively increased by a relative reduction
in the imports of consumer goods. Equally important are imports of raw materials
and intermediate goods and need for such imports is likely to rise at least in the
first phases of development. Even within the reduced imports of consumer goods,
wage-goods that are in short supply in the domestic market will have to be given
a preference over the non-wage-goods which are rightly termed by many developing
countries as "in-essential consumer goods." In any case, it will be surprising if the
composition of imports does not change in favour of producers goods in general.
Secondly, import controls can certainly be used for protecting a domestic industry.
Many times industrialization starts with building industries behind the tariff wall.
However, nicely balanced tariffs to protect home industries is very likely an
obsolete idea today, simply because of the inability of the developing countries
to import consumer goods. In a developing country today the central problem of

---

[4] J. Bhagwati, "Indian Balance of Payments Policy and Exchange Auctions," *Oxford Economic Papers*, N.S., Vol. XIV (February 1962), p. 51ff. Dr. Bhagwati makes a strong plea for
exchange auctions to replace the present method of import licensing. But a policy of auctioning
is not likely to last long as it will bring commercial policy more and more in the political arena.

industrial planning is not that of choosing particular industries for protection from foreign competition but to channel investment into particular industries and to discourage or even to prohibit the establishment of industries that are not essential for the time being. Due to the inability to import consumer goods, the problem of protection is transformed into the problem of investment priorities. Thirdly, import controls can help to create the badly needed savings for economic development. In a backward country a large proportion of people are so poor that it is neither desirable nor possible to extract any savings from them. The upper and middle classes, therefore, have to sacrifice some of their consumption to raise the level of national savings. Except for the consumption of services the consumption level depends on the availability of goods and therefore, when nonessential imports are shut off, the saving potential of the nation can be raised; and commercial policy can be certainly used for this purpose.

(8) As a matter of fact, whenever there is an exchange scarcity, the first thing that a country does is to cut down the imports of nonessential consumer goods. But, generally speaking, such controls are rarely used to raise the saving potential of the country. Especially in a large country like India, as soon as luxury imports are stopped, import-substitute industries are established, and an alternative source of supply is created to maintain expensive consumption. It is easy for a backward country to fall prey to import-substituting industrialization and to saddle itself with industries which are justified neither by a comparative advantage nor by the extent of the domestic market. However, such industries can create broader avenues of consumption by high pressure salesmanship, by keeping up the demonstration effect, and by resisting high excise duties. Once established, these industries compete with others not only for the scarce resources available in the country but also for foreign exchange to import equipment, spare parts, and many intermediate and ancillary goods. Many times these industries are established either by foreign producers or by native producers with foreign collaboration, creating a further drain on foreign exchange for the transfer of profits. So the production of such goods not only reduces savings but also creates a larger demand for scarce foreign exchange which was supposed to have been conserved by the original import restrictions. It is necessary for a developing country, therefore, to discourage *both* the production and imports of luxury goods.

(9) It has been argued[5] that there is no harm if developing countries import luxury goods from each other on a discriminatory basis; so that India can import wines from Tunisia (but not from France) in exchange for exports of cashew nuts, and this trade will help both the countries. This view does not seem to be correct unless two assumptions are made, and they are not likely to be realistic assumptions. First, luxury goods are produced by very specific resources without any alter-

---

[5] I. G. Patel, "Trade and Payments Policy for a Developing Economy," in Roy Harrod (ed.), assisted by Douglas Hague, *International Trade Theory in a Developing World*, Proceedings of a Conference held by the International Economic Association (London and New York, 1963), p. 309ff.

native use; and secondly, demand for such goods is very inelastic in advanced countries. If this is not true, either wage-goods can be produced instead of luxuries or the luxury goods can be exported in exchange for essential imports. Moreover, if one is interested in reducing consumption, to open up new avenues of consumption is not advisable. Probably both countries will soon require both goods, and by promoting exports they will retard each other's development. A reasonable list of underdeveloped countries can furnish any country with almost everything that is desired by well-to-do people. This is especially true when the developing countries indulge in import-substituting industrialization. India alone can produce and export quite a few luxury items to all the backward countries if they open up their markets, even for swapping with their own luxury goods. Because the latter can be re-exported to advanced countries while the modern luxury items have no such export market in advanced countries. Such an arrangement will be very useful for India but not likely to be accepted by other developing countries, because consumption of luxury goods, wherever they come from, will reduce the saving potential and hamper economic growth.

(10) In developing countries today the main barrier to economic development is supposed to be the scarcity of foreign exchange; paucity of domestic savings is not taken that seriously. That is why imports of luxury goods are stopped, but domestic production of such goods is not discouraged. In a country where there is a huge amount of unemployed labour, establishment of any industry is considered desirable. Social cost of unemployed labour is nil, and anything produced by this labour is considered a net gain. Especially if foreign exchange is available, say by collaboration with foreign producers, any industry is established, and increase in any sort of investment is hailed as economic development. This reasoning is simply incorrect in, what may be called, a subsistence economy.

(11) A subsistence economy may be defined as an economy where most of the people, except the small upper and middle classes, are so poor that they spend all their income on bare necessities like food, clothing, and shelter, and consequently their income elasticity of demand for food is very high. A second characteristic of a subsistence economy is that food is produced by the peasants not mainly for the market but for their own consumption, and only a surplus is sold to the market on which the non-farm population has to subsist. Therefore, when the peasant's income increases, either due to higher production or higher prices, he consumes more of his own product and raises his own standard of life and sells only the rest of the extra production. If food prices rise without increasing food production, food supply to the industrial sector may actually fall. In such an economy, industrial employment cannot be increased without increasing food supply, not only for the industrial labour but also for the peasant. As soon as employment and wage-income is increased, a demand is created for wage-goods; and if their supply is not proportionately increasing, there arises not only a fear of inflation but a fear of political unrest and destabilization of the whole social structure. It is somewhat surprising that an equilibrium can be maintained with a huge load

of unemployed and half-starved people but a slightly different redistribution of the given amount of wage-goods takes the system to the brink of disaster.[6] This is a real barrier to the increasing employment, and "unlimited" supply of labour cannot be used for industrialization without concurrently increasing agricultural productivity. In a subsistence economy, therefore, any cutting down of consumption for increasing investment is as essential as in a full employment labour-scarce economy. To produce luxury goods or to maintain a retinue of servants is to use resources that could have created essential investment.

(12) It is easy to come to the conclusion that such a country can import food and other wage-goods and increase its employment potential. If the investment in agriculture and wage-goods industries is taking place, such imports may be useful to tie over the gestation period. But not always are such imports planned that way. One should expect the development effort to start with the protection of and investment in wage-goods industries not only because they are broad-based industries with large home market but also because the larger supply of wage-goods creates immediate possibilities of further investment. However, to protect an industry is to raise the price of the product at least temporarily; and to raise the price of wage-goods is not likely to be a popular policy. Therefore, when foreign exchange is scarce, the axe falls on luxury items; and when their prices rise, import-substituting industries are started, creating larger demand for wage-goods but at the same time creating more pressure to keep their prices down. In this way the wage-goods industries languish and the luxury industries get ample protection, braking up the whole development process.

(13) The imports of wage-goods and especially the imports of food are not possible to maintain on a growing scale for a backward country without reducing the imports of capital goods and intermediate goods necessary for economic development. For example, India would require about 25 per cent of her export earnings to be able to import 5 per cent of her total need of foodgrains. Ghana has found out recently that it is cheaper to produce food in the country than to import from abroad.[7] Food imports, however, are possible for many developing countries without using foreign exchange thanks to the U.S.A.'s PL 480. It is doubtful whether such imports are useful for quickening economic development, unless they are meant for a very short period. They help food prices to remain unduly low and push the agricultural development in the background. If any industry deserves the first priority in the investment programme and in protection, it is the food industry. To keep the prices of food low is to discourage investment in agriculture. Even at

---

[6] K. N. Raj says: "It is true that if the aggregate output and, therefore, the total amount available for consumption remain the same as before, increased consumption on the part of some will necessarily mean that less is available for others. But however much this may appear as a cost to the latter, there is no reason whatever, from the economic point of view, to regard it as a cost to the society as a whole. In fact, insofar as the same volume of output as before is used to sustain a higher rate of investment, which in due course would increase output, it can be legitimately argued that a positive economic gain accrues to the society as a result of the redistribution." K. N. Raj, *Some Economic Aspects of the Bhakra Nangal Project, A Preliminary Analysis in Terms of Selected Investment Criteria* (Bombay, 1960), p. 18. However, such a redistribution may not be politically feasible, as has been shown by the recent events in India.

[7] International Monetary Fund, *International Financial News Survey*, Vol. XV, No. 14, (Washington, D.C., April 12, 1963), p. 121.

the risk of raising prices the food industry has to be protected and food production has to be expanded as this forms a necessary input for all other production due to the high income elasticity of demand for food in subsistence economies. In the hurry of industrializing the country, it is possible to forget this basic fact.[8] It is possible to build up an industrial economy depending on imports of food and raw materials only if the country has an obvious comparative advantage in industrial goods; this is a rare possibility for a developing country today. Industrialization in a subsistence economy, therefore, will have to depend on agricultural productivity, which has to be induced by the planners by keeping the prices of farm products stable and high and by giving priority to agricultural investment.

(14) A decision to concentrate all investment on wage-goods, however desirable, may be very hard to make. In that case it may be better to select only a few luxury industries than to spread investment over the whole range of non-wage-goods. This is desirable not only because limited investment is possible but also because all the industries together will not have enough effective demand for their products to make them viable industries. In a poor country the demand for non-wage-goods is, almost by definition, very small; only a few people are enough well-off to spend on luxuries. If this small demand is diffused over many products, then no industry in this category is likely to flourish. Concentrating this demand on few goods will help to create viable industries. If air-conditioners are not available,

---

[8]This does not mean, however, that all the possible investment must be made to produce wage-goods directly. It may be necessary and desirable to invest in the production of capital goods for increasing the rate of production of wage-goods. Here, the basic point is that continuous growth in investment and production is not possible unless production of wage-goods also proportionately increases.

If a certain amount of investment is going on continuously in the wage-goods industries, income of wage-earners will be stabilized at a certain level, but the productive capacity will rise with each period of investment. If I_1 is such a rate of investment and b_1 is the output-capital ratio, then

$$I_1 b_1 = \Delta P$$

This extra supply of wage-goods can make it possible to invest in other non-wage-goods industries. This investment will create income to wage-earners but will not produce wage-goods. If I_2 is such an investment, it can continuously grow at a certain rate, each time raising the demand for wage-goods. Then

$$\frac{I_2}{S} = \Delta D \qquad \text{where } S \text{ is the MPS}$$

Therefore $C(\Delta D)$ will be the increase in demand for wage-goods, where C is the MPC. The stability condition of such investment is

$$C(\Delta D) = \Delta P$$
$$\therefore I_1 b_1 = C[I_2/S]$$
$$\therefore \frac{I_2}{I_1} = \frac{b_1 S}{C}$$

This means that if I_1 is 10 per cent of wage-goods production and if b_1 is 0.5, then wage-goods production will rise by an absolute rate of 5 per cent. In that case I_2 can grow by about 5.5 per cent of I_1 or by little more than 0.5 per cent of original wage-goods production. This much "unproductive" investment with the multiplier will create just enough income to absorb the continuous rise in the production of wage-goods due to I_1. Any further increase in I_2 will necessarily lead to inflation. Furthermore, it is assumed here that the extra production of I_1 is not absorbed by the rising population. Such are the limitations on the investment that is not meant directly or indirectly for the production of wage-goods.

demand for refrigerators will certainly be larger, there will be less excess capacity in the industry, refrigerators will be cheaper, and industry will be larger than when both refrigerators and air conditioners are produced. Industry with one or two tiny firms is not likely to be efficient enough to dispense with protection. Large industry, moreover, by sustaining ancillary industries, is likely to reduce the import-content of its product and save foreign exchange.

(15) Any successful industry creates an atmosphere for itself in which it flourishes and expands. In such a created atmosphere, the industry, if not individual firms, can reap increasing returns, leading to a fall in costs and expansion of the market. Such atmosphere is cumulative, and it grows with the industry and vice versa. That is how industries acquire their location when it is not dictated by transport costs. Even handicrafts industries presumably create particular atmospheres for themselves, and products come to be identified by locations. The created atmosphere is many times so important that it defies even climatic atmosphere. The Indian sugar industry, for example, has got located in a region which is not the best region in India for growing sugar cane. The atmosphere may be just psychological in the sense that the Schumpeterian swarm of second-best producers follows the innovating entrepreneur and chooses the "correct" location instead of developing a new one. However, the atmosphere consists of real factors also; skilled labour required for that particular industry becomes more easily available; as the centre grows, there is an easy access to raw materials; due to the emergence of ancillary industries, it becomes easy to buy accessories and to sell by-products; there is a possibility of a detailed imitation and emulation of competitors; and so forth. For whatever reason, the firms in an industry tend to come together, and they create an atmosphere that assures the success of the industry. Concentration of demand on few products will make it possible for whatever industry that is started to create an atmosphere for itself. To diffuse the tiny demand for many products is to refuse a fighting chance to any industry. Of course, a group of cognate industries can create an atmosphere for themselves, but then the argument remains the same as between many such groups.

(16) If atmosphere creation leads to increasing returns, then it can be said that comparatively large industries in an economy, supplying either the home market or the export market, tend to acquire comparative advantage and tend to become powerful in the international market.[9] A newly developing country, however, can

---

[9] Cf. Kelvin Lancaster, "The Heckscher-Ohlin Trade Model: A Geometric Treatment," *Economica*, N.S., Vol. XXIV, (London, February 1957), p. 19ff. On p. 20ff., Mr. Lancaster says: "[The classical] comparative costs approach relied on accidents to explain the difference which initiated trade, accidents such as differences in knowledge or skill, there was a reasonable presumption that international trade could ultimately cease to exist. . . . In the Heckscher-Ohlin model . . . trade would continue even if there were perfect transmission of knowledge and techniques and absolute freedom for the costless migration of factors. . . . Factor price equalisation shows that there would be no incentive for factor endowments to become uniform, so resulting in the cessation of trade." In the Ricardian model, with constant costs and only one factor, labour, the reason why the comparative advantage arises seems to be the difference between atmospheres in different countries. All labour is homogeneous, and differences in skill or knowledge are not assumed. It is arguable whether atmosphere or factor endowment is an accidental fact, but it cannot be doubted that the atmosphere is at least as important as the factor endowment. This is quite obvious with physical atmospheres, and it is not difficult to perceive other

rarely build an industry which can successfully compete in the international market without depending on the domestic demand. The newly developing countries will do better if they base their industries on the firm foundation of home demand.[10] Once established, however, such industries may be able to compete in the international market. Even for export promotion, therefore, it is necessary for poor countries to concentrate their demand on comparatively few products. It is now generally believed that backward countries can build up exports of modern manufactured goods that are relatively simple and inexpensive. India has already started exporting bicycles, electric fans, sewing machines, electric motors, oil engines, etc. But the reason for such exports may be that these industries are now well established due to a large home market. That they are simple and inexpensive manufactures is incidental and is probably solely due to high demand for such goods in poor countries. If the home demand for more complicated goods could be concentrated on a few items and if viable industries are established, exports of complicated and expensive goods also will be equally possible for these countries. In some countries like India there is a cheap supply of highly skilled labour like that of engineers, electricians, chemists, metallurgists, pharmacists, and others. Industries that require ample labour of this kind will also be successful in the export market, if they are initially supported by a sizable home demand.

(17) In subsistence economies, paucity of wage-goods and not the shortage of foreign exchange is the main barrier to investment and employment. However, foreign exchange barrier is unduly emphasized, and therefore export promotion is a watch-word of commercial policy in many developing countries. They are all trying to boost their traditional exports like vegetable oils, cotton, tea, coffee, rubber, jute, spices, etc. In good old colonial days exporting raw materials or importing manufactured goods was considered a policy of exploitation of the backward countries. These days are over. Now the backward countries complain that the demand for traditional exports is not sufficiently expanding.[11] Such exports are maintained and promoted irrespective of the terms of trade, interests of other developing countries exporting the same goods, fiscal burden of the subsidies, or even the general effect on economic development. One must remember that export

---

types of it, including the ones created by the industries themselves. The factor-price equalization theorem makes it *unnecessary* for the factors to migrate, but if such a migration takes place, say due to non-economic reasons, the differences in factor-endowments can be nullified, leading to the cessation of trade. But atmosphere in different countries or regions cannot be easily transplanted or wiped out. Factor-price equalization can consider migration from labour-scarce country to labour-endowed country as economically insignificant. But this does not happen. Even inside one country where there is free trade between different regions, migration becomes desirable, industrial centres continuously grow, and the depressed areas remain depressed until they are looked after by the government, either for moving out the people or for bringing in the needed capital. That different regions and countries are either endowed with or create specific atmospheres affecting the production functions is certainly a fact of some economic significance.

[10]Cf. Staffan Burenstam Linder, *An Essay on Trade and Transformation* (Uppsala, 1961).

[11]"Indian exports can only be expected to drift along, as they have done in the past, a downward curve, despite the increasing number of expert bodies and export promotion councils that may be appointed to reverse it. It is better part of wisdom to accept this unwelcome and brutal fact and to prepare to live with it." S. J. Patel, "Export Prospects and Economic Growth: India," *The Economic Journal*, Vol. LXIX (London, 1959), p. 502.

cannot be an end in itself; from any one country's point of view exports are a dead loss. Exports have to be maintained only for financing imports, which, in turn, are mainly required for the development of the economy. In a completely free economy where price mechanism alone can be used even to achieve and maintain full employment, the device of dumping goods in foreign markets may be a small price to pay to get over the slump, instead of making irreversible changes in the institutional structure of the economy. But when there is full or over-full employment, dumping indeed will be a curious policy. A subsistence economy on the path of development has to be considered a full-employment economy, because all the employment that is justified by the supply of wage-goods has been created, and the rest of the unemployed people cannot be given employment before producing more wage-goods. Therefore export promotion, let alone dumping, is not likely to be worthwhile unless export industries use specific resources which cannot be used for the production of wage-goods. If the export industries use the factors in wage-goods industries, then the export promotion policy is very suspect, and it may actually hinder economic development. For example, it is doubtful whether India can export more vegetable oil, sugar, raw cotton, and even jute, without affecting her food production.

(18) Another facet of export promotion is to push raw material exports little further in the production process before they are exported. Thus Ghana exports processed cocoa instead of cocoa beans, and India exports groundnut oil instead of groundnuts. When total possible employment is limited, one cannot be sure that this is the ideal policy for development. The little step toward increasing the export value of traditional goods can be taken any time if such exports are maintained. Meanwhile employable labour can be used in a more worthwhile way. If a steel factory or fertilizer factory or hydro-electric works cannot be built due to the lack of wage-goods, crushing of cocoa beans or groundnuts does not seem to be the best way to use scarce resources. Blind faith in export promotion coupled with the notion of unlimited supply of labour is more likely to do harm than good to a developing country.

(19) In the case of wage-goods more slippery policy than straight-forward export promotion is also possible, that is, to use quantitative restrictions on exports. The simplest way to use such restrictions is to vary the export quotas inversely with the internal price of the commodity, the assumption being that the varying prices are brought about by the forces of supply and demand and they constitute a good index of the need of the commodity to the consumers at home. But such an export policy, instead of stabilizing prices at home and benefiting the consumer and the producer, may inject an extra element of speculation in trading and productive activity. When for some reason international prices rise, the traders may try to acquire more stocks with the hope of getting an export license, and this activity can raise internal prices irrespective of home demand or home production. With prices rising, even some of the farmers can withhold stocks for getting better prices later. But, when the home prices rise, government reduces the export quota. When the international prices fall, traders try to get rid of stocks, and when the domestic prices fall, the government will increase the quota. In this way the

government and the traders may unwittingly cooperate to export more when prices are low abroad and export less when prices are high. By such a preference for bad terms of trade over good ones a country can unnecessarily forego the extra foreign exchange it would have otherwise earned. Such quantitative restrictions on exports do not help the production of wage-goods. If the farmer is not allowed to take the benefit of the higher prices, it is unfair to make him receive the full impact of the lower prices. Price support, however, is not an easy policy to follow in a backward country, both for administrative and financial reasons. But it is certainly possible to devise a more rational export policy than just to vary inversely the exports with the domestic prices. Even to fix per head consumption and to allow exports of the rest of the production irrespective of domestic prices may earn more foreign exchange and also insulate the domestic market from the international price movements. The best policy, however, is to discourage exports of all wage-goods, except those items which can be abundantly produced by very specific resources, such as tea.

(20) The use of quantitative restrictions in the regulation of imports seems to be a mistaken policy also. To liberalize imports in one year when foreign exchange is available and to cut down imports when foreign exchange is scarce does not show any great effort to plan economic development. This sort of policy also amounts to the deliberate preference for bad terms of trade to good ones. Because, when the prices and volume of exports go up, more foreign exchange is earned, and when there is such a booming demand for exports, import prices are also likely to be high. Instead of spending the export earnings immediately, it will certainly be more economic to plan foreign exchange budgets for a little longer time, working with some reserves to keep up the planned import schedule. If the import content of exports is high or if the investment projects are kept in a queue to be served as soon as foreign exchange is available, such a use of quantitative restrictions on imports may be justified, though this may not be an ideal planning for development. But when such restrictions are used for the import of consumer goods, it amounts to a refusal to plan and a willingness to drift with the external forces affecting the foreign trade. After all, to manipulate imports and exports just to maintain an accounting identity of the balance of payments is not worthwhile, unless it is meant for a very short time to avoid extensive and irreversible repercussions in many directions. If things are left to themselves, balance of payments will automatically be adjusted; if tampering with this process is to be justified, the management of foreign trade must have a long-term welfare implication. Adjusting imports and exports each year does not seem to have such welfare content, and the banal accounting identity seems to be modifying the trade policies of the developing countries today.

(21) Especially in the case of nonessential consumer goods the policy of fluctuating restrictions is not likely to help the development effort. Quantitative restrictions indirectly encourage import-substituting industries, unless such industries are prohibited by planners; but the fluctuating imports of these goods fail to give the necessary protection to these industries, and the country is saddled with inefficient industries suffering from excess capacity and producing substandard goods.

To make these industries viable and efficient, it may be necessary to stop the relevant imports altogether and not to whittle the already tiny home market. Fluctuating imports keep up the desire for imported goods, by their demonstration effect; consumers wait till the next liberalization of import quotas, and the domestic substitutes are bought only as a last resort. It is a waste of foreign exchange and domestic resources to create these industries and then to threaten them continually with import liberalization. If these industries are not required, it is better to prohibit such investment and maintain high enough import duties on the goods so as to restrict them to a desired limit. Tariffs, at least, bring in extra revenue to the government, while the quantitative restrictions create huge profits to traders unless the import licenses are auctioned, and auctioning is not necessarily a desirable policy.[12]

(22) Though the developing countries are interested in promoting exports and in discouraging imports, they do this by very complex restrictions instead of a straight devaluation. One may suspect that in some countries at least the bureaucracy and sometimes even political authorities get interested in such manipulations of trade for the sake of enjoying the power that such controls bring, if not for the sake of any direct personal gain. In modern times, however, devaluation does not seem to be popular in any country, advanced or backward. The wheel seems to have come a full circle since the 1930's when many countries indulged in competitive depreciation. Many and possibly all underdeveloped countries today tenaciously hold to exchange rates that overvalue their currencies, not only on the basis of supply of and demand for foreign exchange but also on the basis of purchasing power in the domestic markets. Pakistan, for example, refused to devalue her currency in 1949 when the pound sterling was devalued, and even today her exchange rate is very much overstated. Indian rupee today is at least 30 per cent overvalued by the official rate if the blackmarket rates are any indicators of the real worth of the currency. This overvaluation of currency requires extensive and complex exchange controls, which by the very nature of transactions are not always entirely effective, besides making governmental interference in the economy unnecessarily more comprehensive and conspicuous than it need be.

(23) The best policy for a backward country is to maintain more or less a free market exchange rate, with temporary support for smoothing out erratic fluctuations; this will minimize the use of exchange controls. One of the reasons why a low exchange rate is shunned by the developing countries is, presumably, the fact that the exports become unnecessarily cheap to foreigners, especially to advanced countries who are the main customers for traditional exports. But this is not inevitable. All traditional exports can be taxed, and foreign prices of such exports can be maintained at the desired level even after devaluation. Such an export tax can improve the fiscal position of the government and the development effort can be improved. If Indian government devalues and imposes an equivalent export tax, it will raise its total revenue by more than 25 per cent. This money is lost today to those who import foreign goods because importers are the beneficiaries of the

---

[12]See footnote 4.

high exchange rate, unless an equivalent amount was collected by taxing the imports. Furthermore, high exchange rate is an implicit tax on *all* exports, and this is not an ideal policy. It may be economic to create export markets for modern manufactured goods produced by newly established industries, and such exports need not be taxed. One should expect traditional exports to decline with rising rate of industrialization of a subsistence economy and the exports of modern manufactured goods to increase. Overvalued currency does the opposite; at the least, it does not favour one sort of exports over another. Apart from manufactured goods, a developing country should promote exports of luxury goods both for reducing consumption at home and for earning more foreign exchange. When currency is devalued, almost certainly such exports will increase, and in the home market the prices will rise if the supply is not very elastic. Even if production of such goods is not to be increased, an excise tax compensating devaluation will release a larger part of production for export than when the currency is overvalued. High exchange rate, indeed, amounts to a subsidization of domestic consumption of luxury goods which a developing country can ill afford. India, for example, will be able to export more coffee, cashew nuts, rugs, fancy handicrafts, and spices if the rupee is devalued.

(24) Devaluation will raise the prices of imports not only of consumer goods (which is welcomed by the developing countries) but also of producers goods required to carry on the programme of development. There is a popular fallacy in some underdeveloped countries that low exchange rate makes the country pay more for its imports. The individual importer in terms of his domestic currency certainly pays more, but the country as a whole would be paying more only if exports also are comparatively cheaper in a foreign currency. If the exports can be taxed, the extra money that the importer has to pay comes back by the way of export tax, and the country as a whole is not a loser. Whether the country pays more or not can be found out only by the change in the terms of trade, which are certainly not determined only by the exchange rate.

(25) That the capital goods will cost more to individual producers is not necessarily a disadvantage. To keep the currency overvalued is to give a continuous and indiscriminate subsidy to capital goods imports. This is rather a surprising policy in countries where governments favour labour-intensive methods of production as labour is supposed to be in unlimited supply. To the extent this view is mistaken and scarcity of wage-goods requires capital-intensive methods in subsistence economy, overvalued currencies have unwittingly made them choose more correct methods of production. However, for preferring more capital-intensive methods, no hidden and indiscriminate subsidy is required, and explicit subsidies, if necessary, can be adopted. One of the reasons of foreign exchange barrier is indeed the indiscriminate imports of all sorts of capital goods. When abundant investment projects, that do not require imported machinery, are held up due to a real fear of inflation, none need fear of slackening investment due to high prices of imported capital goods. If imported equipment costs more, the foreign exchange bottleneck can be widened, investment priority can be more clearly determined, replacement will be more cautious, and maintenance will be more careful. However desirable

is the capital-intensive method, as long as capital is more scarce than labour, it is neither possible nor desirable to use indiscriminately capital-intensive methods over the whole range of industries. To use complex automatic machinery to produce soft drinks or cosmetics is to create a foreign exchange barrier for the investment in steel plants or fertilizer factories. In India, for example, old manual method of making carbonated water is already obsolete, and one can see expensive imported machinery producing soft drinks even in small towns. Indian textile mills could find only one way of maintaining competitive prices in the international market— that was by using up-to-date automatic machinery imported from the U.S.A. With lower exchange rate, such use of capital-intensive method may turn out to be uneconomic, and more capital can be used for a better purpose.

(26) Furthermore, cheap imports of capital goods will discourage the domestic production of capital goods, and for the long-run economic development capital goods industry also has to be created and protected. Especially if the export-earnings are likely to remain stagnant—due to either demand or supply limitation— they will make a falling percentage of a rising national income. If investment solely depends on export-earnings, the rate of investment also will continuously decline. To avoid this immiserization of growth, some part of investment has to be diverted to capital goods production. This will mean a smaller rate of growth of consumption for some time but much larger growth once the capital goods industries are built.[13] For a small country it may not be possible to build and

---

[13]If I is the rate of investment in consumer goods and M is the rate of investment in capital goods that will eventually be used for the production of consumer goods, then

$$Ib_1 = \frac{dC}{dt}$$

and

$$Mb_2 = \frac{dI}{dt}$$

where b_1 and b_2 are respective output-capital ratios. If amount of investment is fixed (e.g., by limited imports of capital goods due to stagnant exports) and if all this investment is used for I, the C (production of consumer goods) will go up by a constant absolute rate of Ib_1; for instance, if I is 10 per cent and if $b_1 = 0.5$, then rate of growth of $C = 5$ per cent.

If all the investment is concentrated on M, then rate of growth of C will start at a much lower level, but this rate itself will be continuously rising, and hence eventually C will be much larger than in the previous case. As

$$Ib_1 = \frac{dC}{dt}$$

and

$$Mb_1b_2 = \frac{d^2C}{dt^2} \qquad \text{as } I = Mb_2t$$

For example, if $M = 10$ per cent and $b_2 = b_1 = 0.5$, then in the next period $I = 5$ per cent and $Ib_1 = 2.5$ per cent. If $b_2 = 0.25$, then $Ib_1 = 1.25$ per cent. But now I is not constant but will grow each period by 5 or 2.5 per cent, depending on b_2, and hence with time dC/dt also will rise. Therefore, it is not an ideal policy to confine one's interest to the very short run. Especially if limited foreign exchange is spent on importing consumer goods (or raw materials for the production of consumer goods), then C itself can stagnate and $(dC/dt) = 0$. This indeed seems to be happening in India where the import bill for raw materials and intermediate products is larger than the export earnings, and investment depends to a large extent on the inflow of foreign capital.

It may not be possible to divert all the possible investment in capital goods industries, but whatever the proportion so used, it can be quickly made up by the increasing rate of capital goods production. If sustain capital goods industries, and to that extent a small country will have to make its development programme more export-oriented than is necessary for a large country. However, wherever it is possible, the establishment of such industries need not be ignored. New techniques that are suitable for the particular needs of the backward countries today can rarely be devised unless there is a domestic capital goods industry. A country like India has a great possibility of starting such industries and even to build an export trade in this line. Devaluation will help both to create such an industry and also an export market.

(27) Devaluation may remove many reasons for which exchange controls become necessary. When imports and exports can be regulated by tariffs and excise taxes, and foreign travel of the residents is controlled by the usual passport-issuing authorities, the main need of exchange control may remain for controlling the outflow of capital. If native capital tends to go out, then the developing country must indeed scrutinize all her economic policies; however, as an immediate measure, every sort of control to stop the capital outflow may be justified. Nevertheless, the outflow that is generally feared is that of foreign capital. But, if the private capital has come in the underdeveloped countries when the currency was over-

---

$$I = Mb_2t$$

total I produced by M over a period of time will be

$$\int_0^t Mb_2t \, dt = \frac{Mb_2t^2}{2}$$

The I that is foregone due to continuous investment in M will be compensated at a time when

$$tM = \frac{Mb_2t^2}{2}$$

$$\therefore t = \frac{2}{b_2}$$

That is, investment diverted toward M will make itself good within 10 years if $b_2 = 0.2$ or within 20 years if $b_2 = 0.1$, etc. This result holds true whatever the M, 1 or 10 per cent or any other percentage.

The real problem about making up the lost investment arises in connection with the gestation period. Investment in consumer industries may be fruitful, say, within a year, but investment in capital goods industries may take five years before it produces the capital goods. Suppose gestation period in capital goods industries is K times longer than in consumer goods industries. Then by writing t' for time period in capital goods industry and t for consumer goods industry and M for yearly percentage of investment going into capital goods industry, we can write

$$I = KMb_2t' \qquad \text{and} \qquad Kt' = t$$

Then

$$\int_0^{t'} KMb_2t' \, dt = \frac{KMb_2t'^2}{2}$$

By setting this equal to the I lost over the periods concerned,

$$Mt = \frac{KMb_2t'^2}{2}$$

$$= MKt' = \frac{KMb_2t'^2}{2}$$

$$\therefore t' = \frac{2}{b^2}$$

so that if $t' = 10$ (if $b_2 = 0.2$) and if $K = 5$, then it will take 50 years to recover the investment that had gone into the capital goods. Hence the importance of time preference.

Cf. K. N. Raj and S. K. Sen, "Alternative Patterns of Growth Under Conditions of Stagnant Export Earnings," *Oxford Economic Papers*, N.S., Vol. XIII (1961), p. 43ff.

valued and when foreign exchange transactions were strictly controlled, there is no reason why capital should withdraw when the currency is correctly valued and when foreign exchange controls are removed. The freedom to withdraw the capital and the better confidence in the currency due to correct or even under-valuation of the currency may indeed increase the inflow of capital in the developing countries.

(28) Whether such an inflow is desirable is, however, another matter. Because, when the profits are sent out, the main source of further investment is lost, and even if profits are ploughed back for some time, sooner or later the foreign capitalist has to take back his profits and snap the chain of sustained development. This seems to be inevitable unless the businessmen are motivated by altruistic purpose or they themselves migrate to the developing country along with their capital. This does not mean that temporary foreign capital can never be useful for development. Its use in a crucial industry may justify all the subsequent drain on the savings and the foreign exchange, but by and large it can rarely lead to a sustained growth.[14] If the repatriation of profits and capital is prohibited by the developing country, foreign enterprises may squander the investible funds by giving large salaries to employees and for keeping good connections with the authorities. But most importantly, as foreign capital spreads by using the unrepatriated profits, more and more lines of production are closed to native entrepreneurs, and the development policy that discourages the native entrepreneurial talent is not likely to be correct in the long run. Moreover the dominance of economy by foreign capital is likely to create a popular demand for larger and larger public intervention in the economy if not outright nationalization of industries. For the planning authorities the easiest way to show results is to invite foreign capital irrespective of the long-run effects on investment and native entrepreneurship. Even the advanced countries like England, France, or Germany are chary about American investment in Europe, and the case cannot be much different for backward countries.

(29) Many times foreign capital is invited as a package deal to get not only foreign exchange but also to get the technical skill and managerial know-how in some complex industries. However, it seems like paying a high price if the ownership of the project itself has to be given away to the foreigner. This is especially not justified when the advanced countries are eager to help the backward nations with all the skill and technique that is required. Truman's "point four" programme and Kennedy's "peace corps" are evident proofs of this desire. Moreover, skill can always be hired in the free international market. It seems, therefore, that foreign capital is welcomed in the underdeveloped countries due mainly to their excessive

---

[14]This point is not entirely lost over the governments of the underdeveloped countries. For instance, Maurice Zinkin complains as follows: "Asian governments are apt to treat the foreign investor as a wild beast whom it is necessary to cage; without permission he is normally not allowed to invest at all, and even if he is allowed, he is checked by a whole series of leashes. He must take a proportion, perhaps a majority, of local capital, he must have a certain percentage of local employees, he must get permission to expand, or to locate his factory, or to rationalise his operations. . . . Foreign investment nevertheless continues. There are always some brave pioneers, and some firms who have no option." Maurice Zinkin, *Development for Free Asia*, issued under the auspices of the Institute of Pacific Relations (Fair Lawn, N.J., 1956), p. 52.

concern with the foreign exchange barrier to economic development. This is quite clear in the case where flight of foreign capital is supposed to be catastrophic. Once the industry is established, there is no need to worry even if foreign capital in that industry is pulled out. Due to the loss of foreign exchange required to complete the flight of foreign capital, new investment depending on capital imports may be hampered, but nothing happens to the investment that has already taken place in the country. As a matter of fact, a native entrepreneur will get this investment at a cheaper price from the withdrawing foreigner. It does not seem, therefore, to be a good policy to resort to foreign exchange control with a hope of using the foreign capital for economic development.

(30) This long discussion can be summed up as follows. Many developing countries today can be characterized as subsistence economies in the sense that most of the people in these countries are so poor that the income-elasticity of demand for wage-goods and especially for foodstuffs is very high. Increasing employment in such economies is possible only after increasing the production of wage-goods if inflation and unrest are to be avoided. "Unlimited" supply of labour, therefore, cannot be effectively used for increasing investment without reducing consumption, and conservation of labour is as essential in a subsistence economy as in a full employment labour-scarce economy. The barrier of domestic savings, therefore, is more important than foreign exchange barrier to the development effort. Import policies can be used to elicit larger savings from well-to-do people by shutting off the supply of nonessential consumer goods; for this purpose investment in similar import-substituting industries also has to be discouraged. At the least, demand for different nonessential items should be concentrated on few goods so that it will become possible to establish viable industries that may eventually enter the export market. Export of manufactures is not impossible if these new industries get a firm base of a home market. Export promotion of traditional goods, however, has to be cautious lest they affect the supply of wage-goods to the domestic economy. Indeed, such exports are to be discouraged, if they, directly or indirectly, use the resources required to raise the production of wage-goods. It is better to do this by export taxes rather than the present method of maintaining high exchange rates. Devaluation will help nontraditional exports, will discourage the indiscriminate use of imported capital goods, encourage the domestic production of capital equipment, and reduce the domestic consumption of nonessential exportables. More importantly, devaluation may help to abolish clumsy exchange controls and to reduce the reliance on quantitative restrictions on imports and exports. Abolition of exchange controls may lead to a larger inflow of private foreign capital, though it is doubtful whether the policy of encouraging foreign investment is desirable in the long run. Commercial policy is a beautiful and a delicate tool that can be effectively used for the development of a backward economy by skillful administrators, especially if they have a long-term plan for economic development.

Selection **28**

Exchange Controls
and Economic Development

JORGE MARSHALL

*From: International Economic Association, Economic Development
for Latin America; Proceedings of a Conference Held by the International Economic Association, Howard S. Ellis (ed.), assisted by Henry
C. Wallich (New York: St. Martin's, 1961), pp. 430–438. Reprinted by
permission of St. Martin's Press, Inc., Macmillan & Co., Ltd.*

I. INTRODUCTION AND DEFINITIONS

The expressions economic development and economic development policies
are used today with a variety of meanings.[1] Here, having in mind the economic
structure of most Latin American countries, economic development will be understood to mean the raising of the level of real income *per capita*, mainly through
direct and indirect measures aiming at an increase in the rate of capital formation.
There are three basic elements in the concept thus interpreted: first, a certain
degree of state intervention, in order to promote objectives which would not be
attained by the free play of economic forces; second, the direction of intervention
more towards the increase of real production than towards its redistribution; and
third, the position of paramount importance assigned to changing the institutional
factors, political, administrative, legal, social, educational, or economic, which
in a growing and developed economy can be taken as given, but which in an
undeveloped economy have to be changed if economic development is to be
possible. Recourse to intervention by the state does not necessarily imply regimentation of the economy, the public ownership of enterprises, or even socialism
in the conventional meaning of the word. State intervention or direction can be
made effective by indirect instruments of policy, which are quite compatible with
capitalism or private enterprise. Fiscal, monetary, commercial, exchange, investment, and other policies may be used as instruments for this purpose.

By exchange control is meant here direct government interference with incoming

---

[1] See Jacob Viner, *International Trade and Economic Development* (Oxford, 1953); see also
Celso Furtado, "Capital Formation and Economic Development," in *International Economic
Papers*, No. 4.

and/or outgoing foreign payments through prohibitions, quotas, or licensing, and/or the existence of an exchange rate system in which a single buying and selling exchange rate are not maintained, with a spread no larger than is necessary to pay for the services of brokers and other exchange dealers. The first type of control will be called quantitative restrictions and the second multiple exchange rates. For the purposes of this discussion I shall not attempt to identify these exchange control measures with any kind of legal exchange standard (national or international), nor shall I try to solve the host of problems which may be presented by this concept, such as the differences between exchange and import restrictions, or the question whether, in any given case, an exchange tax creates a multiple exchange rate situation.

It goes without saying that some forms of exchange control are quite strong and elaborate, while others are simple and of little practical significance.[2] Some countries control foreign exchange receipts and payments only for statistical purposes. Others, Peru, for example, have two exchange markets with only a very small spread between the two market rates; while others, Cuba, for example, maintain a tax on foreign exchange remittances. In this paper, when I speak of exchange controls I mean either quantitative restrictions which significantly reduce import demand and/or multiple exchange rates of a rather elaborate nature. It is rather arbitrary to make this distinction, but it seems more appropriate for the purpose of this discussion to consider countries like Peru, Venezuela, or Cuba as, in effect, not having exchange controls.

The discussion throughout will have in mind the condition of a country where the density of population is low, as is usual in Latin America, and in which the capital stock is rather small compared with the labour supply. Disguised unemployment is usually relatively high, and a substantial percentage of the labour force could be removed without causing a large reduction in the national product. In these circumstances, the manufacturing sector usually contributes less to the national income than agriculture and mining. Exports are generally an important part of the total product, consisting for the most part of one or a few agricultural or mining products. Technology is quite advanced in the export industries but much less developed elsewhere, especially in that sector of agriculture which supplies the home market and where rather primitive methods of exploitation prevail.

As part of the general economic policy of the government, exchange controls may be utilized as instruments to foster economic development in the sense indicated above. Methods of using exchange controls for this purpose and their shortcomings will be briefly described in the next two sections.

---

[2] No attempt has been made to measure precisely the tightness of exchange restrictions. One procedure might be to estimate the degree of overvaluation by comparing the actual exchange rate or rates with a computed purchasing power parity exchange rate which also took into account the effects of changes in custom tariffs. This method has two serious drawbacks: first, purchasing power parity rates are poor indicators of equilibrium rates, not only because of the technical deficiencies of price indices, but also because in the long run many changes occur in demand and cost functions; and, second, even if a good measure of currency overvaluation could be obtained, the necessary curtailment of the demand for foreign exchange will depend on the elasticity of demand within the relevant range.

• • •

II. Exchange Controls as an Instrument for Fostering Economic Development

The uses and abuses of exchange controls for the purpose of economic development have already been discussed in many places and specifically in an International Monetary Fund staff paper.[3] Here we shall summarize what has been said and perhaps elaborate one or two points which deserve further attention.

The ways in which exchange controls may be considered as helping economic development may be classified under six headings. First, exchange controls may be used as a balance-of-payments corrective. Exchange controls are likely to be used when balance-of-payments problems result from economic development policies or when a government attempts to improve its foreign exchange reserves position with a view to financing future developmental expenditures abroad.

An economic development programme is bound to produce a rise in domestic prices, even if monetary inflation is not the method selected to finance the programme.[4] Changes produced by the new pattern of income and expenditures may also affect the balance-of-payments unfavourably.[5] Such balance-of-payments problems do not have to be solved through exchange controls. If domestic stabilization policies are not feasible, equilibrium may be restored in the foreign accounts by devaluation of the exchange rate. The use of exchange control measures as a balance-of-payments corrective assumes the desirability of maintaining an over-valued exchange rate.

Examples of attempts to strengthen foreign exchange reserves through exchange controls with a view to financing development are less frequent, but essentially they do not differ from the case just described.

Second, exchange controls may be used to protect domestic economic activities. Exchange controls may be used to exclude foreign competitors in the interests of domestic industries which the development programme wishes to encourage. Protection may be given through straight prohibitions, quotas, or the maintenance of exchange rates which increase the internal supply prices of foreign goods.

Exchange controls, in the form of favourable export rates, may also be used to stimulate the growth of certain industries by enabling them to compete in foreign markets. Export quotas and prohibitions aimed at reserving a certain amount of supplies for the internal market may also be considered as illustrations in this category.

Third, exchange controls may be used to reshape import expenditures. Favourable licensing conditions or overvalued import exchange rates may be established

---

[3] See Margaret de Vries, *Restrictions and Economic Development in Underdeveloped Areas*, International Monetary Fund, ERD/53/1, March 4, 1953.

[4] See Harold Pilvin, *Inflation and Economic Development*, a paper presented to the Fourth Meeting of Central Bank Technicians, held in Washington and New York, April–May 1954.

[5] See Celso Furtado, *op. cit.*, p. 138ff., and R. Nurkse, *Problems of Capital Formation in Underdeveloped Countries* (Oxford, 1953), p. 104ff.

for imported capital goods and raw materials deemed necessary for economic development. The opposite treatment, or even complete import prohibitions, may be applied to nonessential or luxury goods. This policy is based on the assumption that the composition of total expenditure can thus be influenced, decreasing luxury consumption expenditure and increasing investment expenditure. Furthermore, when an overvalued exchange rate is maintained and import demand has to be curtailed, exchange controls may be used to ensure the use of the scarce supply of foreign exchange in the way most consistent with the economic development plans.

Fourth, exchange controls may be used to encourage domestic and foreign investment. Exchange controls were first established in most countries to prevent capital flights during the 1930's. Insofar as they still have that purpose, or insofar as they regulate the rate of remittances of amortization, interest, and profits with a view to having these funds reinvested within the country, they may be thought of as a part of an economic development programme.

Many countries with elaborate exchange control systems have established special treatment for new capital coming into the country, these regulations being intended to promote a larger inflow of foreign investments.

Fifth, exchange controls may be used as revenue-producing instruments. Exchange controls in the form of multiple exchange rates may be a source of fiscal revenue when there is a spread between the buying (or average buying) and the selling (or average selling) exchange rates.

The establishment of preferential exchange rates for government imports and/or payments may also be considered as a method of producing revenue for the government.

Another illustration of this type of exchange control is the widespread use of penalty export rates instead of export taxes, as a means of absorbing the profits of exporters or as an anti-inflationary instrument. If the revenue produced can be used to finance economic development expenditures, this type of exchange control may be considered to be a means of fostering economic development.

Sixth, exchange controls may be used as instruments for enlarging a protected regional market. Exchange control measures may be used to establish discriminatory regional trade and payments arrangements designed to protect certain industries and to enlarge their markets, thus providing economies of scale for new industries which the economic development programme wants to encourage. This type of policy involves the cooperation of at least two countries. It may take the form of a bilateral or a multilateral clearing settlement, especially when imports from the area covered by the payments system are permitted, while other imports are excluded.

III. SHORTCOMINGS OF EXCHANGE CONTROLS

For every exchange control measure there is some alternative which would produce equivalent economic effects which may be more desirable for other reasons. For example, in dealing with a balance-of-payments problem created by internal inflation, the results expected from exchange controls could be obtained by anti-inflationary monetary, fiscal, and wage policies. At the same time some of the shortcomings of exchange control would be avoided, and the problem would receive a more fundamental solution.

The very flexibility which may be regarded as an advantage of exchange controls for one or other of the purposes listed above should in fact be regarded as a disadvantage. The purpose of a policy, the details of which can be readily and quickly changed, will not be understood by the public, and its costs may not be immediately visible. Measures other than exchange controls, particularly taxes and subsidies, are usually less flexible in the sense that they are more difficult to impose, or, when once imposed, to change. This also means that they may be devised so as to give policy a more definite shape, to make its purpose clearer, and to permit an accurate weighing of advantages against costs. For example, if a certain activity is deemed to need a subsidy, it seems more appropriate to give the subsidy through the budget (after parliamentary approval) than by the device of a preferential exchange rate, which easily avoids public scrutiny.

Another general shortcoming of exchange controls in contrast with other measures is that the former throw doubt on the soundness of the currency and the financial policies of the country. This tends to discourage the flow of foreign capital which may be necessary to finance a higher rate of investment. No legal provision guaranteeing remittances of amortization and profits can be more effective in attracting foreign capital than sound financial policies and freedom of exchange. When a country is suffering from inflation, balance-of-payments difficulties, and strict controls, legal guarantees do not accomplish their objectives. Moreover, if the country has a free market parallel to the official exchange market, strict import restrictions may be circumvented.

When exchange controls take the form of quantitative restrictions, and the country lacks efficient or perhaps even honest administrative machinery—as is the case in many Latin American countries—exchange controls are a major disturbing element for the country's foreign trade and for many productive enterprises linked with or dependent on that trade. Foreign supplies are uncertain, export licences and appropriate exchange rates may not be forthcoming, and it may pay to produce for the domestic market rather than for export. Furthermore, the allocation of quotas is usually made on a historical basis, modified by administrative value judgments about essentiality. When exchange receipts decline, the tendency is to maintain the volume of essential imports, thus increasing their relative importance. If the price mechanism is not working adequately because of an overvalued exchange rate for these essential imports, there is likely to be excessive consumption of these imports. The country may thus be deprived of many import goods—such as spares, raw materials, and machinery—which are rated low by the administrative authorities, but which may be more important for development than some of the so-called essential imports.

Moreover, since exchange control authorities are subject to pressure from interested parties, clever entrepreneurs may conclude that it is to their advantage to spend time in obtaining a favourable administrative decision rather than in increasing output, improving the quality, or reducing the cost of their goods.

The difficulties of reaching rational administrative decisions and the inherent temptation to corruption are among the worst features of quantitative exchange controls. They have particularly detrimental effects upon any effort to increase output. These disadvantages can be diminished if a flexible exchange market or a different exchange rate is established. At the same time the unjustified profits which may arise from transactions in import quotas will be diverted to the government.

The effects of exchange controls are sometimes confined to the country applying them. In other cases the advantages which are the purpose of the policy may result in loss or disadvantage to other countries. This is the case when a country attempts to exploit its monopoly power, or depreciates one of its multiple exchange rates in order to get an advantage over foreign competitors. It is therefore always necessary to take into account the possibility of retaliation in one form or another.

The foregoing discussion has shown the disadvantages of exchange controls as compared with other policy measures, which would produce equivalent effects. There are also other shortcomings associated with the use of exchange controls for specific purposes.

The basic problems raised by the use of exchange controls as an instrument for protection need not be discussed here. They are the same as those that arise in any general discussion of tariff policy. It is also clear that exchange controls imposed for other reasons may have unwanted protective effects. If protection for industries which would have no chance of survival without it is condemned as harmful, it makes no difference whether this protection is provided through exchange controls or by other means.

Protective exchange control measures are particularly bad when they completely exclude foreign competition. In many Latin American countries, protection of this kind tends to create highly uneconomic industries and prevents any possibility of future readjustment. The problem is aggravated when the size of the protected market is favourable to a monopolistic structure in the country's industries.

Export quotas or prohibitions intended to protect domestic market supplies usually defeat the objectives of economic development, because their effect is usually to maintain a high level of consumption of certain goods at the expense of exports. But, though the resultant discouragement of exports may intensify balance-of-payments difficulties, it is scarcely possible for a government to ignore the political and social problems which arise if consumption is cut down.

When exchange controls in the form of multiple currency practices are used with the intention of determining the distribution of national expenditures, as between essential consumption, luxury consumption, and investment, they cannot attain their objective unless domestic measures having a similar objective are applied to domestic production. Even if the penalized imports are not domestically produced, there are other alternatives for luxury expenditure which may entirely defeat the purpose of encouraging productive investment. Another significant factor is that favourable import rates may tend to create quota profits in favour of privileged importers, while the abnormally low prices of favoured imported goods may retard the introduction of industries which would have been economically feasible.

One of the strongest cases for the use of multiple currency practices can be made when they have a revenue purpose[6] in a country which does not have a well-developed or well-organized fiscal system. Even under these circumstances, however, the general shortcomings of multiple currency practices remain valid, and it would be in the best interests of the country concerned to develop an adequate tax system as part of economic development itself as soon as circumstances permit.

The idea of widening the market for certain industries is no doubt commendable, and it may be the only way of eliminating inefficiencies resulting from the small size of certain plants producing for limited markets. But it does not follow that this objective can be best attained through discriminatory regional exchange arrangements. It would probably be more effective to adopt fiscal devices, or to give preferential customs treatment to the industries for which a wider market is desired. This could also provide an opportunity for laying the foundations of a regional custom union.[7] In this way the countries concerned might attain their objectives without foregoing the advantages of a fully convertible system of payments.

In reviewing the reasons for including exchange controls in an economic development programme, the correction of balance-of-payments disequilibrium overshadows all the others. Those countries which resort to strict exchange controls are usually those countries with payments difficulties which are the result of strong inflation—whether because of economic development or for other reasons—and an overvalued exchange rate or rates.[8] The exchange control practices of those countries which do not have balance-of-payments problems and which have imposed exchange controls for other reasons are unlikely to be very significant, and they could be readily replaced by other economic policy measures.

Unfortunately, however, exchange controls are an unsatisfactory solution for balance-of-payments problems. The only sound policy is to attempt economic development within a framework of financial stability.

---

[6] To absorb windfall profits accruing to exporters from booming export markets so that their income will be stabilized over time, or to tax export monopoly profits.

[7] For some economic problems raised by custom unions, see J. E. Meade, *The Theory of International Economic Policy*, Vol. II: *Trade and Welfare* (London, 1955), p. 521ff.; and Jacob Viner, *The Customs Union Issue* (New York, 1950), Chap. IV.

[8] The exchange rate or rates may be overvalued without inflation.

Selection **29**

International Commodity Agreements

J. E. MEADE

From: Lloyds Bank Review, *No. 73 (July 1964), pp. 28–42. Reprinted by permission of the* Lloyds Bank Review *and the author.*

THE NEED FOR ACTION

The prices of primary products, when they are traded frccly on uncontrolled world markets, are subject to violent fluctuations. Both the amounts produced and the amounts consumed of such products are typically rather insensitive to price changes, so that quite moderate shifts of world supply or demand may cause very great price changes before supply and demand are brought back into balance. Well-informed professional speculation, by carrying supplies from period of low to periods of high price, can partially, but only very partially, offset these fluctuations. Ill-informed and perverse speculation may accentuate the fluctuations in price.

Moreover, there have in the past been periods of years during which the prices of primary products have shown a perisistent trend (downwards or upwards) relatively to the prices of manufactured products, these price trends being determined by the balance of many structural changes in demand and supply conditions, both in primary production and in manufacture. Such price trends can be of the utmost importance to the countries producing primary products. A downward trend in the price of a particular primary product relatively to the prices of manufactures may well deprive a particular developing country of purchasing power over manufactured imports which is considerably greater than the total financial aid which it has been receiving for its economic development; and in recent years such downward price trends have been much in evidence, though the movement has now been reversed, at least for the time being.

EFFECTS OF PRICE FALLS ON PRODUCERS

The damage which may be done by a price fall to a country which is producing a primary product can take three distinct, though closely related, forms.

First, a fall in a primary-product price can put a very severe strain on the balance of payments of a country whose exports consist very largely of that product.

Secondly, the financial problem of the balance of payments can (though often only with great difficulty) be overcome (1) by a drastic monetary deflation which discourages investment in new machinery and makes the citizens unable to afford the purchase of imported consumption goods or (2) by a governmental restriction of imports which directly deprives the country either of consumption goods or of capital goods needed for economic development or (3) by so great a depreciation of the country's currency in terms of other countries' currencies that the citizens can no longer afford the excessively high prices for imports of manufactured consumption goods or of capital goods for economic development. But in all these cases there would, of course, be a great reduction in the standard of living in the country or in its programme of capital development. Its real income will have been greatly reduced. In the extreme case of Mauritius a single product (sugar) accounts for virtually the whole of Mauritian exports, and these exports account for virtually one-half of the Mauritian national income. A 50 per cent fall in the price of sugar would cause a 25 per cent fall in the real income available in Mauritius for consumption or capital development.

Finally, apart from the general impact on the producing country's balance of payments and real income, there may well be a very serious problem for the particular section of the community which produces the primary product. Even if sugar exports were a relatively small proportion of a country's total exports and total national product, a fall in the price of sugar might inflict great damage on a concentrated and isolated group of producers who were unable to move readily to alternative occupations. This may cause concentrated distress which requires some relief. Fluctuations and uncertainty in selling prices may also discourage efficient planned production in the industry concerned.

These three forms of damage which primary-producing countries may suffer from falls in the prices of primary products have, of course, their obverses in the three forms of damage which the importing countries may suffer from rises in such prices.

How Price Rises Damage Importers

A rise in the price of a primary product will increase the cost of its imports and so the strain on the balance-of-payments of an importing country if it cannot readily produce the supplies for itself or turn to the use of a substitute product. Even, however, if it is successful in meeting the balance-of-payments strain, the rise in the cost of its imported supplies of the product will reduce its real income, while those of its citizens who rely to an exceptional degree on the use of this product may be exceptionally hard hit.

But there are two reasons for believing that the damage done to the importing countries by a given rise in price is much more tolerable than the damage done to the exporting countries by an equal fall in price.

First, in a number of cases the real income per head is higher in the importing countries (which are often the highly developed industrialized countries) than in the exporting countries (which are often the underdeveloped unindustrialized

countries). In these cases, a dollar's loss to the former countries with a high standard of living can properly be counted as of less importance than a dollar's gain
to the latter countries with a low standard of living.

But this argument must be applied with great care. There is a very serious risk
that it may be tragically misapplied in the coming years. For a very large and
important group of primary products (namely, the temperate-zone foodstuffs such
as wheat and similar cereals, meat, and dairy produce) the net exporters are those
wealthy developed countries which are rich both in capital and land (for example,
Canada, the United States, Australia, New Zealand). Many less developed countries with lower standards of living are net importers. Moreover, with the present
population explosion and pressure on natural resources in many of these latter
countries, it is greatly to be hoped that the wealthier temperate-zone countries
will open their markets more and more widely to the simpler labour-intensive
manufactures of the less developed countries and will provide aid to these countries. This will enable the latter to purchase not only the more elaborate manufactured capital goods but also some of their needed supplies of foodstuffs in increasing quantities from the wealthy temperate-zone granaries of the world. It would
be a tragic mistake to regard the maintenance of the prices of temperate-zone
foodstuffs as a way of helping the poor at the expense of the rich; the position is
already the reverse and in a sane commercial world will become increasingly so.

Moreover, within a primary-producing underdeveloped economy there are
quite likely to be much greater disparities in the distribution of income and wealth
than in the industrialized developed economies. In some sugar-producing territories a rise in the price of sugar will raise the real incomes of the extremely poor
cane-cutter and the extremely rich owner of the land and processing equipment
on the sugar estate in a sugar-producing community; in the industrialized importing
countries it will lower the real incomes of many working and middle-class families
who are nothing like as poor as the cane-cutters nor as rich as the estate owners
in the sugar-producing community. A rise in the price of sugar probably transfers
income from the moderately well-off to the very poor and the very rich.

There is, however, a second and much more generally valid reason why the
damage caused to consumers of primary products by a rise in the price of the
product is more tolerable than the damage done to the producers by an equal fall
in price. The former is much less concentrated than the latter. This is outstandingly
true of individuals. The producer, whether he be the poor cane-cutter or the rich
estate owner, may rely almost 100 per cent on the price of sugar for his income;
there is no family in the importing countries which spends the whole of its income
on sugar. A fall in the price of sugar will ruin a limited number of persons. A
rise in the price of sugar will slightly raise the cost of living to a very large number
of persons. This difference in the degree of concentration is true also of whole
economies. Practically 100 per cent of Mauritian export earnings are sales of sugar
and 50 per cent of Mauritian income is derived from sugar production; in an
importing country like the United Kingdom, imports of sugar account for only
small fractions of total imports and of total national expenditure. A fall in the
price of sugar would play havoc with the Mauritian balance-of-payments and

national income, while it would have a very limited effect upon the over-all balance of payments and national income of each importing country.

BUFFER STOCKS

It is for these reasons most desirable that, as part of any new arrangements for world commerce, steps should be taken to offset the damaging effects of sharp fluctuations in the prices of primary products and to mitigate the effects of any persistent downward trends in such prices. What measures could be taken for this purpose? International commodity arrangements in the past have been in the main based upon either or both of two principles.

First, a buffer stock arrangement can be used to mitigate fluctuations in the price of a particular primary product. The management of the stock is endowed in the first place with certain financial resources which can be used to buy up the commodity for storage when its price is abnormally low and for resale later when its price is abnormally high. Such action can undoubtedly be of great use in suitable cases. It is to be hoped that the use of this weapon will be extended in the future. But this weapon has its limitations.

The success of such schemes rests upon the wisdom (and resistance to pressure from interested parties) of the management or the designers of the rules for the operation of the scheme. It can succeed only if there is sufficient foresight and independence of action to ensure that purchases are made only when present prices are low relatively to future prices, and sales are made only when present prices are in fact high relatively to future prices. Such foresight is by no means easy. A buffer stock scheme, moreover, can operate only in the case of commodities for which the cost of storage is not excessive. There is always some cost involved in the interest on the capital invested in the stock; but in the cases in which warehousing space, refrigeration, protection against vermin, and other similar costs are concerned, the scheme may well become excessively costly. Buffer stock schemes should in any case be operated only so as to mitigate fluctuations in price. They cannot be properly used to mitigate or offset the damaging effects of a persistent trend in price. Thus if there is a persistent downward trend in the price of a product, purchases by a buffer stock could reduce the rate at which the price is allowed to fall, but would lead only to an accumulation of stock which must be sold at a still lower price in the future.

RESTRICTION SCHEMES

The second type of arrangement is the agreed restriction of the quantity produced or exported by the primary-producing countries. When a world surplus supply of a product occurs or threatens to occur, the governments of the countries which produce the product can get together and agree that each will intervene in its own national market in such a way as to restrict the amount produced or the amount exported to some agreed quota. By thus restricting the supplies coming forward for sale, the price of the product can be maintained at a higher level; and if, as is usually the case at least in the short run, the demand for the product is inelastic, the exporting countries receive a larger total value for a smaller volume of exports and the producers a larger total income for a smaller volume of output.

If no alternative action is available, such an arrangement may often be better than doing nothing, particularly in an emergency situation in which the price of a product on which many economies largely depend would otherwise totally collapse. In this sense such schemes may often deserve every support. But it will be argued in the next section that the alternative arrangements there described provide a good basis for dealing with situations of this kind, that they may make it unnecessary to resort to restriction schemes, and that they are at the least a most helpful supplement to any restriction schemes.

Restriction schemes are in any case subject to important difficulties. Such schemes are in fact extremely difficult to maintain. Past experience suggests this, and the reason is easy to understand. If all producers are withholding supplies and thus maintaining a profitable price, it becomes exceedingly attractive to any individual producing country to refuse to join the scheme and to enjoy the high price on an unlimited output and export volume. A restriction scheme may start with all the producers in it except for one or two small producers, but this may give an opportunity for these outside producers greatly to expand their output and export. The quotas of the producers in the agreement will have to be reduced to maintain the prices as the sales of the outsiders expand. It becomes more and more attractive to the individual insider to join the outsiders. Attempts may be made to prevent this by means of an agreement which includes the main importing countries, which, in return for the opportunity thus gained in controlling the degree of restriction exercised by the producers, agree to police the scheme by undertaking to purchase only from the inside producers. The outside producers will then be selling at lower prices than the inside producers, and there will be a great incentive on individual importing countries to stay out of the agreement in order to purchase these cheaper supplies. This product may well be a raw material which enables an industrialized country that obtains cheaper supplies to undercut on the export market for manufactures those rivals purchasing their raw material supplies at the higher price, and in such a case there will be a great incentive for the importer countries to withdraw from their obligations to police the scheme. A pure restriction scheme is thus unlikely to be able to maintain for any very long period of time a price substantially above the price which would otherwise clear the world market.

There is a second reason why a restriction scheme, though it may be feasible and necessary as an emergency rescue operation, may be unsuitable for permanent operation. The elasticity of demand for most primary products is certainly small in the short run, but in the long run the response of purchasers to the price may be much greater. A rise in the price of natural rubber in the short run is unlikely to affect very appreciably the amount of natural rubber which is purchased for use in the motorcar and other industries. But if the higher price persists and is expected to persist, it may make profitable a substantial expansion in the manufacturing capacity for synthetic rubber. It is an outstanding feature of modern technological advance to devise alternative ways of producing a needed material or to devise ways in which a need can be satisfied by the use of an alternative material.

Finally, restriction schemes, if they are maintained for long, make it very difficult to prevent serious inefficiencies in the production of the primary product concerned. Production or export quotas are likely to be fixed on the basis of past performance. Each producing country has a limited quota and it is thus impossible for the producing countries in which costs of production are reduced to expand at the expense of those in which costs of production rise or fall less rapidly. Moreover, this phenomenon is likely to appear within each producing country. If the government of a country undertakes that its private enterprise producers will not in total produce or export more than a given national quota, it must introduce some licensing or similar scheme to restrict the output or exports of each individual producer. The allocation of these subquotas within the country, if, as is likely, it is arranged on the basis of past performance, will make it difficult for the progressive producer to expand at the cost of the stagnant.[1] Attempts can be made from time to time to revise the distribution of international quotas between the producing countries and of national quotas between the individual producers with the purpose of allowing low-cost producers to expand at the expense of their high-cost rivals. But attempts to do this by governmental agreement and administrative action are much less likely to be effective than the spur of competition in a world market.

PRICE COMPENSATION AGREEMENTS

The price mechanism always plays a dual role. A rise in a price affects the distribution of income, benefiting producers at the expense of consumers. It also affects the efficiency of the economic system, encouraging the more effective production and the more economical use of what is especially scarce. In no set of markets is this distinction more noticeable than in the world markets for primary products. Because of the concentration of production and the short-run inflexibilities of outputs and of demands, the "distributional" effects of price changes may play havoc with the balance of payments and the real income of whole communities and may thus greatly impede the programmes for economic development of such countries. But, at the same time, to prevent the longer-run trends of supply and demand from determining the prices of the products in world markets may not only be a difficult task but, if successful, may introduce serious "inefficiencies" into the world economy. In any case there is no reason whatever for believing that the prices which are desirable on "distributional" grounds are the same as those which are desirable on "efficiency" grounds.

It is the purpose of this paper to suggest an extremely simple method of divorcing

---

[1] This difficulty could be surmounted by the auctioning of licences to produce to the individual producers. The more efficient would outbid the less efficient. But this method of allocation of quotas is not a popular one, and it would, of course, mean that the actual producers of the product did not get the advantage of the higher price of the product. Their competition for licences could ruin them just as effectively as their competition for markets.

these two aspects of price variation. Consider a case in which one country (Urbania) imports a primary product (that—following Lord Keynes—may be called Commod) which another country (Ruritania) exports. Their two governments agree upon a sliding scale whereby as the world price of Commod falls further and further below a certain figure the government of Urbania will pay an increasing sum of money to the government of Ruritania, and as the world price of Commod rises further and further above a certain figure the government of Ruritania will pay an increasing sum of money to the government of Urbania. One possible sliding scale—but by no means the only possible one—could be devised on the following lines. The two governments would agree on what was a "normal volume" of exports of Commod from Ruritania to Urbania; they would agree on what was a "standard price" to expect for Commod; and they would then devise a sliding scale so that the government of Urbania was paying to the government of Ruritania each month an amount of money which was equal to the shortfall below the "standard price" of the world price of Commod on the "normal volume" of trade in Commod between the two countries. Conversely, the government of Ruritania would pay to the government of Urbania an amount equal to any excess of the world price over the "standard price" as reckoned on the "normal volume" of trade between them.

The scheme has been illustrated in the above example in a form which gives complete compensation. But this is, of course, not necessary. The two governments might agree on a sliding scale whereby, say, only one-half of the variation in the price of the "normal volume" of trade between them was compensated by inter-governmental transfers.

DISTRIBUTIONAL EFFECTS

Arrangements of this kind would directly divorce the "distributional" from the "efficiency" effects of changes in the world price of Commod. The two governments could allow their citizens to buy and sell Commod freely in world markets at the ruling world price. But as far as the balances of payments and national incomes of Urbania and Ruritania were concerned, the effect of a change in the world price of Commod would be entirely or partially offset, insofar as the normal volume of trade between Urbania and Ruritania was concerned. For example, if the world price of Commod fell below the agreed standard, Urbanian citizens would obtain cheaper supplies of Commod, but the government of Urbania would have to raise additional revenue from them to pay over to the government of Ruritania. At the same time the Ruritanian producers of Commod would be receiving smaller earnings from their sales of Commod, but the Ruritanian government would be receiving an income from Urbania. The two governments would be entirely free to raise, and to dispose of, the funds transferred between them in any manner they choose. The Urbanian government could, if it so desired, raise the additional revenue by a levy on its citizens' consumption of Commod, in which case the consumers who would have gained from the fall in price will to this extent no longer do so. The Ruritanian government could, if it so desired, use its receipt of revenue from Urbania to supplement the incomes of its producers of Commod; but, if it so desired, it could use the revenue so received to finance other forms of economic development, or it could use the revenue partly for the one and partly for the other purpose.

The scheme thus copes with the distributional aspects of price changes, but it begs no questions about the efficiency aspects of price changes. What is done in that respect depends upon the action of the national governments concerned. They can offset the price changes to the particular consumers and producers concerned or they can allow world price changes to have their full effect in their own national markets for Commod.

EXTENSION ON MULTILATERAL BASIS

The scheme has been expounded above in the simplest from of a bilateral agreement between one importing and one exporting country. It is a great virtue of the scheme that it could take this limited from without in any way discriminating in world trade in Commod, even if there were many other importers and exporters of Commod. In this case it would simply be an arrangement whereby these two countries agreed to offset the "distributional" impact between them of a change in the price of Commod. But on the other hand there is, of course, nothing to prevent a fully multilateral international agreement on these lines. The governments of all the exporting and all the importing countries of Commod could jointly agree on a standard price and, for each participating country, on a normal quantity of import or of export of Commod for that country (the total of normal imports being equal to the total of normal exports). They could agree on a sliding scale according to which, when the world price of Commod was low, the governments of the importing countries paid contributions into a fund from which the governments of the exporting countries drew out an equal total sum—and conversely, if the price of Commod was high.

Many intermediate groupings are possible, covering more than two countries but less than all the countries concerned. Thus a Commonwealth Sugar Agreement could be arranged in which all Commonwealth imports and exports of sugar take place on the world market at the world price, but in which the governments of the importing members made transfer payments to the governments of the exporting members (and vice versa), according to the world price of sugar at which the trade was actually conducted. An outstanding advantage of the proposed scheme is that a bilateral or limited multilateral arrangement can be maintained without breakdown and can be arranged in such a way that it does no damage to outsiders and in no way discriminates in the flows of world trade.

A further advantage of compensation schemes of this straight-forward direct type is that they are in no way incompatible with other schemes. Thus if the world price of Commod is being partially stabilized by a buffer stock scheme or if it is being maintained by a restriction scheme, this in no way prevents the operation of direct compensation schemes, though, of course, the actual payments of compensation may be smaller because of the effect of the buffer stock or of the production or export quotas on the world price. It is, however, to be hoped that the successful initiation of a compensation scheme might often avoid the necessity for a restriction scheme, thus allowing the "efficiency" effects of price movements to have their full play.

RESTRICTION SCHEMES AND COMPENSATION SCHEMES

It is not, of course, claimed that compensation schemes will automatically make restriction schemes pointless. Thus a fully multilateral compensation scheme for wheat might set as the standard price what was expected to be the price which would equate supply to demand for wheat over the average of, say, the next five years. Its effect would then be to offset the repercussions on balances of payments and national incomes of day-to-day divergencies of the world price from the standard price. But this would not, of course, prevent unforeseen adverse changes in the underlying conditions of world supply and demand from causing a persistently low world wheat price. If, at the end of the five-year period, when the compensation scheme came up for renewal, the "standard price" were not reduced, then the compensation scheme would become one under which the importing countries persistently subsidized the exporting countries. If the "standard price" were reduced to correspond with the now lower expected world price, then a persistently lower value of exports and of national income would be experienced by the producing countries, unless this was offset by a restriction scheme.

There would then be three possibilities: to accept the long-run reduction in the export receipts and incomes of wheat producers; or to maintain these by a compensation scheme which set a "standard price" on the average persistently above the world price ruling over an average of years; or to agree to a restriction scheme. But there is no reason to believe that the importing countries would lose more by accepting a "standard price" rather unduly favourable to the producers (the second alternative) than by accepting the raising of prices against them by the restriction of production or export (the third alternative).

FLEXIBILITY OF COMPENSATION SCHEMES

Thus in its treatment of a persistent trend in the price of a primary product a compensation scheme can be very flexible. For example, the "standard price" could be set at what was initially a generously high level (in order to provide funds to the governments of the exporting countries to maintain the incomes of their producers), but at the same time it could be agreed that this standard price should be gradually lowered from year to year so that this persistent subsidy to the producers by the consuming countries was gradually tapered off. In any case, even if a restriction scheme were operated, it would be possible and perhaps desirable to operate simultaneously a compensation scheme to offset the effects of fluctuations in the world price around the higher average level maintained by the restriction.

There is one other way in which a compensation scheme could show great flexibility. At the one extreme, it might constitute a purely stabilizing device for offsetting the effects of a fluctuation in price on the balances of payments and national incomes of a group of importing and exporting countries. At the other extreme, it could be turned into a device for the grant of financial aid from a group of industrialized importing countries to a group of unindustrialized exporting countries, the amount of the aid varying, however, according to the balance of payments and national income needs of the latter countries.

To take a possible example of the former type of agreement: wheat is a commodity which is produced largely by one group of rich highly developed countries and consumed largely by another group of rich highly developed countries. A compensation agreement for wheat might, therefore, be expected to be based on a sliding scale which, on the average, caused the transfers from exporters to importers (in times of high prices) to be equal to the transfers from importers to exporters (in times of low prices).

But there may be a primary product (let us call it Commod) which is produced by relatively poor underdeveloped countries and consumed by relatively rich developed countries, and it may be the desire of the latter to grant financial aid to the former. Nevertheless, it may be very desirable that more aid should be given if the price of Commod is low and less aid if the price of Commod is high, since the needs of the exporting countries and the ability to pay of the importing countries will both be lower when the price of Commod is high. This result can, of course, be brought about by an appropriate choice of sliding scale under a compensation agreement.

The basic idea of compensation agreements is not, of course new. This was the principle which lay behind the first wheat agreements after the second world war. Trade in wheat could be conducted at world prices, but when the world price fell below a certain level, the governments of the importing countries were obliged to pay a higher price for a certain quota of their imports and exporting countries had the right to sell corresponding quotas of their exports at a similar higher price; and conversely when the world price of wheat rose above a certain predetermined level. In essence, this was compensation by the governments of importing countries to the governments of exporting countries when the price of wheat was low; and vice versa when the price of wheat was high. But the arrangement was unnecessarily complicated by making the government-to-government compensation operate through obligations by exporting governments to provide some relatively cheap wheat when the world price was high and by importing governments to accept some relatively expensive wheat when the world price was low. These provisions constituted a set of quite unnecessary obligations for governmental interventions in the wheat markets. Much simpler is direct financial compensation, leaving it open to national governments to intervene or not to intervene in their national markets as they think fit.

COMPENSATORY FINANCE

More recently, important proposals for more general schemes of compensatory financing have been made by two groups of experts.[2] Under such arrangements countries whose export earnings fluctuated widely as a result of fluctuations in their trade in primary products would receive special financial support in times of low export earnings, all or part of which they would repay in times of high export earnings. Partly in response to these suggestions, the International Monetary Fund has made special arrangements to enable countries whose export earnings decline as a result of fluctuations in the trade in primary products to borrow for short periods more readily from the Fund.[3] These comprehensive and general financial arrangements have one great advantage over the price compensation agreements proposed in the previous section of this paper. They take account of fluctuations in the volume, as well as in the price, of exports of a primary-producing country.

What one wants to offset are fluctuations and declines in the total value of a country's export earnings. The commodity compensation agreements proposed above offset only fluctuations in the price of exports. Whether or not this is satisfactory will depend upon the conditions which have caused the change in export prices. Changes in the world price of a commodity must arise either from changes in conditions of demand or from changes in conditions of supply for that commodity. Insofar as price changes are due to changes in demand in the importing countries, price compensation agreements are bound to be helpful. If the demand for a primary product falls, exporting countries may suffer both from a fall in price and from a fall in the quantity sold. An agreement which compensated for the fall in the price but not for the fall in the volume would at least work in the right direction. Moreover, if the elasticity of supply is small, the price will fall much more than the volume; and a price compensation scheme would, therefore, make a correction in the right direction and for the greater part of the change.

But insofar as a change in the world price of a commodity is due to a change in conditions of supply, a price compensation scheme might conceivably work in a perverse manner. For example, suppose that there were exceptionally good harvests of wheat throughout the world; world supplies of wheat are increased and the price of wheat falls. If, however, the elasticity of demand for wheat were high—as is almost certainly not the case—the price might fall only a little, so that the increased volume of exports of wheat more than offset the fall in the

---

[2] United Nations, *International Compensation for Fluctuations in Commodity Trade* (Report by a Committee of Experts, New York, 1961). Organization of American States, *Final Report of the Group of Experts on the Stabilization of Export Receipts* (Washington, D.C., 1962).

[3] International Monetary Fund, *Compensatory Financing of Export Fluctuations* (Washington, D.C., 1963). The United Kingdom government has put forward proposals to the United Nations Conference on Trade and Development whereby such short-term finance might be supplemented by longer-term finance in those cases in which the export earnings of an underdeveloped country suffered a protracted decline which threatened to impede its programme for economic development.

price of wheat, with a rise in the export earnings of the wheat-producing countries. To compensate for the price fall would add still further funds to their already inflated export earnings. If, however, as is more probable, the price elasticity of demand for wheat is low, the increased volume of exports will lead to a heavy fall in price and total export earnings will fall. Price compensation would supplement the fallen export earnings; but in this case, if price compensation were complete, export earnings would, of course, be overcompensated, since exporting countries would be getting the equivalent of the previous price on the larger volume of exports. A sliding scale which gave only partial price compensation would be needed to stabilize export earnings.

While the elasticity of demand for the world's exports of a primary product is likely to be low, this may well not be true for the exports of a single country. Suppose that as a result of local cyclones Mauritian exports of sugar are halved. This may have only a moderate effect in reducing world supplies and so only a moderate effect in raising the world price of sugar. The value of Mauritian exports would be disastrously reduced, in spite of a small rise in the world price. It would be perverse in the extreme if, because of the rise in the world price of sugar, the Mauritian government had to pay compensation to the United Kingdom government at a time when the value of her exports had slumped.

General schemes for compensatory finance would not be subject to these dangers. They would compensate for a worsening or an improvement in the total *value* of a country's exports and not merely in the *price* of its exports. On the other hand, one of the main attractions of price compensation agreements is their simplicity and ease of administration. Intergovernmental transfers of funds according to changes in a world price index are easy to administer and it would not normally be possible for an individual country to affect the world price in a way which would enable it to gain improperly from the arrangement. This, unfortunately, would no longer be true if the arrangement were based on the value of a country's exports. A country might well be more ready to adopt policies which would in fact result in a decline in the value of its exports if it knew that such a decline would automatically be compensated by an intergovernmental transfer of funds to it.

CONCLUSION

We may conclude (1) that a price compensation agreement is wholly appropriate for a commodity primarily subject to fluctuations on the demand side; (2) that, provided that the elasticity of demand for the world supply is low, a price compensation agreement can be devised to maintain and stabilize total world export earnings in the face of changes in world supply conditions; but (3) that price compensation agreements cannot cope with (and indeed may even somewhat intensify) the problems which arise from local fluctuations in the supply conditions in individual producing countries. Problems of this kind must be covered by other measures. Price compensation agreements have the great advantage of extreme simplicity and flexibility. Above all, they could be started on a very restricted scale but be gradually expanded into a world-wide network covering many products and many countries. The ideal system would no doubt be to combine such a network of particular agreements with a general scheme for compensatory finance. There is no incompatibility between price compensation agreements and a general scheme of compensatory finance. The two measures complement each other; the existence of a network of price compensation agreements would greatly reduce the financial calls on any fund set up to provide general compensation against fluctuations in total export earnings. The fund would thus be able to use its limited resources in a more effective manner to deal with those cases which the network of price compensation agreements did not, and perhaps could not, cover.

Selection **30**

Trade Preferences for Manufactured Goods

HARRY G. JOHNSON

From: Economic Policies Toward Less Developed Countries (*Washington, D.C.: Brookings Institution, 1967*), pp. *163–170, 181–184, and 204–211.* Reprinted by permission of the Brookings Institution.

The preparatory work for the United Nations Conference on Trade and Development, and the conference itself, produced two proposals for changes in policy with respect to trade in manufactured products. The more important, novel, and controversial proposal, on which the conference was unable to reach agreement, was for the establishment of preferences in the markets of developed countries for exports of manufactures and semi-manufactures by the less developed countries. The other proposal was for preferential arrangements for trade among the less developed countries in manufactured products. This proposal attracted relatively little discussion, presumably because it involves no change in the trade policies of the developed countries, but merely an extension of their tolerance of the protectionist policies of the less developed countries to the sanctioning of overt discrimination against their exports.

Both proposals violate the nondiscrimination principle of the General Agreement on Tariffs and Trade and the GATT ban on new preferential arrangements other than customs unions and free trade areas embracing the bulk of the trade of the participating countries. This, however, does not mean that the proposed trading arrangements would necessarily be economically disadvantageous. The postwar development of the theory of customs unions and of commercial policy changes, culminating in the theory of second best, has shown that in a tariff-ridden world economy there is no a priori reason for believing that nondiscrimination among import sources is economically superior to discriminatory trading arrangements. It has demonstrated also that the question of whether a discriminatory tariff reduction improves or worsens the efficiency and economic welfare of the countries involved and the world as a whole depends on the empirical circumstances of the particular case.

Both the theory of second best and modern welfare economics (as well as ordinary common sense) indicate that policy changes that secure desirable results in terms of income distribution or other objectives at the cost of reduced economic efficiency may constitute improvements on a balance of gain and loss and may legitimately be recommended if no more efficient method of achieving the same objectives is feasible or acceptable. Finally, inconsistency with GATT principles is not an insuperable institutional objection to the proposals for changes, since GATT principles may be modified by the contracting parties if such modification serves the basic objectives of the Agreement; under Article XXV of the Agreement a member may be relieved of its obligations under GATT by a two-thirds majority vote of the members, a majority which the less developed countries command.

[The following] considers the two proposals for altering existing arrangements governing trade in manufactured goods. Attention is devoted primarily to the possibilities of preferential treatment of exports of manufactured and semi-manufactured goods by less developed to developed countries as a means of promoting the growth of the less developed countries. Some brief observations only are offered on the subject of preferential arrangements for trade in manufactured goods among less developed countries.

TRADE PREFERENCES IN DEVELOPED-COUNTRY MARKETS

At the United Nations Conference on Trade and Development, the U.S. delegation adopted a position of adamant opposition to the demand of the less developed countries for preferences for their exports of manufactured and semi-manufactured goods. This position has subsequently been reiterated by official spokesmen and defended, supported, or rationalized, at least in broad terms, by various academic experts.[1]

Apart from the traditional commitment of the United States to the principle of nondiscrimination, which is largely responsible for its dogmatic stance on the question, the reasons underlying American opposition to or skepticism about the desirability and probable contribution of preferences to the development of the less developed countries are of two broad sorts: administrative-political and economic. The administrative-political arguments possess a certain prima facie cogency; the economic arguments, on the other hand, appear to have been insufficiently thought out and to have been strongly influenced by the political convenience of the conclusion they arrive at.

Administrative and Political Arguments Against Preferences

The chief administrative and political arguments against the adoption of preferences for manufactured exports by less developed countries are four in number.[2]

---

[1] For a dispassionate exploration of the possibility of assisting the less developed countries by trade preferences in manufactured goods, concluding with extreme skepticism, see Gardner Patterson, "Would Tariff Preferences Help Economic Development?" *Lloyds Bank Review*, No. 76 (April 1965), pp. 18–30. The argument in this chapter draws on Patterson's exposition, though disagreeing with his central theme.

[2] G. Patterson, *op. cit.*, pp. 28–30. Patterson presents these as "costs" of preferential arrangements, rather than as arguments against them.

In the first place it is argued that the establishment of preferences would inevitably generate—and in fact discussion of them has already generated—serious political frictions among and between the developed and the less developed nations. Among the developed countries, some favor preferences for selected products only and others preferences for all manufactures; some favor nondiscriminatory preferences for all less developed countries and others preferences for selected less developed countries or preferences differentiated according to each country's stage of development. Moreover, some developed countries are pecularly vulnerable to the discrimination against their manufactured exports that preferences for less developed countries would invoke. The important cases are Japan, which exports goods of a type closely competitive with the labor-intensive goods in which the less developed countries have a comparative advantage, and countries such as Canada and Australia, which, though developed, tend to be weak competitors in the world market for manufactures.

Among the less developed countries, for their part, there are conflicts of interest between the members of the British Commonwealth and the associated overseas territories of the Common Market, which currently enjoy preferences, respectively, in the markets of the United Kingdom and the Common Market countries that they would stand to lose, and other less developed countries that would tend to gain from preferences, partly at their expense. There are also conflicts between the more advanced and the more backward less developed countries, since the former stand to gain more and the latter less, the freer the competition between less developed countries allowed by the preferential arrangements adopted. A serious attempt to initiate preferences for manufactured exports by less developed countries would undoubtedly exacerbate these frictions. On the other hand, it can be argued that if preferential arrangements promise to yield a significant contribution to the economic development of the less developed countries, these frictions should be resolvable by the normal procedures of international negotiation; if necessary, measures could be devised to compensate developed or less developed countries adversely affected by the arrangements.

In the second place it is argued, quite convincingly, that preferential arrangements of the type proposed would involve a great deal of governmental surveillance and control of trade and correspondingly large administrative costs. The arrangements, it is asserted, would entail exceptions for certain commodities, require validation of the origins of commodities enjoying the preferences, and probably necessitate a complex system of quotas to prevent undue disturbance of domestic markets and to equalize the distribution of the benefits of preferred market entry among the beneficiary less developed countries. These administrative problems and costs, however, have to be weighed against the potential contribution of the arrangements to the growth of the less developed countries.

In the third place, it is argued, the establishment of preferences would create powerful vested interests opposed to further nondiscriminatory tariff reduction through GATT, since such reduction would reduce the value of the preferences enjoyed by the less developed countries. This argument, however, does not present the whole picture. The vested interests would be those of the less developed countries which could only exert political pressure externally on the developed countries. They would be bound to be less powerful than the domestic interests now vested in national tariffs. Moreover, once these national vested interests were subordinated, domestic political pressures for all-round reduction of trade barriers might be strengthened. Further, the argument assumes that in the absence of preferences there would be a strong inclination on the part of the developed countries to pursue trade liberalization through GATT. This is a questionable assumption, for it is very possible that an unsatisfactory outcome of the Kennedy Round and the unwillingness of the United States and other developed countries to reduce tariffs unilaterally on a most-favored-nation basis may leave preferential trading arrangements as the only feasible and acceptable method of assisting the less developed countries through changes in their trade policies.

In the fourth place it is argued that the establishment of preferences for less developed countries' exports of manufactures requires United States participation. Other developed countries presumably will not establish such preferences unilaterally for fear of having their markets glutted by exports from less developed countries, while the less developed countries now enjoying Commonwealth and Common Market preferences will not surrender them unless they receive compensation through preferential access to the American market. From this conclusion it is further argued that while Congress might be willing to empower the Administration to offer preferential access for manufactured exports from less developed countries either unilaterally or by negotiation of a multilateral scheme with other developed countries, a Presidential request for such authority might open a Pandora's box of congressional interventions in the trading privileges of particular less developed countries. It might also offer Congress the opportunity to graft new protective devices for domestic industry onto the arrangements and to use trade policy as an instrument for punishing or rewarding particular developed countries. The fear of what might happen if Congress gained control of a discriminatory United States tariff policy appears to be a powerful underlying factor in the aversion of American officials and academic experts to any form of preferential trading arrangements for less developed countries.[3] How far this fear is justified is a crucial question of political judgment, beyond the scope of this study. Clearly, however, the strength of this argument depends on how great a contribution to development preferential arrangements might make, as well as on how firmly public opinion and the Congress endorse this means of promoting development.

Economic Arguments Against Preferences

All of the political-administrative arguments are inconclusive and depend for their strength on the implicit assumption that the contribution that trade preferences could make to the development of the less developed countries is relatively small. The economic arguments used to support this assumption are

---

[3] Several officials who made this point in discussions cited the administration of the sugar quotas as a leading example of what they feared.

essentially the same as those used to support the assertion that the barriers imposed by the developed countries to the development through trade of the less developed countries are relatively minor. These arguments rest on the small volume of existing exports of manufactures by less developed countries, the small number of the exporters and the narrow range of products exported, the low average tariff levels of the developed countries, and the prospect that these tariff levels will be substantially reduced in the Kennedy Round. On the other hand, the small existing volume of trade may reflect the influence of trade barriers and certainly does not prove inability to benefit from the reduction of trade barriers, especially in the longer run. Reference to tariff averages conceals the tendency for tariffs to be exceptionally high on the labor-intensive, technologically simple products in which the less developed countries are likely to have a comparative advantage. A number of commodities in this category are on the exceptions lists presented by the developed countries to GATT and so will not be included in the Kennedy Round of tariff reductions. Finally, and most important, what matters for trade is not the tariff rates on commodities but the effective rates of protection of value added implicit in the whole tariff schedule. These effective rates tend to be high on exports or potential exports of less developed countries both because the escalation of tariff rates by stage of production makes effective rates on finished goods higher than nominal rates and because the nominal rates on goods of interest to the less developed countries tend to be exceptionally high. Judged in terms of effective rather than nominal rates, preferences are likely to be considerably more effective in improving the competitive position of less developed countries in the markets of developed countries than might appear from consideration of nominal tariff rates alone.

The argument that preferences in industrial products would be unlikely to contribute much to the development of the less developed countries has been presented in the most careful detail by Gardner Patterson.[4] He points out that in order for a preference to be helpful to less developed countries' exports, the exporter's price must be less than the domestic price in the preference-giving country[5] and must exceed competitors' prices by less than the amount of the preference margin given. The room for the latter condition to be fulfilled, he argues, is rather restricted: the tariff levels of the developed countries average about 15 per cent and will, he reckons, be reduced to 10 per cent by the Kennedy Round; moreover, developed countries would be extremely reluctant to grant zero tariffs to the less developed countries and would be more likely to settle for the 50 per cent minimum preference suggested by some of the less developed countries at UNCTAD. He therefore concludes that what is under discussion is a 5 per cent average margin of preference and that even this would be subject to exceptions, notably for cotton textiles. He then poses the question: "How many cases are there where a 5–7 per cent price advantage would be a decisive factor in making it possible for less

---

[4] G. Patterson, *op. cit.*, pp. 25–28.
[5] In this connection, Patterson makes the relevant but frequently overlooked point that the less developed countries will have to compete with the lowest-cost producing countries in the European Economic Community (EEC) and the European Free Trade Association (EFTA).

developed countries to take markets in developed nations away from both domestic producers in those countries (including all members of any regional group) *and* from producers of comparable manufactured goods in other industrial countries?" His answer is "some, but not many." "Excluding those goods for which most-favored-nation reductions would probably be as effective as preferential ones (leather and wood manufactures, some textiles, rugs, some drugs, etc., come to mind) the most likely candidates would seem to be in such products as pottery, toys, sporting goods, footwear and rubber manufactures."[6]

This argument is unsatisfactory even in its own terms as an evaluation of the potentialities of trade preferences for less developed countries. In the first place, it is not legitimate to argue that a policy has limited economic potentialities by assuming that it will be applied only to a limited extent, as Patterson does in assuming preferences of 50 per cent only; to do so is to confuse a judgment about governmental behavior with an assessment of economic facts. In the second place, it is not valid to exclude goods on the grounds that a nondiscriminatory reduction of the tariffs applicable to them would be equally effective; to do so is to assume without warrant that such a reduction will in fact occur, as well as to ignore possible differences in the benefits of the two alternative policies to the less developed countries.[7] The main objections to the argument, however, concern its reliance on average tariff rates and, more fundamentally, its use of nominal rather than effective rates of protection.

· · ·

The Arguments for Preferences

The central argument for tariff preferences for the manufactured exports of less developed countries advanced at UNCTAD was for temporary preferences; the argument was derived from infant-industry considerations and alleged to be a logical extension of the infant-industry argument. In one respect it is not a logical extension, but an empirically motivated analytical revision of the infant-industry

---

[6] Quotations from G. Patterson, *op. cit.*, p. 27.

[7] Grant L. Reuber [*Canada's Interest in the Trade Problems of Less-Developed Countries* (Montreal: The Canadian Trade Committee of the Private Planning Association of Canada, May 1964), pp. 23–27] has compared three tariff strategies for increasing the earnings of less developed countries from exports of manufactures not subject to quantitative restrictions. These are reduction of most-favored-nation rates to zero and elimination of existing preferences, reduction of preferred rates to zero and reduction of most-favored-nation rates sufficiently to maintain existing preferences (both strategies being consistent with GATT), and elimination of tariffs applicable to less developed countries combined with maintenance of tariffs applicable to developed countries (the extreme possibility of trade preferences). He concludes that the third (preferential) strategy would be most beneficial to the less developed countries; using a 12 per cent estimate of average tariff rates and an assumed demand elasticity of two, he estimates that this strategy would increase less developed country's exports of the goods in question (which account for about 5 per cent of their total exports) by 25 per cent (p. 26), or about $600 million per year (p. xii). This estimate is subject to the same major objections as are Patterson's less quantitative arguments and for that reason is probably a substantial underestimate of the possibilities; nevertheless, it does indicate that the possibilities of preferences in industrial products for less developed countries are by no means negligible.

argument, for it incorporates the observation that the process of acquiring efficiency in production through experience requires access to a large competitive market and is unlikely to be carried out successfully in the small national market made available by infant-industry protection on traditional lines. In two significant respects, however, the argument is something different from and more debatable than the infant-industry argument.

Infant-industry preferences—The infant-industry argument envisages a social investment by the consumers of the country imposing the infant-industry tariff, financed and disbursed through higher prices paid by consumers and received by producers as a result of the tariff; in return the country acquires an industry able to compete at world market prices, while the producers earn higher incomes than they would have earned without the social investment. In contrast, the argument for tariff preferences is an argument for a social investment by the consumers of the developed countries, the return on which will accrue to the producers of the less developed countries except to the extent that the maturation of the infant industry actually has the effect of reducing world market prices.

Therefore the argument for preferences is an argument for a particular form of transfer of external resources from the developed countries for investment in the industrialization of the less developed countries. The question naturally arises as to the relative merits of this method of collecting and transferring the resources and choosing the investments, as compared with the more straightforward method of transferring resources as foreign aid and choosing the investment projects as part of the normal routine of development planning. The answer obviously must be that preferences could provide resources that would not be made available through the more orthodox aid alternative.

The more important difference between the tariff-preference and infant-industry arguments concerns the choice of industries and the amount of protection afforded them. Rational implementation of the orthodox infant-industry argument would involve first selecting the industries that could—after an initial period of protection—compete in the world market while yielding a socially satisfactory return on the investment and then granting these industries the temporary protection required to establish them. Under the tariff-preference scheme, however, at least in its more general forms, selection would be based on the extent to which the developed countries protected the industries, those most heavily protected being given the greatest incentive to establish themselves in the less developed countries.

Politically this is a dubious scheme because it would provide maximum incentives for the establishment in the less developed countries of the very developed-country industries that have in the past shown most political power to obtain protection from foreign competition. This would seem likely to militate against preferences unless they were accompanied by quota and other safeguards designed to minimize their inherent threat to existing protectionist interests. The tariff-preference scheme is economically dubious because it provides maximum incentives for the establishment of the industries whose costs will have to fall most below those in the preference-giving countries if they are to survive the termination of the preference. While the most heavily protected industries in the developed countries are likely to include those in which the less developed countries have a potential comparative advantage, it is very unlikely that they generally represent the best infant-industry prospects for the less developed countries. Generally speaking, the developed countries have designed their tariffs to protect their industries from each others' competition, and that competition is at least as likely to be based on abundance of capital or technological superiority as on the low-wage labor and abundance of raw materials that constitute the potential comparative advantage of the typical less developed country.[8]

These doubtful features of tariff preferences relate to a scheme in which a standard preferential margin for less developed countries is applied to the existing national tariff schedule of one or more developed countries. The problems indicated could be avoided by two alternative preferential arrangements. One would involve giving each less-developed-country industry the same absolute preference margin. Ignoring certain difficulties associated with the difference between nominal and effective preference margins, this alternative would be equivalent to an export subsidy on industrial exports by less developed countries or (again with certain obvious qualifications associated with differences in the effects on imports) to a devaluation coupled with an aid transfer. This alternative would ignore differences in the infant-industry potentialities of different lines of production, letting experience determine which industries should survive. The other alternative would be to examine the various industries for infant-industry potentialities and provide the required protection by specific adjustment of the margin and duration of the preference for each product. The difficulty with this alternative, aside from its cumbersomeness, is that existing developed-country tariffs might not be high enough for preferences to provide the required protection,[9] additional subsidies being required. In any case, implementation of the infant-industry argument in the context of a tariff-ridden world market could be more conveniently and simply effected by the use of production subsidies to industries genuinely qualifying as infants.

However, even where infant-industry conditions exist—an empirical issue concerning which the ratio of unsupported assertion to empirical evidence is probably unexcelled in any other field of economics—these conditions do not logically lead to the recommendation of a tariff. Instead, they lead to the recommendation of a subsidy, either on the production of the industry or on whatever aspect of its initial operations (creation of infrastructure, training of labor)[10]

---

[8] These points would lose some of their force if it could be assumed that investment decisions in the preference-receiving countries were guided entirely by consideration of those countries' comparative advantages after the preferences terminated, but this would involve a deliberate decision to renounce opportunities for profits in the interim period (commonly put at a minimum of ten years), which seems very unlikely.

[9] G. Patterson, *op. cit.*, p. 26, emphasizes the point that the levels of developed-country tariffs are now too low to enable as much protection of infant industries to be given through tariff preferences as has in the past been conferred by infant-industry tariffs.

[10] It is frequently argued that the training by a firm of workers who then move on to other employers imposes a private loss on the firm to which there corresponds no social loss (e.g., G. Patterson, *op. cit.*, p. 24). This is only true if the firm, and not the worker, bears the cost of the training; institutional arrangements such as apprenticeship or other means of paying low wages to trainees generally permit the firm to make the worker bear the expense of his training where this risk of loss exists.

generates the difference between social and private return on which the argument depends. The use of the tariff, which entails a distortion of consumption choices contributing nothing to the attainment of the objectives of the policy, has to be justified by the infeasibility of the economically superior subsidy method, so that resort to infant-industry tariffs appears as a second-best policy. Correspondingly, the recommendation of tariff preferences from developed countries, with their inefficiencies, appears as a third-best policy recommendation.

•   •   •

Concluding Observations on Preferences

The proposal for developed countries to extend preferences on imports of manufactures and semi-manufactures to the less developed countries as a means of promoting the economic growth of the latter raises a host of difficult problems. Nevertheless, it has been argued that, contrary to superficial appearances, preferences might be an extremely powerful tool for stimulating industrial development in the less developed countries, the reasons being largely inherent in the recently developed theory of effective protection. Given the emphasis placed by the less developed countries on their need for such preferences and the possibility that the formation and policies of the European Common Market will block further progress after the Kennedy Round toward trade liberalization along traditional GATT lines, the possibilities of using trade preferences to promote development deserve serious consideration.

Unfortunately, it is not possible to estimate how much could be done by this means for the less developed countries, by the United States acting unilaterally or in concert with other developed countries, let alone to produce comparative estimates of the probable effects of alternative systems of trade preferences on the volume and gains from trade of the less developed countries.[11] The conceptual framework required to tackle these empirical questions in the scientifically proper

---

[11]Exploration of these problems would require empirical investigation not only of the effective preference margins the developed countries would give, but of the costs of production in the less developed countries, which would determine their ability to take advantage of preferences. One indication of the potentialities of preferences would be the total customs revenus now collected by developed countries on their imports from less developed countries, which revenue might be transferred back to the less developed countries via preferences. The total customs revenue collected on imports of manufactured goods from less developed countries into the United States, United Kingdom, European Economic Community, and Sweden in 1962 has been estimated at $306 million, made up as follows: United States, $140 million; United Kingdom, $89 million; European Economic Community, $71 million; Sweden, $6 million. The estimate, by V. N. Balasubramanyam, applies Bela Balassa's average tariff rates on industrial products to trade data obtained from the *Foreign Trade Analytical Abstracts* of the Organization for Economic Cooperation and Development. To allow for Commonwealth preference for members and EEC preferential treatment of associated overseas territories, sterling area imports are excluded from the figures for the United Kingdom and imports from Africa from the figures for the EEC; if these imports were not excluded, the estimated total duty collected would be $390 million. Unfortunately, the data required to make the same calculation for Japan are not available.

fashion has only recently been developed, and its empirical application requires extensive collation and manipulation of data on tariff rates and on the industrial input-output structure that are notoriously difficult to mesh together. In addition, much of the argument for preferences as presented at UNCTAD hinges on whether and to what extent preferential market access would permit less developed countries to reap economies of scale in production or to lower costs through the accumulation of experience; this is a question on which, despite the hoary history of the infant-industry argument, international trade specialists have developed neither the theoretical conceptualization nor the empirical evidence that is required to pass an empirical judgment.

If preferences for less developed countries are to be seriously considered, a great deal of theoretical and empirical research needs to be done on the infant-industry and scale-economy arguments. More generally, it is necessary to determine what factors account for the inability of less developed countries, and specifically of the "developing" countries that already produce manufactures for the home market, to export in competition with the developed countries in spite of their comparative advantages in availability of materials and low-wage labor, and how significant these factors are empirically. A major part of the explanation is to be found in the import-substitution and currency-overvaluation policies typically pursued by the governments of less developed countries, and that the cost disadvantages resulting from these policies may frequently be far greater than the competitive advantage that could be conferred by preferences from the developed countries.[12] If this suggestion is confirmed by further empirical research, it would imply that neither preferences nor nondiscriminatory tariff reduction would help the less developed countries unless they were prepared to make major changes in their tariff and exchange-rate policies. Thus, the developed countries could legitimately insist on such policy changes in the less developed countries as a condition for trade concessions.

PREFERENTIAL ARRANGEMENTS AMONG LESS DEVELOPED COUNTRIES

The proposal at UNCTAD for preferential arrangements for trade in manufactured goods among less developed countries was based on the same sort of argument as the case for preferences in developed-country markets: the need for a market larger than the protection of the national market could provide, in order to foster the development of infant industries and to permit the exploitation of economies of scale, and the inability of producers in the less developed countries to export in competition with producers in the developed countries. Such preferences would be negotiated among the countries of a region, or of a like-minded

---

[12]There is some general evidence suggesting that the tax policies of less developed countries may impose especially heavy tax burdens on industries producing potentially exportable manufactures.

group, for the manufactured products they agreed upon, and would stop considerably short of a free trade area. Hence they would be in violation of the principles of GATT. However, there was little discussion of the proposal at UNCTAD, and the reaction of the developed countries to it appears to have been generally sympathetic, presumably because their trade in manufactures with the less developed countries is both relatively unimportant and limited, at least on a superficial view, by those countries' receipts of foreign exchange rather than by their tariffs.

The GATT principle of nondiscrimination and ban on new preferences except for customs unions and free trade areas are not consistent with either the political principle of treating all foreign countries equally or the economic principle of maximizing real income through promoting the most efficient attainable allocation of productive resources in the world economy. There is therefore no compelling reason for opposing the proposal for preferences among a group of less developed countries on grounds of its inconsistency with GATT principles. The facts that these preferences would involve only less developed countries and that prevailing political sentiment favors giving such countries the maximum possible latitude within the GATT system, however, do not provide valid grounds for giving a blanket endorsement to such preferences. There is, in fact, good reason for not endorsing them without investigating their economic aspects in the same way as preferences from developed to less developed countries.

This analytical task can be considerably simplified by assuming, as seems reasonable, that preference-induced changes in the demand of the less developed countries for the manufactured goods to which preferences would apply would be small in relation to total world production and consumption; thus the developed-country producers could shift the goods to other markets, or the resources used in producing them to other activities, without appreciable change in their prices or the incomes of their producers. In other words, it is reasonable to assume that any potential or actual trade diversion resulting from group preferences would inflict no significant damage on the developed-country suppliers, and correspondingly would yield the less developed countries no benefits in the form of improved terms of trade with the developed countries. The analysis then need consider only the effects on the participating countries; the concern of the developed countries in such arrangements can be considered to be confined to their potential effects on development.

From one point of view, of course, it could be argued that if one is prepared to assume that preferential arrangements among less developed countries would impose no economic cost on the developed countries, the latter have no legitimate concern with the terms of the arrangements. The principle of freedom of contract should rule and should by itself guarantee that any resulting preferential arrangements will be beneficial to all participants. This argument, however, assumes that the governments of less developed countries fully understand their own interests and how these will be affected by preferential arrangements; moreover, it ignores the fact that as providers of foreign assistance for economic development, the developed countries have a legitimate concern for the efficiency with which development is planned and promoted in the less developed countries.

Preferences to Expand the Industrial Base

In analyzing the effects of preferential arrangements among less developed countries, it is necessary at the outset to distinguish two alternative standards of economic welfare that might be applied. In the policies of many less developed countries, economic development appears to be identified with expansion of the industrial structure, regardless of whether the cost of production of industrial products is above the price of such products in the world market. If these policies are regarded as representing rational social choice, it must be assumed that the social value of having additional industrial facilities as a symbol of development achievement is worth the loss of material consumption imposed by the higher costs of domestic production as compared with importing. On this basis, anything that lowers the cost of establishing additional facilities for industrial production in the less developed countries increases their welfare and contributes to their development. Preferences in manufactured goods among a group of less developed countries would permit such a reduction in the cost of establishing additional industrial production by the group by enabling the group to produce each industrial good in the member country possessing a comparative advantage in supplying it (instead of each country producing its own requirements) and to enjoy whatever economies of scale and infant-industry maturation the larger size of the pooled markets would allow.

Allowing less developed countries to negotiate whatever such arrangements they considered desirable would therefore contribute to their economic welfare and promote their economic development, in the special sense that identifies development with industrialization. The only problem that would arise on this approach would derive from the fact that, since the granting of a preference to another less developed country entails a sacrifice of actual or potential domestic industrial production by the preference-granting country, which must be compensated by receipt of a reciprocal preference on industrial production in which it has a comparative advantage within the group, the possibilities of improvement depend on the extent to which the preferences can expand the markets for lines of industrial production in which the various countries have comparative advantages within the preferential group. The distribution of comparative advantages in industrial production among the countries of the group might be such that some countries had few or no industrial products they could produce at lower prices than the others, or that cost differences among the countries were so negligible that preferences could not be negotiated to mutual advantage.[13]

---

[13]The problems and possibilities of preferential arrangements among less developed countries envisaged from this analytical point of view, are dealt with in detail by C. A. Cooper and B. F. Massell, "Toward a General Theory of Customs Unions for Developing Countries," *Journal of Political Economy*, Vol. 73 (Oct. 1965), pp. 461–476. In any grouping of countries, it might be possible for the more powerful to exert pressure on the weaker to participate in preferential arrangements that imposed a welfare loss on the weaker countries by obliging them to provide a market for the high-cost products of the more powerful countries even though their industrial products were unable to compete with industrial production in the rest of the region, or to compete on a scale sufficient to be compensatory. For this reason, even if the developed countries accepted the definitions of economic welfare and development employed in the foregoing analysis, they would have some obligation to exercise surveillance over less developed countries' preferential trading arrangements to protect the weaker from the rapacity of the stronger.

Preferences to Establish an Efficient Economic System

The foregoing analysis assumes both that the governments of the less developed countries understand the interests of their peoples and how best to serve them, and that the objectives they define for themselves should be accepted unquestioningly by the developed countries. The alternative analytical approach—which appears more realistic and relevant for the developed countries to adopt in determining their attitude to preferential arrangements among less developed countries—is to assume that, regardless of how governments in less developed countries may visualize their objectives, the true interests of their peoples lie in achieving the most efficient possible economic system, and to evaluate proposed preferential arrangements in that light. This involves applying the economic analysis of preferences for exports of manufactured goods, with the two differences that the effects on outside countries can be ignored and that the effects of the preferences on the joint economic welfare of the preference-giving and preference-receiving countries must be considered.

In terms of the static-efficiency considerations of that analysis, preferential trading arrangements among less developed countries will improve their economic efficiency, and hence contribute to the economic development of the group, to the extent that they create trade by leading to substitution of lower-cost for higher-cost production within the group. Conversely, preferential arrangements will worsen efficiency and retard economic development to the extent that they divert trade from outside sources to higher-cost sources within the group. In terms of the dynamic arguments for preferential arrangements based on scale-economy or infant-industry considerations, preferences will contribute to welfare and development only if, in fact, costs are reduced as the arguments claim they will be, and the cost reduction yields an adequate social return on the investment implicit in the use of preferences.

These propositions imply that the developed countries should favor and seek to promote preferential arrangements among less developed countries for trade in the products of industries already established within the group, particularly products in which the group is close to self-sufficient, since they offer the maximum opportunity of gain from trade creation and the minimum risk of loss from trade diversion. By contrast, the developed countries should regard with extreme skepticism preferential schemes to establish new industries based on scale-economy and infant-industry arguments; the establishment of such industries necessarily involves trade diversion which can be economically justified only by a strong probability that costs will in fact fall sufficiently to make the industry economic.[14] Such a policy stance would, however, be sure to arouse dissension between the developed and the less developed countries, since the governments of the latter

---

[14] Given the distortions of costs in less developed countries introduced by import substitution and currency overvaluation, it is quite possible that the establishment of some such industries would be justified even if costs could not be reduced to the world level. The complications of optimal investment decision in an environment of distorted factor and commodity prices would have to be tackled in any evaluation of such proposals.

generally seek tenaciously to maintain any industrial activity they have been successful in establishing, regardless of its excess cost, and view preferential arrangements as a way of establishing still more industry without sacrificing what they already have.

The protectionist policies of the less developed countries are frequently an important factor in fostering inefficiency in their economies and inhibiting their economic development. The developed countries could probably help to ameliorate this problem by attempting, in connection with any decision to modify the GATT rules to allow preferential arrangements for less developed countries, to establish some sort of internationally agreed maximum rate of protection[15] that could possibly be justified by the familiar arguments for protection in less developed countries, and to insist that it not be exceeded in any new preferential arrangements. In the longer run, the same objective of curbing the excesses of protectionism in less developed countries might be served by the negotiation and implementation of such new preferential arrangements, since this would oblige the participating less developed countries to take a critical interest in each others' protective policies.

---

[15]Ideally, the effective and not the nominal rate.

Selection **31**

External Aid:
For Plans or Projects?

H. W. SINGER

From: the Economic Journal, *Vol. LXXV, No. 299 (September 1965), pp. 539–545. Reprinted by permission of the* Economic Journal *and the author.*

External financial aid to underdeveloped countries is given in diverse forms. Some of it is clearly linked with specific projects; some of it is given in general support of annual budgets or longer-term plans without reference to specific projects; some of it is in a great variety of forms intermediate between these two categories. Such intermediate forms include: specific projects within the framework of a development plan; earmarked aid to be drawn upon only for specific agreed projects; support for groups of projects rather than individual projects; aid for specific import requirements (food, spare parts) not linked to specific projects, etc.

In discussing some issues arising from this wide variety of forms of aid and aid policies, a distinction has first to be made between the *ostensible* tying of project aid to specific projects and the projects which the aid *actually* finances. Provided that the country which receives aid has some additional money of its own (or receives additional aid from other sources), and provided that this additional money is not entirely absorbed in the project or projects selected by the aid donor and to which his aid is tied, the project *actually* financed by aid may be quite different from the one to which the aid is *ostensibly* tied. If the project to which the aid is ostensibly tied is a "high-priority project" which would in any case have been part of the recipient's plan, and which he otherwise would have undertaken with his own money, then obviously the aid given enables the recipient to release his own money from Project A (which is now aid-financed); continue with Projects B, C, and D, which he financed with his own money; and utilise his money now released from Project A in order to add a new Project E to his original development plan or expenditure schedule.[1] This could mean that the donor of aid ties his aid to Project A, studies it minutely, and satisfies himself

---

[1] "Project E" may, of course, consist in an enlargement or acceleration of Projects B and/or C and/or D.

that it is technically sound and economically right, while in reality—as distinct from appearance—his aid may go into Project E, which he may know nothing about, which he does not study, and which may be neither technically sound nor economically right, nor generally the kind of thing that the aid donor would want to support. In effect, he has given plan aid without knowing it—like Molière's prose-speaker.

This situation is basically unsatisfactory. There is an element of make-believe in that the donors of aid, as well as the parliaments and citizens of donor countries, believe or pretend that they are doing one thing when in fact they are doing something quite different. Such self-deception or deception does not strike one as a happy basis for the kind of international cooperation and solidarity which aid should represent and permit. There may be good reasons for this situation. To tie the aid to the "high-priority" Project A may be politically necessary in order to rally support for aid. It may provide the opportunity to render technical assistance in connection with the high-priority Project A, and indeed to improve it or redesign it fundamentally; it may be more important for the development of the recipient country to do this in respect of the high-priority Project A than in respect of the marginal Project E, even though the latter is the project which the aid really finances (in the sense that Project E is the project which would have to be eliminated if the aid did not exist). Project A may enable the aid donor to tie his aid to the supply of his own equipment for Project A. It may be that untied aid[2] would be unacceptable or economically impossible for the donor (because of balance-of-payment difficulties), while Project E (which he really finances) may not need the kind of equipment that he would like (or be able) to supply.

But it still remains true that if specific project aid is viewed not only from the point of view of expediency or popularity but also as a continuing relationship and a contribution to the long-run development and ultimate "take off" of the assisted country, then it is myopic of the aid giver to limit his attention, analysis, and technical assistance to Project A. He should be equally interested in Projects B, C, D, and E—perhaps specially E, since this is the real result of his aid. Even if there is no substitution of resources between Projects A and E, the efficiency of Project A would still depend on the soundness of the recipients' total investment programme. If the aid must be tied for balance-of-payment reasons, it would still be better to seek agreements with other aid-givers so that the receiving country would be able to buy in the cheapest market while the balances-of-payments of the individual donor countries would benefit more or less in proportion to the aid which they give. It would also be more rational to tie the aid to specific items of equipment (or the products of specific depressed areas in the aid-giving country), while still permitting the recipients to use the tied supplies in whatever projects and fields these supplies are cheapest in relation to alternate sources.

So far, we have assumed that the aid-financed Project A is truly a high-priority project which the country would and should have carried out with its own money if the aid had not been forthcoming. It is possible to imagine the worse case where

---

[2] *I.e.*, not tied to the donor's own equipment and supplies (as distinct from aid not tied to specific projects).

project A is not a true high-priority project at all but is put forward only because it is the kind of project which attracts aid from the donor.

Because of the rules of the aid game as at present played, the donor may be prevented from financing local supplies needed for the true priority project, or from financing general supplies of food or raw materials or spare parts, or from taking account of the indirect developmental balance-of-payments needs of the assisted country. Where the project to which the aid is tied has been tailored to meet the needs of the aid-donor rather than those of the aided country, there is not even the consolation that the aided country's own money will be released for Project E and that with good luck and good planning Project E will be exactly the project which, with more sensible rules of the aid game, would have been selected in the first place. The fact is that there may be no true release. On the contrary, Project A, which has been put forward to attract aid, although not among the real top priorities of the country, will also tie down some of the recipient country's own resources, which would otherwise have gone into a real top-priority project (still, for the present assuming good planning). More local cost financing within the framework of project aid would help to eliminate this distortion. The best that can be hoped for in this case is that the value of the aid (which could not have been obtained for any other project) will outweigh the negative effect of the diversion of the recipient country's own resources away from its real priority. This will, of course, often, probably normally, be the case (especially if the aid is on soft terms), so that the net contribution of the aid is positive. But it is hardly an ideal state of affairs and certainly does not maximise the contribution of aid to development.

So far we have implicitly assumed that the aid-giving country and the receiving country are in broad agreement about the priorities and top needs of the aid-receiving country. If this assumption is not true, then of course the case for specific project aid is greatly strengthened. If the donor country believes that Project A is the top priority, but if project A would not be included by the receiving country in its development plans, so that without aid only Projects B, C, D, . . . would be executed, then the situation is fundamentally changed. The fact that Project A (which is not included in the country's own priorities) will be carried out only because aid is available exclusively for it, but not for other projects, ceases to be a vice and becomes a virtue. This is the case at least in the judgment of the aid-giving country which believes that Project A is better than the receiving country's own Projects B, C, D, ... It is also objectively the case if the aid-giving country's judgment of the receiving country's priorities and needs is better than that of the receiving country itself.

This last assumption is, of course, contrary to the polite assumption underlying international economic relations that each country is the best judge of its own needs (or indeed that each government of the day is the best judge of its own country's needs). The opposite assumption that another aid-giving country is a better judge of a receiving country's needs than that country or its government itself will be rarely made explicit, but it will nevertheless sometimes guide the actions of the aid-giving country. In fact, the aid-receiving countries on occasion may recognise this by specifically asking advice from aid-giving sources about their proper priorities. One way in which this can be done without breaking the polite assumption about each country's being the best judge of its own needs is to ask such assistance from international organisations whose advice is not "foreign," but who nevertheless may either themselves dispense aid or whose judgments concerning priorities may stand a better chance of being accepted by aid-giving countries than those of the aid-receiving countries. Thus, where there is some disagreement about priorities, specific project aid may be the only way in which aid can be forthcoming at all. Moreover, in this case there would be little self-deception; the aid will *actually* make project A possible, as well as being *ostensibly* tied to it. The assisted country will still go on with Projects B, C, D, . . . which would also have been carried out without aid (except to the extent that its own resources are tied down in the new aid-assisted Project A).

A somewhat related case for aid tied to the specific Project A can be made where the receiving country does have a general plan and priorities acceptable to the aid-donor but has not worked out its general ideas in terms of specific projects. In that case the tying of aid to specific projects has the advantage of being a convenient way of helping or forcing the assisted country to translate its acceptable development strategy into concrete projects. The element of self-deception will also disappear in this case. For what happens in fact is that the receiving country will carry out its own plans according to its own priorities (accepted by the donor), while if general plan aid had been given, the plan would not actually have been carried out through lack of concrete projects. This is therefore a somewhat paradoxical position where specific project aid is given in order to give effective general plan aid.

The element of illusion or deception inherent in the specific project approach can also be avoided if the donor country or agency picks the marginal project (Project E) which the receiving country is able to add to its plan as the result of the additional aid which it is getting as the project to which to tie its aid. It does, of course, presuppose a certain degree of sophistication on the part of the donor of aid to expect him to tie his aid to a "marginal" project, instead of insisting on iden- tification with a "high-priority project." Perhaps more important, however, this procedure also presupposes a high degree of sophistication in the planning process of the aid-receiving country. In order to identify the marginal project, that country must draw up not one plan but two: one without aid and one predicated on aid. It is difficult enough to draw up one plan, let alone two (or perhaps even several, predicated on different amounts of external aid). The economy of scarce planning capacity is precisely one of the main advantages of plan aid known in advance to the receiving country.

This last point brings us up against the major difficulty of "identifying" aid with any project, whether priority or marginal. So far, we have mechanistically assumed that a plan consists of separate projects, A, B, C, D, E, . . . which can be ranked according to priority, and without "feedback" effects among each other. This view of planning will, however, be rarely accurate, except perhaps in the most primitive conditions. In fact, the whole point about planning is that the developmental impact of any good expenditure pattern *plus* policy package is maximised, if these expenditures and policies are properly related to each other and taken as a whole. Thus, Plan II (prepared on the assumption of some aid and hence larger) will differ from Plan I (prepared on the assumption of no aid and hence smaller) not just by the addition of one or two projects. Rather, if the planning process in the country is at all meaningful, Plan II will be quite different from Plan I. There will be projects in Plan II which are not in Plan I, but there will also be projects in Plan I which are not in Plan II. Moreover, Plan I and Plan II may contain identical projects, but these may well be carried out with a different technology, on a different scale, and on a different time schedule in the larger (aided) Plan II compared with the smaller (unaided) Plan I. Thus, the identification of a "marginal project" for purposes of tying aid to it without illusion or deception does not only require a high degree of sophistication but is really inherently impossible except in rare circumstances. Thus, in the final analysis aid *can* only be given on a "macro" basis, to result in additional output in terms of value, but not on a "micro" basis in terms of specific projects.

It will be remembered that so far we have assumed that the aid given to a country is only part of the total available resources and accordingly that the aided project or projects are not the only developmental activity carried out. Where this assumption is not valid, the problem discussed here can hardly be said to exist. Project A (top priority) and Project E (marginal) are identical, since there is only one single Project A. Thus the question of deception or illusion cannot arise. The aid is bound to be attached to "the" project. The only question which arises in certain circumstances is whether the Project A (aided), which *is* the development plan of the country, is imposed upon the receiving country by the donor by the threat that the aid will disappear if Project A is changed, or whether Project A has been previously selected by the receiving country and is then accepted by the donor. This alternative may look superficially similar to a choice between project aid and plan aid, but it has really little to do with it. The tying of aid in this case may be of legal, political, or administrative importance, but it certainly has no economic meaning, not even the dangers of illusion or deception.

We have mentioned before as a possible advantage of project aid, especially if a high-priority project is selected for attaching the aid, that this may serve as a convenient handle for improving the project or rendering technical assistance. Against this must be set the danger that project aid may lead to delays in negotiation and thus in project implementation, and this would be a greater danger and more harmful if the aid is attached to the high-priority Project A rather than the marginal Project E. Project aid may result in additional aid which would not otherwise be forthcoming at all; but this may be offset by the possibility that project discussions and frictions and differences of opinion concerning specific projects result in delays and pipeline accumulations, so that the actual flow of aid may in fact be smaller than it would have been with plan aid not tied to projects. Even an argument that project aid is good because it forces the receiving country to come up with concrete projects finds its counterpart in the argument that planning aid is good because it forces the receiving country to come up with sound plans and think about the necessary interrelation of its projects and its total development policies. However, a plan solely prepared to please aid-donors would not be likely to rest on a solid foundation.

Plan aid seems to be more popular among the receiving countries than project aid. This would be expected to be considered as an advantage of plan aid, since it may spur the receiving country to greater efforts in order to get the aid, apart from smoothing relations between the aid-giver and the receiver, which is presumably also an objective of aid. However, the recipient's preference for plan aid over project aid is sometimes considered to be an argument in favour of project aid, because it shows that plan aid is "soft" and requires less "discipline."

It may be said that aid tied to specific projects is an inducement or receiving countries to think of development in terms of concrete projects, i.e., specific types of net investment of physical capital. Development is, of course, much more than that, and in fact many expenditures classified as current or as consumption are much more developmental than expenditures classified as "projects" or capital expenditure. From this latter point of view, plan aid, and even more annual budget aid, is clearly preferable if the donor agrees with the recipient on developmental policies and priorities.

Development plans in some countries may be highly unstable, with frequent revisions or even abrupt changes with changes of government. On the other hand, important projects will, or should, figure in all these plans, however frequently revised or upset. Here project aid has an advantage over plan aid. One suspects that much of the preference of donors for project aid has its real, if unacknowledged, basis in some mistrust of the recipient's planning stability.

A difficult problem exists in the case of small aid-giving countries, especially in relation to large receiving countries. (Aid by Luxembourg to India, shall we say.) The paradox consists in the fact that the aid-giver will not want to go to the trouble of examining specific projects to which the aid would be tied, since the cost and delays of the examination would be out of proportion to the aid available. On the other hand, aid tied to the plan would make the aid appear too insignificant. The answer will usually lie in pooling the contributions of small donors with contributions of larger donors, both through international organisations and through participation of small donors in aid consortia.

Our discussion has not resulted in any clear-cut statement on the superiority of plan aid over project aid, or vice versa. That was not to be expected. The rather tangled relationships which have been discussed reflect the state of the whole business of aid which has grown haphazardly and in a rather wild and disorderly manner. At present there certainly seems room for both kinds of aid. There seems some justification for the economist's instinctive preference for plan aid, but this preference may have to wait for a tidier period in the aid business. There are some indications that such a tidier period is on the horizon. One feels that the scope for plan aid through aid consortia combined with technical planning and project assistance to developing countries, with some emphasis on multilateral assistance, may be on the increase in the next phase. This could result in greater effectiveness of aid than uncoordinated project aid.

Selection 32

Project Versus Program Aid

ALAN CARLIN

from: "Project Versus Programme Aid: From the Donor's View-point," the Economic Journal, *Vol. LXXVII, No. 305 (March 1967), pp. 48–58. Reprinted by permission of the* Economic Journal *and the author.*

H. W. Singer has recently reopened one of the longest-standing controversies in the administration of foreign aid, the question of project versus programme aid.[1] Unfortunately, his analysis is limited largely to the much discussed fungibility issue.[2] While this is an important issue, it is far less so than Singer's treatment implies. As will be brought out later, there are even some major aid recipients, such as India, where it is not a major problem. Singer's conclusion, that there is something to be said for both types of aid, has some merit, but is inadequately supported by the remainder of the paper. This is almost entirely concerned with pointing out some (but by no means all) of the problems with project aid. Little is said concerning the drawbacks of programme aid. In brief, the project-programme question is just much more complex than Singer suggests. Before attempting to bring out these added complexities, it is useful to make several initial distinctions that set the problem in a more meaningful context.

The most basic of these distinctions is between the interests of the aid-donor and the recipient. Singer addresses the project-programme question with an implied recipient-country welfare function. This gives rise to the question of whether the donor or recipient government knows what is "best" for the recipient country. But, much more important, it ignores the fact that the form of external assistance is determined largely by the donor rather than the recipient. An attempt either to understand or to influence the choice between the two approaches can much more usefully examine the donor's point of view.[3] Perhaps the least interesting point

---

[1] H. W. Singer, "External Aid: For Plans or Projects?" *Economic Journal*, No. 299 (Sept. 1965), pp. 539–545.

[2] See, for example, Thomas C. Schelling, *International Economics* (Boston: Allyn and Bacon, Inc., 1958), especially pp. 441–457. Fungibility will be discussed in more detail below.

[3] Although this paper assumes that the donor's primary objective is to promote the recipient's economic development, many of its conclusions are applicable either directly or with minor changes to aid given for other objectives, such as to increase the recipient's military capability or to compensate him for foreign military installations on his soil.

of view is that of the recipient government, which will almost always prefer programme aid because of the increased flexibility it confers.

Once it has been decided that the relevant viewpoint is that of the donor, a
related distinction arises between the domestic political motivations of the donor
for the two types of aid and his objective reasons for adopting them in terms of
his national (or institutional) self-interest.[4] Here the interesting question from
an economic standpoint is which approach would be more suitable if the donor's
domestic political considerations were ignored.

Before examining the relative merits of the two alternatives it is worthwhile
clearing up another source of confusion on the subject—the definitions of the
terms involved. Project aid can be defined as assistance whose disbursement is
tied to capital investment in a separable productive activity. Programme aid is
assistance whose disbursement is tied to the recipient's expenditures on a wide
variety of items justified in terms of the total needs and development plan of the
country rather than any particular project. The important distinction is that project aid carries added restrictions on its use. Because aid has usually been project-
tcd where possible, programme aid has become identified with aid not nominally
used in investments in productive activities, or, in other words, with that used for
maintenance imports. Nevertheless, there is an important conceptual difference
and sometimes a practical difference between programme aid and aid used for
maintenance imports. It is quite possible, for example, to supply free foreign
exchange (such as would be likely to be used for maintenance imports) with
project aid.[5]

It is often difficult to classify some capital assistance, particularly that given
by the United States Agency for International Development (A.I.D.), as either
project or programme. Thus A.I.D. has given substantial assistance to meet the
foreign exchange needs of the Indian Railways. Although most of this assistance
is tied to foreign exchange expenditures for a number of different railway capital
projects, A.I.D. has made little effort to document the returns from each particular
project,[6] even though such loans are considered project loans to India. They are
really programme loans to the Indian Railways for capital projects of their choosing
and are justified on the basis of the overall performance and needs of the Railways.

---

[4] One of the strongest reasons for the continued partial use of the project approach by the
United States Agency for International Development is undoubtedly the strong support for this
type of assistance in Congress. This support is to a considerable extent based on the identification
of project aid with traditional banking activities. The project approach of the International Bank
for Reconstruction and Development may also be partly motivated by the conservative image
that it helps to create in financial circles.

[5] The procedure is to tie the aid (assumed to be in the form of foreign exchange) to more than
the foreign-exchange costs of projects. Part of such local cost financing will, of course, serve
only to cover the increased imports indirectly resulting from the local currency expenditures.
But the remainder (if any) will amount to a net increase in the foreign exchange available for
other purposes. This remainder is not entirely hypothetical, since the International Development
Association has on occasion supplied a significant amount of free exchange in connection with
some projects in India and perhaps elsewhere, while A.I.D. has done so in some Latin American
countries.

[6] This paragraph is based on Alan Carlin "An Evaluation of U.S. Government Aid to India,"
(unpublished doctoral dissertation, Massachusetts Institute of Technology, 1964), pp. 47–137.

Another example of assistance in the grey area between project and programme aid is aid to intermediate credit institutions.

With these definitions in hand, it is possible to reformulate the original question somewhat more precisely. The objective of this paper is to set out the more important considerations that a rational donor should take into account in deciding whether it is more advantageous to give aid as project or programme assistance. Since project assistance can be considered programme aid with certain additional restrictions on its use, a convenient way of reviewing the arguments on each side is by looking at the additional benefits and costs of these added restrictions.

BENEFITS OF THE PROJECT APPROACH

The more important potential benefits[7] of the project approach are:

1. Direct control by the recipient over the selection of projects *in certain circumstances*;
2. Greater opportunity of influencing, in both their design and implementation, those projects nominally financed by the aid donor;
3. Increased ease of influencing the recipient's policies in those sectors of the recipient's economy for which project aid has been made available;
4. Incentives for improving the quantity and quality of projects;
5. Better opportunities for publicising the donor's aid programmes;
6. Increased access to information on sectors of the recipient's economy in which projects are financed;
7. If aid is also tied on a country-of-origin basis a somewhat less adverse effect on the balance of payments of the donor nation.

Micro-influence

The first three benefits are related and involve the exercise of micro or project influence over the recipient. As many have pointed out, the fungibility problem greatly limits the effectiveness with which project controls can influence the recipient's allocation of resources. The fungibility problem arises because the particular project with which the aid is identified may or may not represent the actual use of the added funds provided by the aid.[8] This problem has often been overemphasised by economists, however, since there are a variety of circumstances in which influence can be exercised over the allocation of resources despite it. One such case arises when the donor offers aid for a project that the recipient regards as sufficiently marginal so that he would not finance it out of his own resources if the aid were not made available. This means that if the donor can find what he considers worthwhile projects neglected by the recipient he can

---

[7] Throughout the paper the discussion of benefits will be in terms of potential benefits. Since donors vary greatly in the extent to which they actually achieve these benefits, it is best to discuss the optimum case and allow readers to apply their own discounting factors for the donor in which they are interested.

[8] Thus, although expenditures for imports for a power plant may be reimbursed by the aid-donor, the plant might well have been built even if total aid had been reduced by the amount reimbursed. The funds can then hardly be said to have financed the power plant at all, but rather the use of the funds that would have been sacrificed if the aid had not been extended.

influence the recipient's allocation of resources. Despite Singer's doubts on the subject, a number of aid-donors have been able to identify marginal projects when they have set out to do so. In the early 1960's, for example, the International Development Association attempted to locate a number of such projects in India and chose projects in the areas of highway development, telephone service, irrigation, and drainage to receive credits.

In the extreme case all of a donor's projects can be considered marginal, and he can effectively determine the recipient's allocation of investment resources provided through project support. This occurs when the recipient's free foreign-exchange resources are already tied down to uses given relatively high priority by the recipient while not including any of the projects financed by the donor. If no foreign private or public investment body is willing to finance a given project, the country must usually abandon it. This situation occurs most commonly when the recipient country cannot meet all of its essential "maintenance imports" out of its own foreign-exchange holdings or earnings. India provides a good illustration within recent years. Her debt repayments and imports of food, essential consumer goods, and raw materials needed to keep existing industrial capacity in production exceed her free foreign exchange. Failure to meet the more basic of these requirements would have worse political and economic repercussions than failure to expand capacity, so that it is probable that the latter would be sacrificed should India have to choose between the two. As a result, the use of project aid can substantially influence the allocation of India's developmental resources. As long as the sum of available free foreign exchange plus untied programme aid is less than essential maintenance imports, no project requiring substantial amounts of foreign exchange will normally be undertaken without some public or private international financing.

India's efforts to find a donor for its seventh steel mill (fifth in the public sector) illustrate the point involved. Since she has been unable to find a donor, the project has been delayed for lack of foreign exchange. Current Indian thinking centres on one possible loophole in the donor's ability to influence India's resource allocation, namely, the possibility of financing the project through short-term supplier's credits arranged by a consortium of foreign equipment suppliers with maximum reliance on domestically produced equipment. But given a determination by the aid-donors to avoid such an end run, which could ultimately be financed only through larger programme loans, this loophole should not prove impossible to close.

Besides enabling the donor to exercise some influence over the recipient's allocation of resources, at least in some cases, the use of project aid also enables the donor to influence more easily the projects nominally financed, whether or not they happen to be the projects that the aid actually makes possible. If the donor's goal is the recipient's economic development, this influence will presumably be directed towards improving the economic viability of the projects. The influence can be exercised in a number of ways, particularly by insisting on higher standards of project preparation, by introducing technical aid as part of the project, by imposing various conditions on the execution of the project, or, in the extreme case, by partial supervision of the project itself. Much more than capital is usually needed by less developed countries. In many cases technical aid and other influences do more than improve the economics of a project; without them, the project may not be economically viable.

One striking example is provided by the contrast between the steel mills erected in India in the late 1950's with British and German assistance and that erected with Russian aid. The markedly superior performance of the Russian-built mill (Bhilai) in the years following its completion can be ascribed in considerable measure to the close and constant supervision and aid furnished by the Russians after the mill went into operation.[9] The British and Germans did not insist on such supervision because of Indian reluctance to accept it. Not until the mills they built deteriorated to such a point that they became national issues did the Indian Government and the foreign equipment suppliers agree to meaningful foreign participation in the direction of the mills.

Investment in physical capital is only one essential requisite of industrial growth; it is also necessary to develop various skills, particularly managerial skills, to use the capital efficiently once it is built. Capital projects are an effective way to provide this form of technical aid. Most L.D.C.'s are reluctant to admit that such aid is vital to the success of many projects; project aid provides the donor with some leverage for insisting that it is accepted.

In addition to making possible the exercise of greater influence on the allocation of resources between projects and on individual projects, the project approach also opens up opportunities for exercising greater influence than would be possible with programme aid on policies in sectors related to the projects nominally financed by the aid. This can often be done by arguing that changes in these policies are necessary for the success of the project. For example, in the case of a railroad project, the donor might be able to insist on changes in the railroad's rate structure, or in the case of a fertiliser plant, a change in fertiliser prices or distribution practices.

Unfortunately, much of this section on the benefits of micro-influence has had to be rather general because so few examples are available of its effective use. One of the major conclusions of an earlier study of the United States aid programme to India was that little micro-influence has been exercised through project restrictions on capital aid.[10] Although A.I.D. and I.B.R.D. projects in India appear to be worse in this respect than the average in other countries, the difference does not appear to be very great, particularly with respect to influencing policies not directly related to aid projects in sectors for which aid has been made available. Recently, however, the I.B.R.D. has shown what can be done in the way of significantly improving the design of a project by insisting on an improved project report on the proposed Halida port in India. Since the benefits from exercising micro-influence are undoubtedly the most important potential benefits of project lending, their frequent absence in practice greatly diminishes the case

---

[9] See William A. Johnson, *The Steel Industry of India* (Cambridge: Harvard University Press, 1966), pp. 178–179 and 183.

[10] See Alan Carlin, *op. cit.*, pp. 232–234 and 241–242. The study includes detailed analyses of U. S. aid to Indian irrigation and transport and the extent of micro-influence through it.

for the project approach in those cases. It is certainly not an easy task to create an organisation sufficiently competent to exercise much useful influence. Those donors that are unable to do so should certainly seriously question the wisdom of pursuing the project approach.

Other Benefits

One important, but largely overlooked, potential benefit of project lending is the incentive which it can provide for recipient countries to develop a larger number of acceptable projects than they otherwise would.[11] This is desirable not only because of the favourable economic effects of the additional projects that may be engendered but also because it provides, to some extent, a meaningful measure of the recipient's performance and "absorptive capacity" as an objective guide[12] to donors in setting country aid levels. As long as there is a relationship between project approval and project preparation, the country that is able to increase its generation of acceptable projects can increase its share of the available funds. This can provide a significant built-in incentive to recipient countries in marked contrast to programme aid, where the incentives normally work in the opposite direction, since the larger the balance-of-payments or budget deficit (the usual criteria, in the absence of any objective criterion of performance), the larger the aid. While it might be possible to impose conditions on programme aid dealing with the number and acceptability of available projects, this type of incentive can be more efficiently applied by the use of project aid in the first place. Experience also suggests that there is indeed ample opportunity for many aid recipients substantially to increase their total aid receipts by increasing the number and quality of projects they prepare. There are a number of countries (such as India) where pledges of project assistance by various aid-givers have gone unused because the potential recipient fails to come up with an adequate number of acceptable projects. The use of project assistance can have an important educational effect by emphasising the importance of developing this often neglected but critical capability.

The added publicity value derived from identifying aid with particular projects (which might be termed the "billboard effect") can be of importance. The Russians, for example, appear to place considerable emphasis on this gain from project lending and have used it with unusually good effect. By identifying their aid with certain prominent or "impact" projects in a number of countries, they have greatly increased the publicity value of their aid.[13] The best-known examples are

---

[11] This is not to say that all aid-donors have given, or are likely to give, project aid in a way that will always provide such incentives. In many cases there are significant administrative and political pressures to maintain previous levels of assistance to particular countries, with the result that project standards suffer.

[12] This is not meant to imply that the level of aid suggested by the availability of acceptable projects is "optimum" (say in terms of minimum discounted total cost to the donors to achieve some development goal), but that it is not (or at least less) influenced by considerations other than the economic performance of the recipient.

[13] By way of illustration, most people are surprised to learn that the Soviet Union has contributed less than 6 per cent of total aid utilised by India from 1950 through 1963, and ranks as the fifth largest donor.

the Bhilai and Bokaro steel mills in India, the Aswan dam in the United Arab Republic, and the Kabul street-paving project in Afghanistan. Clearly, project aid, especially if attributed to such carefully chosen projects, greatly increases the publicity value of the donor's aid.

Still another potential benefit of project aid is that it often provides the donor with an opportunity for obtaining detailed information concerning at least the principal techno-economic problems of the sectors in which the projects are located. Because of both the association of aid financing with bank financing and the desire of the country to receive the aid, it is often possible, with a minimum of hard feelings, to use the project application as an excuse for obtaining information not only about the project itself but also about related activities. This can be useful for suggesting specific conditions to attach to the approval of the project, conditions that will improve the efficiency of the sector concerned. It can also be useful in analysing in greater detail the development prospects and performance of various sectors, which can, in turn, form the basis of a more general analysis of the development prospects of the country and, therefore, the desirability of giving it aid in the first place.

With country-of-origin tying, as in the case of A.I.D. loans, the addition of project restrictions to aid generally results in a larger net increase in the donor's exports per dollar of his aid than in the case of programme aid. This, in turn, will mean that project aid has a somewhat less adverse effect on the balance of payments of the aid-giver per dollar. Although the recipient usually suggests that aid be nominally ascribed to projects where the largest percentage of imported goods would be purchased from the aid-giver if the project were financed from free foreign exchange, it is likely that a somewhat lower percentage of the goods purchased under a project loan would have been purchased from the aid-giver in any case compared with the purchases under a programme loan. It is not usually possible to find projects that consist entirely of goods normally or most advantageously purchased from any one donor country. On the other hand, from a long list of maintenance imports, from apples to oil, it is fairly simple for the recipient to pick out those goods that would normally be purchased from the aid-giver anyway.

It has often been alleged that the project approach is also less likely to lead to a "politically frozen" aid level. A programme aid level maintained over several years can take on a political status that makes for inflexibility. In contrast, project aid is at least theoretically tied directly to the submission of eligible project proposals by the recipient government. Either slow submission of good proposals or slow utilisation of funds already obligated will automatically result in lower assistance levels, besides signalling inadequate performance by the recipient country.

COSTS OF THE PROJECT APPROACH

The potential costs of project aid can be grouped into the following categories, roughly in the order of their importance:

1. Possibility of reduced leverage over aggregate policies of the host country;

2. Introduction of incentives favouring the construction of new capacity rather than providing raw materials that would make it possible to use existing capacity better;
3. Intergovernmental problems arising from the bureaucratic frictions created by detailed supervision of project formulation and execution;
4. Increased costs of aid administration;
5. Increased real cost (to the recipient nation) of borrowing.

These costs are likely to be present even where the technical expertise and administrative efficiency associated with project aid are beyond reproach. An additional set of costs emerge if there are administrative or analytical failures on the part of the aid-giver. Since it is doubtful whether any organisation can avoid all mistakes, costs in this second category ought also to be considered. In particular, these are likely to arise from delays in the recipient's capital projects as a result of review and supervision by the donor, as well as in categories 3 and 4 above.

Many of these costs also depend in magnitude on the assiduity with which the aid-giver attempts to exercise influence over the recipient. There are no costs in terms of macro-bargaining opportunities forgone if no bargaining would be attempted anyway, and few costs if no attempt is made to exercise project influence. Costs arising from the frictions involved in project scrutinisation will be unimportant if the review of project proposals and the monitoring of project implementation is largely permissive. Assuming away the problem of creating an effective control system, the most important potential cost of giving aid in the form of projects is the loss of bargaining power over aggregate economic and political policies of the borrower. The intergovernmental *cum* interbureaucratic frictions of effective project control are chiefly important because they result in an erosion of host-country willingness (and ability) to agree to restrictions on its freedom of action implied by aggregate performance criteria.

To the extent that project aid reduces the potential leverage per dollar of aid over broader policies,[14] this is indeed an important consideration. Such a reduction might occur for two reasons. First, project aid may be worth less to the recipient government, especially if there is a squeeze on maintenance imports. Second, any attempt to exercise micro- or project influence will tend further to decrease the attractiveness of the aid to the recipient, and hence the potential macro-leverage available per dollar. It should be pointed out, however, that the use of macro-leverage on the L.D.C.'s has been something less than wholly successful to date. Despite increasing interest and efforts in this direction in the early 1960's, it has been used successfully only in a few cases in the last decade. The problems arise mainly because of the administrative difficulties of making the criteria meaningful and the political difficulties of making conditions effective.

It is assumed here that it is quite possible to exercise macro-influence with project aid, preferably by bargaining over groups of projects or project packages. Given this, it can be argued that to some extent micro- and macro-influence exercised through project assistance are complements rather than substitutes for each other.

---

[14]If the donor's objective is the economic development of the recipient, the donor will often be most interested in affecting fiscal and monetary policies.

In fact, a considerable portion of the benefits from project level influence can be obtained without the recipient feeling that he has been asked to make a major concession that greatly decreases the value of the aid. To a considerable extent this influence is quite similar to technical aid—suggestions for relatively minor improvements in a project or its operation, or perhaps insistence on certain standards in project submission and preparation. In addition, attempts at micro-influence can be partly justified by the "normal" banking practice of attempting to ensure the credit-worthiness of a given project, and hence may not be considered as great an interference in the internal affairs of the recipient country as they might otherwise.

Project aid undoubtedly introduces a number of biases into country development. Perhaps most important, it favours building new capacity rather than making better use of existing capacity. Since project aid is often more readily available than programme aid, there are built-in incentives for the potential recipient to accept additional project aid even if his resources could be better devoted to fuller utilisation of present capacity. The result is likely to be overbuilding of infrastructure and expansion of the public sector. Once again perhaps the best example is India. Because her free foreign exchange and non-project aid receipts are less than her non-project needs, there is considerable underutilisation of industrial capacity. Yet she continues to accept project-tied aid to build new industrial capacity, some of it in the same industries which are now suffering from a shortage of maintenance imports.

Even if project influence is inherently more palatable than programme influence, project assistance may also give rise to a number of interbureaucratic frictions, often of the most nonsubstantive, petty type. These sometimes arise in the case of A.I.D. because of a number of specific prohibitions written into foreign aid legislation by Congress.

The real costs of loans to the recipient may be increased by the project approach in the case of country-tied aid from individual countries for the same reason that the foreign exchange costs to the aid-giver are reduced—the recipient is forced to buy some items for a given project from a country other than the lowest-cost producer. If the objectives of the donor include a concern for the economic welfare of the recipient, this may represent a cost to the donor as well.

CONCLUSIONS

The general conclusion from this analysis, that there is something to be said on both sides, is much the same as Singer's. But unlike Singer, it stresses that the particular objectives of the donor in giving aid, and to some extent the particular circumstances of the recipient, are likely to make it advisable to pursue a project approach in one case, a programme approach in another, and some combination in still others. This paper has attempted to outline what some of the more important considerations are. Undoubtedly the most important of these is whether the objectives of the donor can be best served by attempting to exercise influence on the macro- or the micro-level.

Although micro-influence can result from programme aid and macro-influence from project aid (properly "packaged"), such influence is usually more effectively exercised by project and programme aid, respectively. The primary question is the level on which influence can most usefully be focused; the choice of type of aid is generally a second-order issue that follows from the first.

If, for example, the donor's objective is the recipient's economic development, and the donor believes that it is by influencing project preparation and execution and related sectoral policies that he can most fruitfully use the limited leverage provided by his aid, then the project approach would be preferable. If, on the other hand, the donor believes that his objectives can best be served by concentrating his influence on broader, more aggregate issues, programme aid offers some advantages. If some mixture is desired in the direction of donor influence, project aid can be "packaged," with emphasis on macro-bargaining over the packages.

There are other considerations in selecting one or the other aid instrument besides the relation of donor objectives to the optimum level of influence. Another, for example, is the competence of the donor in exercising influence through project aid. In general, there are a number of factors to be taken into account in each donor-recipient relationship, and it is a question of weighing one against the other. The significant aspect of this (and Singer's) conclusion is that it differs markedly from the prevailing view of many economists that programme aid is to be preferred. All too often this judgment is based solely on the fungibility argument, which is but one of several important considerations to be taken into account.

Rejoinder

H. W. SINGER

From: "Project Versus Programme Aid: A Rejoinder," the Economic Journal, *Vol. LXXVII, No. 308 (Dec. 1967), pp. 963–964. Reprinted by permission of the* Economic Journal *and the author.*

I do not feel there is enough difference in the views or conclusions of Mr. Carlin[1] and my own article on the same subject,[2] on which Mr. Carlin commented, to justify a long substantive debate. However, I may perhaps just make four brief points.

Mr. Carlin's article is explicitly written from the donor's point of view, and he

---

[1] "Project *versus* Programme Aid: From the Donor's Viewpoint," March 1967 issue of this Journal.
[2] September 1965 issue.

believes that I have looked at the problem too much from the recipient's point of view. However, when you deal with true development aid, as distinct from political subsidies, military aid, etc., the broad and ultimate objectives of the recipient and donor should coincide, and differences in exposition from the donor's or recipient's end become more semantic than real. Of course, the donor and the recipient may differ as to the best means by which to reach the common purpose of development in terms of concrete projects, and such differences constitute a basis for project aid, as I stated in my article.

Even if we adopt a "tough" donor's point of view, it is fallacious to assume—as Mr. Carlin seems to do—that the preference of the recipient for untied aid generally, and programme aid over project aid specifically, becomes any less relevant. If, because of its increased flexibility, the value of each aid dollar given in programme aid is equivalent to the recipient to $1.25 in project aid, then the donor, if he is willing to give the aid in the preferred and more acceptable form of programme aid, can cut down on his aid total by 25 per cent and still achieve the same aid effect as before. Hence, the question of toughness does not really enter—it does only if one assumes that the aid total is a fixed sum in money terms and not dependent on the form in which the aid is given.

Mr. Carlin thinks that I overstated the fungibility issue in my article, and he writes in support: "As long as the sum of available free foreign exchange plus untied programme aid is less than essential maintenance imports, no project requiring substantial amounts of foreign exchange will normally be undertaken without some public or private international financing." Wish it were so! Unfortunately, the industrial landscape of the underdeveloped countries provides sad evidence that Mr. Carlin is wrong. In many countries where there is not enough foreign exchange for essential maintenance imports, new projects are going up and are being planned even without external financing. Governments in their development plans clearly tend to identify development with new projects and new capacity rather than with increased output from existing capacity; quite apart from development plans, foreign exchange is being allocated and licences given much more readily for new projects in the name of "development" and/or "import substitution" than for essential maintenance imports. Similar factors are at work on the side of external financing also, both public and private. It is with such circumstances in mind that I attribute importance to the fungibility issue, even under the conditions which Mr. Carlin has in mind.

The project approach has a weakness, not mentioned by Mr. Carlin, nor in my earlier article. This is the corollary of its advantage—mentioned by both of us—of high visibility and publicity impact of project aid. The other side of the coin which we should perhaps not fail to emphasise is that any failure of the project will also discredit the aid and have an *adverse* publicity impact. This can happen even if the failures and deficiencies of the project lie on the side of the recipient country and become apparent only at the subsequent stage of operating the project. This also is by no means a theoretical construct, but all too frequent in real life.

Selection **33**

Technical Assistance

I. M. D. LITTLE and J. M. CLIFFORD

From: International Aid; a Discussion of the Flow of Public Resources from Rich to Poor Countries (*Chicago: Aldine Publishing Co., 1966*), *pp. 174–180.* © *1965 and 1966 by George Allen and Unwin, Ltd. Reprinted by permission of George Allen and Unwin, Ltd., Aldine Publishing Company, and the authors.*

TECHNICAL ASSISTANCE AS TIED AID

We have said some harsh things about the practice of tying aid, but there is one form of tying which in present circumstances actually tends to increase the usefulness of aid. This happens when aid is provided in the form of the services which we are accustomed to call "technical assistance."

Technical assistance from the donor's point of view takes two main forms. First, people are recruited in the donor country for service overseas, partly, often largely, at the expense of the donor government; second, scholarships and training facilities are provided in the donor country. Why is technical assistance singled out for special treatment in this way, when recipient governments might equally well be given more financial assistance and left to decide for themselves what fraction of their aid should be spent on the services of foreign experts, and on education and training overseas?

The reason why "tying" aid to technical services is acceptable to recipients is that it tends to increase the value of the nominal amount of aid spent on technical assistance; technical assistance contrasts strongly in this respect with financial aid tied to procurement in the donor country, and with commodity aid, both of which tend to be worth less than their nominal value. The contrast exists because many of the services provided under technical assistance programmes are scarce or unobtainable on the world market and can be secured by recipients only with the help of donor governments.

Donor government assistance in recruiting is most important when the experts (or training facilities) to be supplied can be found only within central government departments or within organizations like the post office or the army which are ultimately subject to central government control. If an expert is needed to set up or reorganize post office services overseas, or if on-the-job training is needed in

361

the post office, then clearly this can be arranged only through the central government. If technical assistance is needed in decentralized fields of government, like training town clerks, or in school-teaching, or even in non-government fields like university teaching or medicine, the central government can still be an almost indispensable intermediary; in school-teaching, for instance, the British Government has encouraged and helped representatives of the teachers' organizations and local authorities to work out a code of secondment, which enables a teacher to work overseas for at least five years, without losing his pension rights, and with the certainty that he will have a job to return to. Although these arrangements do not depend upon the donor government having a financial interest in the technical experts and training facilities that are provided for overseas governments, a donor government is likely to make a more serious attempt to recruit people, and find training places, that will carry a British (or German, or Russian) technical assistance label than if it merely recruits on behalf of overseas governments.

A further useful attribute of technical assistance, when it takes the form of educational and training facilities in donor countries, is that since both donor and recipient governments take part in the choice of courses and selection of candidates, the types of training offered can be more closely geared to the needs of the recipient economy (and the capability of the donor) than education which is paid for privately or by the recipient government. Ideally, part at least of the training provided should be linked with technical assistance on the "expert" side and even with capital assistance. For example, if an expert is provided to reorganize and expand a recipient's postal services, training should be provided for the men to run the new service; or if financial aid is provided for a new oil refinery, both experts and training facilities should be provided in engineering, management, and the other skills needed to operate the refinery. Donors have found in the past that, left to themselves, recipients have been reluctant to spend enough of their own resources on the technical expertise demanded by a new installation, and offers of free or subsidized technical assistance are therefore extremely useful in persuading recipients to accept the necessary advice and training.

The independence of former colonies, especially those which were formerly British, has seriously reduced the supply of foreigners prepared or able to make their careers in developing countries. Under current conditions, advisers and teachers for work overseas are recruited on contract, for a maximum of three years (though with the possibility of renewed contracts in some cases), because neither donor nor recipient government wishes to be committed for longer periods. Recipient governments are afraid of barring promotion for local people by taking foreigners on career terms, and donor governments have felt unable to set up career services for expert advisers. The result is that expert advisory or even operational work overseas is regarded by the employee as a temporary interruption to his career at home, and he is not willing to stay abroad for more than a few years for fear of losing promotion in his real career. For instance, a young and ambitious doctor, who works overseas soon after he qualifies, is more than likely to miss any chance of becoming a consultant, which he might have had if he had stayed in England.

However great the probability that foreign advisers, teachers, etc., will make mistakes, foreign influence cannot be avoided. Few societies are so isolated that they have been unaffected by contact with the products, ideas, and techniques of richer countries, and most are already changing so fast, economically and socially, that they could not restore their traditional institutions even if they wished to do so. Population growth is perhaps the most obvious stimulus to continued change, but new material and social ambitions of all kinds are close competitors. Whatever the potential dangers of foreign influence, developing countries must import foreign skills and education at the moment if they are to achieve economic progress. Isolation on the Russian or Japanese models would not be a feasible policy for any of the developing countries at this stage, because they do not yet possess the numbers of trained and skilled people, or the determination to introduce technical change, that the Russians and Japanese possessed in the late nineteenth century.

THE NEED FOR TECHNICAL ASSISTANCE AND FORMS OF TECHNICAL ASSISTANCE

Technical assistance represents only a small fraction of the total transfer of skills from rich to poor countries. But, as we have said already, it is the form of transfer most amenable to selective control by the recipient government. It is important that governments and individuals in poor countries should learn to consider more carefully the likely effects of innovations that appeal to them and should be more selective in their choice of foreign influences to be encouraged or discouraged.

This process of selection itself, however, requires a certain level of sophistication and understanding of the scientific approach to decisions, which is lacking in many recipient countries. Especially in Africa, there are many countries which need technical assistance not only to transfer new skills, but, temporarily at any rate, to operate the whole machinery of government, educational institutions, and that part of productive capacity which is on a scale larger than the family farm. This means that the process of selecting and adapting foreign influences to local conditions is very largely neglected, and that institutions are modelled very closely (if at times unsuccessfully) on the institutions of a European country, usually the former colonial power. This situation could hardly have been avoided, but unless the institutions of such countries are gradually adapted to fit local traditions and needs, they will continue for a long time to depend on foreigners or foreign-trained nationals for survival.

Technical assistance therefore varies in form and function, depending on the type of country receiving it. At one end of the scale are countries which can fill ordinary government posts, and many specialist appointments, from among their own nationals, but which occasionally have to import highly specialized skills for particular jobs, like designing an oil refinery or setting up an industrial research department. The most efficient of these countries can identify for themselves which jobs need to be done and the type of experts needed to fill them and are capable of arranging job specifications and recruitment: technical assistance for them means simply that they pay less for an expert and are helped with recruitment; the latter may be especially useful if there are no consulting firms capable of doing the particular job needed. But few countries possess government machines efficient enough for technical assistance to be so simple. Most need help with "pre-investment" surveys, feasibility studies, pilot projects, and the like, and, pushing the process one stage further back, with economic planning and project selection in general. Efficient donor administration of aid can help, by means of careful project selection and by drawing attention to the need for surveys and planning.

But technical assistance can stop at the planning stage only if the government machine is capable of implementing the planners' decisions, and in many countries this condition is not fulfilled. In some countries the most essential form of technical assistance is providing people to fill "operational" posts, including teaching, in the ordinary government establishment. While technical assistance comes up against political and personal difficulties at every level, filling operational posts presents by far the most delicate problem. Civil servants in a newly independent country dislike taking orders from a foreigner. Citizens outside the civil service dislike dealing with foreigners. Ambitious subordinates resent foreigners who appear to stand in the way of their promotion. Sometimes the position can be made easier by appointing a foreign "adviser" who will in effect do an operational job, but this may create personal difficulties with the titular "operational" employee. An advisory appointment is, of course, appropriate and preferable to an operational appointment, if there is a suitably qualified, but inexperienced local man who can be trained on the job by the foreign adviser to fill the operational vacancy once the adviser has left.

The notion of absorptive capacity applies as much to the various types of technical assistance as to financial assistance. Specialists doing "once and for all" jobs can be employed only to the extent that there are identifiable jobs for them to do and when there are people capable of running the installations and services that these experts set up. Absorptive capacity for such specialists can be increased by appointing foreigners to help with economic planning, feasibility surveys, pilot projects, and professional and technical training for running new projects. Absorptive capacity for advisers on planning and for professional training is in turn limited by the capacity of government and by the output of secondary and higher education institutions. It can be raised by appointing foreigners to government and teaching posts. The ultimate limit to absorptive capacity for technical assistance is therefore set by the acceptability and suitability of foreigners in government and teaching.

In the short run, the acceptability and supply of foreigners are the restraints which are obvious to all those who have been in contact with post-colonial governments. Many government departments in Africa would run a great deal more smoothly if they were not understaffed. Many more East Africans could be found placed in higher education if there were more places for secondary school pupils. But in the longer run a more serious restraint, which may underlie some of the hostility to foreigners in the civil service establishment of these countries, is the difficulty of adapting institutions—from legal procedures to school curricula—to local conditions. The more a government depends on foreign experts and foreign training courses to staff and teach its civil service, the more difficult adaptation becomes.

This brings us to the final function of technical assistance—research. As the above remarks suggest, not nearly enough is known about the degree to which the institutions and traditions of rich countries—their legal and social systems, their languages, philosophical systems, educational methods, etc.—are necessary for any society which hopes to achieve material prosperity, and how far they are merely accidental results of European history. Many other types of research are also needed, especially into the application of natural science to problems of developing better seeds, methods of husbandry, methods of birth control, and so on; and in the application of social science to finding ways of persuading people to adopt new crop rotations, fertilizers, etc. Much of the research needed can be done only in developing countries and must often be specific to quite small areas, bounded by climatic or tribal differences.

Even more important than new research, at any rate in Britain, is the need to draw upon the experience of people who have lived and worked in developing countries. There is a great deal of knowledge and expertise among ex-colonial civil servants, consulting firms, missionaries, technical experts, and teachers, who have worked overseas on contract, which is exploited in an informal way by means of personal contacts and in conversation but which could be used more systematically.

Technical Assistance and Financial Aid

... We have shown that technical assistance is by no means a homogeneous activity, but that the usefulness of the various types of technical assistance may in turn be limited by absorptive capacity. In countries where this is the case, that is, in countries which lack the educated manpower to staff government or teaching posts or to take up offers of specialized technical and professional training, technical assistance in the form of teachers and staff to fill operational posts in government may reasonably be administered independently of financial assistance.

But other types of technical assistance—the supply of experts to carry out surveys and research, to design installations and services, or to staff planning departments—should usually be related to financial assistance. The main reason for this is that recipient governments tend to overestimate their own efficiency and to ask for financial help with projects that are ill-chosen, badly designed, or wrongly located and which they will be unable to run efficiently when they have been completed. Providing technical and financial assistance in a "package" tends to increase the efficiency of both. It can ensure that a project for which a loan or grant is made is properly designed and costed and is feasible. Conversely, a technical expert's or survey team's advice is far more likely to be taken if related financial aid can be made dependent on measures to follow such advice. When a donor government is supplying substantial amounts of money for a number of projects, it is also in a position to insist that the recipient employ well-qualified staff (not necessarily provided by the donor or of the donor's nationality) in government posts closely concerned with these projects: and if it thinks it necessary to insist on such appointments, it should do so. Combining technical and financial assistance in these ways is useful in combating corruption as well as inefficiency. To some extent, a donor's aid advisory staff can themselves provide technical assistance, as well as examine proposals and supervise expenditure. Britain's Middle East Development Division (M.E.D.D.) and some of the U.S. A.I.D. Mission staff do just this, and the arrangement seems to work reasonably well.